TRANSNATIONAL SOLIDARITY

This book analyses the concept and conditions of transnational solidarity, its challenges and opportunities, drawing on the diverse disciplines of history, law, philosophy, political science, psychology and sociology. In the contemporary world, we see two major opposing trends. The first involves nationalistic and populistic movements. For more than a decade, global economic and migration crises have put transnational solidarity under pressure leading to the rise of populistic and authoritarian leadership in some European countries, the USA and Brazil. Countries withdraw from international commitments on climate, trade and refugees, and the European Union struggles with Brexit. The second trend, partly a reaction to the first, is a strengthened transnational grass-root community – a cosmopolitan movement – which protests primarily against climate change. The book uses interdisciplinary reflections on the concept of transnational solidarity to analyse its challenges and opportunities, drawing on Europe as a focal case study to reach a broader, global perspective.

HELLE KRUNKE is Professor of Constitutional Law at the University of Copenhagen. She is First Vice President of the International Association of Constitutional Law. She has published extensively on Constitutional Law and EU Law and was invited to present papers at the University of Oxford, University of Sorbonne and European University Institute.

HANNE PETERSEN is Professor at the Faculty of Law, University of Copenhagen. She is the first Nordic Professor of Legal Cultures and has previously held positions as Jean Monnet Scholar at the European University Institute, Florence, Professor at University of Greenland and Professor of Greenlandic Sociology of Law at the University of Copenhagen. Her publications relate, among others, to labour law, gender, religion, the Arctic and China.

IAN MANNERS is Professor in the Department of Political Science at the University of Copenhagen. He has previously been Professor at Roskilde University, Head of the unit at DIIS, Associate Professor at Malmö University and at the University of Kent at Canterbury. Professor Manners' research interests lie at the intersection of critical social theory, the European Union and planetary politics.

TRANSNATIONAL SOLIDARITY

Concept, Challenges and Opportunities

Edited by

HELLE KRUNKE
University of Copenhagen

HANNE PETERSEN
University of Copenhagen

IAN MANNERS
University of Copenhagen

CAMBRIDGE
UNIVERSITY PRESS

CAMBRIDGE
UNIVERSITY PRESS

University Printing House, Cambridge CB2 8BS, United Kingdom

One Liberty Plaza, 20th Floor, New York, NY 10006, USA

477 Williamstown Road, Port Melbourne, VIC 3207, Australia

314–321, 3rd Floor, Plot 3, Splendor Forum, Jasola District Centre,
New Delhi – 110025, India

79 Anson Road, #06–04/06, Singapore 079906

Cambridge University Press is part of the University of Cambridge.

It furthers the University's mission by disseminating knowledge in the pursuit of education, learning, and research at the highest international levels of excellence.

www.cambridge.org
Information on this title: www.cambridge.org/9781108487368
DOI: 10.1017/9781108766593

First published 2020

A catalogue record for this publication is available from the British Library.

Library of Congress Cataloging-in-Publication Data
Names: Krunke, Helle, 1970– editor. | Petersen, Hanne, 1951– editor. | Manners, Ian, editor.
Title: Transnational solidarity : concept, challenges and opportunities / edited by Helle Krunke, Hanne Petersen, Ian Manners.
Description: Cambridge, United Kingdom ; New York, NY : Cambridge University Press, 2020. | Includes bibliographical references and index.
Identifiers: LCCN 2019053363 (print) | LCCN 2019053364 (ebook) | ISBN 9781108487368 (hardback) | ISBN 9781108766593 (ebook)
Subjects: LCSH: Transnationalism – European Union countries. | International cooperation – European Union countries. | European Union countries – Emigration and immigration – Social aspects. | European Union countries – Social policy. | European Union countries – Economic policy.
Classification: LCC JV7590 .T734 2020 (print) | LCC JV7590 (ebook) | DDC 305.80094–dc23
LC record available at https://lccn.loc.gov/2019053363
LC ebook record available at https://lccn.loc.gov/2019053364

ISBN 978-1-108-48736-8 Hardback

CONTENTS

FIGURES

TABLES

PREFACE

It has been a privilege to edit this book. Transnational solidarity in Europe and the World is one of the most topical, exciting, important and fundamental themes. The chapters' authors have shared their rich and inspiring ideas on the topic from their varied academic fields, including history, law, philosophy, political science, psychology and sociology. While we were writing this book together, the theme developed around us: trends which drew the World closer together, and trends which drew the World further apart. Young people, including Greta Thunberg, co-created a transnational movement protesting against climate change and for a future for their generation. Brexit has finally become a formal reality with the UK leaving the European Union. Furthermore, global transnational solidarity experiences a new challenge – and opportunity – with the COVID 19 crisis. We have been on an amazing journey together over the past four years. We owe all of our excellent and patient authors our deepest and warmest thanks. It has been wonderful working together with all of you, and the result of all your hard work is a truly unique interdisciplinary approach to transnational solidarity.

We have had an excellent co-operation with Cambridge University Press all through the publishing process and we warmly thank Tom Randall, Gemma Smith, Anjana Karikal Cholan, Raghavi Govindane and Jeremy Toynbee. We would also like to thank project students Benjamin Muschinsky, Rasmus Glud Madsen, Anna Carolina Jensen and Djellza Fetahi for their assistance with finding sources, editing the manuscript and creating an index for the book. A special thank you to Roberta Mungianu, our former colleague, for your contribution to organising the international interdisciplinary colloquium on transnational solidarity in Copenhagen in 2016, which kick-started this project.

This project would not have been possible without the support of the University of Copenhagen and the Centre for European and Comparative Legal Studies (CECS), Faculty of Law. The last year of the project, we also received inspiration and support from the European Union's Horizon2020 project DEMOS (grant agreement No. 822590). Thank you.

Introduction

HELLE KRUNKE AND HANNE PETERSEN

1 Conception

This book has been conceived in a period where transnational solidarity and co-operation seemed to be moving backwards rather than forwards. A prime example of this decline of transnational solidarity being the so-called refugee crisis in Europe in 2015. After the Brexit referendum in the UK in June 2016, and presidential elections in the USA later the same year, the political agenda turned inwards, focusing primarily on internal national perspectives in relation to areas such as environmental protection, aid to countries in the Third World and trade with the outside world. Recently, the EU has experienced a number of crises, among others an economic and financial crisis and later the refugee crisis. These crises have challenged transnational solidarity in Europe. This development in Europe and the wider world raises the question of whether (and how) transnational solidarity is possible. This book is motivated by these developments and discusses and attempts to answer this question. Our main presumption is that solidarity can create stability and sustainability (social, economic, environmental and peace), within states, regions and globally, and that is why it is crucial to gain more knowledge about it. Realisation of the UN's Sustainability Goals 2017 and 2030 go hand in hand with solidarity at local, regional and global levels. In this book, we do of course build on earlier discussions and investigations of solidarity.

2 The Concepts of Solidarity and Transnational Solidarity

Solidarity refers to relations and ties in society that bind people together. Its origins are found in the Roman law of obligations. Since the classic definition of solidarity as the relationship between entities belonging to a group,[1] focus has been on different characteristics of solidarity,[2] distinguishing between affectional, conventional and reflective solidarity,[3] understanding solidarity as involving an inherently oppositional nature and mutually shared vision,[4] constructing solidarity through a public sphere of discourse and cultural interpretation, and through participation of civil society associations.[5] Owing to global developments and the challenges they raise, recent focus has turned to transnational solidarity with an emphasis on democracy,[6] ethics,[7] empathy and gender,[8] inclusion/exclusion and equality/inequality,[9] a performative theory of assembly (Butler 2015) and identification, transcendence and interpenetration (Somek 2007).

We have borrowed the term 'transnational solidarity' from Carol Gould.[10] Gould also reflects on the concept of transnational solidarity in this book. Her definition of transnational solidarity is a connecting thread throughout the book. Many chapters apply Gould's understanding of transnational solidarity or discusses it. Other chapters present other understandings of transnational solidarity or pick out specific elements, which they find especially fundamental to the understanding of transnational solidarity. This way the book presents a rich and dynamic approach towards the concept and an openness to develop our understanding of it.

1 Émile Durkheim, *The Division of Labour in Society* (*De la division du travail social*) (Paris: Félix Alcan, Éditeur, 1893).

2 Kurt Bayertz, ed., *Solidarity. Philosophical Studies in Contemporary Culture* (Groningen: Kluwer Academic Publishers, 1999); Patrick Doreian and Thomas Fararo, eds., *The Problem of Solidarity: Theories and Models* (Amsterdam: Gordon and Breach Publishers, 1998).

3 Jodi Dean, *Solidarity of Strangers: Feminism After Identity Politics* (Berkeley, CA: University of California Press, 1996).

4 Chandra Talpade Mohanty, *Feminism Without Borders: Decolonizing Theory, Practicing Solidarity* (Durham, NC: Duke University Press, 2003).

5 Craig Calhoun, 'Imagining solidarity: cosmopolitanism, constitutional patriotism, and the public sphere', *Public Culture*, 14(1) (2002), 147–71.

6 Carol Gould, 'Transnational solidarities', *Journal of Social Philosophy*, 38(1) (2007), 148–64; Carol Gould, *Interactive Democracy: The Social Roots of Global Justice* (Cambridge: Cambridge University Press, 2014).

7 Janusz Salamon, ed., *Solidarity Beyond Borders: Ethics in a Globalising World. Bloomsbury Studies in Global Ethics* (London: Bloomsbury Academic, 2015).

8 Gould, *Interactive Democracy*; Hauke Brunkhorst, *Solidarity: From Civic Friendship to a Global Legal Community* (Cambridge, MA: MIT Press, 2005).

9 Nathalie Karagiannis, ed., *European Solidarity. Studies in Social and Political Thought* (Liverpool: Liverpool University Press, 2007); Marion Ellison, ed., *Reinventing Social Solidarity Across Europe* (Bristol: Policy Press, 2011).

10 Gould, 'Transnational solidarities'.

3 Analysing Transnational Solidarity with an Interdisciplinary Approach

If we turn to recent literature on cross-border solidarity. We see a growing interest in this field of research. However, we also see that many of the books on cross-border solidarity represent a specific discipline or focus on solidarity within a specific field. Many books are purely focused on solidarity within the EU[11] and several on the social dimension of the EU.[12]

Whereas the books by Floris de Witte, Michael Dougan and Elanor Spaventa, and Andrea Biondi, Eglė Dagilytė and Esin Kücük have a (dogmatic) legal approach, other books are centred on other disciplines such as philosophy,[13] sociology[14] and political science.[15]

Excellent work has been written on cross-border solidarity, and with this book we have an ambition of taking research in this field further through focusing on 'transnational solidarity' and 'interdisciplinarity' as key words.

While using Europe as our 'research lab' our ambition reaches beyond Europe in trying to answer whether transnational solidarity is possible and how. Hence, it is the cross-border element, which is at the heart of our analysis and not, for instance, how to build national solidarity amid diversity.[16] One more distinction is necessary in order to explain the precise focus of the book. We distinguish between 'transnational solidarity' and 'global justice'. Contrary to transnational solidarity, global justice is often normative in the sense that its focus is on how to create 'just' international institutions or 'just' international human rights. We do not engage in this discussion in our book.

While the EU is an important player in creating cross-border solidarity among European countries, our focus also reaches beyond the EU as an

[11] Andrea Biondi, Eglė Dagilytė and Esin Kücük, *Solidarity in EU Law. Legal Principle in the Making* (Cheltenham: Edward Edgar, 2017); Floris de Witte, *Justice in the EU. The Emergence of Transnational Solidarity* (Oxford: Oxford University Press, 2015); and Malcolm G. Ross and Yuri Borgmann-Prebil, eds., *Promoting Solidarity in the European Union* (Oxford: Oxford University Press, 2010).

[12] Ellison, *Reinventing Social Solidarity*; and Michael Dougan and Eleanor Spaventa, eds., *Social Welfare and EU Law* (Oxford: Hart Publishing, 2005).

[13] Gould, *Interactive Democracy*; Karagiannis, *European Solidarity*; and Salamon, *Solidarity Beyond Borders.*

[14] Brunkhorst, *Solidarity.*

[15] Keith Banting and Will Kymlicka, *The Strains of Commitment. The Political Sources of Solidarity in Diverse Societies* (Oxford: Oxford University Press, 2017).

[16] See Banting and Kymlicka, *The Strains of Commitment.*

international organisation in our analysis of transnational solidarity. Transnational solidarity can also be created outside the institutional and political setting of the EU. This becomes clear in the first part of the book, which considers the concept and conditions of solidarity, and in the second part of the book, which analyses some of the current crises Europe faces with regards to solidarity and the proposed solutions to these challenges. Solutions that are proposed both within the existing European institutional and political setting but also beyond it.

No single discipline owns the definition of solidarity and neither the challenges to solidarity nor the possible solutions are to be found within a specific discipline. Therefore, we take an *interdisciplinary approach* on the topic. We are to some extent inspired by the classic work of Kurt Bayertz from 1999,[17] who also recognises the importance of interdisciplinarity in this field. However, whereas his book is structured around specific disciplines, we *structure our book across disciplines on four topics*: (1) the concept and conditions of transnational solidarity; (2) the current challenges to and pressure on transnational solidarity; (3) reflections on how to (re)establish transnational solidarity within existing institutions and political settings; and (4) reflections on how to create new forms of transnational solidarity outside the established institutional and political settings. This way we are allowing for interdisciplinarity to flow more freely. The group of authors who have contributed to this book represent the disciplines of history, law, philosophy, political science, psychology and sociology.

4 Scope and Structure

The book is structured in the following way. First, we analyse and discuss the concept of transnational solidarity, its expressions and its conditions in general (Part I). Second, as already mentioned, we have chosen Europe as our 'research lab'. We try to answer the book's main question by first analysing some of the contemporary challenges facing transnational solidarity in Europe (Part II), and then analyse whether transnational European solidarity can be (re)established within the existing institutions and political settings (Part III). Finally, new forms of transnational solidarity emerging outside the traditional institutions and political settings in Europe are analysed (Part IV). In Concluding Thoughts: Concept, Challenges and Opportunities, we discuss our findings from

[17] Kurt Bayertz, *Solidarity* (Groningen: Kluwer Academic Publishers, 1999).

Parts I, II, III and IV and attempt to answer our main question in the light of this.

Part I analyses the concept, conditions and expressions of transnational solidarity across history, law, philosophy, political science and psychology. We start in Chapter 1 with a *historical* analysis of the concept of solidarity by **Sven-Eric Liedman,** which leads up to present day and claims that in a globalised world, the concept of solidarity only seems to get its full meaning if all of humanity is included. This naturally leads us to Chapter 2 by **Carol C. Gould,** who introduces the reader to a conceptual framework for understanding transnational solidarity and suggests that the *justification* for giving priority to solidarity with members of one's own nation state has to comport with cosmopolitan principles of universal human equality. The discussion on transnational solidarity continues in **Hauke Brunkhorst's** Chapter 3, in which Brunkhorst claims that we cannot reconstruct national democracy within the rise of global societal constitutionalism. The transnationalisation of democratic power inter alia is a *necessity.* By applying psychoanalytical theory, **Nathalie Karagiannis** in Chapter 4 shows how violence is a fundamental *condition* for solidarity, including the original violence, which produces it, and the violence it produces. Finally, Part I of the book is concluded by Chapter 5 by **Ian Manners**, who explores the symbols and myths of contemporary solidarity. His chapter builds on the assumption that the politics of solidarity are never over and he shows the vital role that symbols and myths play in the expression of solidarity. He concludes that symbols and myths of solidarity in the twenty-first century are increasingly transcending simple juxtapositions between cosmopolitan/communitarian understandings of solidarity, as agonistic cosmopolitical confrontations between cosmopolitan ethics and communitarian politics proliferate.

In Parts II, III and IV, Europe is used as a lab in which to study transnational solidarity. With the co-operation among European countries fostered by, among others, the EU it seems that Europe forms a good basis for analysis. European solidarity has been institutionalised almost since the end of the Second World War. In Part II of the book, we explore some of the major contemporary challenges to transnational solidarity in Europe. In Part III, we discuss whether the existing institutions and political settings can contribute to (re)building European transnational solidarity. And finally in Part IV, we explore the new opportunities for transnational solidarity in Europe coming from outside existing institutions and political frameworks.

In Part II of the book, both lawyers and political scientists contribute to the analyses. In Chapter 6 the *economic crisis* of the EU is analysed in the light of EU solidarity and from a legal perspective by **Ulla Neergaaard**. This is followed, in Chapter 7, by an analysis by **Graham Butler and Holly Snaith** of solidarity within the EU's legal and political framework, in the context of the *financial crisis*. The *refugee crisis* in Europe is analysed in Chapter 8 by **Eiko Thielemann. Alison L. Young** analyses the EU Brexit crisis following the outcome of the UK referendum on EU membership in 2016 in Chapter 9. Finally, we turn to the challenges facing the EU arising from regionalisation. In Chapter 10, **Antoni Abat i Ninet** analyses the impact of *regionalisation* on cross-border solidarity in the EU focusing primarily on Catalonia.

Part III combines legal, philosophical and sociological perspectives. Having analysed in Part II some of the current challenges to transnational solidarity in Europe, we discuss in Part III whether and how transnational solidarity can be (re)established through the existing institutional and political setting. **Alexander Somek** discusses the importance of 'friendship' for solidarity, how solidarity is established within nation states, through the creation of a shared cultural heritage, and whether this can be applied to the EU in Chapter 11. From discussing the possibilities of creating transnational solidarity through political discourse and processes, we move to the creation of solidarity through the case law of the European Court of Justice in the EU. **Dagmar Schiek**, in Chapter 12, explores whether and how far the case law of the European Court of Justice supports solidarity as an EU legal principle. Schiek explores whether solidarity as a transactional category between citizens of different nationalities is supported. Finally, **Christian Lahusen's** Chapter 13 analyses transnational civic solidarity in the EU. He finds that it is fragmentary and fragile because of a low degree of institutionalisation of civic society at the EU-level (in contrast to the level of institutionalisation of civic society at the national level).

Finally, in Part IV of the book we explore the possibilities of building new forms of transnational solidarity outside the traditional institutions and political setting. This part combines legal, sociological and political science perspectives. **Chenchen Zhang** discusses the judicial politics of free movement and *social rights* in the EU in Chapter 14. She argues in favour of a politically construed understanding of solidarity across borders applying the political philosophical theories of Étienne Balibar to the debate on post-national forms of solidarity and the question of social Europe. Critical citizenship theory focuses on acts, performances and claim-makings outside formal institutions of participation. **Hans-Jörg Trenz**, in Chapter 15, discusses the role of the *media*, including social media, in establishing solidarity relationships among Europeans as members or as citizens of a shared polity and thereby creating new opportunities for European solidarity. The emergence of *trans-religious* solidarity is studied in **Hanne Petersen's** Chapter 16. Her chapter is inspired by a trans-religious memorial service held at the Copenhagen Cathedral in solidarity with all afflicted by, and condemning, terrorism. Petersen presents religious solidarity across different religions and between secular and religious values as a new kind of transnational solidarity. Finally, we focus on transnational solidarity between *cities*. Whereas, states represented by heads of states are normally seen as the primary political actors in establishing solidarity across European countries, European cities are increasingly taking such a role upon themselves. Cities in Europe and beyond co-operate on environmental initiatives and create new transnational solidarity. This new form of transnational solidarity is analysed in Chapter 17 by **Helle Krunke** and **Katarina Hovden.** The internal tension in many countries, between cosmopolitan big cities with a global out-view open to transnational solidarity and smaller towns and rural areas with a more nation state oriented conception of solidarity is also discussed in their chapter. This chapter combines sociological, legal and political science perspectives.

In **Concluding Thoughts: Concept, Challenges and Opportunities** the editors engage in a general discussion of the chapters in the four parts of the book aiming to answer the main question of the book, namely whether and how transnational solidarity is possible.

The interdisciplinary approach in the book reflects the way we have worked with solidarity over the past four years. Almost all the authors have been part of interdisciplinary international conferences, workshops and lecture series and they have all been attracted to and inspired by the interdisciplinary approach. Hence, the book is not a result of conference papers from one specific conference (which is often the case in an edited volume) but rather the *result of the thoughts, inspiration, developments and outcome of a long four-year process* in which we have been working on this topic as a group. The purpose of the book is to offer a *timely* and *interdisciplinary perspective* on transnational solidarity, the challenges currently facing it and possible solutions to those challenges, and this reflects the originality of the project.

Interdisciplinarity is furthermore reflected in the group of editors, who together represents law (Helle Krunke), political science (Ian Manners) and legal sociology and legal culture (Hanne Petersen). We have worked in close co-operation with Carol Gould, who has a background in philosophy. She has been closely connected to our solidarity project throughout the past four years and we wish to express our deep gratitude for this co-operation.

PART I

Transnational Solidarity

Concept and Conditions

1

Solidarity

A Short History from the Concept's Beginnings to the Present Situation

SVEN-ERIC LIEDMAN

In this chapter,[1] I will trace the history of the concept of solidarity back to its historical roots in French jurisprudence, and then follow its development as a political and social catchword used by so-called utopian socialists and then by the labour movement. In the Catholic Church, solidarity has been given a prominent place from the late nineteenth century up to the present time, but in sharp contrast to the socialists, who saw solidarity as typical of the modern age, it was here identified with the age-old Christian notion of charity. A rather recent example of an effort to make the concept useful to a very modest political agenda is found in so-called New Labour politics under Tony Blair. Much more radical, however, is the campaign led by young people to save the climate for future generations, with the sixteen-year-old Swedish schoolgirl, Greta Thunberg, as its figurehead. In this context, the concept of solidarity has been given new vitality.

The word 'solidarity' comes from the French. Its roots go further back to the Latin *solidus*, which means sturdy, firm and undivided. As early as the sixteenth century, French lawyers spoke of *solidarité* in a sense that is still current in many languages today. If a loan has multiple guarantors and the borrower defaults, one of them pays the entire amount and is subsequently reimbursed by the others. English jurisprudence uses the phrase 'joint and several liability', but the concept is the same as what we in common parlance call 'all for one and one for all'.

[1] This chapter is partly based on the first part of the book, Sven-Eric Liedman, *Att Se Sig Själv I Andra – Om Solidaritet* (Stockholm: Bonnier Essä, 1999).

Solidarity appeared in *Code civil*, Napoleon's famous statute book of 1804.[2] A few years later, Charles Fourier incorporated the word into his vocabulary, lending it the political and ideological nuances that it has retained to this day.

Though opinionated and eccentric, Fourier was a brilliant and ground-breaking social philosopher. In addition to playing a decisive role in early socialism in general and for Marx in particular, Fourier's vision of a harmonious new society spawned a large coterie of devotees ready and willing to put it into practice.

Théorie des quatre mouvements (*Theory of the Four Movements*), Fourier's first major work, came out in 1808 when Napoleon was at the height of his power. In it he sketches the contours of a totally new society. The civilisation that so smugly looks down on barbarians and savages is, in reality, a hodgepodge of blind and anarchistic competition, large-scale excess and a scandalous waste of talent and emotion. It singles out reason as the most important human attribute and passion as the quality that propels humanity forward and enriches our lives. Associated with faith in reason is the concept that all people are basically equal. Fourier, however, maintains that we are unequal and that it is our very differences that permit us to cooperate with each other. Such collaboration would be most fruitful in small, independent ideal communities that he calls phalanxes. Not only will they prohibit duplication of labour, but nobody will have to do the same thing from dawn to dusk. People will switch tasks several times throughout the day and everyone will be dependent on their fellows.[3]

The word solidarity slinks almost unnoticeably in and out of his writing. As the supreme coiner of words and concepts, Fourier did not attach undue significance to a term that had been borrowed from legal jargon.

The word remained in the background until the 1840s, when it became a political catchword. In Europe, the 1840s were incomparable years, particularly when it came to political ideas. Utopias were designed, ideal communities were founded on faraway continents and many European countries advanced ineluctably towards revolution. The word solidarity took on a new lustre, signifying a free and blessed country that stood in

[2] *Code civil*, art. 1211. See *Trésor de la langue française*, Vol. 15 (Paris: Centre de Recherche pour un Trésor de la Langue Française, 1992), pp. 623–6.

[3] C. Fourier, *Théorie de quatre mouvements et des destinées générales* (1808), in C. Fourier, *Oeuvres complètes de Charles Fourier*, Vol. 1 (Paris: Aux bureaux de la phalange, 1861), pp. 272–85.

opposition to the stagnation that obstructed society's view of the glorious future.

Its use was not limited to political radicals; conservatives could and did use it, as we will see. A decisive point came in 1864, when the First Workers' International was founded in London. The provisional rules of the International spoke of 'solidarity among workers of various trades in every country'.[4]

To all appearances, Marx did not play a decisive role in altering the terminology from 'brotherhood' to 'solidarity'.[5] But a brush maker by the name of Johann Philipp Becker was an ardent champion of the word solidarity. Though he was much less well known, he had long been close to Marx. Given that Becker accorded greater significance to trade unions than Marx, he gravitated towards Mikhail Bakunin's anarchists at a certain point. He eventually returned to the fold when the schism between the Marxists and anarchists brought down the entire International.

Becker's greatest influence was as editor of the journal *Der Vorbote* (*The Harbinger*). In it, he made a noble attempt to draw a clear conceptual distinction between brotherhood and solidarity. According to him, solidarity is *Brüderlichkeit der Tat* (the brotherhood of deeds) and should not be confused with the bourgeoisie's *Brüderlichkeit der Phrasen* (the brotherhood of words). Rather than being a moral issue, solidarity is a matter of reciprocity and affinity.[6]

The international aspect of the solidarity concept nurtured by the workers' movement was to be crucial for the future. Of equal significance is that the concept remained outside the scaffolding of Marx's theories. Furthermore, thinkers such as Karl Kautsky, Vladimir Ilyich Lenin, Antonio Gramsci, Mao Zedong or Jean-Paul Sartre, who subsequently enlarged upon Marx's ideas, did not ascribe solidarity much theoretical importance. It was a straightforward word to be used in the realm of political rhetoric, union meetings and one-to-one conversations.

[4] 'Inauguraladresse der Internationalen Arbeiter-Assoziation', in *Marx Engels Werke*, Vol. 16 (Berlin: Dietz, 1964), p.12.

[5] On *brotherhood* as a concept, see Wolfgang Schieder, 'Brüderlichkeit', in Reinhart Koselleck et al. (eds.), *Geschichtliche Grundbegriffe*, Vol. 1 (Stuttgart: Ernst Klett, 1972), p. 577f. For Marx on brotherhood see his 'Inauguraladresse der Internationalen Arbeiter-Assoziation', p. 12.

[6] Johann Philipp Becker (ed.), *Der Vorbote, Politische und Sozial-ökonomische Monatsschrift*, vol. 8 (1866), p. 18.

The power of the word stemmed from its flexibility, durability and emotional intensity. 'Real socialism', as practised in the Soviet Union and its border states, harboured few compunctions about dropping solidarity when it suited. When used at all, it became synonymous with 'socialist internationalism', a concept used by the Soviet Union when invading both Czechoslovakia and Afghanistan.[7]

Thus, the Polish labour movement took a bold step by calling itself *Solidarność* (*Solidarity* in Polish). Quite simply, workers adopted a word that rulers had jealously guarded for their own purposes. In doing so, they gave it back the meaning that Becker and the International had in mind. As a matter of fact, the word had been entrenched among workers ever since that time.[8]

Christianity, particularly the Catholic Church, also got in on the act well before the turn of the twentieth century. German theologians and social philosophers led the charge. Two influential German Catholic thinkers were Franz Hitze and Heinrich Pesch. Spurning both the workers' movement and capitalism, they envisioned a society in which competition would make way for solidarity. Their ideal was the cohesion that characterises a well-adjusted family. By extension, an entire society could function in a similar manner.

Though not new in themselves, these ideas took on fresh implications by linking up with the view that the church should enter into a dialogue with modernity instead of dismissing it. Solidarity appeared in Pope Pius XI's (papacy 1922–39) famed encyclical of 1931,[9] which advanced the principle of subsidiarity as the solution to key social problems. Pius was proposing a structure in which decisions would be made at the lowest possible level, be that the international community, the nation, the region or the family. Thanks to the European Union, subsidiarity is now a firmly established word.

Ever since the 1931 encyclical, popes have had a good deal to say about solidarity. Although *solidarietas* did not find its way into Latin until 1964, modern languages had adopted it much earlier. John Paul II (papacy

7 For example, in Georg Klaus and Manfred Buhr (eds.), *Philosophisches Wörterbuch*, Vol. 2 (Leipzig: Bibliographisches Institut, 1975), p. 1,110, where solidarity is defined exclusively as international solidarity.

8 There is a wealth of literature on the Polish Solidarity movement. See, for example, T. Garton Ash, *The Polish Revolution: Solidarity*, 3rd edition (New Haven, CT: Yale University Press, 2002).

9 Pius XI, *Quadragesimo anno* (Roma, 1931).

1978–2005) was a specialist, of sorts, on the Catholic conception of solidarity.

John Paul II frequently related solidarity to his concept of personality. The individual is in danger of melting into the crowd, becoming faceless and replaceable, but by cultivating your personality you can remain autonomous while contributing to the cohesion of the larger group. In learning to identify that which binds you to others, you develop a sense of solidarity.[10]

Such an approach eschews not only the collectivism espoused by socialism, but the individualism that is the hallmark of liberalism. In the commonwealth foreseen by the Pope John Paul II (papacy 1978–2005), rich and poor are aware of their dependence on each other which leaves no room for either class struggle or the merciless competition of market liberalism.

The Christian solidarity of his late-nineteenth-century predecessors was special in a number of respects. Up until that time, the word had referred to a wholly new possibility – whether it be the phalanxes, the role of the working class or the interdependence that would characterise an enlightened state. However, popes, since Pius XI, linked it to the Christian tradition, in particular Jesus' declaration to his disciples that '(i)nasmuch as you have done it for the least of My brothers, you have done it unto Me'.[11]

Furthermore, while Fourier and later socialists had made a clear-cut distinction between solidarity and philanthropy, according to the papacy, helping the poor is the highest manifestation of Catholic theology's concept of *caritas* (love for one's neighbour).

From this, it is clear that we have two different concepts of solidarity. According to the first, the socialist or working-class concept, solidarity belongs to the modern society with its far-reaching division of labour and the necessity for people who would otherwise be exploited or oppressed to band together. According to the other, the Catholic concept, solidarity means just as much as age-old Christian charity.[12]

[10] On the Catholic tradition and especially Pope Jean Paul II, see Kevin P. Doran, *Solidarity: A Synthesis of Personalism and Communalism in the Thought of Karol Woytila/Pope John Paul II* (New York: Peter Lang, 1996).

[11] Matthew 25:40.

[12] Two influential German Catholic social philosophers, Franz Hitze and Heinrich Pesch, seem to have been the founders of this tradition. Most important is Franz Hitze, *Kapital und Arbeit und die Reorganisation der Gesellschaft* (Paderborn: Druck und Verlag der Bonifacius-Druckerei (J. W. Schröder), 1880). On solidarity, see, for example, p. 435f.

Let me immediately declare that I am not an adherent to the Catholic idea of solidarity as charity. We live in a time when it would often be heartless if we refused to give alms to beggars or to make a contribution to organisations that make life somewhat more bearable for poor people. In the present situation, when millions of refugees are trying to rescue their children and themselves from the burning hells in Syria or Afghanistan, it is even our moral duty to try to help at least a few of them.

It is, however, quite another idea that society must forever be at a stage where we have some relatively stable roles as, on the one hand, the benevolent rich and, on the other, the help-seeking poor. On the contrary, we still need a provisional utopia in which charity would be, at most, an accidental exception. This is the dream of a relatively egalitarian and free society and was also the original socialist conception of a good future.

In recent times, however, many socialists and social-democrats have adopted much more modest and limited, even bleaker, perspectives. Let me give just one example: the famous British sociologist, Anthony Giddens. In the heyday of the British New Labour Party, Giddens was an important intellectual adviser to Tony Blair, the man who had taken it upon himself to transform Britain. In 1998, Giddens published a book called *The Third Way: The Renewal of Social Democracy*.[13] Giddens cites a typical statement by Blair on the very first page of this book. Whereas globalisation elicits dogged resistance among the old Left and a spirit of laissez-faire in the new Right, Blair summons adherents of the Third Way to strive for 'social solidarity and prosperity'.

Though the book mentions the word 13 times in 150 pages, it never lets the reader in on what non-social types of solidarity may entail. Nonetheless, a certain pattern begins to take shape. Whenever associated with collectivism, solidarity takes on a negative connotation. One of the whipping boys of political terminology nowadays, collectivism was part and parcel of the traditional workers' movement. As a result, the solidarity propounded by the Third Way must join forces with contemporary individualism. According to Giddens, '(s)olidarity has long been a theme of social democracy';[14] however, he goes on to say that Marxism was ambivalent when it came to individualism and collectivism. Marx wrote

[13] A. Giddens, *The Third Way: The Renewal of Social Democracy* (Cambridge: Polity Press, 1998).

[14] Ibid., pp. 34–7.

that a socialist society would allow each person to fully and freely develop his or her individual gifts. Still, both socialism and communism, as practised in the real world, emphasised the role of the state in forging equality and solidarity. Giddens claims that such a strategy is futile in our times. The world of today fosters a non-egoistic 'new individualism', which poses no threat to social solidarity. Rather, our challenge is to find new ways of ensuring that cohesion.

Giddens refers to the modern phenomenon as 'institutionalised individualism', arguing that it is a product of the institutions associated with the welfare state. For him, the primary beneficiary of these institutions is not the family but the individual. Each person is dependent on employment, which in turn stands or falls with education and mobility. In other words, an individual chooses his or her own profession and place of residence regardless of tradition or family considerations.

Paradoxically, the same collectivism that contributed so much to the emergence of the welfare state has spawned a new type of individualism.

Giddens is also guided by another idea. He maintains that once a relatively prosperous democracy has ensured people's basic necessities, they tend to seek a better quality of life (which he defines as the opportunity for self-realisation, meaningful work and satisfying leisure activities) as opposed to additional material advantage. The new spirit of individualism is accompanied by greater scepticism towards political authority.

Rather than an adversary to solidarity and individualism, Giddens regards globalisation as a possible ally. He wants to curb market forces, restrain unproductive currency trading and rectify an irrational state of affairs in which only 5 per cent of financial transactions involve goods and services. However, he likes the fact that each point on earth is increasingly linked to the whole. According to Giddens, the very process of globalisation accords greater importance to local and regional entities, but he readily admits that national institutions will continue to play a key role; some decisions that were once the purview of the state will now accrue to global organisations, whereas others will fall to regions, municipalities or individuals.[15]

Some of today's most pressing problems – 'the weakening sense of solidarity in some local communities and urban neighbourhoods, high level of crime, and the breaking up of marriages and families' – can be alleviated accordingly. Instead of harkening back to the old type of

[15] Ibid., pp. 78f.

affinity, local communities will be better able to mobilise their resources in order to improve the material and social condition of deteriorating areas. Education, universal healthcare and crime fighting will liberate people from oppression. The society envisaged by the Third Way ascribes great importance to the family – not the patriarchal setup of the past, but as a new (by definition good) entity based on equality between the sexes.[16]

Perhaps Giddens' book must first of all be seen as an example of the optimism that was typical of the 1990s, after the end of the Cold War. To many, a good, harmonious society seemed almost within reach. Welfare society served as the midwife of a sound individualism characterised by a sense of trust and security. Russia, already almost a fully fledged democracy, would soon come close to the Western lifestyle and social life. With globalisation, wealth and welfare would soon be realised in a not-too-distant future in Latin America, South Asia and Africa. In such a world, the very modest ideas of a good future, as presented by Anthony Giddens, could be seen as highly appropriate, at least from the vantage points of the leaders of the New Labour Party. Today, they stand out as both futile and naïve.

With the benefit of hindsight, we can say that the optimism of the 1990s was not built on adequate foundations. In 2019, if the word solidarity can have any meaning at all, it is not in accordance with Anthony Giddens' proposals. After 9/11 in 2001, and more so after George W. Bush's and Blair's invasion of Iraq in 2003, the idyllic prospects from 1998 seem totally out of date. The financial crisis that culminated in 2008 meant another incredibly substantial change. The tax payers in many countries had to pay for the adventurous financial manoeuvres of the economic elite. From the so-called 'Panama Papers', which were leaked a few years ago, we know that the same economic elite escaped from their own tax paying by sending money to tax havens including Switzerland, Cyprus and the British Virgin Islands, and the British Crown dependencies of Guernsey, Jersey and the Isle of Man.

At the same time, millions of refugees from the burning hells of Syria, Iraq, Afghanistan and other countries are trying to rescue themselves by fleeing to Europe. At first, they seemed to be relatively successful but now they are met by closed borders, fences and walls. Those who are already

[16] Ibid., pp. 105ff.

settled in Europe, are facing increasingly visible right-wing populism, chauvinism, xenophobia and even racism.

Atop all this, more ominous than anything else, comes the climate crisis which is the most challenging part of today's universal environmental crisis. This crisis has been recognised by experts for decades and has more recently been widely acknowledged by most politicians and, finally, by the person in the street. However, some leading politicians, such as Donald Trump and the new Brazilian president, Jair Bolsonaro, continue to hold a position of denial of the imminent threat. Above all, the road from insight to efficient action turns out to be critically long for most governments, just as it is for big companies and even most ordinary consumers.

In reaction to this situation, a young Swedish schoolgirl, Greta Thunberg, started her own school strike in August 2018. In a short time, her example has inspired other young people to a near-global movement of protest against the lack of initiative and stubborn egotism exhibited by those in power. In this action, the concept of solidarity has become quite central. Many people declare that they will live and act 'in solidarity with Greta Thunberg', and others talk about a solidarity with young and future generations that makes it necessary for everybody to change habits and lifestyles.[17]

It is impossible today to forecast the future impact of Thunberg's and her sympathisers' actions. Thunberg is, however, not alone among young people protesting against a political and economic order that threatens both social coherence and nature. Another example is Alexandria Ocasio-Cortez, who at the age of twenty-nine became the youngest woman ever to serve in the United States' Congress. She has already become an influential member, focusing upon both environmental issues (especially climate threats), and to rapidly increasing inequality in the USA and across the world.[18]

Evidently, an increasing number of people are now aware of the ominous importance of climate change and realise that it is not enough

[17] A Google search that combines Thunberg's name with the word 'solidarity' already gives good examples of this, and even if the word 'solidarity' is not very frequent, the phenomenon of acting together for a better future for people and nature in coming generations is decisive. On her international impact, see the English Wikipedia article on her: https://en.wikipedia.org/wiki/Greta_Thunberg.

[18] Alexandria Ocasio-Cortez, often refer to as AOC after her initials, has been treated, hailed and criticised in a large number of articles. See the many references in the English Wikipedia article on her: https://en.wikipedia.org/wiki/Alexandria_Ocasio-Cortez.

to change their own consumption pattern – they must also influence politicians and corporations. In the last analysis, this is most of all an act of solidarity with the generations that follow us. If both corporations and politicians only focus on what is coming up in the next few months or couple of years, ordinary people have a duty to be more farsighted and sagacious.

Today, this seems to be the most imminently important aspect of solidarity, whereas the New Labour meaning (as formulated by Anthony Giddens) of idyllic, welfare state individualism, already looks both provincial and outdated two decades later. The lifestyle typical of northwestern Europe and the USA is more and more untenable, not only due to the global situation but also to imminent internal problems, such as a steady over-consumption of both personal and social resources.

In short, welfare state individualism does not seem to be the nearest future of humankind. An alternative kind of solidarity that is thriving, not only across the Western world but all over the globe, is a-nationalistic and excludes forms of solidarity that make a sharp dividing line between 'real' inhabitants of a country and those seen as foreigners who do not belong to the true *Gemeinschaft*. What is the awful Mr Trump if not a reactionary chauvinist, and what do we see in India, China, Japan and all over Europe if not intolerant nationalism? Furthermore, there is just as exclusive a solidarity inside many religious communities, culminating in the terrible terrorism of Al Qaida and Daesh (ISIS).

I think that the only honourable solidarity in this situation is the absolute opposite of chauvinist and other kinds of militantly excluding unity. In a globalised world, those who are superficially or more substantially different must meet and join forces against all the imminent threats that we are facing today. We already have a set of good strategies to fight both racism and sexism. The differences between languages and cultures are more difficult to overcome. English as *the* language of a globalised world is, of course, an excellent tool for fostering solidarity but still only one of many requisite means. The difference between those who have English as their mother tongue and those of us who do not is already important. Besides, the rich variety of different languages is also part and parcel of human culture; every language being a world in itself with its own folklore, poetry, art, way of living and so on. What is impossible to grasp immediately will, in due time, open up its hidden richness to the diligent foreigner.

There are two typical attitudes towards 'the foreign' – one is fear, the other curiosity. Today, fear is dominant. Many try to find their own hidden place inside their nation, their religion and their way of living. Curiosity about that which is different and even alien is the only remedy and the only safe way to foster both more wisdom and more tolerance.

Of course, what I am saying is quite utopian. Impeding the realisation of such a utopia lies the abyss between the rich and mighty and the poor, wars and deepening conflicts, the enormous environmental problems and so on. We must fight the economic inequality that causes so many of the other problems. At the same time, we have to change the ways of thinking that make people foreigners to each other. The opposite of chauvinism, racism, sexism and religious intolerance is real human solidarity that must today extend to all nature of which we, as physical beings, are part and parcel.

2

Solidarity Between the National and the Transnational

What Do We Owe to 'Outsiders'?

CAROL C. GOULD

Recently, people in countries on both sides of the Atlantic have been wrestling with questions concerning the priority they should give residents of their own country versus distant others. In Europe, the issue of the acceptance and treatment of migrants from the Middle East and North Africa came to prominence; although the numbers of migrants are down to pre-2015 levels, the issue continues to affect politics there, with nationalist and nativist parties on the rise. Likewise, in the USA, President Trump attempted to bar Muslims from entering the county at all, increased the deportation of undocumented Mexicans and people fleeing violence and hardship in Latin America (including separating children from their parents), and drastically cut the number of refugees that could be admitted. The issue of priority to 'countrymen' has also arisen there in debates about international trade and its impacts on jobs for Americans, as well as in regard to foreign aid and also the obligation to maintain regional and global alliances.

These various practical contexts, so salient in contemporary politics, raise questions of what we owe 'outsiders', whether they be distantly situated or attempting to migrate to our own or to a different state, and these questions raise difficult issues of conflicting solidarities. Should we always stand in solidarity with fellow citizens or other members of our own political communities, or should we equally prioritise solidarity with oppressed or suffering others outside our borders? In this chapter, I want to make some progress towards clarifying this issue, if not solving it, by analysing the two main senses of solidarity involved here and then going on to discuss the question of negotiating between them when they conflict. I will not focus directly on the problem of migration in this chapter but will take it as one of the most important domains that call for solidarity with outsiders. Indeed, even if the contemporary causes of migration are eventually mitigated, the challenge posed by climate refugees – of migration due to climate change – is certain to become more pressing in the coming decades. With the differential impacts of climate change, including the likely eventual disappearance of entire island nations, the problem of obligations to admit outsiders or at least to solidaristically aid them will confront more favoured communities worldwide. (Of course, eventually, climate change will also pose grave danger for the world as a whole.)

In fact, the term solidarity has been widely, and perhaps carelessly, used over the past period to refer to a host of possible relations to others. Notably, it has been applied to express how we feel in relation to the victims of terrorist attacks elsewhere, and their fellow nationals impacted by these attacks, with whom we frequently say that we stand in solidarity. What do we mean by this? Is it more than an expression of sympathy? Increasingly, the notion of standing in solidarity with the victims of oppression or exploitation is used in ways that harken back to earlier Marxist notions of labour movement solidarity. Solidarity in this sense is also implicit in the recent attention theorists have given to our responsibility to attempt to remedy various forms of structural injustice, whether through boycotts or protests, or other ways of expressing solidarity with others, many of whom live beyond our national borders. Recent feminist movements, notably the #MeToo movement, have taken on a distinctly transnational dimension, fuelled in part by social media attention to various cases, initially of prominent men but extending to women's experiences in all walks of life.

It is evident that these senses of solidarity – which pertain to distant people or transnational social movements – go beyond the traditional conception that applies among the members of a given group; the latter represents a type of unitary solidarity that (putatively, at least) binds the members of a given community to each other. This unitary form has been most often applied to the relations among citizens within a nation state, as well as to smaller groups, though it has also increasingly been used in the context of the obligations of members of the EU to each other.

In previous work, I have delineated a new conception of transnational solidarities, understood in terms of overlapping networks of relations between individuals or groups and distantly situated others (again, individuals or groups), in which the former aim to support the latter through actions to eliminate oppression or reduce suffering. We can discern networks of this sort in social movements as well as in civil society organisations, where those joining in these networked relations aim at the fulfilment of justice or the meeting of basic needs. These solidarity networks may be based on empathy or fellow feeling with these affected others, or else on shared interests. Although often taking the form of advantaged groups helping disadvantaged ones, in theory at least these forms of solidarity involve some notion of potential reciprocity or mutual aid, particularly when the connections are founded on shared interests. Normatively, moreover, we can say that such transnational solidarities ought to exemplify deference to those they are endeavouring to aid, taking their lead from these affected others.[1]

Labour movement solidarity is a classic case of network solidarity, but such forms of solidarity are also found in social movements like Occupy Wall Street, the Indignatos in Spain, and in Latin America groups organizing against dictatorships or oriented to achieving social justice with regard to food, water and other needs. Another example, explicitly focused on countering oppression, is the anti-sweatshop movement. And although solidarity is not the same as humanitarian aid, solidarity networks can also be found among some civil society organisations that attempt to relieve the suffering of people subject to natural disasters. Examples are those that followed the Haitian earthquake or the Asian tsunamis. It should be noted that this type of solidarity, namely, network solidarity, is not necessarily transnational, though it often is. The recent Resistance movement in the USA, including the Indivisible movement, though more narrowly political, takes a similar networking form, as I shall describe further below. Likewise, there have been forms of solidarity established among cities and some nation states who are committed to achieving a reduction in carbon emissions to counter climate change, sometimes involving a sharing of useful information and strategies, if not yet of other resources. A new social movement initiated by children who skipped school to protest and highlight the need for climate action also shows potential to spread transnationally.

I have suggested that such network solidarities can be analysed as differing in important ways from the classic forms of solidarity thought to bind individuals to each other within social groups, for example, in

[1] Carol C. Gould, 'Transnational solidarities', *Journal of Social Philosophy*, Special Issue on Solidarity, 38(1) (2007), 146–62; Carol C. Gould, *Interactive Democracy, The Social Roots of Global Justice* (Cambridge: Cambridge University Press, 2014), 99–131.

families or tribes, as well as within broader political communities. In these more traditional contexts, the groups are thought to manifest the spirit evident in the slogan of the Three Musketeers – 'all for one and one for all'.[2] Needless to say, this spirit can have problematic consequences when the groups in question are gangs or clans, where loyalty to fellow members tends to be placed above considerations of justice or moral rightness. It is also problematic when it takes nationalist forms, as has become widespread again of late. But related ethical issues can impact network or transnational solidarities as well, to the degree that they may sometimes disregard questions of justice entirely, or adopt faulty and exclusionary understandings of it, for example, among white supremacy groups. Even movements oriented towards justice can be exclusionary, at least to a degree, when they centre on the realisation of shared interests that necessarily oppose the interests of those engaged in exploitation or other forms of injustice.

Although these potential negative impacts of solidarity pose difficulties for theory, I want to focus here especially on the hard question that arises when the two main contexts of solidarity – the national and the transnational – conflict with each other. That is, what are we to do when the obligation to stand in solidarity with members of one's own community conflicts with the call to participate in transnational solidarity networks that themselves aim at justice? In order to address this question, I think we first need to get clearer on these possible forms of solidarity and the demands they make on us. To this end, we will have to bring in some normative perspectives concerning our local and global responsibilities, if we are to successfully deal with the problem raised by such conflicts. Effectively addressing this problem (or beginning to address it) promises to have practical significance in regard to evaluating the contemporary treatment of migrants in Europe and the USA, as well as for the obligations to fellow nationals posed by international trade, as this has been discussed in recent US politics. Similar conflicts have been posed in the discussion of the viability and desirability of the European Union (EU), and on the other side of the Atlantic, in regard to the acceptability of the ill-named and, indeed, also ill-conceived, 'America First' policy, both in international affairs and as it affects those within US borders.

[2] It should be noted that this slogan has older roots than Alexandre Dumas's novel of 1844, apparently going back to at least the seventeenth century, and serving as the traditional motto of Switzerland.

1 Types of Solidarity

So far, I have suggested that a conflict can exist between (1) a group-binding notion of solidarity, evident in communities at local and national levels, and (2) a notion of overlapping solidarity networks, most often found in transnational contexts. But we can see already that this dichotomy needs to be qualified in various ways. For one thing, the first sense – of social bonds and unified commitment within an existing community – can itself extend transnationally, as in some regional applications, although these bonds tend to remain rather weak there, notably in the EU. More importantly, the networked sense of solidarity also exists within the borders of nation states, for example, within subnational social movements and in connections among civil society organisations in the national context. This suggests that we should not define these alternative conceptions primarily in geographical terms, but rather as ideal types of social and political organisation of solidarities. This observation will have import in what follows.

Another proviso concerns the very concept of a network as applied to (mostly transnational) solidarity movements or to the interrelationships among civil society organisations. Although I continue to rely on this notion of a network in my own account of transnational solidarities, as have others (for example, Sally Haslanger in her analysis of the distribution of roles within institutional social structures[3]), we can wonder whether it is fully adequate for these purposes.

The advantage of the network notion is the focus it places on the way groups or individuals link up with diverse others for various purposes, where these others are most often not members of the same group or even the same encompassing group (such as a nation). Yet, the notion of a network has disadvantages as well, and perhaps a different metaphor can better suggest the diverse interrelationships between groups or within a social structure. In particular, it may be that the metaphor of a *web* may be better than that of a network. The problems with the notion of a network are threefold.

1. Although we may acknowledge the differential power that usually accompanies certain positions within a network, the idea of a network normally implies that the nodes are in an important sense equal in status and access. (This equality is precisely the characteristic

[3] Sally Haslanger, 'What is a (social) structural explanation?', *Philosophical Studies*, 173(1) (2016), 113–30.

of the design of the Internet that appealed to its developers. It can be entered from anywhere and no node has priority over others. Unfortunately, this openness has lately been curtailed, largely by the effects of commercialisation.)

2. The notion has its original home in computer networking, and brings certain limitations when transferred to social relations. Like all technological and scientific metaphors, it may be compelling in its original domain, but can reify social relations, in this case by omitting their internality and their embeddedness. The latter qualities are perhaps better captured by the idea of a web (though of course, that too is derived from elsewhere – from biological nature in this case). We can note that even the notion of 'interlocking' positions or roles suggests chains, and therefore remains a technologically freighted metaphor.
3. A final drawback is that networks most often suggest openness to new participants in their membership. But in fact, many social networks are not open, but rather closed to outsiders. (Perhaps this deficiency can be remedied by distinguishing between open and closed networks.)

While the idea of a 'web' is itself a metaphor drawn from nature, it suggests the interrelations and overlapping that we are getting at with the idea of a network and may better reflect the interrelatedness of people and groups within social movement contexts or even in social structures. It points to the embeddedness and particularity of human relations, while networks are inherently replicable and also schematic. The notion of a web also has the advantage of connoting something spun, which is suggestive of agency (that is, a spinner in this case). Still, the metaphor of a web, like that of a network, does not do justice to the power discrepancies that mark human social relations, and especially, the relations between groups in society.

Turning to network solidarity, we can note that it generally has a positive sense in referring to individuals or groups who are ready to offer each other mutual aid, whether within a nation state or across borders. The relations among the entities are normally cooperative, rather than antagonistic, which is not to say that they cannot also sometimes evince negative forms of relationships. Examples of the network or web forms include labour movement solidarity between unions; social movement solidarity, for example, among transnational justice or democracy movements in Latin America, as in the Via Campesina; feminist solidarity movements, for example, against female genital cutting, or in some ways the recent #MeToo movement with the mutual support it can engender among women (both individually and in groups); and finally, cooperative relations among civil society or aid organisations to ameliorate natural disasters or social harms, whether across borders or within them.

These forms of solidarity are distinguished from national solidarities, which are understood as more unitary phenomena in which individuals (or sometimes groups) bind themselves to each other (and feel themselves bound in this way), in view of their shared language, history, traditions and practices. In this latter case, each is thought to bear the same relation to the others, and stands together with them, as members of a unitary group. Subnational solidarities, by contrast, can either take such unitary forms or may constitute themselves as overlapping solidarity networks. The unitariness of the solidarity involved exists in the understanding of the participants, despite the actual diversity of their backgrounds and interests. It can also exist, though to a lesser degree, in the actual relations of interdependence among the members of this group, as they act in economic and social contexts. Yet, at the national level, these solidarities are in fact rarely fully unitary, except perhaps in some situations of defensive war. Moreover, the unitary understanding is often accompanied by exclusionary definitions of who is a true member of the nation in question or by notions of a pre-existing community and history that grounds the solidarity of the (often national) group. Despite the non-solidaristic aspects that may be evident in practice, we can see that the idea of the nation or of the unity of the more local group in question retains a normative force that undergirds this type of solidarity.

Unitary solidarities can be found outside the national level, and in fact can be characteristic of local or regional groupings, such as towns and municipalities. In fact, they often mark the relations among small groups, whether of friends, or co-workers, or a gang, or in broader contexts, a tribe. These groups are not necessarily based on ethnicity, or even a single goal, although they tend to involve some shared goals and practices. At the most general level, solidarity in this sense can be seen to emerge in the context of what I have elsewhere designated as common activities, which are groups oriented to shared ends, sometimes explicitly constituted and bound by those, but most often taking the form of a community or set of co-ordinated and integrated activities that are aimed at sets of shared or overlapping ends over time. This sense of solidarity will also have importance in what follows, since the success in achieving the shared goals depends in part on reciprocal and co-operative relations among the members of the group and community. It also depends on the ability of the members to meet their own basic needs, most often through the support of the group, whether understood locally, nationally or in other ways. In cooperating to achieve shared goals and in offering each other mutual support, such forms of solidarity (ideally at least) go beyond mere feelings of togetherness or of a shared fate to actions that work to advance the interests of the community or group as a whole.

In contrast, the networked (or webbed) forms that characterise many transnational social movements or associations are distinguished by the fact that they are based on a relation to groups outside a given set of common activities. Moreover, the groups that make up the network link up with each other and attempt to co-operate in specific and varied ways to achieve a shared goal (in broadest and normative terms, that of achieving justice or countering oppression, or perhaps also alleviating suffering). They may divide up the project and each may do part of the tasks required, or they may perform overlapping tasks. They do not necessarily agree on the importance of all parts of the plan, or on the specific ways in which the goals are to be achieved. The groups constitute themselves as a network – or perhaps better, a web – of co-operation.

Clearly, the solidarity groups here are inter-constituted in virtue of sharing common goals, as well as in the explicitly co-operative forms of planning and execution of the projects they undertake. We can say then that these groups or the individuals that make them up are internally related and inter-defined, but generally not as strongly or enduringly as are groups or individuals within a unitary solidary community. The unity among them is explicitly constructed and sustained rather than regarded (at least most often) as pre-existing, or pre-constituted. The unions, movement groups, or civil society organisations that stand together in solidarity networks may have other projects that they undertake singly – even ones they regard as more significant – beyond the solidarity project at hand, and in this respect they may remain relatively unchanged by their interrelations with each other. Nonetheless, to the degree that they see their work as aimed at a comprehensive goal like global justice, they will likely try to ensure that their various separate projects and their participation in the transnational solidarity network will be in some sort of harmony, certainly more so than can be found among a group of organisations with divergent goals and plans.

More could be said about the forms of decision making that transpire within such transnational solidarity movements or networks, especially as to whether they operate democratically or not, and if so, whether they use consensual forms of decision making or representative ones.[4] The effect of institutionalisation of these solidarity groups has been studied and the contrast drawn with more aggregative forms of social change, for example, through internet crowdsourcing or crowdfunding.[5] The latter – more aggregative – type of organisation tends to emerge from and reinforce relatively external relations among participants, though it can also evidence certain instrumental forms of co-operation for specific purposes. Still, these crowd-sourced forms of interaction do not manifest the stronger inter-constitutive types of solidarity that I am highlighting here.

An important difference between the unitary and the network forms of solidarity is that the unitary sense of social bonds and commitment normally presupposes the prior existence of a social group, whereas the networking form endeavours precisely to create or construct such a group through activity linking the single individual, institution or group with others. An important feature of this latter form of solidarity is that it is, as Klaus Rippe puts it, 'project oriented', aiming at the realisation of shared goals.[6] Moreover, such groups may work at countering oppression, meeting basic needs or fulfilling human rights, thereby aiming to realise the requirements of justice. These solidarity groups may not share a single conception of justice, although they take justice as their aim. Moreover, such groups may strive to be inclusive and to operate consensually or democratically, though they most often fail to measure up to these desiderata.

The sort of transnational network that aims at the elimination of oppression or the establishment of justice differs in some significant ways from those networked civil society solidarity groupings whose primary aim is the alleviation of suffering. The first of these types, exemplified by labour solidarity or, in a different way, the #MeToo movement – involves groups most often organised around shared interests, which tend to stand against or opposed to other groups or social structures that they view as oppressive or exploitative. Nonetheless, in the labour case, it is possible to distinguish between the exploitation that attends the performance of a role within the capitalist economy and the

4 Gould, *Interactive Democracy*, chapters 5 and 12.

5 See Jeffrey S. Juris, 'Reflections on #Occupy Everywhere: social media, public space, and emerging logics of aggregation', *American Ethnologist*, 39(2) (2012), 259–79.

6 Klaus Peter Rippe, 'Diminishing solidarity', *Ethical Theory and Practice*, 1(3) (1998), 355–74.

people themselves performing this role who may not have explicit motives or intentions to oppress. This raises difficult issues of responsibility for exploitation, which I will return to later.

The second sort of solidarity grouping, which aims to alleviate suffering, in contrast, exemplifies the forms of activity involved in providing humanitarian assistance or aid. This differs from simply providing charitable aid in maintaining an implicit notion of reciprocity with those they seek to aid. That is, there is the implicit understanding that what is involved is potentially mutual aid, given the shared humanity and contingent circumstances of those who aid in relation to those they help. Like the first type of network solidarity, the groups in this second case are project oriented, and they may also be directed to the achievement of justice, and especially the rectification of historical injustice.

Whereas the first of these two networking types of solidarity has as its original model labour union solidarity, the second type tends to arise from Catholic models of solidarity with those who suffer. Nonetheless, from a normative perspective, in order to be effective, as well as to count as solidarity in a full normative sense, both forms need not only to implicitly involve reciprocity and even mutual aid, but also need to engage in social critique, in order to understand the concrete context of those they are assisting or the context of oppression that they oppose. This sort of social understanding can enable the solidarity groups to avoid reduplicating forms of oppression or offering unwanted or humiliating forms of aid. In all cases, the assistance or co-operation in question must be desired and perhaps even solicited by the distant others.

Finally, I have suggested that the networking forms of solidarity aimed at justice reveals what we can call a connection between particularity and universality. That is, transnational or networked solidarity always involves feelings and actions directed towards particular others (whether individuals or groups). Yet these solidarity actions can be undertaken with universalistic intent, when they are motivated by the aim of achieving justice. Moreover, such groups normatively ought to be inclusive and to welcome the participation and support of other like-minded groups. In this way, they eschew exclusivism and other forms of narrowness. Yet, to the degree that the solidarity groups in question may be organised around shared interests, they stand opposed to other groups representing the interests of those hostile to their aims, though they may also link up with the members of the groups they oppose in a range of other ways and seek to persuade them to share their vision of equality and the elimination of oppression and exploitation.

Both types of solidarity analysed above can be seen to display what have been called pro-social motivations and feelings oriented to supporting or aiding others. Yet, normatively at least, to evince solidarity of either type, people would need to go beyond feeling or sentiment to practical action in support of others. In this connection, Barbara Prainsack and Alena Buyx have recently proposed that the relevant sorts of action necessarily involve a willingness to incur costs on behalf of others, where these others are perceived as similar to one in a relevant respect.[7] Clearly, if we use the language of 'costs', this need not be understood only, or even mainly, in financial terms, since networking solidarities aiming at overcoming injustice most often involve the expenditure of time and energy in projects or movements. Moreover, to the degree that such movements are oriented around shared interests (rather than simply focused on providing aid to needy others) and indeed may operate against a background of mutual aid, those involved may not perceive any trade-offs between the interests of the individuals and the groups they belong to, or again, among the various groups making up solidarity networks.

Nonetheless, whatever harmony these observations may establish in theory, they do not obviate the problem of conflicting solidarities and their associated obligations, especially those arising from the conjunction of the national and transnational contexts of contemporary social life. We can now turn to further characterising these increasingly pervasive conflicts and considering whether there are ways to effectively deal with them.

2 Negotiating the Conflicting Demands of Multiple Solidarities

The problem posed for an account focused primarily on the recent growth of transnational solidarities is that national solidarity remains the central form in contemporary politics. Indeed, as already suggested, such solidarity is sometimes very necessary, particularly to support economic redistribution within still mainly national economies, and also at the times (hopefully, rare) when a state may need to defend itself against aggression. As we are keenly aware, these nation-based solidarities are widely valued

[7] Barbara Prainsack and Alena Buyx, *Solidarity in Biomedicine and Beyond* (Cambridge: Cambridge University Press, 2017), 52. I present some criticisms, along with an appreciation, of their approach in Carol C. Gould, 'Solidarity and the problem of structural injustice in healthcare', *Bioethics*, Special Issue on Solidarity: New Frontiers, 32(9) (2018), 541–52.

by people in many countries around the world, even if they most often are not conceived to extend to all the residents of the countries in question. These national forms of solidarity would seem to pose demands or obligations on citizens that conflict with the requirement to stand in solidarity with distant others who are oppressed or suffering.

We have noted that similar unitary forms of solidarity can be found within localities and municipalities and at regional levels. These can represent important foci for people's activities and can be analysed as common activities that themselves demand allegiance. Although often identified as constituting an older, historically important form of solidarity, these local or regional varieties in fact remain highly significant as contemporary contexts for mutual identification and mutual aid. As spheres of particular association and affiliation, they represent significant ties that bind people to others, and that help the members of these groupings to meet their basic needs. For these reasons, these more local solidarities need to retain a central place in our analysis.

How, then, can we decide between these various demands of solidarity when they conflict? And even if we undertake to stand in solidarity with distant others, which of these solidarity movements or networks should we participate in? Are there principles that enable us to decide whether to participate and how to choose among the various groups or networks, in terms of which to join and whose causes are the most urgent? These questions concerning transnational solidarity in some ways replicate those posed by the requirements of global justice relative to those of distributive justice at the national level. Yet, given the particularist nature of solidarities, some distinctive questions arise beyond those of balancing the global and the national as in the case of justice.

I have previously proposed that individuals' participation in particular transnational solidarity networks can be regarded as voluntary in the sense that it is up to them to choose which network or project to participate in. What is needed, I have suggested, is a disposition to solidarity, which can be cultivated through education and upbringing. It involves developing faculties of both empathy and reasoning, and also calls for understanding something of the concrete context in which oppression or suffering specifically arises. Given that the disposition to solidarity can (at least in principle) be cultivated generally and widely, we can say that it introduces a universal moment, open to all, although the forms of solidarity to which the disposition will be directed and realised remain particular and diverse. That is, it is possible in principle (however difficult in practice) to have a very wide cultivation of the disposition to solidaristic action, although the particular groups supported by such action are likely to vary widely.

In view of the priority this account gives to fulfilling the aims of social justice on both local and global scales, we can wonder what serves to justify giving priority to national solidarity from a moral point of view. Insofar as many, if not most, states have historically been formed with highly contingent boundaries, often owing their origins to war or to violence more generally, can national solidaristic feelings and actions be justified in wholly particularist and nation-centred terms?

Here I would like to propose that any justification for prioritising solidarity with co-nationals has to comport with cosmopolitan principles of universal human equality, where, moreover, this equality involves more than simply an abstract moral regard (for example, treating all humans as ends and not as means only, in one's personal affairs or interactions with others). It has to be understood in terms of social and political equality as well. A suggestion along similar lines may be implicit in Robert Goodin's analysis in his classic article, 'What is so special about our fellow countrymen?' Goodin presents an account of our duties to co-nationals in terms of a notion of *assigned responsibility*, that is, as an application of what he regards as general duties we owe to everyone. The devolution of those general duties to nation states is at least in part instrumentally justified, that is, the devolution is acceptable as a practicable way by which the general duties can be met, at least in principle.[8]

Although I am wary of Goodin's overall consequentialist framework, we can nonetheless argue in a related way that the fulfilment of human rights (including economic and social rights) by nation states, rather than by the world as a whole, can be justified as a way of realising human rights if these states (and the societies that make them up) can plausibly be expected to do so effectively for their own members. However, it also follows from this contingent priority of the nation state as an avenue for rights fulfilment that if a given state is unable or unwilling to provide for the human rights of its residents, then others (whether states or individuals) have an obligation to step in to help realise these rights. This requirement to step in is entailed by the supremacy of the universal principles of human rights and justice (in my view, to be understood as equal positive freedom[9]). But the fulfilment of the needs and human

[8] Robert E. Goodin, 'What is so special about our fellow countrymen?', *Ethics*, 98(4) (1988), 663–86.

[9] Carol C. Gould, *Rethinking Democracy: Freedom and Social Cooperation in Politics, Economy, and Society* (Cambridge: Cambridge University Press, 1988), ch. 1.

rights of distant others where nation states fail to do so can be seen to require transnational solidarity, as we have been discussing it, as well as the development of standing institutions that can effectively meet these basic needs and rights. In this way, the justification of nation state priority is only a practical and instrumental one, and does not exhaust the obligations involved, in those multifarious cases in which human rights remain unfulfilled. Of course, this does not yet address the precise balance between the various national and transnational obligations, and it also does not speak to the role of more local solidarities. But it does require that national commitments need to be supplemented by (and also qualified by) transnational commitments, if everyone's human rights are to be met, at least at a basic level.

A related normative basis for standing in solidarity with others, whether near or distant, arises from the requirement to address specific injustices such as exploitation, along with instances of large-scale suffering. Often, the solidarity required is the transnational or networked sort (though it could also be met by enhanced traditional solidarity within nation states or newer regional associations).

In regard to economic concerns, the issue of the potential conflict between efforts to rectify injustices in national versus transnational contexts is somewhat different. If we take solidarity movements oriented to countering exploitation as a case in point, we can see that there is a potential for considerable harmony between subnational, national and transnational foci. This occurs where the exploitation in question derives from capitalist economic functioning that is relatively similar in all these contexts, whether within borders or across them, and that has been operating in increasingly global ways with the growing power and scope of transnational corporations. In a related way, labour solidarity should in principle be similar and interrelated across both national and international contexts. In practice, however, and understandably, unions in various countries often take conflicting positions on matters like international trade. Different countries, along with the economic sectors within them, most often differentially benefit from trade, so the problem of the national versus the transnational re-emerges there.

Although the above theoretical considerations provide some modest guidance in understanding the normative relation between national and transnational solidarities, they do not yet address the question of what the focus should be for any given individual or group. Yet, it is not clear how much can be said in general about this question of normative priorities among solidarity efforts as it applies to specified individuals or groups.

Some forms of solidarity may derive from a person's particular job or functioning, as in the labour case. Other forms may be suggested by the practical matter of what people are in fact able to accomplish (given that ought implies can), such that if someone or some group or institution is well situated to provide assistance, they might well choose to prioritise efforts along those lines.[10]

An important set of cases are solidarity efforts designed to rectify historical injustice, or addressing needs in contexts where there is a historical connection between the agents in question. These include colonial relations between nations or peoples in the past, but it might also extend to helping those affected by more recent forms of intervention by powerful states, as in the case of the USA vis-à-vis Iraq. An argument can be made that rectifying historical injustice by those responsible for creating it provides an appropriate focus for assistance and solidarity actions. Very often, however, the historical injustices and their contemporary effects remain obscure to contemporary actors, and especially to the more powerful agents in the contemporary world. They are often unaware that their power and wealth often depends on previous colonial or exploitative relationships. To the degree that they have unjustly benefited from these relationships, they have special obligations to these others, which in turn support solidarity efforts towards them with the aim of working to meet their needs.

In a similar way to the case of historical injustices, it can be argued that those implicated in systems of structural injustice are obligated to stand in solidarity with those most oppressed or exploited by these systems. An argument along these lines was advanced by Iris Young, but she eschews notions of liability for these injustices and instead proposes that all who are implicated in the social connections involved should work to remedy the injustices from a forward-looking perspective. She also mentions the notion of solidarity in this connection.[11] Certainly, the fact that we operate in ways that sustain these unjust structures by participating in them gives us all a reason to work to eliminate the injustices they involve. But I think it is nonetheless the case that those in whose interest these systems function, notably the capitalist class (as we may still want to call

[10] A related point is made by Iris Marion Young in regard to the differential forward-looking responsibilities that may accrue to people in virtue of their various social positioning from a social connections perspective. See Iris Marion Young, 'Responsibility and global justice: a social connection model', *Social Philosophy and Policy*, 23(1) (2006), 102–30.

[11] Ibid.

it) have the greatest responsibility for the exploitation or other forms of oppression that may occur. In my view, this responsibility includes both the putative backward-looking liability (in Young's terms), along with very substantial forward-looking obligations as well, even if they are unlikely to take them on and act to meet them. Yet, although workers are not responsible for their own exploitation, nonetheless both in practical terms and because of their direct experience with the exploitation involved, workers and others who share their interests should be deferred to as leaders in these social and political processes of transformation. We have to acknowledge, however, that the contemporary situation gives little cause for near-term optimism about the required solidaristic actions and institutional transformations, particularly across borders.

Accounts that emphasise such responsibilities to remedy injustice and the resultant solidarities that derive from our actual ties or social connections to others include both those that highlight historical injustices and those that focus on structural or institutional injustices. Unlike truly cosmopolitan perspectives, they tend to eschew universal claims, although they may evidence what I previously characterised as a *concretely universalist* perspective, one that emphasises the concrete social relations among people or groups and that views universality as constructed on the ground, as it were. The account of solidarity that I have offered in this chapter remains primarily on this same terrain of actual social relations. This applies both to the construction of just interrelations through solidarity movements and actions transnationally and also to the understanding of solidarities among the members of one's own state. In this connection, the actual economic and social interdependence with others resident there, and the benefits one derives from those, give rise to the solidarity obligations as much as and indeed probably even more than do people's status as fellow citizens.[12]

However, I have suggested here and elsewhere that solidarity movements and the disposition to solidarity also can have a universalistic intent when they aim at egalitarian and inclusive forms of justice and at promoting the fulfilment of human rights. In my view, solidarity movements and solidarity groups need to be oriented to such norms of justice. This does not mean that all these movements need to have the very same concept of justice in view. But they do need a commitment to equality

[12] A related view of social membership is advanced by Joseph Carens, *The Ethics of Immigration* (Oxford: Oxford University Press, 2013).

and to the elimination of oppression. Moreover, cosmopolitan principles are also required as a framework within which state-based solidarity can be regarded as legitimate. This has important implications for the analysis of responsibility as well. As noted previously, the priority to the nation state has to be qualified by the requirement to stand in solidarity with people in profound need and to work to rectify unjust situations even outside one's nation state or where basic human rights are violated or, in the economic case, unfulfilled.[13] This cosmopolitan requirement derives from people's fundamental equality and interdependence, such that we are all obligated to help construct systems that will work to fulfil everyone's human rights.

Sometimes, the most needy or unjust situations that require assistance may not be related to one's job, or even to historical injustice, or to what one is in a position to provide. Yet, in these cases, one nonetheless has an obligation to stand in solidarity with such needy or oppressed people, even apart from any specific social connections with the people in question.[14] While the particular types of assistance are voluntary, some participation is required. We can say that urgent cases of poverty or other deprivation, situations that result from war and violence of various sorts, as well as natural disasters, call for solidarity by outsiders that may well overwhelm state-based solidarities and rightly take priority over them.

It also needs to be recognised, however, that people who lack basic needs locally are often not in a position to support others at a distance. This suggests that the more unitary solidarity involved within a given domain of common activity retains an important role. It is apparent that if people have their basic needs met, they will be more likely to have the time, resources and opportunities to engage in solidarity networks in support of distant others. However, since economic co-operation to meet these basic needs remains primarily local and national at present, standing in solidarity with co-members of these groups is still very much required.

Although most contemporary national forms of solidarity, understood as unitary, presuppose pre-existing communities, with a (putatively) shared history and set of traditions (however diverse they may be in fact), we can suggest that these national groups would themselves benefit

[13] For an argument along these lines, see Carol C. Gould, 'Varieties of global responsibility: reflections on Iris Marion Young's last writings', in Ann Ferguson and Mechthild Nagel (eds.) *Dancing with Iris: Between Phenomenology and the Body Politic in the Political Philosophy of Iris Marion Young* (Oxford: Oxford University Press, 2009), 199–211.

[14] Ibid.

from adopting some of the openness, constructivist character and orientation to justice that we have highlighted in many transnational solidarity movements. As is apparent, existing local and national solidarities are increasingly marked by harsh tendencies to exclusion, not only of outsiders but of some 'insiders', that is, of minority groups who are regarded as not fitting into the nation, or are regarded as inauthentic members in some sense, if not as complete interlopers.

To take the national community as constructed and open, in contrast, would involve seeing it as a project, and a (relatively) inclusive one at that. Although clearly not everyone can be admitted and made a citizen, efforts need to be made to incorporate not only those who are perceived as like those already present, or those who will work hard, but also many of those who need to be admitted simply in order to be able to fulfil their basic human rights. Ideally, fairness across states would require new agreements to share in these admissions. Such agreements would need to be based on transnational co-operation that is in short supply as present, even though it is normatively and practically urgently required. Even absent such agreements, however, the obligation to admit exists, at least up to the point of foreseeable adverse impacts on the capacity for human rights fulfilment by the existing population. Using such a standard would, however, clearly support many more admissions than at present.

3 Some Remarks About Cases

We may conclude with some brief remarks about the two contemporary cases we highlighted at the outset. Although we cannot settle the issue of priorities of solidarity as they apply to the difficult situations of displaced workers in the USA in relation to international trade or the urgent issue of entry and treatment of refugees and other migrants in Europe and the USA, the above analysis suggests some implications for these cases.

In the case of trade, the US discussion has most often been framed in terms of protectionism to remedy the situation of US workers who have lost their jobs due to globalisation and to protect against future losses for similar reasons. The focus has been almost exclusively on the national impact on US citizens to the disregard of the impacts of globalisation or of policies to address it on people elsewhere. Where the effects on outsiders comes into play, these have most often been framed in entirely positive terms, such that the harms to US workers are understood as partly justified because of the benefits to workers elsewhere, giving them employment and raising them from poverty. The problem with such analyses, however, is that little or no attention is given to the detrimental effects of globalised trade on these foreign workers themselves. These include the infamous 'race to the bottom' in working conditions and wages, the commercialisation of land and water, the growth of emissions worldwide, and other deleterious effects.

The analysis offered in this chapter suggests that we have to take seriously the full range of these consequences on people at home and abroad. Moreover, if one adopts a generally critical stance to capitalist globalisation, including its emphasis on capital mobility at the expense of labour mobility, one can see that both US and foreign workers are subject to this same system, and that countering it will require the old fashioned but still relevant idea of international solidarity among workers in both contexts. Of course, implementing such solidarity poses profound challenges in the present, largely nationalist, framework for action and it is also complicated by the diffusion of work, for example, in manufacturing with its global supply chains, across numerous and ever-changing sets of countries.

The current problem of large numbers of refugees attempting to enter Europe and the treatment of migrants in the USA can also be helpfully viewed through the lens of solidarity. Without undertaking any sort of full analysis, we can note that these cases counterpose national (and in the European case, some degree of regional) solidarity with the need for transnational solidarity with the refugees and other migrants and the requirement to aid them. The latter can be framed in terms of fulfilling their human rights (including the range of civil, political, and economic rights), but it also can be understood in terms of historical injustice, given the role that Europe (and the USA) played not only in colonialism but also more recently in the Middle East and North Africa. As far as climate refugees are concerned, the responsibility would seem to be ongoing for countries (like the USA) that continue to emit on a massive scale. Indeed, rather than only being historical, the responsibility of large emitters can be expected to grow over time, with the predictable vast increase in the number of refugees fleeing on account of climate change. Another factor supporting this sort of obligation on powerful countries arises from their having the ability to pay and to assist in mitigation and adaptation.

Needless to say, efforts need to be made to deal with the impacts that large numbers of refugees (from whatever cause) will have on current workers and citizens in the countries admitting these refugees. Economic policies of austerity and cuts in welfare support have not been helpful along these lines. Indeed, policies that would boost these welfare levels – perhaps through basic income, among other methods – would be important for both citizens and new entrants. Yet none of this settles the issue of conflicts of solidarity, which will continue to pose hard questions for theoreticians and activists. But it is clear from the analysis in this chapter that we need to go beyond traditional national solidarities, however important they may be, to take into account and to address our justice obligations to distant others. This will require new forms of transnational solidarity to help fulfil their human rights if necessary, as well as new efforts to cultivate the disposition to join with others to build a more equal world.

3

Democratic Solidarity Between Global Crisis and Cosmopolitan Hope

HAUKE BRUNKHORST

The first section of this chapter offers a brief diagnosis of modern society under conditions of global crisis (11 theses), and then the second section draws some political conclusions (related to four fundamental problems). The final section tries to specify four changes political agencies need to adopt to save democratic solidarities under stress from globalisation. These changes advocate global expansion of democratic solidarity rather than a retreat to the national state.

1 Solidarity as Comprehensive Democratic Inclusion?

Solidarity – as I understand it – is *comprehensive democratic inclusion*, and I use the multilayered concept primarily as a legal notion.[1] *Solidarity* is complementary to *justice*, and a principle of democracy that is *self-legislation* or *autonomy*, includes both sides.[2] Self-legislation, solidarity and justice are equally universal concepts. Self-legislation means that *all* (and not only all national citizens) affected by a legal norm should be able to understand themselves as authors of that norm. Therefore, self-legislation from the beginning implies the ideal a cosmopolitan democracy. Whereas justice refers to universaliable, and therefore, unconditionally (absolutely/*unbedingt*) binding norms (such as in international law the ban on torture, or in the German Basic Law human dignity that forbids any utilitarian calculus, such as shooting down a hijacked plane and sacrificing the passengers to save thousands of people). *Solidarity* refers to *equally universaliable interests*

[1] Hauke Brunkhorst, *Solidarity – From Civic Friendship to a Global Legal Community* (Cambridge: MIT Press, 2005). This wide notion of solidarity fits to very different theories of solidarity as those of Marx, Dewey and Parsons.

[2] See also Jürgen Habermas, 'Gerechtigkeit und Solidarität', in Jürgen Habermas (ed.), *Erläuterungen zur Diskursethik* (Frankfurt: Suhrkamp, 1991), 49–76, at p. 70ff.

and feelings (for example, 'moral resentments'), which are the moving power of the utopian, cooperative project of a planetary community.[3]

This concept of solidarity emerges from old Roman civil law. Solidarity is solid. *Solidus* is dense and firm. The Roman legal concept *in solidum* means an obligation for the whole, cooperative liability, common debt and solidarity obligation: *obligation in solidum*. One for all, all for one. The bond of solidarity is solid not only for the debtor community itself but also for the creditor, who can if necessary turn to the surrogate who is able to pay. Thus, *obligatio in solidum* already binds together unfamiliar people in complementary roles and heterogeneous interests in the medium of abstract law. Solidarity, therefore, is *solidarity among strangers*.[4]

However, our use of the term 'solidarity' is not older than the French Revolution. During the Revolution, intellectuals such as Danton and Mirabeau used the word 'solidarity' sometimes but the masses still were mobilised by the slogan of brotherliness and brotherly love (*fraternité*) with its Christian roots in a *universal* community of love or agape.[5] Then in the course of the nineteenth century, the concept of solidarity initially continued alongside that of fraternity, only to replace it after the European Revolution of 1848. At first in the workers' movement under the influence of Marx and Lassalle, then at the end of the century in sociology and jurisprudence, and today even in the texts of constitutions and international human rights pacts.[6] The *solidarité républicain* that arises in the late

[3] On universaliable, *moral resentments* see Peter F. Strawson, 'Freedom and resentment', in Gary Watson (ed.), *Proceedings of the British Academy, 48* (1962), 1–25. On the planetary community see Richard Rorty, 'Menschenrechte, Vernunft und Empfindsamkeit', in Jörg Huber and Alois Martin Müller (eds.), *'Kultur' und 'Gemeinschaft'* (Frankfurt: Stroemfeld and Roter Stern, 1994), 99–126, at p. 115.

[4] Andreas Wildt, 'Solidarität', in *Historisches Wörterbuch der Philosophie, Bd. 9* (Darmstadt: Wiss. Buchges, 1995), p. 1004f.; see Ulrich K. Preuß, 'Solidarität unter Bedingungen von Vielfalt', in Johannes Bizer and Hans-Joachim Koch (eds.), *Sicherheit, Vielfalt, Solidarität. Ein neues Paradigma des Verfassungsrechts? Symposium zum 65. Geburtstag Erhard Denningers* (Baden-Baden: Nomos, 1998), p. 129ff.; Hasso Hofmann, 'Vielfalt, Sicherheit und Solidarität statt Freiheit, Gleichheit, Brüderlichkeit?', in Bizer and Koch, *Sicherheit, Vielfat, Solidarität,* p. 111ff.; Hasso Hofmann, *Einführung in die Rechts- und Staatsphilosophie* (Darmstadt: Wiss. Buchges, 2000), p. 193ff.; Karl-Otto Hondrich and Claudia Koch-Arzberger, *Solidarität in der modernen Gesellschaft* (Frankfurt: Fischer, 1992), pp. 12ff., 114ff.; Hauke Brunkhorst, *Solidarität unter Fremden* (Frankfurt: Fischer, 1997).

[5] See Charles Taylor, *Ein säkulares Zeitalter*. Trans. Joachim Schulte (Frankfurt am Main: Suhrkamp, 2009). Critical see Hauke Brunkhorst, 'Die große Geschichte der Exkarnation', in Michael Kühnlein and Matthias Lutz-Bachmann (eds.), *Unerfüllte Moderne? Neue Perspektiven auf das Werk von Charles Taylor* (Berlin: Suhrkamp, 2011), pp. 44–77.

[6] See Wolfgang Schieder, 'Brüderlichkeit', in Otto Brunner, Werner Conze and Reinhart Koselleck (eds.), *Geschichtliche Grundbegriffe, Bd. 1* (Stuttgart: Klett-Cotta,

nineteenth century out of the constitutional revolutions of the eighteenth century transforms the old aristocratic-elite form of civic solidarity into a democratic-egalitarian form. The latter can no longer fixate on the ethos of city life, but encompasses the 'large solidary community of the nation' (Ernest Renan), in America even an unbounded, communicatively expanding 'Great Community' (John Dewey). What already 'was and is still revolutionary' in the Christian message that all men are brothers, which finds its secular political form in the freedom–equality–fraternity triad, 'is the idea that strangers are bound to one another by a universal bond of civility and can be brought into relations of reciprocity'.[7]

Only reciprocal relations are compatible with democracy's postulate of autonomy. Fraternity is not compassion, and solidarity is not mercy but a right.[8] Unlike the classical political concepts of (substantial) justice, of the good life and of the common good, the revolutionary slogans of fraternity and solidarity refer directly to the specifically modern combination of freedom and politics.[9] Solidarity is nothing but the democratic realisation of individual freedom.[10] If the classic republican formula of the common good refers to an objectively recognisable collective good, 'solidarity' has from the start an individualistic quality.[11] But solidarity is supposed to guarantee the equal enjoyment of individual rights within the medium of the political equality of every subject under the law, along with the 'participation of each individual in

1972), pp. 552–581, at pp. 565ff.; Émile Durkheim, *The Division of Labor in Society* (Free Press, 1893); Dieter Grimm, *Solidarität als Rechtsprinzip. Die Rechts- und Staatslehre Léon Duguits in ihrer Zeit* (Frankfurt: Athenäum, 1973), p. 38ff.; Erhard Denninger, *Menschenrechte und Grundgesetz* (Weinheim: Beltz, 1994), p. 23ff.

7 Ulrich Preuß, 'Verfassungstheoretische Überlegungen zur normativen Begründung des Wohlfahrtsstaates', in Christoph Sachße and H. Tristram Engelhardt (eds.), *Sicherheit und Freiheit. Zur Ethik des Wohlfahrtsstaates* (Frankfurt: Suhrkamp, 1990), p. 131.

8 Preuß, *Solidarität unter Bedingungen von Vielfalt*, p. 129.

9 On the latter, see also Hannah Arendt, 'What is freedom?', in *Between Past and Future* (New York: Viking Press, 1961); Hannah Arendt, *On Revolution* (New York: Penguin, 1965), p. 141ff.; Hannah Arendt, *The Life of the Mind, vol. 2: Willing* (New York: Harcourt Brace Jovanovich, 1978), p. 195ff.

10 As it is in Hegel, in the only place in his work in which he uses the word solidarity, found in the notes from the lectures on the philosophy of right in winter semester 1819–20. To 'join in solidaristic union' [*sich 'solidarisch zu verbinden'*] is the 'right' of the 'individual', if his freedom in civil society is to 'have not only possibility, but also reality'. G.W.F. Hegel in Dieter Henrich (ed.), *Philosophie des Rechts, Transcription of the Lectures of 1819–20* (Frankfurt: Suhrkamp, 1983), p. 203f.

11 See Franz-Xaver Kaufmann, 'Sozialpolitik zwischen Gemeinwohl und Solidarität', in Herfried Münkler and Karsten Fischer (eds.), *Gemeinwohlrhetorik und Solidaritätsverbrauch. Integrationsprobleme moderner Gesellschaften* (Berlin: Akademie, 2001).

public affairs'.[12] Thus, in the equality of public freedom, which is required for 'preserving the potential for social self-change', there also lies the only foundation in constitutional theory for the social-welfare state.[13] In the modern constitutional regime, common good, justice and solidarity coincide with the democratic legitimation of normatively binding decisions. There is in the constitutional state neither a common good nor a justice beyond democratic legislation and, therefore, also no constitutional state without democracy.

Democratic solidarity must stand up to two crucial experimental checks, one is *normative* and the other *factual*, and only if democratic solidarity passes both, it becomes an 'existing concept'.[14]

(1) The *normative experimentum crucis* of democratic solidarity is the extensive and transgressive *inclusion of the (material) other.*

The democratic inclusion of the other is 'material' because it – different from Kant – includes our 'external', 'wild lawless Freedom'. Kant had suggested 'that the individual' should abandon 'his wild lawless Freedom wholly' in exchange for (at any rate) 'all his proper Freedom (*Freiheit überhaupt*)'. All proper freedom, Kant explains, means his 'entire and undiminished' freedom 'regulated by laws of Right', which 'arises out of his own law-giving Will'.[15] Whereas Kant's transformation from the entire wild and lawless freedom to the entire freedom of civic (common, and not commercial) self-legislation loses the bodies that matter (Judith Butler) on the way to autonomy because in fact it is a dualistic transubstantiation.[16] The theory of deliberative democracy, in contrast, *includes all movements of bodies that matter*, of their legs, hands, heads, eyes and tongues, which act and communicate within the 'wild complex that resists organization as a whole'.[17] Only 'on the basis of an anarchic, unfettered communicative

[12] Preuß, 'Verfassungstheoretische Überlegungen', p. 117; see also Ernst-Wolfgang Böckenförde, 'Demokratie als Verfassungsprinzip', in Ernst-Wolfgang Böckenförde (ed.), *Staat, Verfassung, Demokratie* (Frankfurt: Suhrkamp, 1991), p. 327f.; Joshua Cohen and Charles Sables, 'Directly-deliberative polyarchy', *European Law Journal*, 3(4) (1997), 318f.

[13] Preuß, 'Verfassungstheoretische Überlegungen', pp. 115, 119f., 131.

[14] G.W.F. Hegel, Wissenschaft der Logik II, Frankfurt: Suhrkamp 1971, 481; s.a. Hegel, Grundlinien der Philosophie des Rechts, Frankfurt: Suhrkamp 1971, § 20, § 66, § 217,

[15] Immanuel Kant, *Metaphysik der Sitten* (Frankfurt: Suhrkamp, 1977), §47, p. 434, English quote from Kant, *The Philosophy of Law* (Edinburgh: Clark, 1887), §47, 169–70, available at: https://oll.libertyfund.org/titles/kant-the-philosophy-of-law (accessed 19 August 2019).

[16] On the important distinction between common (communio) and commercial (commercio) in Kant's *Critique of Pure Reason* (A 213–6/ B 260–3) see Christoph Menke, *Kritik der Rechte* (Berlin: Suhrkamp, 2015), pp. 350–1.

[17] Jürgen Habermas, *Facticity and Normativity* (Cambridge, MA: MIT Press, 1996), p. 307.

freedom' that is performed in the legally enabled public sphere, common will-formation and self-legislation is socially possible.[18]

(2) The factual experimentum crucis of democratic solidarity (as of any other political regime in modern societies) is the capacity to solve societal problems produced by functional differentiation, which cannot be solved by functional differentiation alone.[19]

A classic example for the latter is Marx's thesis that the self-referential closure of economy can solve *all* problems of *exchange-value* and *dead labor* (capital) through the expanded reproduction of exchange-value but cannot solve the problems, which its own reproduction causes in an environment that is a social lifeworld where *use-value* and *living labor* matter. Because modern capitalism relies on the solution of environmental problems, which capitalism generates but cannot solve, a *political solution* is needed.

This problem, which Marx described as the contradiction between living and dead labor, became urgent in the middle of the nineteenth century when the economic system became the leading system of society – due to the unprecedented punctual burst of all industrial productive forces.[20] At the same time the constitutional regime that was established in the course of the Atlantic Revolutions of the eighteenth century already existed in many places, usually in the form of a constitutional monarchy dominated by bourgeois (and often still hegemonial aristocratic) class interests.[21]

My *first thesis* is that the constitutional regime of anti-democratic bourgeois class rule that was established after the great legal revolutions of the eighteenth

18 Habermas, *Facticity and Normativity*, p. 186.

19 Brunkhorst, *Solidarity*, pp. 81–101.

20 Charles Bright and Michael Geyer, *Benchmarks of Globalisation: the Global Condition, 1850–2010*, electronic-paper (Chicago and Berlin, now published in Blackwell Companion to World History, 2011). On punctuational bursts see: Quentin D. Atkinson, Andrew Meade, Chris Vendetti, Simon J. Greenhill and Mark Pagel, 'Languages evolve in punctuational bursts', *Science*, 319 (2008), 588; Connie J. G. Gersick, 'Revolutionary change theories: a multilevel exploration of the punctuated equilibrium paradigm', *The Academic Management Review*, 16(1) (1991), 10–36; Steven Jay Gould and Richard Lewontin, The spandrels of San Marco and the Panglossian paradigm', available at: www.aaas.org/spp/dser/03_Areas/evolution/perspectives/Gould_Lewontin_1979.shtml (accessed 4 April 2012); Hauke Brunkhorst, *Critical Theory of Legal Revolutions – Evolutionary Perspectives* (New York: Bloomsbury, 2014), 33–8.

21 The term Atlantic Revolution is used in the rapidly growing branch of world history, and it includes all revolutionary activities in the Atlantic Region including in particular the Caribbean Revolution (Haiti), but also the many follow-up revolutions in Latin-America, insurgencies and revolutionary activities in Ireland, Greece and so forth.

century was not capable of solving the environmental and, in particular, the social problems of the capitalist system.

This immediately leads to my *second thesis*: if a solution to the environmental problems caused by modern capitalism is possible at all, then – and this was the truth of 1848 – only through a *fundamental democratisation* of the existing constitutional regimes and the abolishment (or at least neutralisation) of bourgeois class rule.

The democratic solution depends on a couple of societal conditions. First, modern societies – independent of their constitutional regime – *cannot preserve themselves without growth*, and growth comes regularly together with *enlargement*, transgressing borders and boundaries.[22] Moreover, as Durkheim, Parsons and Luhmann have shown, not only the efficiency and viability of the economy but also the efficiency and viability of all important social systems is *dependent on growth* – such as medicine, science, education, political power and law (but also art, sports and so on). By all means, the successful solution of problems, for example of health care, regularly has unplanned side effects, causes succession-related problems and also reflexive problems such as medically induced epidemics. Their solution needs ever more medical and therapeutic technologies and inventions, and that means growth not only in medicine but also in other systems (in this case especially of science, economy, administrative power and traffic) and vice versa, scientific inventions, industrial diseases, war injuries and car accidents stimulate medical growth and enlargement.

Moreover, the dependence of functional differentiation on growth is not only due to *factual* but also to *normative* reasons. There is at least one *ethical premise of good life* shared by all modern societies, and it is general and negative: *nobody* really wants to live *without* the great inventions of electricity, running water, chemistry, pharmaceuticals, mass-communication and mass-transportation, which all were made between 1870 and 1940.[23]

There is, as John Dewey rightly explained from an evolutionary perspective, an internal relation between *democratic solidarity and quantitative growth and enlargement*. On the road to the Great Community *growth and enlargement are unqualified goods*, and they are unqualified because, for the sake of democracy, they must be kept open for

22 I am thankful to Regina Kreide for a controversial discussion of this point.

23 See Robert J. Gordon, *Rise and Fall of American Growth: The US Standard of Living since the Civil War* (Princeton, NJ: Princeton University Press, 2016).

democratically self-determined qualifications and revisions (democratic experimentalism) any time.[24]

Therefore, my third thesis is that there is no modern society, in particular no socially inclusive democratic society, and hence no democratic solidarity that is beyond *growth* and *enlargement*.

Bourgeois class rule was celebrated as the revolutionary subject of growth by Marx and Engels, and Marx's admiration for the achievements of modern capitalism never ended.[25] However, as the young Marx rightly observed, only the emergence of 'true democracy' in the course of class struggles could solve the environmental, at least the social problems of capitalism.[26]

True democracy for Marx and Engels, in the 1840s, is the same as *communism*, and true democracy and communism are not an '*ideal*' but the '*real* movement which abolishes the present state of things'.[27] To determine the constitutional ('Staatsrecht') conditions of the real movement that solves the 'riddle of all constitutions',[28] Marx distinguishes the *power-limiting* constitution of *liberalism*, which *limits* the 'political state' by the 'limiting intelligence (*Verstand*)' of 'liberal property, contract, marriage, civil society', from the *power-founding* constitution of *democracy*.[29] He calls the latter 'true democracy'. Why true? For Marx democracy is the historical 'truth' of 'all forms of the state' because it *constitutes* 'law', 'state' and 'constitution' through the procedural performance of the 'self-determination of the people'.[30]

24 Dewey's idea of democratic solidarity is not legal but Aristotelian, targeting a concrete but (and this goes beyond Aristotle) indeterminate form of life.

25 Marx and Engels, Communist Manifesto, Chap. I. Available at: www.marxists.org/archive/marx/works/1848/communist-manifesto/ch01.htm#007 (accessed 4 July 2019). For the late Marx see Marx, *Grundrisse*.

26 Karl Marx, *Zur Kritik der Hegelschen Rechtsphilosophie: Kritik des Hegelschen Staatsrechts*, MEW 1 (Berlin: Dietz, 1972), pp. 201–33, at pp. 231–2.

27 Karl Marx and Freidrich Engels, *Die deutsche Ideologie*, MEW 3 (Berlin: Dietz, 1973), p. 35, original emphasis.

28 Marx, *Kritik des Hegelschen Staatsrechts*, p. 231; for a further discussion of the riddle see Susan Marks, *The Riddle of All Constitutions* (Oxford: Oxford University Press, 2000).

29 Marx, *Kritik des Hegelschen Staatsrechts*, p. 233. On the difference between *herrschaftsbegrenzender Verfassung* and *herrschaftsbegründender Verfassung* see Christoph Möllers, 'Verfassungsgebende Gewalt – Verfassung – Konstitutionalisierung. Begriffe der Verfassung in Europa', in Armin von Bogdandy (ed.), *Europäisches Verfassungsrecht* (Berlin: Springer, 2003).

30 Marx, *Kritik des Hegelschen Staatsrechts*, p. 233. This use of 'true' is different from the predication of truth to sentences ('p is true') and resembles the use in practically orienting sentences such as the biblical 'Jesus says, I am the truth', which opens a path of religious, ethical or political change on the basis of some (true or false) insight in the course of history.

In his brief reconstruction of the constitutional evolution, Marx explains the historical truth of democracy by means of an *immanent criticism* of the constitutional law of liberalism (as it is represented by Hegel's theory of constitutional monarchy).[31] All that is needed for such critique is already present within the *existing contradiction* of constitutional history between power-limiting and power-founding constitutions. This pragmatic contradiction is 'charged with moral energy', and therefore, the driving force of the *real movement* of true democracy (communism).[32] As Marx has shown in his 18th Brumaire, this constitutional contradiction appears in public class struggles *once the parliamentary constitution is completed by universal suffrage and decoupled from the monarchic constitution.*[33] Together with its democratisation constitutional and public law overcomes – and here Marx anticipates Dewey *and* Kelsen – the old-European 'dualism' of subjective and objective law, private and public law, subjective rights and democratic self-legislation.[34] Therefore, the *real movement* of true democracy or communism is not beyond modern law but nothing else than the *dynamic procedure of the existing contradiction of modern law* between a *law of domination that is civil law*, grounded in subjective rights and *public law*, which is *emancipatory* because it enables the *self-determination of the addressees of law.* From Marx over Kelsen to Habermas, therefore, it is the procedural paradigm of egalitarian and inclusive democratic self-legislation (Kant's 'communio', Marx' 'communism') that overcomes constitutional welfarism (and bureaucratic socialism) as well as liberal capitalism.[35]

True democratic solidarity that is socially inclusive, egalitarian and power-founding and, therefore, the *real movement of communism* began in the middle of the nineteenth century. A century later democratisation and democratic class struggle, reforms and revolutions (closely connected with the world wars of the twentieth century that were at

[31] Marx, *Kritik des Hegelschen Staatsrechts*, pp. 230–2.

[32] The quote is from Jürgen Habermas, 'Dialektischer Idealismus im Übergang zum Materialismus', in *Theorie und Praxis* (Frankfurt: Suhrkamp, 1972). On existing contradiction see G. W.F. Hegel, *Wissenschaft der Logik II* (Hamburg: Meiner, 1975), p. 59. In his worthwhile interpretation of Marx's theory of law, Robert Fine makes the important point that Marx does not understand the legal ideas of freedom and equality as a (however necessary) illusion (and in that sense as 'superstructure' and 'ideology'), but as a contradiction, Robert Fine, *Democracy and the Rule of Law. Marx's Critique of the Legal Form* (Caldwell: Blackburn, 2002), pp. 5, 159 et seq.

[33] See Karl Marx, *Der 18. Brumaire des Louis Bonaparte* (Frankfurt: Suhrkamp, 2007).

[34] Marx, *Kritik des Hegelschen Staatsrechts*, p. 232.

[35] See Habermas, *Facticity and Normativity*, pp. 388–445.

the same time global civil wars) had largely overcome, or at least curtailed and weakened bourgeois class rule, and transformed the constitutional state into egalitarian mass-democracy.

Thesis 4 is that for almost half a century (between 1940 and 1990) the democratisation of the constitutional state (more or less) solved the twofold problem of growth *and* social exclusion (economic exploitation) *through social inclusion.*

However, from the beginning this solution suffered from two problems. The first problem was the gloomy *heritage of colonialism.* Moreover, affirmative action of national welfarism was white, male and heterosexual. Egalitarian democracy was realised only in a small global segment of rich and highly industrialised countries, which all belonged to the former world of global empires, and it ended everywhere at the color line and the gender line. It is hardly surprising, therefore, that the revolutionary victory of democratic egalitarianism was largely at the expense of the formerly colonised world, and the vast majority of world population. Nevertheless, normatively the democratic nation state was bound to the '*exclusion of inequalities*'.[36] This refers not only to national solidarity but (since the American Declaration of Independence) also to universal moral and legal commitments to 'expand' democratic solidarity 'as far as we can'.[37] Rorty's utopia of a 'planetary community' is an unfinished and ever again expandable project of a 'democratic *civitas peregrina*' that – as in the science fiction movies – will 'carry' democratic solidarity 'to the stars'.[38] This utopia is not imperial (as in most of the science fiction movies) because Rorty understands it as the expansion 'of us at our best', and we are at our best if we de-center our self-understanding in reciprocal expansion of our different horizons in a 'free and unforced talk' of many, finally all cultures.[39] However, Rorty agrees with the thesis that this kind of global democratic solidarity can only be realised if 'we stop yearning for an impossible global *Gemeinschaft*. For a global legal community (*globale Rechtsgenossenschaft*) would suffice to ensure

[36] Rudolf Stichweh, *Die Weltgesellschaft* (Frankfurt: Suhrkamp, 2000), p. 52.

[37] Richard Rorty, 'Putnam and the relativist menace', *Journal of Philosophy* 90(9) (1993), 452; Richard Rorty, 'Erwiderung auf Kettner', in Thomas Schäfer, Udo Tietz and Rüdiger Zoll (eds.), *Hinter den Spiegeln* (Frankfurt: Suhrkamp, 2001), pp. 287–91, at p. 229.

[38] Rorty, *Menschenrechte, Vernunft und Empfindsamkeit*, p. 115; Richard Rorty, 'Heidegger wider die Pragmatisten', *Neue Hefte für Philosophie* 23 (1984), 20.

[39] Rorty, 'Relativist menace', p. 452; Rorty, 'Erwiderung auf Kettner', p. 229.

both liberty and equality, even in the absence of anything much like *Bruderschaft*'.[40]

Normatively, modern state formation from the beginning had a cosmopolitan side that is constitutive.[41] Moreover, latest since the middle of the nineteenth century world society factually is a single community of fate, and a community of fate, a *Schicksalsgemeinschaft* in the terminology of Right-Hegelian German *Staatsrecht* is a nation.[42]

Therefore, my *thesis 5* is that the exclusion of the majority of world population from democratic welfarism poses a *serious problem of legitimisation* that is *internal* to all members of the rich and (more or less) democratic family of nation states.

Philosophically speaking, a regime that cannot solve the (factually and normatively) universal problem of democratic legitimisation *should* not exist.

The name of the second problem is *secular stagnation*. The great inventions of the present, the Internet, the mobile phone and the personal computer, are all at best *low-growth inventions* with (probably dramatically) *negative effects on the future of employment*.[43] Even if one considers that the new media are *social* media of dissemination, which soon might become the cornerstone for an effective continentalisation

[40] Richard Rorty, 'Solidarity: From Civic Friendship to a Global Legal Community (review)', *Common Knowledge*, 12(2) (2006), 305.

[41] On the co-evolution thesis see: Hauke Brunkhorst, 'Die Legitimationskrise der Weltgesellschaft. Global rule of law, global constitutionalism und Weltstaatlichkeit', in Matthias Albert and R. Stichweh (eds.), *Weltstaat und Weltstaatlichkeit* (Wiesbaden: Verlag für Sozialwissenschaften, 2007), pp. 63–108; Brunkhorst, *Critical Theory of Legal Revolutions*; Albert Matthias, 'Politik der Weltgesellschaft und Politik der Globalisierung: Überlegungen zur Emergenz von Weltstaatlichkeit', in Bettina Heintz, Richard Münch and Hartmann Tyrell (eds.), *Zeitschrift für Soziologie. Sonderheft Weltgesellschaft* (Wiesbaden: Verlag für Sozialwissenschaften, 2005), pp. 223–39; Thornhill, *A Sociology of Constitutions* (Cambridge: Cambridge University Press, 2011).

[42] Jürgen Osterhammel and Niels P. Petersson, *Geschichte der Globalisierung* (Wissen: C.H. Beck, Petersson), p. 63. On the Staatsrecht side of Schicksalsgemeinschaft see Ernst-Wolfgang Böckenförde, 'Demokratie als Verfassungsprinzip', in *Staat, Verfassung, Demokratie* (Frankfurt: Suhrkamp, 1991).

[43] Nicolas Crafts, 'Is secular stagnation the future for Europe?', CAGE Working Papers Series 225 (Warwick: University of Warwick, 2015); Gordon, *Rise and Fall of American Growth*; see Gordon, 'Is US economic growth over?', Working Paper 18315 (2012). Available at: www.nber.org/papers/w18315.pdf (accessed 4 July 2019); Gordon, 'The demise of U.S. economic growth: restatement, rebuttal and reflections', NBER Working Paper19895 (2014). With emphasis on the more utopian aspects of a post-capitalist transformation of unemployment see Paul Mason, *Post-Capitalism* (London: Penguin, 2015).

and globalisation of egalitarian democratic constitutions (and this is a great hope), there remains a problem. There is little evidence that new media will change the world as fundamentally for the better (at least in technical concerns of material living conditions) as the great innovations (running water, electric light, combustion engine, mass-culture, pharmacy/manipulation of molecules) between 1870 and 1940 did, and that was the age of John Dewey's twentieth century of egalitarian democracy.

Therefore, my thesis 6 is that *secular stagnation* is a challenge modern society has never before had to face.[44] Secular stagnation *first and foremost* is due to the (temporary) *finalisation of the great industrial inventions* in 1940, and *secondly* to the *secular increase of inequality* since the late 1970s.[45]

Sociologically speaking, a complex society that cannot solve the problem of secular stagnation *cannot* exist. The bicycle stops; the bicycle falls.

The secular growth of inequality was the result of, first, a critical situation of democratic welfarism at the *end of the great push of technological, infrastructural and industrial growth, enabled by the great inventions* (1870–1940). Second, political, not always (Chile, Argentina) democratic *decisions of world politics*, triggered by the USA and the UK, and driven by the religious fundamentalism of free but virtual markets.[46] The relations of dependency were turned upside down. First the *tax state* that (as democratic legislator) takes the money away from the rich, was replaced by the *debt state* that is dependent on the generosity of the investors. Then the same happened to the working class, they lost their right to strike and blackmail the owners of productive forces factually, and in exchange got credits unlimited for the expense of a new form of debt slavery. After 40 years of politically implemented neoliberal globalisation, capitalist world economy has itself dissolved from state-control and turned *state embedded markets* into *market embedded states.*[47]

[44] Between 2000 and 2016 (after already 30 years of stagnation) *real investment* in Germany declined close to 20 percent, see Claus Offe, 'The dynamic of secular stagnation', paper presented at a conference on the topic *Jenseits des Kapitalismus* in Wuppertal, 4 February 2016.

[45] See Gordon, *Rise and Fall of American Growth.*

[46] On the quasi-religious side of neoliberalism see Miguel Vatter, 'Foucault and Hayek: Republican law and liberal civil society', in Vanessa Lemm and Miguel Vatter (eds.), *The Government of Life: Foucault, Biopolitics, and Neoliberalism* (Fordam, NY: Fordham University Press, 2014), pp. 163–86.

[47] Wolfgang Streeck, 'Sectoral specialization: politics and the nation state in a global economy', paper presented at the 37 World Congress of the International Institute of Sociology, Stockholm 2005; see Streeck, *Gekaufte Zeit.*

From a well-founded perspective of democratic progress (theses 2–4), *thesis 7* follows, that the globalisation of disembedded markets structurally is a *regression* to the political state of the nineteenth-century's bourgeois constitutionalism.

No wonder that in nearly all OECD-countries we now have an extension of social differences that mirrors exactly that of 1900.[48] Within the neoliberal political-economic regime, high profit rates can be maintained only at the expense of growing social differentiation.[49] But increasing inequality has strong negative effects on growth rates. This gives Paul Sweezy's theory of under-consumption surprising actuality.[50] It was carved out for the monopoly capitalism of the 1960s, which was dominated by the car industry. Sweezy predicted in 1966 the coming stagnation of monopolistic capitalism because it 'tends to generate ever more surplus, yet it fails to provide the consumption and investment outlets required for the absorption of a rising surplus, . . ., it follows that the *normal* state of monopoly capitalist economy is stagnation'.[51] Under conditions of a neoliberally *monopolised* world economy *market competition becomes largely virtual.*[52] Prices are decoupled from markets, profits are stable, their rate of increase is predictable and can be planned, the cyclic (sine curve like) fall

[48] Thomas Piketty, *Capital in the Twenty-First Century* (Cambridge, MA: Harvard University Press, 2014).

[49] The *Institut der deutschen Wirtschaft Köln* (IW) is cynical enough to tell the brutal truth: 'For industrial nations as Germany the *inequality has a positive effect on growth because inequality increases the incentives for entrepreneurship and innovation*' (quoted from *Süddeutsche Zeitung*, 22 March 2016, 17). The latter is, by the way, the basic categorical mistake of neoliberalism and the very reason for its imperialistic claim to subsume all spheres and systems of society under the logic of markets (its commodity fetishism). In particular, the great technical innovations of modern society are not due to market competition but to scientific research that is functionally differentiated from the economy and operating under a logic and rationality that is completely different from the logic and rationality of the market. On logic and rationality of science see Karl-Otto Apel, 'Einführung: Der philosophische Hintergrund der Entstehung des Pragmatismus bei Charles S. Peirce', in Charles S. Peirce (ed.), *Schriften I Zur Entstehung des Pragmatismus mit einer Einführung herausgegeben von Karl-Otto Apel* (Frankfurt: Suhrkamp, 1967), pp. 11–153; Karl-Otto Apel, 'Peirces Denkweg vom Pragmatismus zum Pragmatizismus', in Charles S. Peirce (ed.), *Schriften II Vom Pragmatismus zum Pragmatizismus* (Frankfurt: Sughrkamp1970), pp. 11–211. The logic of science is much closer to socialism than to capitalism, see Gerd Wartenberg, *Logischer Sozialismus. Die Transformation der Kantischen Transzendentalphilosophie durch Charles S. Peirce* (Frankfurt: Suhrkamp, 1971).

[50] Paul A. Baran and Paul M Sweezy, *Monopoly Capital: An Essay on the American Economic and Social Order* (New York: Monthly Review Press, 1966), pp. 76–111.

[51] Baran and Sweezy, *Monopoly Capital*, p. 108.

[52] Herzog, 'Markt und Gerechtigkeit im *Neoliberalismus*'.

and rise of profits suddenly comes to an end, and the profit margins of the 500 biggest US-firms remain consistently high since 2008 – to the horror of Goldman & Sachs.[53] Today, the social class at the top holds nearly all assets, and the lower and middle classes at the bottom have insufficient money to buy the most urgent consumer goods, including in particular education (tuition), private health care, decent housing and so on. The result is a crisis of under-consumption, as Marx had already written in *Capital*: '[T]he ultimate reason for all real crises always remains the poverty and restricted consumption of the masses as opposed to the drive of capitalist production to develop the productive forces as though only the absolute consuming power of society constituted their limit.'[54]

For capitalist economy after the end of the great inventions and under neoliberal conditions of increasing social differentiation (thesis 7), it follows – thesis 8 – that secular stagnation with high profit rates and increasing social differentiation causes a *crisis of under-consumption.*

For inclusive and egalitarian mass-democracy, big differences between the social classes have disastrous causal effects.[55] Theses 9 and 10, therefore, are

Thesis 9: Increasing social inequality causes increasing *political inequality*, and *Thesis10*: Political inequality finally causes a *crisis of legitimisation.*

Not absolute poverty but relative inequality *discourages* the people, resulting in a *crisis of motivation* that explains the dramatic decrease of the voter turnout for middle and underclasses down to 30 percent and less in nearly all OECD-countries.[56] Leftist parties lose their voters and turn steadily farther right whereas right-wing parties stay where they are.

[53] Joe Weisenthal, 'Goldman and Sachs says it may be forced to fundamentally question how capitalism is working. The profit margins debate could lead to an unsettling conclusion', Bloomberg Markets, 3 February 2016. Available at: www.bloomberg.com/news/articles/2016-02-03/goldman-sachs-says-it-may-be-forced-to-fundamentally-question-how-capitalism-is-working; see the summary of the internal study of Goldman & Sachs in Claus Hulverscheidt, 'Kapitalisten zweifeln am Kapitalismus', *Süddeutsche Zeitung*, 4 February 2016. They should have read (and may be they have) Paul A. Baran and Paul M Sweezy, *Monopolkapital* (Frankfurt: Suhrkamp, 1967), pp. 63ff.

[54] Karl Marx, *Das Kapital*, Bd. 3 (Berlin: Dietz, 1968), p. 501. English translation quoted from www.marxists.org/archive/marx/works/1894-c3/ch30.htm

[55] Armin Schäfers, *Der Verlust politischer Gleicheit; Warum die sinkende Wahlbeteiligung der Demokratie schadet* (Frankfurt: Campus, 2005); see Richard Wilkinson and Kate Pickett, *The Spirit Level: Why Greater Equality Makes Societies Stronger* (New York: Bloomsbury, 2010); see Tony Judt, *Ill Fares the Land* (New York: Penguin, 2010).

[56] The typology of crises in Jürgen Habermas, *Legitimationsprobleme im Spätkapitalismus* (Frankfurt: Suhrkamp, 1972) is still actual.

Finally, we are left with *no alternative to austerity* politics, at best with the gloomy alternative between *right parties* of market fundamentalism plus a culture of political correctness and *far right parties* of market fundamentalism plus a neoconservative cultural background that is nationalist, racist and religious fundamentalist (reaching from the German Alternative für Deutschland [AfD] to the American Republican Party).

However, for the established political parties of (far or less far) right-wing market fundamentalism the effects of their own political decisions and the strong and powerful drive of capitalist economy have led to a global situation where no way back seems possible.

And this is *thesis 11*: globalisation has led to an ever denser functional (global systems), cultural (global memory, global human rights) and normative integration (global law) of world society that is now not only a *functionally founded community* of fate but a normatively founded and culturally backed *single legal community* with a strong trend towards *constitutionalism.*

However, the rise of global societal constitutionalism comes with a fall of global (and national) democracy.[57] *Civil law successively subverts and replaces international and national public law.* Different from public law that has an inbuilt emancipatory potential, civil and private law is – in the old Roman Empire as well as in global capitalism – nothing else than a law of coordination of the material interests of the ruling classes.[58] The surprising but expectable effect of the publication of the Panama Papers was that most of the offshore companies and tricky money transactions were completely legal – thanks to civil law's legal construction.

The conclusion of our theses can only be that the project of nation state-based democracy to exclude inequalities finally failed. Even a strong advocate for an *alternative* reconstruction of the system of national welfare states *from the bottom* such as Wolfgang Streeck, has given up on the present system of national democracies. For a long time he argued that in the world of globalised capitalist markets only small and rich countries like Denmark or Netherlands had a chance to survive as (nationally closed) democracies, if (and only if) they transform themselves into *globally operating conglomerates.* Some, at least one big and rich country, such as Germany, can survive only as the *hegemon of a transnational system* of de

[57] Brunkhorst, Solidarity; Hauke Brunkhorst, *Legitimationskrisen. Verfassungsprobleme der Weltgesellschaft* (Baden-Baden: Nomos, 2012).

[58] Gunther Teubner, *Constitutional Fragments. Societal Constitutionalism and Globalisation* (Oxford: Oxford University Press, 2012).

facto mandates.[59] Only *continental regimes* like China (which is not democratic) and the USA (and in the near future also India and Brazil) still seem to have alternatives of political choice but big problems to implement their choices once they endanger market radicalism (such as paradigmatically in the case of the US health care bill).

2 Four Problems of any Political Regime

If this diagnosis is halfway plausible, then there are at least four actual problems that must be solved by *any* political regime, and *none* of it can be solved by national states and international politics alone. They need regional (continental) and global solution, and these solutions need legally binding decisions on continental and global levels. They need legislative majority decisions, and not only contractually consented decisions. The four problems are that

(1) Secular stagnation (theses 3, 6, 8) under conditions of increasing *social differentiation* (theses 6–11) results in a threefold crisis of under-consumption (thesis 8), motivation (thesis 9) and legitimisation (thesis 10).
(2) The *differentiation of center and periphery* generates ever higher rates of *exclusion* (theses 4, 5) along national (suburbs of Paris), continental (European South) and global lines (Global South).[60]
(3) The differentiation of system and environment (theses 1) causes ecological devastation of unknown measures.
(4) The *globalisation of all functional systems* results in a successive replacement of international and national public law by *civil law* (theses 7, 11).

It follows politically, first, that the preservation of the present state of globally disembedded market economy that is the *political project of neoliberalism* has no alternative except authoritarianism.[61]

59 Wolfgang Streeck (interviewed by Michel Feher), 'The life and time in the European consolidation state', *Near Futures Online 1 'Europe at a Crossroads'*, March 2016. Available at: http://nearfuturesonline.org/the-life-and-time-of-the-european-consolidation-state/ (accessed 4 July 2019); see Streeck, *Gekaufte Zeit*.

60 National exclusion rates grew since 2000 between 22 percent and 40 percent, see Offe, The Dynamic of Secular Stagnation, paper presented at a conference in Wuppertal 2014, quoted from memory and handwritten notes.

61 See Immanuel Wallerstein, 'Structural crisis, or why capitalists no longer find capitalism rewarding', in Immanuel Wallerstein, Randal Collins, Michael Mann, Georgi Derluguian and Craig Calhoun (eds.), *Does Capitalism Have a Future?* (Oxford: Oxford University

We are already approaching a new kind of a hypermodern double state.[62] Without reduction of inequality and exclusion high rates of profit can be maintained only by *constitutional regression* from normative to nominal constitutions: *over-integration of the ruling classes* (they appear only as plaintiffs before court) and *under-integration of the lower classes and excluded populations* (they appear only as defendants before court, if they appear at all).[63] Prerogative law and the declared or undeclared state of siege are becoming unavoidable. The war on terror at home and abroad, the legal construction of the public enemy, in case of doubt the frequently renewal of the state of siege (as now in France), and last but not least the emergence of smart and flexible border regimes (Australia, Europe and the USA) consist in *bracketing the constitutional rights of all citizens living within the border region.* In the USA, this affects already two-thirds of the entire population (Coast Region and Great Lakes).[64] Finally mass-incarceration may not remain an American exception.[65] Europe is already experimenting with detention camps for illegal refugees. AfD, Front National and Donald Trump are the logical consequence of market fundamentalism in a permanent crisis. To avoid expenses for the solution of ecological problems *science must be silenced* as it already happens in the USA. Finally, the global double state is stabilised through the complete subsumption of constitutional and public law under the priority of civil and private law. In case of doubt, private *contract law derogates parliamentary and constitutional legislation*, which

Press, 2013), pp. 9–36. Still actual: Herbert Marcuse, 'Der Kampf gegen den Liberalismus in der totalitären Staatsauffassun', in *Marcuse, Kultur und Gesellschaft I* (Frankfurt: Suhrkamp, 1999), pp. 196517–55.

[62] The double state is a mix of (inclusive) norm-state (or *Rechtsstaat*) and (exclusive) prerogative state (or police-state), and there are more formations of the double state than pre-war fascist regimes, on the paradigm case of the latter see Ernst Fraenkel, *The Dual State* (New York: Octagon, 1969).

[63] Still paradigmatic: Marcelo Neves, *Verfassung und positives Recht in der peripheren Moderne* (Berlin: Duncker & Humblodt, 1992); see M. Neves, 'Zwischen Subintegration und Überintegration: Bürgerrechte nicht ernstgenommen', *Kritische Justiz* 4 (1999), 557–77.

[64] See Ayelet Shachar, 'New border and citizenship constellations: implications for law and justice', paper presented at the WZB Workshop 'Critical Theory and Constitutionalism', Berlin, 11 December 2015, 32–35 (at file with the author); Sonja Buckel, *'Welcome to Europe' – Juridische Auseinandersetzungen um das Staatsprojekt Europa* (Bielefeld: Transcript, 2013).

[65] Naomi Murakawa, *The First Civil Right: How Liberals Built Prison America* (Oxford: Oxford University Press, 2014); Bernard E. Harcourt, *The Illusion of Free Markets: Punishment and the Myth of Natural Order* (Cambridge MA: Harvard University Press, 2011).

has a long tradition that (if we only take some landmark decisions of the US Supreme Court) reaches in the USA from *Fletcher* v. *Peck* (1810) and *Dartmouth College* v. *Woodward* (1819) over *Lochner* v. *New York* (1905) to *Citizens United* v. *FEC* (2009). The last is paradigmatic for the present trend. Neither the tradition nor its neoconservative renewal is an American exception.[66]

3 Conclusion: Saving Democratic Solidarity

It follows politically, second, that only the *cosmopolitan project of democratic socialism* to *carry* the legal form of democratic solidarity *to the stars*, can save egalitarian mass-democracy.[67] Facing the nearly unresolvable accumulation and reciprocal reinforcement of problems, the question, if their democratic solution will finally save capitalism from itself, or transform capitalism into democratic socialism, seems to be secondary.

(1) To save growth and democracy in times of secular stagnation, *massive redistribution of wealth to the lower and middle classes is the only hopeful perspective.* Only massive redistribution in favor of the middle and lower classes can *keep growth running* because only lower and middle classes buy masses of consumer goods, and growth in post-industrial societies *based on industry* (electricity, pharmacy, mass-transportation, etc.) still comes from *mass-consumption.* The solution of the problem of social differentiation would solve both problems at once, the problem of growth and the problem of social and political inequality. Unfortunately, there are many more problems to solve.

(2) To include the dramatically growing *domestic* (national and regional) periphery of excluded surplus populations and countries (Greek) there is need for *massive investments in educational and socialisation agencies of all kind, together with a decent basic income.*[68] Nothing else will work. If the following problem (3) could be solved, even a solution for the global, in particular the African problem of exclusion (and migration) could become possible.

[66] See above, and for a brief reconstruction: Brunkhorst, *Critical Theory of Legal Revolutions*, 296–300.

[67] Rorty, *Menschenrechte, Vernunft und Empfindsamkeit*, p. 115 (see above).

[68] Here are well-calculated models available: Bruce Ackerman and Anne Alstott, *Die Stakeholder-Gesellschaft. Ein Modell für mehr Chancengleichheit* (Frankfurt am Main: Campus, 2001). Gerd Grözinger, Michael Maschke and Claus Offe, *Die Teilhabegesellschaft. Modell eines neuen Wohlfahrtsstaates* (Frankfurt am Main: Campus, 2006).

(3) The only realistic solution for the environmental problems (if there is any) is *green growth*. The enormous proportions of the problem come to the fore once we take into account that even the most realistic programs for CO_2-reduction (carbon capture and storage) are possible only with *far reaching public infringements of land ownership worldwide*, which partly are entangled with the results of post-colonial land grabbing.[69]

(4) To keep the tremendously grown blackmailing power of global capitalism in check, there is no alternative but transferring real power – still called with an outdated term 'sovereignty' – to *democratically legitimated and controlled transnational governmental structures*. Intergovernmental governance without government is over. Governance is the cure that is worse than the ailment, in particular if we take not only capitalist economy but also private law and structures of (ever more informal) political hegemony in account, not to talk about the anti-democratic side effects of many other functional systems (for instance, the globalised sport system, global media and cultural industries).

Nobody knows if there is any possible democratic solution to the cumulating problems, and one has to face the gloomy perspective that 1989 was not the advent but the decay of global constitutionalism.[70] But nothing will work without the thrust of a *real movement* towards cosmopolitan democracy, and as Marx and Engels I mean with 'real movements' not only movements of social groups and people in streets and halls but also emerging organisations and institutions, in particular those of public law. There are already some important international organisations, which are bodies of public law and not of civil law. They reach from the UN General Assembly to the European Parliament and their many commissions. There is already a growing number of courts of international public law such as the old international and the new criminal court in The Hague, a couple of Inter-American courts, and

[69] See Ottmar Edenhofer et al., 'Die Gretchenfrage des Klimaschutzes: Nun sag, wie hast Du's mit dem Eigentum?', in Thorsten Müller (ed.) *20 Jahre Recht der Erneuerbaren Energien* (Baden-Baden: Nomos, 2012), 34–50; Jochen von Bernstorff, 'Landgrabbing und Menschenrechte', INEF Forschungsreihe Menschenrechte, Unternehmensverantwortung und Nachhaltige Entwicklung (2012). Available at: www.humanrights-business.org/landgrabbing_final_1.pdf (accessed 4 July 2019); Thore Prien (2014) 'Landgrabbing', *Prager Frühling* (July 2014), available at: www.prager-fruehling-magazin.de/de/article/1148.landgrabbing.html (accessed 8 January 2020).

[70] See Huake Brunkhorst, 'Democratic solidarity under siege – decay of constitutionalization and the crisis of public law and public opinion', in Poul Kjaer and Niklas Olsen (ed.), *Critical Theories of Crisis in Europe* (London: Rowman & Littlefield, 2016).

the courts of the EU and the Council of Europe.[71] Insufficient, decoupled from democratic legislation and often mentally complying to the interests of the global ruling and propertied classes as they are, *they are there* and we can convert them into institutions of increasing and improving democratic solidarity. Even if transnational social movements still are marginal, there is already a real movement of an emerging global civil society (with hundreds and thousands of international non-governmental organisations [INGOs]). They virtually represent 99 percent of the world population compared with the 1 percent of the Wall Street and the World Economic Forum of Davos communities of the world, and there are at least beginnings of transnational social and ecological movements and organisations of workers (international trade unions) and excluded populations. Social movements today are ever more movements of superfluous academics. In a world society where between 20 percent and 50 percent of the younger generation have an academic training, individualistic and universalistic orientations, post-conventional lifestyles and use-value oriented practices are spreading rapidly, and they are already a serious alternative to neoconservative lifestyle reforms, which go global and split the new academic class formations. Together with ever more people grown up with the Internet, nothing seems more predictable than the end of narrow national bounds and nationalist mentalities – on the left but also on the right (global fundamentalism). Finally, when Marx and Engels in 1848 referred to the real movements of true democracy and communism, they referred to a concept, whose existence was not much further (probably even less) developed than that of cosmopolitan democracy today.

[71] Armin von Bogdandy, 'The European lesson for international democracy: the significance of Articles 9–12 EU Treaty for International Organizations', *The European Journal of International Law*, 23(2) (2012), 315–34; Armin von Bogdandy and Ingo Venzke, *In Whose Name? A Public Law Theory of International* Adjudication (Oxford: Oxford University Press, 2014).

4

Chains of Solidarity

Violence and Debt

NATHALIE KARAGIANNIS

1 Law, Europe, Social Thought

Even though we think of our Western societies as disenchanted, rational systems of practices and functions, these societies emerge from a set of dogmas, a certain *dogmatique*. This dogmatique is a cultural foundation that cannot be proven, its reason and profound logic cannot be shown, it is, as it were, axiomatic. This dogmatique is (the origins of) our law – and that is what, at its very source, makes it different from another society's law. However, the need for a common representation of justice, the need for a bridging of the gap between 'being' and 'should be' is common to all human agglomerations.[1]

From an anthropological point of view, when applied, law is a language; it is a language that separates those from whom the law *emanates* (the people, even in parliamentary or representative democracies) and those who *use* the law (practitioners of law and politicians). This gap is related to the gap in democracy between the people as instituting subject and as instituted subject, which is often referred to as the democratic paradox.[2] For our current purposes, this gap should be kept in mind as producing a tension between the social – that which is instituted – and the political – that which institutes.[3] This gap is thus enacted by the language of law, and

[1] Pierre Legendre, one of the great thinkers of the anthropology and psychoanalysis of law, is the author of the expression 'dogmatique'. See, for instance, his *Sur la question dogmatique en Occident* (Paris: Fayard, 1999); it is on this basis of his thought that Alain Supiot develops his own work around solidarity, see Alan Supiot, *La solidarité: enquête sur un principe juridique* (Paris: Odile Jacob, 2015).

[2] See Chantal Mouffe, *Democratic Paradox* (London: Verso, 2000).

[3] Nathalie Karagiannis, 'Multiple solidarities: autonomy and resistance', in Nathalie Karagiannis and Peter Wagner, *Varieties of World-Making. Beyond Globalisation* (Liverpool: Liverpool University Press, 2006).

insofar as the subject from whom it emanates and the subject who mainly uses it are different, this is a language that creates hierarchy. This practical hierarchy, which is also reflected in psychoanalytical thought around the law, ascribes, as its first source, the (name of the) father.[4]

Our context for considering transnational solidarity is the European context, a context with a certain dogmatique, a specific foundation in law, an internalised (or suppressed) violent hierarchy and a general[5] aspiration to peaceful equality. It is certainly both inwardly and outwardly a transnational context, and one in which the violent, colonial past of several European countries and the past and present debts at play among European countries, and between them and their former colonies echo incessantly. In this context, it is possible to plead *for* Europe, a Europe which, borrowing from British psychoanalyst Winnicott,[6] could be called a good enough Europe. A good enough Europe would be a Europe that acknowledges its limits and failings – and attempts to find cures and remedies for them – and, at the same time, does not renounce being Europe because of those limits and failings.

The cohesive, collaborative, ordering, positive effect of the European polity must be seen as going hand-in-hand with aspects of social anomy: violence, revolt and disorder. To think of these two aspects as contradictory and mutually exclusive is an impoverishment, both theoretically and practically. Thus, if Europe has indeed constructed itself on the ruins of the world wars, and the Second World War in particular, with an objective of pacific cohabitation and economic empowerment and has managed to achieve extraordinary successes with regard to welfare state and culture, for instance, it has also had and still has to deal with its colonies, refugees and its internal discriminations. Often, these two aspects (external and internal) are pitched as mutually exclusive.[7] However, that which in psychoanalytical parlance would be called the impulses of *eros* and *thanatos* are not

[4] For instance, Sigmund Freud, *Totem and Taboo: Resemblances Between the Mental Lives of Savages and Neurotics* (Leipzig and Vienna, 2013).

[5] With always more exceptions gesturing either openly to the violence of hierarchy (with charismatic figures of the extreme right) or to an exclusively dissenting equalisation of conditions (with nationalistic/populistic movements).

[6] Winnicott's good enough mother is a mother who augment's her child capacity to frustration (acknowledgement of her failings) progressively, thus allowing the smooth autonomisation of the child. Donald Winnicot, *Playing and Reality* (London: Tavistock, 1971).

[7] Nathalie Karagiannis, 'Solidarity within Europe, solidarity without Europe', *European Societies*, 9(1) (2007), 3–21.

contradictory and Europe makes itself as a world, as a collective social and political subject, in that original gap between being (in all its disorder and attempts to order) and should be. To miss this – for example, to condemn Europe because of its failing refugee policy and to turn to nationalism as an answer – is to miss the extraordinary aspect of Europe as a political community in the making. It is to disown it, in the sense of either considering it fit for utter condemnation or for utopia. Neither is true or desirable and the same goes for solidarity.

Before going on, let us note that solidarity centrally and unequivocally poses one important question that is often ignored: how does the passage from the individual/person/subject to society/polis/social contract occur? It is interesting to look at theoretical efforts, the starting points of which are opposed in this respect, in order to work one's way from one pole towards the other: thus, for instance, whereas psychoanalytical thought starts out from the unique psyche and branches out to the family and wider social constellation, anthropology takes social, moral, economic relations as its basic unit. Likewise, within disciplines such as political philosophy, some thinkers have taken 'the human being' or 'the individual' as their starting point whereas others begin with the enigma of the collective political self. In all cases, the distance between the *I* and the *we* is not easy to bridge, and despite our efforts to elucidate it, it is perhaps better if we admit that it is not always entirely possible to do so.[8] For the moment, nevertheless, it is most useful to think of solidarity as derived from the Roman law responsibility *in solidum*, applied to debtors and creditors: solidity, the block, of creditors in front of the debt or of debtors in front of a demanding creditor. This block, the solidity, belongs to a cluster of concepts such as society, community, communism and social cohesion.

Solidarity (and the cluster of concepts associated to it) cannot be thought of without the original violence which produces it and without the violence it produces. The roots of the still-vigorous paternalistic and patriarchal tradition of solidarity and how they mingle with the similarly vigorous fraternal tradition of solidarity will first be explored; then, through correlation to anthropological research on the debt, a specific kind of debt that demands repayment will be adjoined to each type of solidarity.

[8] As Cornelius Castoriadis suggests in *Les carrefours du labyrinthe ii* (Paris: Seuil, 1986), pp. 42–3.

2 Solidarity, Violence, Revolt

In the socio-political imaginary concatenation that Europe is right now, different types of solidarity co-exist and sometimes clash with each other. This is often not acknowledged because solidarity is usually assumed to be opposed to revolt and violence in keeping with Durkheim's sketch of the evolution of solidarity – going from mechanic (automatic, community style) to organic (reflexive, society-style) – instead of observing that various types of solidarities co-exist in the same space, which they occupy *coevally,* and because we do not see that these multiple solidarities are related to fundamental and deep-seated senses of debt, which involve different temporalities or regimes of historicity[9].

Europe comes out of the ashes of the Second World War, and is an experiment that is exceptional in its width and its collective basis, but relatively similar to other situations in terms of how a city is founded. Strife, war, sacrifice, in other words violence, are often to be found at the source of the emergence of a polis. Almost every myth of the origins of the polis has at its basis an original violence.

In the ancient Greek myths of the beginning of communities of gods, there are at least two major series of patricides. The most known is the patricide of Cronos, by his son Zeus, but this event is preceded by the patricide of Uranus, Cronos's father, who is the first male element of the universe in the Hesiodic account. Uranus had many children with Gaia – Earth – among whom were the Titans, including Cronos. He hated his children and imprisoned them in the Tartars, the jail under the Earth. However, Gaia, their mother, was very angry about this and freed them, asking them to kill Uranus. The only one who could summon the courage to act was Cronos, who severed his father's genitals while the latter was asleep and was able to rule from then onwards, with his closest brothers the Titans (the Cyclops and the Hecatoncheires) as his allies.

When Cronos himself had children, he grew afraid of succumbing to the same fate as his father, so ate the babies that his wife, Rea, delivered one after the other until one day, she gave him a stone wrapped in clothes in the place of the newborn baby. Zeus, who grew up to be strong and powerful, administered poison to his father. The poison made Cronos regurgitate Zeus' siblings, the Olympian Gods, who then waged a war against their father and his allied siblings (the Titans, the Cyclops, etc.).

[9] The phrase is François Hartog's in *Régimes d'historicité: présentisme et expériences du temps* (Paris: Seuil, 2003).

These two patricides – one complete, one attempted – are fundamental in ancient Greek mythology and they are, to a more or less dramatic extent, reproduced in other more minor myths and in tragedy. In this scheme, the hierarchical relation to, and the killing of, the father figure is that which permits the constitution of the group, that is, the group is held together in the name of the father by virtue of being the father′s sons. This identity has absolute precedence over any other but more than bringing about an identity, the scheme of *hierarchy and patricide* must be considered *as a kind of moral economy* (or a world-making).[10] Here, I follow Didier Fassin′s broad understanding of moral economy, that is; a system of practices, relations and exchanges in which the moral gains and losses of each participating member take on a particular meaning because of the existence of the system.[11] Therefore, here, a hierarchical-patricidal moral economy is at the root of a solidarity that is patriarchal and paternalistic. The patriarchal aspect is quite clear: the patricides are acts – or crimes – that take place within a framework where the father is the *arche*, the chief. All practices and relations are to be understood as deriving from that *arche* and the respect, response and/or revolt that this figure elicits.

The paternalistic aspect has to do with such a solidarity locking those who are solidary into the position of children. This opens up the question of the violence against the children, which in actual, but not often-noted, fact precedes the patricides: the father isolates, eats or kills his children, and one could say that therein lies the primordial violence – in the violence against the children or those who are locked into the position of children. Colonial systems of law and social practices have, for example, operated on this basis. Looking at the literature of the Balkans, the sacrifice of the child, the young woman or the wife (the last two being in the position of children) in order for a bridge,[12] a house or a village to be built on solid grounds is an interesting *topos* in this respect.

[10] Freud's *Totem and Taboo* is an inescapable reference here. Freud′s text has two main aspects (sexual competition, Oedipus) which are not of central relevance here. In *Totem and Taboo,* sacrifice is normally understood as an offering of favours, but the first sacrifice was an act of *social fellowship* between the deity and his worshippers, that is, something which was committed in order for the social relations of the participants to be acknowledged. An interesting commentary on *Totem and Taboo,* which insists on the aspect of violence and revolt is Julia Kristeva's *Sens et non-sens de la révolte. Pouvoirs et limites de la psychanalyse I* (Paris: lib. Fayard, 1996). In these pages, Kristeva deploys the reverse, as it were, argument: that revolt is possible because the social exists.

[11] Didier Fassin, 'Moral economies revisited', *Annales. Histoire, Sciences Sociales*, 6 (2009), 1237–66.

[12] For a well-known example, see Ismail Kadaré, *Avril Brisé* (Paris: lib. Fayard, 1978).

In the fraternal type of Ur-violence that brings about solidarity, the killing happens between brothers. Well-known fundamental myths in this vein are Romulus and Remus, Cain and Abel, and Atreus and Thyestes in the Atrides family. In a nutshell, the three pairs of siblings confront each other over superiority and the fraternal killing gives rise to the founding of a city. The details of each story would be worth dwelling on, but for the current purposes, we should remember that: before Remus is killed by Romulus, who is then able to found the city of Rome, both brothers fight against the brother of their grandfather who usurped their grandfather′s throne, a *mise-en-abîme* of fraternal competition; that before Cain killed Abel, and was then able to found his own city, his offering ('sacrifice') had been rejected by God (the father), a *mise-en-abîme* of paternal then fraternal competition; and that Atreus and Thyestes had been exiled by their father as a punishment for having killed their other brother, while later it is Thyestes′s incestuous son who kills Atreus (a double *mise-en-abîme* of paternal-fraternal competition). These *mises-en-abîme* or repetitions of the same theme of the story within the story are reminders that the violence at the origins of that which will hold things together: solidarity, is inescapable.

In Freud's *Totem and Taboo*, the basic idea underlying the violence between brothers is that when the young male becomes adult, he kills and drives away the other young males, since it is ultimately impossible that two become head of the group: for the polis or the community to exist, there must only be one ruler. Clear-cut as this idea may seem, we cannot help but immediately notice that the result of the fraternal competition and killing is that the *arche* goes back to being in the hands of one male, that is, we are back to a hierarchical moral economy. It is clear that, unlike in *Moses and Monotheism*, in *Totem and Taboo,* Freud is interested in myth and its potential when not suppressed historical memory, and what he gives us is, to use Weberian vocabulary, an ideal-typical description. However, for the Freud of *Totem and Taboo*, there is an evolution from patricide to fratricide and then to general law. In turn, writing on the evolution of solidarity within law, Alain Supiot traces the passage of the notion from civil law to social law as breaking with the figure of the father and introducing the Third Man (le Tiers).[13] This 'rise in abstraction' (which Arendt also refers to) introduces the unknown other into solidaristic relations.

[13] Alain Supiot, for example: www.college-de-france.fr/media/alain-supiot/UPL4163552085711608777_0805_0824_Supiot.pdf

Now, if, on the one hand, what we called the *mises-en-abîmes* recall different moral-economic situations – repetitions of fraternal conflict, fraternal conflict with hierarchical conflict preceding it, or fraternal conflict with backgrounds of both fraternal and hierarchical conflicts – and if, on the other hand, the fraternal conflict always serves to the reinstatement of one man as *arche,* then the least that can be said is that these two types of Ur-violence show no straight evolution even at the mythical level.

Furthermore, I would like to suggest that the killing of the brother is the original violence producing solidarity between the *non*-brothers; that the notion of brother extends here to the unknown other, the stranger and that, in effect, we are in the presence here of another kind of moral economy, which includes and asks the question of the unknown other (Supiot's Third Man), rather than the familial and familiar.[14] In a different theoretical language, that of political philosophy, this is the double question of the size of the community and of its centre. First, the fraternal killing and the solidarity between *non*-brothers raises the issue of the borders of the community. Where are the borders of the community? With whom is the community insider solidary? How far does the community extend? What of the stranger inside the community? All these queries have been posed and variously answered by different strands of political philosophy, and must be attached to that first issue.[15] Second, the other side of the question posed by the elimination of the brother in this context is that of central legitimacy: around what emptiness will solidarity be built? This question is not broached straightforwardly in the patricide solidarity, because the father is substituted by the object and eaten (its children assimilate him and become him). At the political level, democracy stems from this question, from the fact that the place of power is empty[16] and undecided – and the social question is unsubstantiated.

Under these types of violence, there lies revolt. In his famous *L'homme révolté*, Albert Camus has an astonishing line: 'je me révolte, donc nous

[14] This also poses directly the question of the competition between groups. In *Totem and Taboo*, Freud notes that, according to Fraser, totemising, that is, not eating the totem may also correspond to a complementarity, a survival between groups.

[15] Nathalie Karagiannis and Peter Wagner, 'The stranger in synagonistic politics', in Andrew Schaap (ed.), *Law and Agonistic Politics* (Farnham: Ashgate, 2008).

[16] It is to Claude Lefort we owe the thought and expression 'empty place of power' in democracy, which replaces the mystic, enigmatic magma in which the *arche* is enveloped in monarchy or similar regimes. See C. Lefort, *L'invention démocratique: les limites de la domination totalitaire* (Paris: Fayard, 1994).

sommes' ('*I* revolt, therefore *we* are').[17] In other words, the constitution of a collective 'we' is subsequent to the individual revolt. The interesting steps taken here concern, on the one hand, the step from the individual to the collective and, on the other hand, the relation between the *action* of revolt and the constitution of an *identity;* in other words: the origins of violence in the emergence of a collectivity. Let us follow his text, which starts a page earlier than this line:

> Human solidarity is based on the movement of revolt and this movement, in turn, finds its only justification in this complicity ... every revolt which permits itself to negate or destroy this solidarity loses in that very moment the name of revolt and coincides with a murderous consent. In the same way, this solidarity, outside of the field of the sacred, acquires life only at the level of revolt. The true drama of the revolted thought is then announced. To be, the human being must revolt, but its revolt must respect the limits that it discovers in itself and where human beings, coming together, start existing ... In the experience of absurdity (the absurd), suffering is individual. From the moment of revolt, suffering gets a collective conscience, it becomes the adventure of all. Thus, the first progress of a spirit seized by estrangement is to recognise that it shares this estrangement with all human beings and that human reality, in its totality, suffers from this same distance to itself and to the world.[18]

Revolt is described by Camus as being founded on human solidarity, the solidarity that unites all those who feel estranged – strangers to themselves and to the world. This solidarity is also called complicity, pointing to Freud's fundamental idea in *Totem and Taboo*: that which holds society together is complicity in the common crime. Complicity, or guilt due to violence, is indeed the spring of solidarity, according to the Freudian account – and it points to Nietzsche's well-known syllogism on

[17] Albert Camus, *L'homme révolté* (Paris: Gallimard, 1951), p. 36, emphases added.

[18] My translation 'La solidarité humaine se fonde sur le mouvement de révolte et celui-ci, à son tour, ne trouve de justification que dans cette complicité.... toute révolte qui s'autorise à nier ou à détruire cette solidarité perd du même coup le nom de révolte et coïncide en réalité avec un consentement meurtrier. De même cette solidarité, hors du sacré, ne prend vie qu'au niveau de la révolte. Le vrai drame de la pensée révoltée est alors annoncé. Pour être, l'homme doit se révolter, mais sa révolte doit respecter la limite qu'elle découvre en elle-même et où les hommes, en se rejoignant, commencent d'être .... Dans l'expérience absurde, la souffrance est individuelle. A partir du mouvement de révolte, elle a conscience d'être collective, elle est l'aventure de tous. Le premier progrès d'un esprit saisi d'étrangeté est donc de reconnaître qu'il partage cette étrangeté avec tous les hommes et que la réalité humaine, dans sa totalité, souffre de cette distance par rapport à soi et au monde' (Camus, *L'homme révolté*, pp. 35–6).

the derivation of guilt from debt in the Genealogy of Morals[19], which will become relevant to our purposes in the next section.

Interestingly, however, complicity and revolt can also be thought of as distinct, if revolt is understood as an event which breaches the received account of time, history or the origins. In that case, the 'way of living well' *together* would be founded on a reconciliation between that breach in the narration and an uninterrupted flow of time. Commenting on Derrida's 'Spectres of Marx', the historian of psychoanalysis Elisabeth Roudinesco, quotes the poet René Char: 'notre héritage n'est précédé d'aucun testament' ('our heritage is not preceded by any testament').[20] Breach caused by revolt *and* flow of the past into the present are upheld at the same time. Camus's warning of the de-coupling of revolt from solidarity, with its murderous undertones, may actually not actually have a different intention.

Camus wrote against a particular historical background in which violence was being theoretically justified in the West and the non-West in the name of class revolution or decolonisation (famously, by Fanon[21]), an era reminiscent of our own from a certain perspective. However, if Camus saw a clear link between solidarity and revolt, he also clearly distinguished between revolt and violence, since revolt finds its own limit within itself: respect for the other human being.

Can violence be easily disengaged from solidarity? The view of Camus himself was a cosmopolitan (ex-communist) republican-liberal left view that is close to the thinking of late modern/contemporary philosophers – starting with Hannah Arendt, and more recently Jürgen Habermas, followed by Nancy Fraser and Axel Honneth – for whom solidarity is defined as social esteem. In an older text, I have criticised Arendt's definition of solidarity on three grounds: abstraction, reason, equality.[22] Briefly, I argued that it is politically inoperative to found solidarity on an abstract idea rather than showing it is constantly there in practices; that it pertains to the realm of the emotions as much as that of reason; and that it is to be found in situations of inequality too. Regarding the last point, Camus's thought on revolt is very similar: '[i]n society, the spirit of revolt is possible only in groups where theoretical equality covers great de facto

[19] F. Nietzsche, *On The Genealogy of Morality, Second Essay: 'Guilt', 'Bad Conscience' and Related Matters* (Cambridge: Cambridge University Press, 1887), pp. 33–67.

[20] Elisabeth Roudinesco 'Jacques Derrida: spectres de Marx, spectres de Freud', in *Un jour Derrida* (Paris: Bibliothèque publique d'information, 2014), pp. 51–60.

[21] Frantz Fanon, *Les damnés de la terre* (Paris: Maspero, 1961).

[22] Karagiannis, 'Multiple solidarities'.

inequalities'[23] and in this we recognise the gap between what there is and what there should be as the dogmatique we started with.

3 Solidarity and Debt

Solidarity and debt are intricately related, not only because of juridical-etymological reasons, but also because they can both be thought of as the cement or the glue that holds the relations between people. Solidarity as glue or as cement, or as that which holds society together, is a *topos* of social-theoretical thought.[24] But the same metaphor of cement can be found in the most unexpected of places in order to describe debt. Hear what Rabelais says:[25]

> You ask me when I will be out of debt. Well, to go yet further on, and possibly worse in your conceit, may Saint Bablin, the good saint, snatch me, if I have not all my lifetime held debt to be as a union or conjunction of the heavens with the earth, and *the whole cement whereby the race of mankind is kept together*; yea, of such virtue and efficacy that, I say, the whole progeny of Adam would very suddenly perish without it. Therefore, perhaps, I do not think amiss, when I repute it to be the great soul of the universe, which, according to the opinion of the Academics, vivifieth all manner of things.

So, solidarity and debt have this feature in common. Let us now look a little bit more carefully at debt, while keeping in mind that one of the earliest social-theoretical justifications for the institution of a system of social solidarity is that social beings have a debt towards society.[26]

If one looks at debt from an anthropological, non-utilitarian point of view, contrary to the received view, debt will appear as a mode of relation between human beings that is out of the market, which extracts the human being from (capitalistic, nowadays) market relations, and which appeals *both to human beings' historicity* (their sense of being inscribed in a time and of creating time) *and their a-historicity.* This latter also forms the context of the dogmatique we were referring to earlier, that is, it

23 Camus, *L'homme révolté*, p. 33. *En société l'esprit de révolte n'est possible que dans les groupes où une égalité théorique recouvre de grandes inégalités de faits.*

24 For example, see Kristeva, *Sens et non-sens de la révolte*, p. 22: Dès lors, la culpabilité et le répentir *cimentent* le lien, le pacte social, entre les fils, entre les frères . . .; or Randall Collins's glue of solidarity in e.g. *Interaction Ritual Chains* (Princeton, NJ: Princeton University Press, 2004).

25 François Rabelais, *The Complete Works*, trans. Donald M. Frame (Berkeley, CA: University of California Press, 1999), p. 267.

26 Karagiannis, 'Multiple solidarities'.

invokes a link to an axiomatic set of principles that are linked to the sacred, whether this is acknowledged or not/suppressed or not, and that are expressed in a reasonable[27] manner. This double belonging of the debt to the historical and to the a-historical universes is fundamental to understanding the co-existence of different types of solidarity.

Looking at ethnography from other societies, however ancient, may be extremely illuminating as to the alternatives that our societies have.[28] It is important to know and express that our current way of comprehending solidarity is not the only one, that even in our own society (in our own dogmatique), there may be others.

The great French ethnographer, Charles Malamoud, finds four categories of theological debt in ancient Indian Brahmanism. After convincingly showing that the notion of debt is first autonomous and non-decomposable (that is, it cannot be derived from any other term or concept),[29] Malamoud states that if the notion of debt cannot be explained, it explains everything. One of the Sanskrit texts that Malamoud quotes, says: 'Every being by being born is born as a debt towards the gods, the saints, the fathers, the fellow human beings. If one sacrifices, that is the debt due from birth to the gods; it is for them that one does it, when one offers a sacrifice, when one offers them libations. And if we recite sacred texts, then this is a debt due from birth to the saints, it is for them we do it, and he who recites ancient texts is called the guardian of the saints' treasure. And if we desire progeny, then this is a debt due from birth to the fathers; it is for them we do it, so that their progeny will be continuous and uninterrupted. And if we offer hospitality, then this is a debt due from birth to human beings; it is for them that we do it when we offer them hospitality, when we offer them to eat. He who has done all this has done all what he had to do.'[30] So the four types debts one is born into, so to say – to the gods, to the saints, to the fathers, to fellow human beings – each have an equivalent way to be repaid; sacrifice(killing), the word, children and hospitality respectively.

[27] Both Camus and Supiot use the notion of reasonableness; when concretely dealing with a complex of solidarities of different kinds, this notion (by opposition to reason) might prove useful.

[28] David Graeber, 'On the moral ground of economic relations: a Maussian approach', *Journal of Classical Sociology*, 4(I) 2014, 65–77.

[29] Charles Malamoud, 'Théologie de la dette dans les Brāhmaṇa', in *La dette* (Paris: Editions de l'EHESS, 1980), p. 45.

[30] Ibid., pp. 49–53, my translation.

Malamoud insists on two points, which are relevant for our purposes. The first point is that behind the debt to the gods (the most important, let us say, and in our words, the most hierarchical) stands the debt to the stronger creditor, death or the god of death, Yama. Thus, the human being from birth owes to death, it is born like a debt to death. Through sacrifice, says an interpretative Indian text, the human being redeems its person from death. Sacrifice allows the sacrificer to ascend to the sky and come back to 'a world that he has done on his own'. Sacrifice usually entails the burning of plants, but we can extend the idea to the killing of an animal, as in ancient Greece, or even the (aborted) killing of a child, as in the Old Testament, in any case, the annihilation of the substitute of the sacrificer. The payment of the debt through sacrifice makes a world (or, in another vocabulary, a moral economy).

The second point is that this world-making can also be achieved by having a child. For as long as the human being does not have a child, s/he does not have a world. The human being is in full coincidence with her or himself when they have a child, and the reason why the child inherits the father′s wealth upon his death is because s/he also inherits his debts.

So even though these are four theological debts, the last point shows the constant interplay between the spiritual or a-historical world and the material, historical world. The Sanskritic texts' insistence on the world-making of the (repayment of the) debt indicates the closeness between the latter and solidarity. After all solidarity, just as debt, is nothing other than the making of a world.

There are certain similarities between these four debts and their modes of repayment and the two types of solidarity we have encountered. On the one hand, the debts towards the gods, the saints and the fathers all pertain to a hierarchical type of solidarity and, at another level, to Durkheim's mechanical solidarity, a solidarity whose cohesion and integration is due to the homogeneity and similarity of its members. In this type of correspondence, the moral economy – the making of a world – at stake plays out issues of reciprocity and exchange in a more explicit and power-laden manner. In this moral economy, the reason of law refers directly to the sacredness of certain duties.

On the other hand, the debt towards one's fellow human beings pertains to a fraternal type of solidarity and, at another level, to Durkheim′s organic solidarity, where social integration is due to complementarity owing to differentiation. Because the conceptual nucleus of the dogmatique here is not similarity/identity, the other extends to the more abstract other of the stranger, that is, the brother can be the stranger. The issue of the limit of the community is pivotal and contestable in this solidarity: the moral economy that is developed contains hospitality, and the theme of the stranger is central and is therefore likely to be a more democratic moral economy (which does not of course exclude violence).The suspension of time operated by the a-historical understandings of debt and solidarity may be remarkably 'modern' if seen through the lenses of globalisation, simultaneity of decision making and action, the explosion of centres of domination and so forth. People's old traditions and religious faith may actually explain a lot about what is or will be happening.[31] Psychoanalytical thought – with the *Zeitlosigkeit* of the unconscious – and anthropological thought with its insistence on non-utilitarian approaches to exchange (that is, exchange which expands across important stretches of time, like in the gift or certain kinds of very long-term debt) play witness to the vital presence of the sacred or the axiomatic or the dogmatique as keeping us together, both as individuals and as members of society.

This is equivalent to saying that while the inscription and creation of historical time may well express an evolution from a more concrete, family/community-bound (hierarchical) solidarity to a more abstract (fraternal) form of solidarity, *coevally*, a-historical time is at stake in the relation between a certain debt and a certain solidarity.

4 The Chains of Solidarity

Chains are things that limit freedom, that keep things imprisoned. Solidarity can take the form of oppression if some aspects of it are not acknowledged and represented. Unless we see in solidarity things other than trade unionism and the welfare state, we will not be able to keep up with discourses that use the concept in a different way than the way we are used. Most of this chapter is dedicated to such chains.

Thus, solidarity is founded in violence and bears the signs of violence and revolt. The creation of community in innumerable foundational myths results from a terrible killing. According to whether this killing is of the father or the brother, I suggested that solidarity is either hierarchical, and geared towards those strictly understood to be children

[31] An idea not unusual for anthropologists, historians or philosophers, for example, from Mircea Eliade, 'Introduction', in *Images et symboles: essai sur le symbolisme magico-religieux* (Paris: Gallimard, 1951) to Giorgio Agamben, *The Kingdom and Glory. For a Theological Genealogy of Economy and Government*, trans. Lorenzo Chiesa (Stanford, CA: Stanford University Press, 2011).

of the father, or fraternal, in the sense of geared towards the stranger, the non-brother. I also suggested that both these solidarities can exist in combined forms, even within the same foundational myth. Revolt is violence-in-solidarity and it reconciles, that is, it allows for simultaneity of the event (or suspension of time, which happens in the area of the sacred, the religious, or the Durkheimian mechanic) and the historical, continuous flow of time (which happens in the area of the reasonable, or the Durkheimian organic).

In our contemporary world, different types of solidarity constantly overlap and although some of them may not acknowledge their part in violence, inequality and impulse, others do. The non-acknowledgement of violence and revolt, and of inequality and passions (rather than reason), in our own ways of understanding solidarity blinds us to social phenomena which clash with our sense of a common world, but which are also forms of solidarity. Acknowledging the repressed constitutive elements in our sense of solidarity is a first step to acknowledging the oppressions and exclusions it operates to then reverse process with regard to other social phenomena, observing the violence and oppression they operated and understanding the solidarity that they produce.

Solidarity has nothing to do with equality. It may be an instrument of equalisation of conditions, but it is based on the fact of inequality. If it is insisted upon here – with the support of Camus referring to the spirit of revolt – it is because it is an indispensable acknowledgement in two necessary, but opposite, directions: both the recognition that there should be more or better solidarity (*better* goes in the direction of Axel Honneth's understanding of solidarity) and the recognition that, unacknowledged by the privileged and by those high up in the social ladder who see themselves as givers, there are humbler and effective small-scale solidarities at work, as David Graeber suggests.[32]

Chains are also events or beliefs that follow from one another and it is therefore possible both to establish chains of solidarity and to interrupt them and cut them away. For instance, solidarity might be an issue at stake in grand political frames and in overall progressive politics, like the European project (and there are good arguments about the overall diminishing importance of social solidarity in the practical passage of competences from the states to the Community), but it is also often present in nationalist and populist feelings and expressions, which can,

[32] Graeber, 'On the moral ground of economic relations'.

as a second step, be politically stirred, enhanced, mobilised and manipulated, or interrupted.

There are at least two ways that seem to offer such possibilities of (but also point to the absolute need for) interrupting chains of solidarity.

First, any community problem seems trivial compared to the problems that human communities – humanity – are facing because of the degradation of the climate. Keeping in line with the acknowledgement of the original violence upon which our communities are built and subsequently kept *in solidum*, we should make an effort to identify and symbolically represent the violences we keep on perpetrating in order to stay together. Starting thus anew with the notion of sacrifice, which at the largest scale today concerns animals and human beings far away, we must turn unequivocally towards the anthropocene in order for other less fundamentally costly solidarities to be developed.

Second, taking up the idea of sorority (Bonnie Honig's work on the relation between Antigone and Ismene[33]) and matching it to an unfailing concern for the more vulnerable (as was and is the foundation of the European welfare state) turns us rather radically away from patriarchy but also fraternity.

Both these foci (environment and sorority) radically alter our understanding of how solidarity might manifest itself. Why? Because they radically alter the very language in which solidarity is described and lived. Thus, the overwhelming awareness and response of artists to the problem of climate change and to feminism, and the eagerness of thinkers in these areas to find an active public which will further their case has given rise to an innovative mix of scientific-activist-artistic languages, which far from being totalitarian (that is, aspiring to treat everything through the same prism), are collaborative, complementary and 'processual', in that they arise from their own making. These languages are not yet admitted as legitimate in most academic publications – which is why this chapter has not used them – but if there is any way forward for thinking and practising transnational solidarity, it passes through forging new languages of that type.

33 Bonnie Honig, *Antigone Interrupted* (Cambridge: Cambridge University Press, 2013).

5

Symbols and Myths of European Union Transnational Solidarity

IAN MANNERS

1 Introduction

The treaties of European Union (EU) contain twenty-nine references to 'solidarity' with a wide variety of meanings and consequences for the study of transnational solidarity. This contribution takes a step back from the policy detail of these treaty- and policy-based understandings of solidarity to consider the constitutive effects of EU symbols and myths in a wider understanding of transnational solidarity within, across, and beyond the EU. The EU's Europe Day Poster celebrating '50 Years of Solidarity, Prosperity and Peace' on 9 May 2000 illustrates (Figure 5.1) that the status of solidarity in the EU is one of considerable importance in terms of symbols and myths of EU transnational solidarity.

This chapter explores the symbols and myths of EU transnational solidarity through a threefold analysis of transnational solidarity within, across, and beyond the EU. Based on post-Cold War study of the EU in global politics over the past three decades, the chapter compares and contrasts transnational solidarity from communitarian and cosmopolitan perspectives before advocating a cosmopolitical understanding of EU transnational solidarity in a global context. The chapter proceeds by delineating and theorising the concepts used, including symbols and myths, European integration, and transnational solidarity in order to prepare the ground for the next three analytical sections. Section 2 examines transnational solidarity within the EU by looking at symbols and myths of communitarian, cosmopolitan, and cosmopolitical solidarities. Section 3 looks across the borders of the EU to consider the symbols and myths of communitarian, cosmopolitan, and cosmopolitical solidarities within the European neighbourhood. Section 4 goes beyond the EU to analyse the symbols and myths of communitarian, cosmopolitan, and cosmopolitical solidarities

Figure 5.1 European Union, Europe Day Poster, 2000[1]

with distantly situated others through EU external actions. The chapter concludes by arguing the need to clearly identify, in line with Carol Gould,[2] transnational EU solidarities as overlapping networks of relations that share and support actions to eliminate oppression or reduce suffering. It is furthered argued that cosmopolitical solidarities that network and share

[1] European Union, '50 Years of Solidarity, Prosperity and Peace, 9 May 1950–2000' (2000) Europe Day Poster, available at: https://europa.eu/european-union/about-eu/symbols/europe-day_en).

[2] C. Gould, 'Transnational solidarities', Journal of Social Philosophy, 38(1) (2007), 148; C. Gould, 'Solidarity between the national and the transnational: what do we owe to "outsiders"?', in H. Krunke, H. Petersen and I. Manners (eds.), *Transnational Solidarity* (Cambridge: Cambridge University Press, 2020).

global ethics with local politics are more likely to take actions in concert that are caring and empathic towards distantly situated others.

The chapter draws upon material from a four-year project on symbols and myths in European integration to analyse the roles of symbols and images, myths and narratives, in this solidarity. Collective symbols and myths are fundamental to our understanding of issues such as European social solidarity, citizens feeling of belonging to the EU, political advocacy for and resistance to European integration, and concrete political actions in global politics. It is important to clarify that symbols are understood not just as the official 'icons' of the EU (the flag, the motto, the anthem, the day, or the euro), but as including official and non-official images and representations of the EU.[3] Similarly, myths are understood not as imaginary or unreal folklore, but as cultural and political narratives that provide meaning of the EU in society.[4] Symbols and myths include performative 'rituals' (such as ceremonies and commemorations), 'totems' (such as the capital of culture), and 'taboos' (such as exiting the euro/EU). These rituals and practices of meaning-making ensure that symbols and images, myths and narratives are represented and inscribed with particular understandings for the producers and consumers of European (dis)integration. The final step is to realise that such symbols and images, myths and narratives, rituals and practices are read, and must be interpreted, through political psychology.[5]

The chapter compares and contrasts symbols and myths of EU transnational solidarity within, across, and beyond the EU. The chapter makes a unique contribution to the volume by raising questions about communitarian, cosmopolitan, and cosmopolitical understandings of solidarity and the way they travel over distance within, across, and beyond the EU. European integration is understood as the social, economic, and political processes of mutual accommodation and inclusion by European states and peoples.[6] This definition of European integration is more accommodating and inclusive to social, economic, and political processes than the conventional definition of political integration defined by one of the

[3] I. Manners, 'Symbolism in European Integration', *Comparative European Politics*, 9(3) (2011), 243.

[4] I. Manners, 'Global Europa: Mythology of the European Union in World Politics', *Journal of Common Market Studies*, 48(1) (2010), 67; I. Manners and P. Murray, 'The end of a noble narrative? European integration narratives after the Nobel Peace Prize', *Journal of Common Market Studies*, 54(1) (2016), 185.

[5] I. Manners, 'Political psychology of European integration: the (re)production of identity and difference in the Brexit debate' *Political Psychology*, 39(6) (2018), 1, 213.

[6] Ibid., p. 1, 214

earliest theorists of European integration, Miriam Camps, as a 'new form of "action in common" among governments' merging their 'sovereignties to form a new political unit'.[7] The notion of solidarity in the EU has become expansive in the seventy years since the Schuman Declaration (1950) and Treaty of Paris (1951) aimed at taking 'concrete actions which create a real solidarity'. This diversity of solidarities is captured in the Treaty of European Union's (TEU) emphases on 'solidarity between ... peoples', 'solidarity ... between women and men', 'solidarity between generations', 'solidarity among Member States' and 'solidarity ... among peoples [of the wider world]' in the Preamble, and Articles 2 and 3.[8] With twenty-nine references to solidarity in the TEU and Treaty on the Functioning of the EU consolidated after the Treaty of Lisbon, it is clear that the term is used in a wide variety of ways and contexts. For example, previous research on the EU's normative power over the past two decades has analysed the promotion of social solidarity, in particular through development and trade policies, in global politics.[9]

As the other contributions to the volume demonstrate, conceptualising and defining transnational solidarity within and without the EU is challenging, especially given the expansive understandings of solidarity found in the EU. What is equally clear is that these understandings of solidarity depend heavily on positions taken within communitarian and cosmopolitan views of the world. In order to address these questions throughout the rest of the chapter, Carol Gould's conception of transnational solidarities is adopted, understood in terms of 'overlapping networks of relations between individuals (or groups) and distantly situated others (again, individuals or groups), in which the former aim to support these latter through actions to eliminate oppression or reduce suffering'.[10] This conception of transnational solidarity has four particulars of interest in this chapter: (1) it consists of **networks** of relations between individuals or groups; (2) it has **shared** goals of eliminating

[7] M. Camps, 'The European Common Market and American policy', Memorandum No. 11, Center of International Studies, Princeton University (1956), p. 3 and M. Camps, 'The European Common Market and free trade area: a progress report', Memorandum No. 15, Center of International Studies, Princeton University (1957), p. 7 in I. Manners, 'European communion: political theory of European Union', *Journal of European Public Policy*, 20(4) (2013), 473.

[8] TEU 2016: Art. 5 and 17.

[9] I. Manners, 'Normative power Europe: a contradiction in terms?', *Journal of Common Market Studies*, 40(2) (2002), 235, 242; I. Manners, 'Normative ethics of the European Union', *International Affairs*, 15(1) (2008), 45, 53.

[10] C. Gould, 'Solidarity between the national and the transnational'.

oppression or reducing suffering; (3) it is based on **empathy** between distantly situated others; and (4) it takes place through taking **action** in support of others.[11] Having set out the central concepts of symbols and myths, European integration, and transnational solidarity, the next section proceeds to use these ideas to analyse symbols and myths of transnational solidarity within the EU.

2 Transnational Solidarity within the EU

Discussions of solidarity in the EU have grown exponentially in the two decades since the Treaty of Maastricht.[12] Similarly, the growth of normative political theory and critical social theory applied to the study of global ethics and global justice of the EU has occurred at the same time.[13] While most accounts of EU solidarity tend to fall within communitarian approaches based on mutual concern, a few stray into cosmopolitan approaches emphasising reciprocal arrangements of mutual aid and duties. In almost all cases, this dichotomisation into communitarian versus cosmopolitan approaches tend to rule out the possibility of other approaches such as transnational solidarity or

[11] Gould, 'Transnational solidarities', 148.

[12] F. Scharpf, 'The European social model', *Journal of Common Market Studies*, 40(4) (2002), 645; J. White, 'Rethinking transnational solidarity in the EU', *Perspectives*, 20 (2003), 40; G. De Burca (ed.), *EU Law and the Welfare State: In Search of Solidarity* (Oxford: Oxford University Press, 2005); M. Krajewski, U. Neergaard, and J. van de Gronden (eds.), *The Changing Legal Framework for Services of General Interest in Europe: Between Competition and Solidarity* (The Hague: Asser Press, 2009); M. Ross and Y. Borgmann-Prebil (eds.), *Promoting Solidarity in the European Union* (Oxford: Oxford University Press, 2010); J. Hayward and R. Wurzel (eds.), *European Disunion: Between Sovereignty and Solidarity* (London: Palgrave, 2012).

[13] I. Manners, 'The European Union as a normative power: a response to Thomas Diez', *Millennium*, 35(1) (2006), 167; I. Manners, 'European Union, normative power and ethical foreign policy', in D. Chandler and V. Heins (eds.), *Rethinking Ethical Foreign Policy: Pitfalls, Possibilities and Paradoxes* (London: Routledge, 2006), p. 116; I. Manners, 'Another Europe is possible: critical perspectives on European Union politics', in K. E. Jørgensen, M. Pollack, and B. Rosamond (eds.), *Handbook of European Union Politics* (London: Sage, 2007), p. 77; I. Manners, 'The European Union's normative power: critical perspectives and perspectives on the critical', in R. Whitman (ed.), *Normative Power Europe: Empirical and Theoretical Perspectives* (London: Palgrave, 2011), p. 226; I. Manners, 'Un-national normative justification for European Union foreign policy', in J. Neyer and A. Wiener (eds.), *Political Theory of the European Union* (Oxford: Oxford University Press, 2011), p. 47; I. Manners, 'European communion: political theory of European Union', *Journal of European Public Policy*, 20(4) (2013), 473; I. Manners, 'Assessing the decennial, reassessing the global: understanding European Union normative power in global politics', *Cooperation and Conflict*, 48(2) (2013), 304–29.

cosmopolitics.[14] As the recent European Commission booklet on 'Solidarity in Europe: Alive and Active' illustrates (Figure 5.2) solidarity within the EU has at least three different meanings: communitarian

Figure 5.2 European Commission, Solidarity in Europe, 2018.[15]

[14] I. Manners, 'Normative ethics of the European Union', p. 47; I. Manners, 'European communion: political theory of European Union', pp. 482–3.
[15] European Commission, *Solidarity in Europe: Alive and Active* (2018).

national/European, cosmopolitan/universal, and some aspects of cosmopolitical/transnational.[16]

2.1 Communitarian Solidarities within the EU

The EU may best be conceived as a political object constituted through 'European communion' understood as the extent to which individuals or groups believe themselves to be sharing relations (or not), and the consequences of these beliefs for European political projects, processes, and products.[17] European communion involves processes of communitarian, cosmopolitan, and cosmopolitical solidarity.[18] Communitarian theories represent the predominant approach to understanding the EU, with international political theorist Molly Cochran arguing that 'communitarianism is particularist and oriented to shared community life',[19] while critical social theorist Craig Calhoun comments that communitarianism suffers from a 'tendency to elide the differences between local networks of social relationships and broad categories of belonging like nations'.[20] Writing over four decades ago, Carole Webb introduced a distinction between intergovernmental cooperation, supranational community, and transnational processes in the European Communities, which tends to assume communitarian understandings of how communities or groups serve to aggregate their interests.[21]

The myths and narratives of intergovernmental cooperation and solidarity within the EU place emphasis on the idea and motto of being 'united in diversity'. Within the EU the symbols and images of solidarity between Member States are particularly strong in single market, economic, social and territorial cohesion, and energy areas of shared and supporting competences. The iconic images are of geographical maps of the EU setting out the different Member States in bright colours, the sight

[16] European Commission, *Solidarity in Europe: Alive and Active* (2018), pp. 3 and 9. https://ec.europa.eu/research/social-sciences/pdf/policy_reviews/solidarity_in_europe.pdf

[17] I. Manners, 'European communion: political theory of European Union', pp. 474–5.

[18] Ibid., pp. 486–7.

[19] M. Cochran, *Normative Theory in International Relations: A Pragmatic Approach* (Cambridge: Cambridge University Press, 1999), p. 8.

[20] C. Calhoun, 'The class consciousness of frequent travelers: towards a critique of actually existing cosmopolitanism', in D. Archibugi (ed.), *Debating Cosmopolitics* (London: Verso, 2003), pp. 86, 96.

[21] C. Webb, 'Introduction: variations on a theoretical theme', in H. Wallace, W. Wallace, and C. Webb (eds.), *Policy-Making in the European Communities* (Chichester: John Wiley & Sons, 1977), p. 1.

of twenty-eight flags outside EU buildings, together with matching rituals and practices of prime ministers and ministers arriving at the Council of Ministers and European Council to take EU decisions. As the chapters in this volume by Young and Abat Ninet on the Brexit crisis and regionalisation crisis illustrate, these symbols, myths, and rituals of Member State communitarian solidarity soon break down when devolved countries, such as the UK or Spain start to break down.

The myths and narratives of supranational community and solidarity within the European community place emphasis on the idea and objective of an 'ever closer union of the peoples of Europe'. Within the EU the symbols and images of European community solidarity goes beyond Member State communities to emphasise solidarity between the peoples of the EU, between women and men, and between generations. In treaty terms, the most iconic symbol of European community is the solidarity clause compelling the Union and its Member States to act jointly in a spirit of solidarity in the event of a terrorist attack, natural- or human-made disaster. In contrast to the Member State iconography, here the symbolism is of maps of European sub-national regions with brightly coloured regions eligible for structural and cohesion funding. Similarly, the 'symbols of the EU' (flag, anthem, currency, and Europe Day) and their ritualistic use throughout the EU and Eurozone are intended to represent a sense of European community solidarity. Within this volume the chapters by Butler and Snaith on the financial crisis, and Neergaard on the economic crisis, illustrate the way in which the global financial crisis and Eurozone sovereign debt crisis exposed serious differences and absence of European community solidarity on questions of financial regulation and intra-Eurozone transfer mechanisms.

2.2 *Cosmopolitan Solidarities within the EU*

Cosmopolitan theories of the EU have become more important since the end of the Cold War. They involve defining cosmopolitanism as 'universalist and individualist in orientation'[22] and argue that 'cosmopolitan means belonging to all parts of the world; not restricted to any one country or its inhabitants'.[23] Cosmopolitan theories thus differ from communitarian theories in arguing that concerns for humanity as a whole, or the rights of the individual within humanity, should provide

[22] Cochran, *Normative Theory in International Relations*, p. 8.
[23] Calhoun, 'The class consciousness of frequent travelers', p. 105.

the basis for understanding solidarity. Cosmopolitan solidarities within the EU tend to be closely associated with liberal rights and mobilities, such as the free movement of goods, persons, services, and capital. A second strand of liberal cosmopolitan theory has focused on Jürgen Habermas's advocacy of deliberative politics through 'communicative action' within the EU public sphere.[24]

The myths and narratives of cosmopolitan solidarity through rights and freedoms within the EU emphasise citizenship of the Union, fundamental rights, and free movement rights. Within the EU the symbols and images of cosmopolitan solidarity are, first, iconographised through the granting of citizenship of the union that is additional to national citizenship, including rights to stand and vote in European Parliament (EP) and local elections, to petition and be heard by the EP and the Ombudsman, and to consular access of any EU consulate around the world. Second, the Charter of Fundamental Rights acts as a touchstone of cosmopolitan solidarity, drawing on treaty references to the 'indivisible, universal values' of human rights, freedom, equality, and solidarity. Third, cosmopolitan solidarity is found in the iconic symbol of the right to free movement found in the absence of border controls across the Schengen Area, as well as the symbols of this freedom in standardised border and road signs, drivers' licences and passports. Within this volume, the chapters by Lahusen on civic solidarity and Trenz on transnational solidarity mobilisation illustrate the way in which civic solidarity and the public sphere in Europe are important for fostering cosmopolitan solidarity in transnational spaces.

2.3 Cosmopolitical Solidarities within the EU

Twenty-first-century critical theories of EU solidarity argue that 'cosmopolitics combine communitarianism with cosmopolitanism . . . If cosmopolitanism relies on a discourse of individual rights; communitarianism is based on a discourse of social rights that is often expressed in exclusive and localist terms. Both run the risk of substituting ethics for politics'.[25] Cosmopolitical solidarities combine

[24] J. Habermas, *Europe: The Faltering Project* (Cambridge: Polity Press, 2009).

[25] C. Kinnvall and P. Nesbitt-Larking, *The Political Psychology of Globalization: Muslims in the West* (Oxford: Oxford University Press, 2011), p. 92; Manners, 'Normative ethics of the European Union', p. 67; Manners, 'European communion: political theory of European Union', p. 483.

agonistic understandings of 'respect' taken from Nietzsche by Connolly,[26] of 'pluralism' taken from Gramsci by Chantal Mouffe,[27] and of 'contest' taken from Arendt by Bonnie Honig.[28] Thus, agonistic, or radical, cosmopolitical solidarities link local politics with global ethics to provide spaces and places where transnational acts of sharing and contestation between the global and the local are performed.[29]

The myths and narratives of cosmopolitical solidarity within the EU go beyond those of communitarian or cosmopolitan approaches to place emphasis on a 'destiny henceforth shared' between ordinary individuals and groups rather than Member State or supranational communities, or citizenship and individual rights. Within the EU the symbols and images of cosmopolitical solidarity are not produced at the EU or Member State level, but instead are the result of treaty commitments to subsidiarity, local and regional governance. More importantly, genuine acts of cosmopolitical solidarity are at the grass-roots level where non-institutionalised organisations and activists spontaneously take actions in common out of shared concern for fellow human beings in Europe. In treaty terms, the most iconic symbol of cosmopolitical solidarity is found in the principle of subsidiarity where 'decisions are taken as openly as possible and as closely as possible to the citizen'.[30] This implies that local, grass-roots democracy, policymaking, and action in common are preferable to higher levels of political abstraction. The principle of subsidiarity also suggests a counteracting principle of 'supersidiarity' where 'the Union shall act only if ... the proposed action cannot be sufficiently achieved by the Member States, ... but can rather, ... be better achieved at Union level'.[31] In other words, this means that 'the Union acts to better achieve together what cannot be achieved apart'.[32]

[26] W. Connolly, *Identity/Difference: Democratic Negotiations of Political Paradox* (Ithaca, NY: Cornell University Press, 1991), pp. xii–xv.

[27] C. Mouffe, *The Return of the Political* (London: Verso, 1993), pp. 4–6.

[28] B. Honig, Political Theory and the Displacement of Politics (Ithaca, NY: Cornell University Press, 1993), pp. 15–16.

[29] B. Honig, 'Another Cosmopolitanism? Law and Politics in the New Europe', in S. Benhabib and R. Post (eds.), *Another Cosmopolitanism* (Oxford: Oxford University Press, 2006), p. 117; J. Ingram, *Radical Cosmopolitics: The Ethics and Politics of Democratic Universalism* (New York: Columbia University Press, 2013), p. 18; C. Mouffe, *Agonistics: Thinking the World Politically* (London: Verso, 2013), pp. 43–64.

[30] TEU 2010: Arts. 1 and 10

[31] TEU 2010: Art. 5

[32] Manners, 'European communion: Political theory of European Union', p. 487.

The iconography of cosmopolitical solidarity is different to the symbols and rituals of communitarian Europe found in maps, flags, anthems, currency or commemoration day, and is different to freedoms and movements of cosmopolitan Europe found in the technologies of mobility. Instead, the formal EU policy of encouraging interregional co-operation through Interreg Europe and the European Regional Development Fund provides the local imagery of projects in research and innovation, small- and medium-sized enterprise competitiveness, low-carbon economy, and environment and resource efficiency. However, since 2016 more grass-roots acts of cosmopolitical solidarity have been driven by the concerns of ordinary people to speak out and take action in common against the reactionary rise of nationalism and the far right across Europe. The 'Pulse of Europe' grass-roots organisation originating in Frankfurt in 2016 has spread political action through regular city demonstrations in favour of a united Europe and opposition to the decline of European democracy.[33] In Britain similar grass-roots pro-EU organisations and activists erupted in the aftermath of the 2016 advisory referendum in favour of remaining in the EU and opposed to the widespread illegalities, disinformation, and lies of the anti-EU 'Leave' networks of power.[34] The largest of these activist groups was the 'People's Vote' group advocating a second referendum and organising a London anti-Brexit demonstration of approximately one million people in March 2019.[35] What these movements, and the myriad of pro-unity movements such as Another Europe is Possible, DiEM25, Volt Europa, European Democracy Lab, My Country? Europe, 89 Initiative and many others suggest is that there is some evidence of genuine acts of cosmopolitical solidarities within the EU.[36] The chapters by Schiek on solidarity

[33] Pulse of Europe 'What is at Stake?' (2019), available at: https://pulseofeurope.eu/en/what-is-at-stake/; M. Cottakis, 'Can Europe save itself?', *Washington Post, 1 October 2018.*

[34] Z. Williams, 'There's only one way to stop Brexit: from the ground up', *The Guardian*, 29 August 2018.

[35] J. Chaffin, 'Britain's Europhiles splinter into dozens of grassroots movements', *Financial Times*, 8 December 2016; A. Rawnsley, 'The anti-Brexiters can get by without a leader. But not without a plan', *The Guardian*, 25 November 2018; B. Mueller and P. Karasz, 'Angry over Brexit stalemate, huge crowds march in London to demand second vote', *New York Times*, 23 March 2019; P. Mason, 'To defeat an insurgent far-right, Labour must resist Brexit with all its force', *New Statesman*, 27 March 2019; People's Vote, 'Who we are' (2019), available at: www.peoples-vote.uk/who_we_are.

[36] H. Kaschel, 'The pro-Europe grassroots movements aimed at saving the EU', *Deutsche Welle*, 1 April 2017; 'Volt wants to become the first pan-EU political party', *The Economist*, 1 November 2018; Y. Varoufakis and D. Adler, 'The European spring holds the answer to the fragmenting EU's plight', *The Guardian*, 11 March 2019.

in the case law of the European Court of Justice and Zhang on free movement and social citizenship in the EU both illustrate the way in which solidarity between citizens and contestation of the social rights of migrants can contribute towards a more critical, cosmopolitical understanding of transnational solidarity from the ground up.

3 Transnational Solidarity across the EU's Borders

Discussions of solidarity across the borders of the EU have grown in the study of EU relations with, and concern for, its neighbours through the European Neighbourhood Policy (ENP) since 2004 and the European refugee crisis of 2015.[37] The European External Action Service Fact Sheet on 'Europe – the Continent of Solidarity'[38] (Figure 5.3), together with an accompanying 'Joint Statement on the occasion of International Migrant Day',[39] illustrate how the analysis of transnational solidarity within the EU must also take account of transnational solidarity across the EU's borders, including communitarian, cosmopolitan and cosmopolitical dimensions.

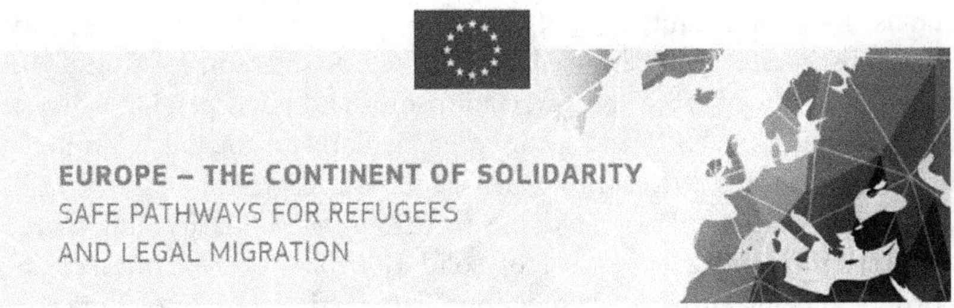

Figure 5.3 EEAS, Europe – the Continent of Solidarity, 2018.

[37] R. Whitman and S. Wolff (eds.), *The European Neighbourhood Policy in Perspective: Context, Implementation and Impact* (London: Palgrave, 2010); S. Poli (ed.), *The European Neighbourhood Policy: Values and Principles* (London: Routledge, 2018); A. Grimmel and S. Giang (eds.), *Solidarity in the European Union: A Fundamental Value in Crisis* (Berlin: Springer, 2017); D. della Porta (ed.), *Solidarity Mobilizations in the 'Refugee Crisis': Contentious Moves* (Basingstoke: Palgrave, 2019).

[38] European External Action Service (EEAS), 'Europe – the Continent of Solidarity', 28 March 2018, available at: https://eeas.europa.eu/sites/eeas/files/migration_opportunities_protection_us.pdf.

[39] European Commission, 'Europe – the continent of solidarity: Joint Statement on the occasion of International Migrant Day' (2017) Statement/17/5344, 18 December.

Analyses of solidarities across the borders of Europe are further complicated by the fact that the EU is not the only pan-European regional organisation. The Council of Europe (CoE), the Organization for Security and Co-operation in Europe (OSCE), and the North Atlantic Treaty Organization (NATO), as well as many other social and cultural organisations all have cross-cutting membership across the EU. Therefore, the apparently simple question of transnational solidarity across the EU's borders immediately runs into the challenge of whether this includes solidarity with the four European Free Trade Association members of Schengen, the other nineteen members of the CoE, or the other members of organisations such as the OSCE/NATO? This question is further complicated by social, cultural, and sporting associations that reach far beyond a narrow EU understanding of Europe including, for example, Armenia, Azerbaijan, Georgia, Israel, Russia, Turkey, and Ukraine participating in events such as the UEFA football championships and the Eurovision song contest.

3.1 Communitarian Solidarities across the EU's Borders

The myths and narratives of communitarian solidarities across the EU's borders expose a series of sharp distinctions between Member State versus EU communities, and between partnership versus security. These distinctions are captured in TEU Art. 8 and Commission document on ENP declaring special relationships and good neighbourliness, but focusing on stability and security, particularly for the EU.[40] Similarly, the Commission's 2015 'European Agenda on Migration', as well as its 2017 Joint Statement declared the principles of solidarity and shared responsibility and a continent of solidarity, but focused on securing borders and international protection. The iconic imagery of the crises of solidarity across the EU's borders are represented by the Arab uprisings of 2010/11 and the related refugee crises of 2015/16. The symbolism of North African and Middle Eastern peoples' rising up against twenty governments is captured by the images of massed protesters in places such as Tahir Square, Egypt.

[40] European Commission, 'European Neighbourhood Policy Strategy Paper' (2004) COM (2004) 373 final, 12 May 2004; European Commission and European External Action Service, 'Neighbourhood at the Crossroads: Implementation of the European Neighbourhood Policy in 2013', Joint Communication JOIN (2014) 12 final, Brussels, 27 March 2014.

Following the repressive reactions to these protests and related civil wars in Yemen, Libya, Iraq, and Syria, from 2014 the symbolism increasingly became of refugees and asylum seekers crossing the Mediterranean in rubber boats or washing up drowned on European coasts. In the uprisings and the refugee crisis, the communitarian solidarities within the EU, between Member States, and across the EU's borders, raised the question of whether EU transnational solidarity has left 'Europe at Sea'?[41] As the chapter by Thielemann on making responsibility-sharing initiatives more effective in the context of the refugee crisis illustrates, these symbols, myths, and rituals of EU communitarian solidarity soon break down under fast-moving conditions of crisis.

3.2 Cosmopolitan Solidarities across the EU's Borders

Similar to the previous discussion, the myths and narratives of cosmopolitan solidarities across the EU's borders are found in the questions of neighbourliness and migration. However, here the distinctions are between Member States, governments, and political parties who take a more cosmopolitan approach to the rights and concerns of non-EU citizens versus those who take a less cosmopolitan approach to excluding foreigners and denying rights. The responses to the 2015 refugee crisis demonstrate these distinctions through open arms and signs of 'refugees welcome', swiftly followed by razor-wire fences and signs of 'refugees not welcome'.

The data from 2015 tells this story well: over 1.2 million asylum seekers registered in the EU, mostly from Syria (363,000), Afghanistan (178,000), and Iraq (121,000).[42] Of those asylum seekers, the largest number registered in Germany (442,000), Hungary (174,000), Sweden (156,000), Austria (85,000), Italy (83,000), and France (71,000). In per capita terms (per million inhabitants), the greatest number of asylum applications was in Hungary (18,000), Sweden (16,000), Austria (10,000), Norway (5,900), Finland (5,900), and Germany (5,400).[43] In September 2015 EU ministers reached agreement on relocation of asylum seekers and burden sharing in the EU.[44] This meeting and subsequent disagreements represents an iconic moment in the collapse of cosmopolitan solidarity across the borders of the

[41] A. Piras (director), *Europe at Sea* (London: Journeyman Pictures, 2017).

[42] Eurostat, 'Asylum in the EU Member States: Record number of over 1.2 million first time asylum seekers registered in 2015' 44 (2016), 4 March news release.

[43] Ibid.

[44] Council of the EU, 'Justice and Home Affairs Council', 22 September 2015.

EU. In terms of per capita asylum seekers (per million inhabitants) Czechia (100), Hungary (18,000), Romania (60), and Slovakia (50) voted against the relocation plan, Finland (5,900) abstained, while the UK (600), Ireland (700), and Denmark (3,700) opted out of burden sharing.[45] In October and November 2015 Member States from north to south introduced restrictive border controls on refugees, while in March 2016 the EU negotiated an agreement with Turkey to restrict refugees reaching Greece.[46] These Member State disagreements, the closing of borders, and the EU–Turkey agreement marked the end of cosmopolitan solidarities for refugees across the borders of the EU. The associated growth of far-right movements and parties in most EU Member States has affected government formation in Hungary, Poland, Italy, France, Sweden, and the UK, and shapes internal politics across Europe.

3.3 *Cosmopolitical Solidarities across the EU's Borders*

Unlike communitarian or cosmopolitan approaches, agonistic cosmopolitics demand a radically different approach to transnational solidarities across the EU's borders. Instead of prioritising the local of communitarian solidarities or prioritising the global of cosmopolitan solidarities, radical agonistic cosmopolitical solidarities link global ethics of emancipation and empathy with local politics of relationships and actions. Within the approach, the myths and narratives of cosmopolitical solidarities across the EU's border are driven by grass-roots activists and groups rather than EU institutions, as six examples of refugee rescue, solidarity, youth response, welcome, artistic response, and activism illustrate.

European non-governmental organisations (NGOs) and volunteer associations run search and rescue ships such as *The Aquarius* operated by SOS Mediterranee and Médecins sans Frontières; the *Mo Chara* operated by Refugee Rescue; the *Open Arms* operated by Proactiva Open Arms; the *Sea-Watch 3* operated by Sea-Watch; the *Alan Kurdi* operated by Sea-Eyes, and at least 15 NGOs recognised by the Search and Rescue Observatory for the Mediterranean.[47] European city authorities and universities organise

[45] S. Erlanger and J. Kanter, 'Plan on migrants strains the Limits of Europe's unity', *New York Times*, 22 September 2015.

[46] European Council, 'EU-Turkey statement', 18 March 2016.

[47] T. Embury-Dennis, 'Médecins sans Frontières forced to pull rescue boat from Mediterranean after being stuck in port for months', *Independent,* 7 December 2018; L. Tondo, 'Italian authorities order seizure of migrant rescue ship', *The Guardian*, 20 March 2019.

solidarity and support for refugees. The Eurocities' 'Solidarity Cities' initiative provides refugee reception and integration with thirty-eight European cities signing the 'Eurocities Integrating Cities Charter'.[48] Similarly, the European University Association 'Refugees Welcome' initiative help to provide shelter, advice and support in 350 intuitions spread across thirty-two countries.[49] Youth associations such as 'Time to be welcome', made up of ten European youth organisations (in particular the Scouts) welcome youth refugees, as well as other grass-roots organisations such as 'Welcome Refugees International' encouraging flatsharing with refugees in thirteen European countries.[50]

At the same time, an interesting reversal of 'welcomeness' has recently occurred alongside negative responses to overtourism and private tourist exploitation with graffiti announcing 'tourists go home, refugees welcome' in Barcelona, Malaga, Berlin, Venice, Amsterdam, Lisbon, and beyond.[51] The art world has also had a more welcoming approach to refugees, with a series of symbolic interventions on refugees and their art. Installations have included Ai Weiwei's 2016 'translocation – transformation' discarded life jackets floating in the pond at Vienna's Belvedere Palace; Doris Salcedo's 2018 'Palimpsest' stone-water memorial for drowned migrants at Madrid's Palacio de Cristal; Amnesty International's 2019 projection of 'refugees welcome' on the Athen's Acropolis; and the Venice Biennial's 2019 'Rothko in Lampedusa' refugee art display.[52] Banksy's graffiti art is significant in this respect with the 2014 racist pigeons graffiti in Clacton-on-Sea, England; the 2015 Steve Jobs Syrian migrant in 'the jungle' Calais; the 2015 raft of refugees in Calais inspired by Gericault's 'Raft of the Medusa'; Weston-Super-Mare's 2015 'Dismaland' refugee boats installation; and the 2018 graffiti critical of the French response to the refugee

48 Solidarity Cities. 'About' (2016), available at: https://solidaritycities.eu/about; Integrating Cities, 'Eurocities Integrating Cities Charter' (2018), available at: www.integratingcities.eu/integrating-cities/charter.

49 European University Association, 'Refugees Welcome Map' (2018).

50 Time to be Welcome, 'Background: Migration in Europe' (2018), available at: http://timetobewelcome.eu/the-project/migration-in-europe/; Refugees Welcome International, 'Refugees Welcome' (2018), available at www.refugees-welcome.net/.

51 S. Burgen, '"Tourists go home, refugees welcome": why Barcelona chose migrants over visitors', *The Guardian*, 25 June 2018; 'Wish you weren't here: the backlash against overtourism', *The Economist*, 25 October 2018.

52 E. Povoledo, 'Wreck of migrant ship that killed hundreds will be displayed at Venice Biennale', *New York Times*, 6 May 2019.

crisis in Paris.[53] The symbols and myths of this cosmopolitical transnational activism and actions in support of solidarity across the EU's border illustrate the ways in which the rescue of, youth support for, and artistic production produce solidarity and welcome refugees, often against the wishes of EU Member States.

4 Transnational Solidarity beyond the EU

Discussions of solidarity beyond the EU pre-date those of solidarity within and across the EU's borders with, for example, extensive post-Cold War examinations of EU 'social solidarity' in the context of the normative power approach to the EU.[54] The symbol and myth of the solidarity jar acted as the banner and icon of the 2000 Cotonou Agreement between the EU and the African, Caribbean, and Pacific (ACP) countries (Figure 5.4). The accompanying description illustrates how symbols and myths of transnational solidarity beyond the EU are important:

> **The symbolism of the solidarity jar**
> The symbol chosen by the host country to illustrate the Cotonou Agreement simultaneously embodies the power of union and the importance of solidarity – the pierced jar will hold water only if all the people come together to plug its holes with their fingers. This symbolic image, borrowed from Ghezo, former king of Dahomey (as Benin used to be known), fits perfectly with the values which have always underpinned relations between the European Union and the ACP countries – values which are now more than ever crucial to the success of the future partnership.[55]

The symbolism and myth of the solidarity jar illustrate how the analysis of transnational solidarity beyond the EU must include the communitarian 'power of union', the cosmopolitan 'importance of solidarity', and cosmopolitical acts when 'people come together'.

[53] H. Ellis-Petersen, 'Banksy uses Steve Jobs artwork to highlight refugee crisis', *The Guardian*, 11 December 2015.

[54] I. Manners, 'Normative power Europe: a contradiction in terms?', *Journal of Common Market Studies*, 40(2) (2002), 242–43, 235; Manners, 'Normative ethics of the European Union', pp. 46–53; C. Bretherton and J. Vogler, *The European Union as a Global Actor*, 2nd edition (London: Routledge, 2005); R. Whitman (ed.), *Normative Power Europe: Empirical and Theoretical Perspectives* (London: Palgrave, 2011); A. Hadfield, I. Manners and R. Whitman (eds.), *Foreign Policies of EU Member States* (London: Routledge, 2017).

[55] European Commission, 'The symbolism of the solidarity jar' (2000) September ACP-EU Courier, Special Issue on the Cotonou Agreement.

Figure 5.4 European Commission, ACP–EU Courier, 2000.[56]

4.1 Communitarian Solidarities beyond the EU

The myths and narratives of communitarian solidarity beyond the EU demonstrates the politics of European communion through the tensions, for example, between Member State solidarities with non-members and EU solidarities with other regional integration organisations. These

[56] European Commission, 'The symbolism of the solidarity jar' (2000) September ACP–EU Courier, Special Issue on the Cotonou Agreement.

myths are given iconic status within the TEU that now states under the general provisions on the Union's External Action that:

> The Union's action on the international scene shall be guided by the principles which have inspired its own creation, development and enlargement, and which it seeks to advance in the wider world: democracy, the rule of law, the universality and indivisibility of human rights and fundamental freedoms, respect for human dignity, *the principles of equality and solidarity*, and respect for the principles of the United Nations Charter and international law.[57]

In this communitarian reading of its external actions, the principle of solidarity is part of promoting principles which have inspired the EU's creation, development, and enlargement, rather than an explicit act of transnational solidarity. It is within this context that the tensions arise between Member State foreign policies through the Common Foreign and Security Policy, and EU external actions through the broader development and enlargement policies of the European External Action Service (EEAS).[58] In this respect the EU's development policy symbolises communitarian solidarity beyond the EU with its emphasis on addressing the 2015 UN Sustainable Development Goals through development assistance, in particular through the narrative of 'Europe remains the world's biggest development donor'.[59]

4.2 Cosmopolitan Solidarities beyond the EU

While the myths and narratives of cosmopolitan solidarities beyond the EU are also given iconic status in the TEU within the common provisions, their emphasis is different:

> In its relations with the wider world, the Union shall uphold and promote its values and interests and contribute to the protection of its citizens. It shall contribute to peace, security, the sustainable development of the Earth, *solidarity and mutual respect among peoples*, free and fair trade, eradication

[57] TEU, Art. 21.1 (2016), emphasis added.

[58] A. Hadfield, I. Manners, and R. Whitman (eds.), *Foreign Policies of EU Member States*, pp. 10–16.

[59] I. Manners, 'The normative power of the European Union in a globalised world' in Z. Laïdi (ed.), *EU Foreign Policy in a Globalized World: Normative Power and Social Preferences* (London: Routledge, 2008), pp. 24–31; I. Manners, 'Den Europeiska unionen i en globaliserande värld', in Rikard Bengtsson, Ian Manners, Hans-Åke Persson, Linda Gröning and Ola Zetterquist (eds.), *Det europeiska projektet: politik och juridik – historia och framtid* (Malmö: Liber, 2013), pp. 216–230, 209; European Commission (2019) 'Europe remains the world's biggest development donor – €74.4 billion in 2018', DG DEVCO, 11 April 2019.

> of poverty and the protection of human rights, in particular the rights of the child, as well as to the strict observance and the development of international law, including respect for the principles of the United Nations Charter.[60]

In a cosmopolitan reading of the EU's relations with the wider world, the aim is not simply to promote its own communitarian values and interests but to also promote cosmopolitan solidarity and mutual respect among peoples (not states), protect human and children's' rights, and to observe and develop international law and the principles of the UN charter. Thus, the communitarian emphasis on the EU's own principles, values, and interests are tempered by the cosmopolitan contribution to the wider world led by the principles of the UN emphasising mutual respect, equality, and solidarity, as well as human rights, democracy, and the rule of law more generally. An iconic illustration of cosmopolitan solidarity is the attempt by Sweden's first EU presidency, and subsequent foreign policy, to place an emphasis on 'an internationally active union based on the principle of solidarity'.[61] This notion of solidarity in EU foreign policy included an equal emphasis on human rights, European security and defence policies, and development cooperation, with a particular emphasis on gender equality.

4.3 *Cosmopolitical Solidarities beyond the EU*

Radical or agonistic cosmopolitical approaches to transnational solidarities beyond the EU shift the focus away from the Member States, institutions, and treaties of the EU. Instead, the focus is placed on networks and actions that are distinctly translocal in terms of principles, actions, and impact. Within this approach, the myths and narratives of cosmopolitical solidarities beyond the EU are not a function of the EU, its Member States, or its policies, but are the ongoing result of millions of EU citizens trying to raise consciousness and change policies on the greatest global political challenge of the twenty-first century; climate crisis.

Since the stark inevitability of 2°C, with an increased probability of 3°C, global warming was made clear in 2018, increasingly numbers of grassroots activists and groups are taking a lead in Europe in trying to change minds and policies.[62] The School Strike for Climate movement, started by

60 TEU 2016, Art. 3.5, emphasis added.
61 Swedish Minister for Foreign Affairs, *Programme of the Swedish presidency of the European Union, 1 January to 30 June 2001*. Draft 2000-07-07.
62 Intergovernmental Panel on Climate Change (IPCC), *Global Warming of 1.5°C* (Geneva: IPCC, 2018); A. Raval and L. Hook 'Paris climate pact aims fading, warns IEA', *The Financial Times*, 15 May 2019.

Greta Thunberg in August 2018, and the Extinction Rebellion (XR) launched in October 2018 both serve as illustrations of how symbols and myths of transnational solidarity are enacted within and beyond the EU.[63] Since November 2018 over a million school children in 2,000 cities have participated in school strikes worldwide, accelerated by the first Global Climate Strike for the Future on 15 March 2019 and their call for politicians to listen to the 'climate crisis and a betrayed generation'.[64] In addition to school strikes in the majority of EU Member States, there have been strikes in at least twenty non-EU countries around the world. Remarkably, these networks of school student solidarity have been coordinated via social media by youth groups such as 'Fridays for Future', 'School Strike 4 Climate', and 'Youth for Climate'.[65] These school strikes appear to be having some effect with Greta Thunberg being asked to speak in the European Commission, the EP, and the UK Houses of Parliament.[66]

At the same time as the school strikes for climate were spreading across the world, the XR movement started taking non-violent direct action in the UK during 2018, spreading across Europe and beyond in 2019. While similar to the school strike movement, XR is a grass-roots mass political direct action movement with three specific aims:

01. **Tell the truth:** Government must tell the truth by declaring a climate and ecological emergency, working with other institutions to communicate the urgency for change.
02. **Act Now:** Government must act now to halt biodiversity loss and reduce greenhouse gas emissions to net-zero by 2025.
03. **Beyond Politics:** Government must create and be led by the decisions of a Citizens' Assembly on climate and ecological justice.[67]

[63] G. Thunberg, 'Vi vet – och vi kan göra något nu', *Svenska Dagbladet,* 30 May 2018; A. Green, M. Scott Cato, *et al.* 'Facts about our ecological crisis are incontrovertible. We must take action', *The Guardian*, 26 October 2018.

[64] Global coordination group of the youth-led climate strike, 'Climate crisis and a betrayed generation', *The Guardian,* 1 March 2019.

[65] S. Laville, M. Taylor and D. Hurst, '"It's our time to rise up": youth climate strikes held in 100 countries', *The Guardian,* 15 March 2019.

[66] G. Thunberg, '"You did not act in time": Greta Thunberg's full speech to MPs', *The Guardian,* 23 April 2019; G. Rankin, 'Greta Thunberg tells EU: your climate targets need doubling', *The Guardian,* 21 February 2019; G. Rankin, 'Forget Brexit and focus on climate change', Greta Thunberg tells EU', *The Guardian,* 16 April 2019.

[67] Extinction Rebellion, 'Our demands' (2018), available at: https://rebellion.earth/the-truth/demands/.

In December 2018 XR expanded beyond the UK to include a call to action by 100 academics, authors, politicians, and campaigners from across the world to address climate crisis, with XR events in the Netherlands, Germany, Austria, Belgium, Sweden, Spain, Switzerland, and outside Europe to large actions in Australia, the USA, and beyond.[68] The combination of school strikes and XR appear to be having some effect in some EU Member States with European Commission President, Jean-Claude Juncker telling Greta Thunberg that his proposal for the coming EU budget (2021–27) had a target of 25 per cent of spending to go on 'action to mitigate climate change'.[69] In May 2019 eight Member States at the forefront of climate change (Belgium, Denmark, France, Luxembourg, the Netherlands, Portugal, Spain, Sweden) subsequently supported Juncker's 25 per cent climate change spending target and pushed for net-zero EU emissions by 2050, while the UK became the first country in the world to declare a climate emergency.[70]

These grass-roots organisations and networks of school strikes and XR direct action illustrate the ways in which cosmopolitical transnational activism within the EU is directly linked to action and concern beyond the EU. The centrality of myths and narratives such as 'school strike', 'Fridays for future', the 'betrayed generation', and well as XR and 'system change not climate change', go hand-in-hand with the images of thousands of school children on the streets and XR direct action against unsustainable practices.

5 Conclusion: Symbols and Myths of EU Transnational Solidarity

This chapter has drawn on three decades of analysing the EU in global politics in order to analyse and differentiate between solidarities within, across the borders of, and beyond the EU. It argues the need to use the work of Carol Gould in order identify transnational EU solidarities as overlapping networks of relations that share and support actions to eliminate oppression or reduce suffering within, across the borders of, and beyond the EU. As the three

[68] V. Shiva, N. Klein, et al., 'Act now to prevent an environmental catastrophe', *The Guardian*, 9 December 2018; J. Watts, 'Extinction Rebellion goes global in run-up to week of international civil disobedience', *The Guardian*, 10 December 2018.

[69] C. Roth, 'Swedish student leader wins EU pledge to spend billions on climate', *Reuters*, 21 February 2019.

[70] R. Toplensky, 'Eight EU nations push for net-zero emissions in bloc by 2050', *The Financial Times*, 8 May 2019; 'UK Parliament declares climate change emergency', BBC News, 1 May 2019.

examples of grass-roots activist groups and networks in support of the EU, in support of refugees, and in support of climate action have illustrated, there is evidence of cosmopolitical transnational EU solidarities that network and share global ethics with local politics that are more likely to take actions in concert that are caring and empathic towards distantly situated others.

The final symbol and myth of EU transnational solidarities is of Aylan Kurdi's aunt, Tima Kurdi and Luis Morago, campaign director for Avaaz, standing in front of the 'Welcome Wall' on Rond Point Schuman in September 2015 to deliver a 1 million signature online petition to the EU to take action to welcome refugees (Figure 5.5). This petition, demonstration, and action helped push the EU Council President Donald Tusk to convene an extraordinary informal European Council meeting on 23 September 2015 to address the 'unprecedented number of migrants and refugees arriving in Europe'.[71] What this symbolic image of Aylan

Figure 5.5 Avaaz, EU: Welcome Refugees, 2015.[72]

[71] European Council, 'Statement on the Informal meeting of EU heads of state or government on migration', 23 September 2015.

[72] Avaaz, 'We're in Brussels delivering over 1M voices calling on the EU to make #RefugeesWelcome today with Aylan Kurdi's Aunt', 14 September 2015, available at: https://twitter.com/Avaaz/status/643341985647075328.

Kurdi, the million messages of welcome, the Welcome Wall, the online activism, and the media event in front of the European Commission and Council of Ministers' buildings on the EU's most central roundabout show is that with the facilitation of Avaaz, a powerful online activist network, genuine transnational EU solidarity is possible.

The examples discussed throughout this chapter help demonstrate the importance of networks of relations, shared goals, empathy with distant others, and action in concert in support of others. But the symbols and images, myths and narratives, of such acts of transnational solidarity are not simply propaganda, media manipulation, or false consciousness of solidarity with others. They are a central component of mobilising, expressing, and demonstrating transnational solidarity in order to eliminate oppression or reduce suffering, whether through discrimination, exclusion, or ecological catastrophe.

PART II

Transational Solidarity in Europe

Under Pressure and Change

6

Solidarity and the Economic and Monetary Union in Times of Economic Crisis

ULLA NEERGAARD

1 Introduction

In times of crisis, solidarity is increasingly challenged both nationally and internationally. Since the onset of the economic crisis, therefore, clear signs in that regard have also been present in Europe. They have in here appeared in many different forms, where one could simply refer to the fears in some Member States of abuse by non-citizens of their national welfare systems, growing Euroscepticism and increased levels of nationalism,[1] as well as an almost paralysis as regards responding to the refugee situation. All these examples represent phenomena pointing at a lack of willingness to demonstrate solidarity with others in need, especially across countries and especially when it requires an economic contribution, that is, not simply an expression of emotional sympathy. In the context of the Economic and Monetary Union (EMU) and the problems it has faced, among others due to a lack of solidarity among Eurozone countries, the famous, Nobel prize-winning economist, Stiglitz, has crucially pointed out that:

> When a group of countries shares a common currency, success requires more than just good institutions . . . For reforms to work, decisions have to be made, and those decisions will reflect the understandings and values of the decision-makers. There have to be common understandings and values of the decision-makers of what makes for a successful economy and a minimal level of '*solidarity*', or social cohesion, where countries that are in a strong position help those that are in need. Today, there is no such understanding, no real sense of social cohesion. Germany says repeatedly that the Eurozone is not a 'transfer union' – that is, an economic grouping

[1] As most significantly expressed by the In/Out referendum in the UK ('Brexit') on 23 June 2016 and the consequential expected exit of the UK from the EU.

> in which one country transfers resources to another, even temporarily in a time of need.[2]

The inherent critique here appears as widely acknowledged, but one may nevertheless question whether it is really true that *legally* there were never – and still are not – any intentions of such kind of solidarity as a guiding mechanism in force, perhaps even combined with actual obligations.[3] In that light, the aim of this chapter is to analyse how solidarity in actual fact has been addressed in the context of the EMU and especially as a response to the economic crisis, where an analysis of ten years of EU reactions is undertaken to obtain a deeper understanding of how solidarity may have materialised. As a basis for the analysis, I first examine how solidarity has developed over time in the overarching primary EU law. Although the overall context thus is of interest, the primary object of analysis is the kind of solidarity referred to in Stiglitz's statement, which may be understood as solidarity in the sense of explicit obligations of the stronger Member States to help those in need by transfers of resources.[4]

Against this background, the intention is to address more precisely the following issues of pivotal interest: solidarity in the general context of primary EU law (section 2); solidarity in the specific context of the EMU (section 3); and conclusions (section 4).

2 Solidarity in the General Context of Primary EU Law

This section outlines the development of solidarity generally within the EU as a whole, as primary EU law may be said to embrace the EMU. The overall aim is to explore where and how solidarity explicitly is present. It is thus limited to an analysis of the treaty texts (that is, the Treaty of Rome, the Treaty of Maastricht, the Treaty of Amsterdam, the Treaty of Nice and finally the Treaty of Lisbon).

The origins of the EU are to be found in the establishment of the original European Economic Community (EEC) pursuant to the Treaty

[2] J. E. Stiglitz, *The Euro and Its Threat to the Future of Europe* (London: Penguin Random House, 2016), p. 22, emphasis added.

[3] For recent legal analyses of solidarity generally in EU law, see A. Biondi, E. Dagilytė and E. Küçük (eds.), *Solidarity in EU Law. Legal Principle in the Making* (Cheltenham: Edward Elgar,2018); and E. Küçük, Solidarity in EU Law. An Elusive Political Statement or a Legal Principle with Substance?, *Maastricht Law Journal*, 23(6) (2016), 965–83.

[4] See further e.g. I. Goldner, 'The EU financial and migration crises: two crises – many facets of EU solidarity, in A. Biondi, E. Dagilytė and E. Küçük (eds.), *Solidarity in EU Law* (Cheltenham: Edward Elgar, 2018), p. 139.

of Rome, which came into force on 1 January 1958. As the name itself indicates the EEC was largely only of an economic character. An explicit use of solidarity therefore not too surprisingly only appears in one place, namely in the Seventh Recital of the Preamble, which states: 'Intending to confirm the *solidarity* which binds Europe and overseas countries, and desiring to ensure the development of their prosperity, in accordance with the principles of the Charter of the United Nations . . .' (emphasis added). The Preamble in its entirety could be understood as solidarity among the Member States ('an ever closer union among the European peoples', 'Community', etc.) rather being understood as referring to solidarity structures within Member States. One way to consider the explicit reference in the Seventh Recital is as an attempt to refer to solidarity among the founding Member States as if it had already been present, but perhaps it would be more correct to view it as an expression of a hope or vision. However, it is definitely not to be seen as anything like an intention of a protection of such a mechanism or implying any kind of obligation. Nevertheless, no doubt solidarity appears as an important term already at this early stage of the development of the EU, signified by a reference made at this prominent place in the original treaty.

In the Preamble of the Treaty of Maastricht, which came into force on 1 November 1993, there is once again a reference to solidarity, namely in the Fourth Recital, which says: 'Desiring to deepen the *solidarity* between their peoples while respecting their history, their culture and their traditions . . .' (emphasis added). Thus, solidarity is again assumed as pre-existing, which is more likely now given that the co-operation had already existed for several decades, and was intended to deepen further. Also, in Article A, in Title I concerning 'Common Provisions', a reference to solidarity appears in the following manner: 'The Union shall be founded on the European Communities, supplemented by the policies and forms of cooperation established by this Treaty. Its task shall be to organise, in a manner demonstrating consistency and *solidarity*, relations between the Member States and between their peoples' (emphasis added).

In addition, and most importantly, for the present context, solidarity is here linked with the EMU, according to Article G in 'Provisions amending the Treaty establishing the European Economic Community with a view to establishing the European Community' Article 2 in the Treaty establishing the EEC was to be amended into the following:

> The Community shall have as its task, by establishing a common market and an economic and monetary union and by implementing the common

> policies or activities referred to in Articles 3 and 3a, to promote throughout the Community a harmonious and balanced development of economic activities, sustainable and non-inflationary growth respecting the environment, a high degree of convergence of economic performance, a high level of employment and of social protection, the raising of the standard of living and quality of life, and economic and social cohesion and *solidarity* among Member States. (emphasis added)

Furthermore, in Article J1(4), in Title II concerning 'Provisions on a common foreign and security policy', it is stated that:

> ... The Member States shall support the Union's external and security policy actively and unreservedly in a spirit of loyalty and mutual *solidarity*. They shall refrain from any action which is contrary to the interests of the Union or likely to impair its effectiveness as a cohesive force in international relations. The Council shall ensure that these principles are complied with. (emphasis added)

Solidarity features in the Treaty of Amsterdam, which came into force on 1 May 1999, mentioned in the Preamble and in Article 1 EU (previously Article A) in the same way as before. In addition, it appears in Articles 11 EU (previously Article J.1)[5] and 23 EU (previously Article J.13).[6] In the Treaty on the European Community, the same sentence which appeared already in the Treaty of Rome is maintained ('INTENDING to confirm the *solidarity* which binds Europe and the overseas countries and desiring to ensure the development of their prosperity, in accordance with the principles of the Charter of the United Nations ...' [emphasis added]). Also, although Article 2 EC was altered, this does not include changes regarding the solidarity reference ('... economic and social cohesion and solidarity among

[5] The relevant part stipulates that: '2. The Member States shall support the Union's external and security policy actively and unreservedly in a spirit of loyalty and mutual *solidarity*. The Member States shall work together to enhance and develop their mutual political *solidarity*. They shall refrain from any action which is contrary to the interests of the Union or likely to impair its effectiveness as a cohesive force in international relations. The Council shall ensure that these principles are complied with.' (emphasis added)

[6] The relevant part stipulates that: 'When abstaining in a vote, any member of the Council may qualify its abstention by making a formal declaration under the present subparagraph. In that case, it shall not be obliged to apply the decision, but shall accept that the decision commits the Union. In a spirit of mutual *solidarity*, the Member State concerned shall refrain from any action likely to conflict with or impede Union action based on that decision and the other Member States shall respect its position. If the members of the Council qualifying their abstention in this way represent more than one-third of the votes weighted in accordance with Article 148(2) of the Treaty establishing the European Community, the decision shall not be adopted.' (emphasis added)

Member States'). The changes, which took place with the Treaty of Nice, which came into force in 2003, did not include new references to solidarity. Thus, altogether, the role of solidarity was not really changed in the process going from the Treaty of Maastricht to the Treaty of Nice.

As to the Treaty of Lisbon, which came into force on 1 December 1999, again a certain degree of continuity is present. Thus, in the Preamble to the Treaty on European Union, a reference to solidarity is again included. This reference is identical to what was included since the Treaty of Maastricht. Regarding values, the new Article 2 TEU stipulates that: 'The Union is founded on the values of respect for human dignity, freedom, democracy, equality, the rule of law and respect for human rights, including the rights of persons belonging to minorities. These values are common to the Member States in a society in which pluralism, non-discrimination, tolerance, justice, *solidarity* and equality between women and men prevail' (emphasis added).[7] Hereby, a change occurs because solidarity now is something the societies of the Member States have in common. The dimension is not so much on some kind of a mutual relationship, but rather on solidarity as one of the characteristics that is common to the Member States. Also Article 3 TEU is of interest here, as it stipulates inter alia that the Union:

> . . . shall combat social exclusion and discrimination, and shall promote social justice and protection, equality between women and men, *solidarity* between generations and protection of the rights of the child.
>
> It shall promote economic, social and territorial cohesion, and *solidarity* among Member States . . .
>
> In its relations with the wider world, the Union shall uphold and promote its values and interests and contribute to the protection of its citizens. It shall contribute to peace, security, the sustainable development of the Earth, *solidarity* and mutual respect among peoples, free and fair trade, eradication of poverty and the protection of human rights, in particular the rights of the child, as well as to the strict observance and the development of international law, including respect for the principles of the United Nations Charter. (emphasis added)

In this provision, solidarity is that of a term regulating a variety of mutual relationships (that is, between generations, among Member States and among peoples). In addition, it should be mentioned that references to

[7] Also see e.g. Leino and Petrov, 'Between "common values" and competing universals – the promotion of the EU's common values through the European Neighbourhood Policy', *European Law Journal*, 15(5) (2009), 654–71.

solidarity are made in Articles 21 and 24 of the TEU, both of which concern the EU's external relations.[8] However, now solidarity becomes a principle, which is stated to have inspired the Union's own creation and which has to be advanced in the wider world.

In the Treaty on the Functioning of the EU (TFEU), solidarity is mentioned in the Preamble in the same formulation as it was since the Treaty of Rome. In addition, solidarity is mentioned in Article 67 TFEU in the context of provisions concerning an area of freedom, security and justice. Here, the reference is made to: '... solidarity between Member States'. Article 80 TFEU, stipulated in the context of policies on border checks, asylum and immigration, states that: 'The policies of the Union set out in this Chapter and their implementation shall be governed by the principle of *solidarity* and fair sharing of responsibility, including its financial implications, between the Member States. Whenever necessary, the Union acts adopted pursuant to this Chapter shall contain appropriate measures to give effect to this principle' (emphasis added). Also in Articles 122, 194 and 222 TFEU, reference is made to: '... a spirit of *solidarity* between Member States ...' (emphasis added).[9]

Finally, it is of great importance that pursuant to Article 6 TEU, the Union recognises the rights, freedoms and principles set out in the Charter of Fundamental Rights of the European Union of 7 December 2000, as

[8] In Article 21 it is, e.g. stipulated that: 'The Union's action on the international scene shall be guided by the principles which have inspired its own creation, development and enlargement, and which it seeks to advance in the wider world: democracy, the rule of law, the universality and indivisibility of human rights and fundamental freedoms, respect for human dignity, the principles of equality and *solidarity*, and respect for the principles of the United Nations Charter and international law.' (emphasis added) It is in Article 24, among others, stipulated that: '2. Within the framework of the principles and objectives of its external action, the Union shall conduct, define and implement a common foreign and security policy, based on the development of mutual political *solidarity* among Member States, the identification of questions of general interest and the achievement of an ever-increasing degree of convergence of Member States' actions. 3. The Member States shall support the Union's external and security policy actively and unreservedly in a spirit of loyalty and mutual *solidarity* and shall comply with the Union's action in this area. The Member States shall work together to enhance and develop their mutual political *solidarity*. They shall refrain from any action which is contrary to the interests of the Union or likely to impair its effectiveness as a cohesive force in international relations. The Council and the High Representative shall ensure compliance with these principles.' (emphasis added)

[9] Also see Declarations 37 and 62, and Protocol 28, as well as the Decision of the heads of state or governments of the twenty-seven Member States of the EU, meeting within the European Council, on the concerns of the Irish people on the Treaty of Lisbon, Section C and Solemn Declaration on workers' rights, social policy and other issues.

adapted at Strasbourg, on 12 December 2007, which shall have the same legal value as the treaties. It is here of significance that an entire chapter carries the headline 'Solidarity', namely Title IV. It contains twelve provisions, namely Articles 27 to 38. These concern the following subjects: Workers' right to information and consultation within the undertaking (Article 27); Right of collective bargaining and action (Article 28); Right of access to placement services (Article 29); Protection in the event of unjustified dismissal (Article 30); Fair and just working conditions (Article 31); Prohibition of child labour and protection of young people at work (Article 32); Family and professional life (Article 33); Social security and social assistance (Article 34); Health care (Article 35); Access to services of general economic interest (Article 36); Environmental protection (Article 37); and Consumer protection (Article 38). Indeed, these subjects reflect a very wide understanding of solidarity. The rights may be classified as a rather heterogeneous mishmash of the predictable and the unexpected.[10] A large part may be said to deal with working conditions. However, solidarity originally known internally in Member States is also to a very large degree put into focus. In addition to this it should be mentioned that the Second Recital of the Preamble refers to solidarity: 'Conscious of its spiritual and moral heritage, the Union is founded on the indivisible, universal values of human dignity, freedom, equality and *solidarity*; it is based on the principles of democracy and the rule of law. It places the individual at the heart of its activities, by establishing the citizenship of the Union and by creating an area of freedom, security and justice' (emphasis added). Importantly, solidarity is here viewed as an indivisible, universal value, upon which the Union is founded. The importance thereof has been stressed by Menéndez, who has stated that the affirmation of solidarity as one of the founding values of the Union might be the most innovative feature of the Charter.[11] In this regard, it should be considered as having significance that solidarity is mentioned along with such prominent values as human dignity, freedom and equality. The mentioning of freedom in the same sentence –thereby probably to be considered on a more or less equal footing – is worth emphasising because freedom and solidarity at times may be in direct conflict with one another.

[10] See S. O'Leary, 'Solidarity and citizenship rights in the Charter of Fundamental Rights of the European Union', in de Búrca G. (ed.), *EU Law and the Welfare State. In Search of Solidarity* (Oxford: Oxford University Press, 2005), p. 60.

[11] A. J. Menéndez, 'The rights' foundations of solidarity: social and economic rights in the Charter of Fundamental Rights of the European Union', *ARENA Working Papers WP 03/1* (2003), p. 15.

Altogether, a significant increase in the explicit use of solidarity over the years is evident in primary EU law. Also, a change from a more 'external' dimension to an 'internal' dimension occurs so that a kind of protection or at least acknowledgement of the latter dimension with the Treaty of Lisbon and the Charter of Fundamental Rights now appears. Solidarity is thus, among other things, to be understood in the context of what it is connected with. Therefore, it can be observed that it is no longer only the relationships among Member States, among the peoples of the EU, and between the Member States and the EU, and between the EU and the wider world, that is, transnational solidarity, which are of interest. Solidarity 'internally' in Member States is also becoming of interest as worthy of protection. Importantly in the context of the present analysis, solidarity among the Member States has been a kind of a binding glue from the very beginning.

Solidarity is not only to be understood in playing a role regarding these relationships. It also plays an important role in the definition of the European identity. Thus, solidarity is viewed as a special and important virtue of what Europe – including both the EU as such and the individual Member States – is about; something which apparently is viewed as distinguishing it from other entities. At the same time, it seems to be indicating an ideal, a programmatic commitment, an expression of a value or even an aspect of an ideology, which may be given weight.

Importantly, in the Treaty of Maastricht (in Article 2 of the Treaty on the European Community), references to both the EMU and solidarity appeared together, which may be understood as establishing that the former is a tool to promote the latter among Member States (rather than the EMU being based on a principle of solidarity among the Member States). Otherwise, the EMU and solidarity are not closely connected in primary law.

In sum, a rather significant re-orientation at the explicit level has taken place. However, even now, nearly ten years after the Treaty of Lisbon came into force, it still remains to be seen more exactly how these grand treaty amendments will work out in practice, but this does not change the fact that the range and proliferation of references to solidarity should not be viewed as accidental.[12]

[12] M. Ross, 'The value of solidarity in European public services law', in M. Krajewski, U. Neergaard and J. van de Gronden (eds.), *The Changing Legal Framework of Services of General Interest in Europe – Between Competition and Solidarity* (The Hague, T.M.C. Asser Press, 2009), p. 88.

3 Solidarity in the Specific Context of the EMU

In contrast to the previous section, the focus here is limited to the evolution of solidarity in the context of the EMU in the period since the beginning of the economic crisis and ten years ahead. However, at first, the more general construction of the EMU is briefly presented, which then is being followed by an analysis of how references to solidarity have evolved in that context.

3.1 *The EMU in General*

The EMU has a long history, but its legal origin lies in the Treaty of Maastricht. In general terms, as it is stated in the Preamble of the TEU, the Member States wish to achieve the strengthening and convergence of their economies and to establish an EMU including, in accordance with the provisions of this Treaty and of the TFEU, a single and stable currency. Thus, the EMU envisages a single monetary policy conducted by a single monetary authority and with a single currency.[13] Exchange rates became fixed in 1998 and the common currency, the euro, was introduced in 1999 and came into circulation in 2002.[14] In addition to the relevant treaty provisions, among the early supplements the Stability and Growth Pact, which was enacted in 1997 and based on TFEU Articles 121 and 126, is of particular importance.[15] It may be seen as supplementing the treaty provisions and constitutes the essential framework of the European Semester.

The design with regard to the distribution of competences contains strong tensions as monetary policy for the Eurozone Member States is the exclusive competence of the EU, whereas the national economic policies can only be co-ordinated by the EU, as these as a point of departure are in principle the responsibility of the Member States (see Article 2(3) TFEU). Regarding this complicated and asymmetric scenario Craig explains that it was integral to the Maastricht settlement that monetary policy was

[13] A. Hinarejos, 'Economic and monetary union', in C. Barnard and S. Peers (eds.), *European Union Law* (Oxford: Oxford University Press, 2014), p. 567.

[14] Ibid., p. 567.

[15] Originally it consisted of the following two regulations: Regulation (EC) 1466/97, O.J. 1997, L 209, on the strengthening of the surveillance of budgetary positions and the surveillance and coordination of economic policies (the so-called preventive arm of the Stability and Growth Pact), and Regulation (EC) 1467/97, O.J. 1997, L 209, on speeding up and clarifying the implementation of the excessive deficit procedure. It has subsequently been revised.

Europeanised, which was reinforced by the Lisbon Treaty provisions on competence.[16] As he also states, the Maastricht settlement in relation to economic policy was markedly different as it was built on two related assumptions – preservation of national authority and preservation of national liability, the message being that national governments retained authority over national economic policy.[17] The design has therefore continuously been criticised, in which respect the historian Tooze sums up in relation to the conception and initial life of the EMU: '[T]he euro was clearly unfinished ... There was no unified economic policy. No unified regulatory structure for banking. Nor, however, was there much urgency in moving to further integration. In its early years, the new currency zone performed tolerably well. European growth accelerated. After an initial hike in prices following the adoption of the single currency, inflation remained moderate. Capital markets were calm.'[18]

At the overarching level, the EU has the power to lay down budgetary discipline and balance rules, which Member States must comply with, but as a point of departure it lacks the power to impose socio-economic redistributive choices on them.[19] However, the consequences of the former rules may in actual fact be that national socio-economic redistributive choices may have to be taken in order to fulfil them.[20]

As stipulated in the leading provision regarding the EMU, Article 119(1) TFEU, EMU is based on an open market economy with free competition. It is stated that for the purposes set out in Article 3 TEU, the activities of the Member States and the Union shall include, as provided in the treaties, the adoption of an economic policy that is based on the close co-ordination of Member States' economic policies, on the internal market and on the definition of common objectives, and conducted in accordance with the principle of an open market economy with free competition. Also, in Article 119(2) TFEU, a similar reference is found where it is stipulated that concurrent with the foregoing, and as provided in the treaties and in accordance with the procedures set out

16 P. Craig, 'Keynote address – the financial crisis, the EU institutional order and constitutional responsibility', in U. Neergaard et al. (eds.), *Proceedings: Speeches from the XXVI FIDE Congress* (2014), p. 69, available at: fide2014.eu/post-congress-materials/.

17 Ibid.

18 A. Tooze, *Crashed. How a Decade of Financial Crises Changed the World* (London: Viking, 2018), p. 93.

19 K. Lenaerts, 'Economic integration, solidarity and legitimacy. The EU in a time of crisis', *Euroforum Lectures* (2013), p. 3, available at: kuleuven.be/euroforum/viewpic.php?LAN=E&TABLE=DOCS&ID=860.

20 Ibid., p. 3.

therein, these activities shall include a single currency, the euro, and the definition and conduct of a single monetary policy and exchange-rate policy, the primary objective of both shall be to maintain price stability and, without prejudice to this objective, to support the general economic policies in the Union, in accordance with the principle of an open market economy with free competition.

The construction from the Treaty of Maastricht was left largely unaltered in the Treaty of Lisbon, and it was, according to Craig, only when the financial crisis hit the EU, that Member States were willing to accept that greater control over national economic policy was a necessary condition for the monetary union and for the enacting of many important measures, such as the Six-Pack, the Two-Pack and the Fiscal Compact.[21] In general terms and in accordance with the statement of Stiglitz introducing this chapter, the architecture of the EMU was not truly founded on solidarity in the sense of explicit obligations of the stronger Member States to help those in need, but certain changes in support thereof may after all be considered to have been implemented piecemeal.[22] In the following sections, these steps will be explored further to examine how solidarity may have been materialised in the context of the EMU after the crisis broke and played out over approximately a ten year period.[23]

3.2 *The Period Under the First and Second Barroso Commissions*

This first phase to be analysed here is defined as beginning on 15 September 2008 (the date on which the American bank, Lehmann Brothers, went bankrupt), which is often considered to have been the starting point of the banking and financial crisis.[24] It is defined as lasting

[21] Craig, 'Keynote address', p. 70.

[22] See further e.g. Goldner, 'The EU financial and migration crises', p. 139.

[23] Considering the enormous and nearly endless amount of actions taken, the analysis in the present as well as the following section is founded on a selection of examples rather than on an exhaustive analysis of all regulation, etc. To give a fuller picture of the situation and political visions at hand, important speeches, notes and the like, have also been included. Importantly, country-specific measures and such related to the banking sector/union have in principle not been included.

[24] For an overview of initiatives, see e.g. the tables in B. Laffan and P. Schlosser, 'The rise of a fiscal Europe? Negotiating Europe's new economic governance', *Research Report at Florence School of Banking and Finance*, 2015/01 (2015), p. 13, available at: cadmus.eui.eu/bitstream/handle/1814/36482/FBF_RR_2015_01.pdf?sequence=1. For a chronological review of the events since 2008, see ec.europa.eu/economy_finance/crisis/2008-10_en.htm; and for an account of the causes of the crisis, see e.g. Commission, *Economic*

until the end of the second Barroso Commission, that is, until 31 October 2014. During the period of the first Barroso Commission, the original measures taken at the EU level were mainly concerned with the financial institutions and markets. Thus, the initiatives in this initial period are not of great interest here.[25] Also, solidarity is generally not really significantly addressed.[26]

In contrast, during the second Barroso Commission, which started on 1 November 2009, measures addressing solidarity were adopted more profoundly and references thereto made elsewhere as well. This development will be analysed further in the following.

A hesitant first step might be viewed as having been taken in March 2010 with *Europe 2020* in the shape of a communication from the Commission, in which a ten-year jobs and growth strategy was launched.[27] Importantly, it is not limited to the Eurozone, but rather concerns the entire EU. There is here one single, rather general reference to solidarity: '[w]e can … count on our strong values, democratic institutions, our consideration for economic, social and territorial cohesion and *solidarity*, our respect for the environment, our cultural diversity, respect for gender equality …' (emphasis added) Concretely, the communication builds on a set-up of stronger economic governance, which is implemented through the so-called European Semester. It relies

Crisis in Europe: Causes, Consequences and Responses, European Economy 7|2009, available at: ec.europa.eu/economy_finance/publications/publication15887_en.pdf. Finally, it may be mentioned that pursuant to e.g. D. Chalmers, G. Davies and G. Monti, *European Union Law. Text and Materials* (Cambridge: Cambridge University Press, 2014), p. 714, the starting date for the European sovereign debt crisis itself is usually seen as starting about a year later, namely in October 2009.

[25] Ibid. Also see Commission Memo, 'A comprehensive EU response to the financial crisis: substantial progress towards a strong financial framework for Europe and a banking union for the Eurozone', 28 March 2014, available at: europa.eu/rapid/press-release_MEMO-13-1168_en.htm, from where it is understood that legal action was initiated from 2010 and onwards.

[26] See however e.g. Council, *Presidency Conclusions*, 29 April 2009, available at: consilium.europa.eu/uedocs/cms_data/docs/pressdata/en/ec/106809.pdf, in which it among other things is stated that: 'Macro-financial stability is an essential element for the resilience of the European economy as a whole. Stressing the solidarity between Member States as a fundamental value of the EU, the European Council invites the Commission and the Council to take the necessary measures in order to be prepared, if needed, to act on a case-by-case basis, on the basis of all available instruments and where appropriate in close cooperation with International Financial Institutions.'

[27] Commission Communication, *Europe 2020. A Strategy for Smart, Sustainable and Inclusive Growth*, COM(2010)2020 of 3 March 2010, available at: eur-lex.europa.eu/LexUriServ/LexUriServ.do?uri=COM:2010:2020:FIN:EN:PDF.

on an approach, which combines priorities and headline targets, as well as on country reporting, helping Member States to develop their strategies to return to sustainable growth and public finances.[28] Thus, country-specific recommendations are to be addressed to Member States and policy warnings could be issued in case of inadequate response.[29]

To give assistance to those Member States, which faced severe economic difficulties as a result of the crisis, a little later, in May 2010, the European Financial Stability Mechanism (EFSM) was established to preserve financial stability in Europe.[30] Shortly after, in June 2010, the European Financial Stability Fund (EFSF) was created as a temporary crisis resolution mechanism.[31] There are no explicit references to solidarity in any of the two constructions (that is, the regulation and the agreement), but self-evidently they are created on the basis thereof.

An annual European Semester for economic policy co-ordination, which was also briefly mentioned above, is a cornerstone of *Europe 2020*, and was established as such in September 2010.[32] It was formalised on the basis of Regulation 1466/97 and is thus related to, among others, the Stability and Growth Pact.[33] The fundamental idea behind the set-up is that all the Member States of the EU have to present their budget plans every year, which are then evaluated in the equivalent semester.[34] The first of these European Semesters was in 2011. The range of activities considered is fairly manifold, and covers in principle many aspects of fiscal, economic and social policy.[35] It is in this context crucially explained by the European Commission that:

28 Ibid., p. 6.
29 Ibid., p. 6.
30 Regulation (EU) 407/2010, O.J. 2010, L 118/1, on establishing a European financial stabilisation mechanism, available at: eur-lex.europa.eu/legal-content/EN/TXT/?uri=celex:32010R0407.
31 See further especially efsf.europa.eu/about/index.htm, available at: esm.europa.eu/content/efsf-framework-agreement, and efsf.europa.eu/attachments/EFSFStatusCoordonnes%2023AVRL2014.pdf.
32 Chalmers, Davies and Monti, *European Union Law*, p. 745. See generally hereec.europa.eu/europe2020/index_en.htm.
33 Ibid. The Stability and Growth Pact is discussed further both above as well as below.
34 See further e.g. European Commission, 'EU Economic governance: a major step forward', MEMO/11/364, 31 May 2011, available at: europa.eu/rapid/press-release_MEMO-11-364_en.htm?locale=en, and ec.europa.eu/info/business-economy-euro/economic-and-fiscal-policy-coordination/eu-economic-governance-monitoring-prevention-correction/european-semester_en.
35 Chalmers, Davies and Monti, *European Union Law*, p. 746.

> Financial assistance can be provided to a euro area Member State which requests it, subject to strong conditionality reflected in an economic adjustment programme to be negotiated by the Commission and the International Monetary Fund (IMF), in liaison with the European Central Bank (ECB). With such mechanisms, the EU has the capacity to act to defend the euro, even in the most stressed scenarios. They are a clear reflection of the common interest and *solidarity* within the euro area, as well as the individual responsibility of each Member State before its peers.[36]

The next important incident to mention – after the introduction of the European Semester – is that at a European Council Meeting in March 2011, the Member States of the Eurozone and six other Member States decided to adopt the Euro Plus Pact (EPP) as an international agreement.[37] Its purpose is to strengthen the economic pillar of the EMU, achieve a new quality of economic policy co-ordination, improve competitiveness, thereby leading to a higher degree of convergence. It is explicitly stated in the EPP that it focuses primarily on areas that fall under national competence and are key for increasing competitiveness and avoiding harmful imbalances. There is no explicit mention of solidarity.

The abovementioned Stability and Growth Pact was reformed in November 2011 through the introduction of the so-called Six-Pack of measures, thereby indicating that it consists of six measures (that is, five Regulations and one Directive).[38] Four out of six measures apply to all Member States, but the two Regulations, which lay down sanctions, only apply to the Eurozone Member States.[39] It not only covers fiscal

[36] European Commission, 'EU Economic governance: a major step forward', MEMO/11/364, 31 May 2011, available at: europa.eu/rapid/press-release_MEMO-11-364_en.htm?locale=en, emphasis added.

[37] 'Annex 1: The Euro Plus Pact. Stronger Economic Policy Coordination for Competitiveness and Convergence', in Council, 'Conclusions of the European Council 24/25 March 2011', 20 April 2011, available at: consilium.europa.eu/uedocs/cms_data/docs/pressdata/en/ec/120296.pdf.

[38] See e.g. ec.europa.eu/info/business-economy-euro/economic-and-fiscal-policy-coordination/eu-economic-governance-monitoring-prevention-correction/european-semester/framework/eus-economic-governance-explained_en. They are enacted pursuant to Articles 121, 126 and 136 TFEU.

[39] Lenaerts, 'Economic integration, solidarity and legitimacy', p. 8. More precisely, it consists of the following six legislative acts which came into force on 13 December 2011: (1) Regulation (EU) 1173/2011 on the implementation of efficient budgetary surveillance in the euro area (O.J. 2011, L 306/1), available at: eur-lex.europa.eu/legal-content/EN/TXT/PDF/?uri=CELEX:32011R1173&from=EN; (2) Regulation (EU) 1174/2011 on enforcement measures to correct excessive macroeconomic

surveillance, but also macroeconomic surveillance. One of the measures consists of the amendment of the abovementioned Regulation (EC) 1466/97 (the so-called preventive arm of the Stability and Growth Pact) as it is amended by Regulation (EU) 1175/2011. Only one of the six measures explicitly refers to solidarity as it is here stated that:

> The Commission shall give due and express consideration to any other factors which, in the opinion of the Member State concerned, are relevant in order to comprehensively assess compliance with deficit and debt criteria and which the Member State has put forward to the Council and the Commission. In that context, particular consideration shall be given to financial contributions to fostering international *solidarity* and achieving the policy goals of the Union, the debt incurred in the form of bilateral and multilateral support between Member States in the context of safeguarding financial stability, and the debt related to financial stabilisation operations during major financial disturbances.[40]

The Treaty on Stability, Coordination and Governance, also known as TSCG, is not in a strict sense a Eurozone regulation as it, besides the Eurozone Member States themselves, was also signed by Member States outside the zone.[41] It was signed in March 2012 and came into force in January 2013. According to Article 1(1) TSCG, the contracting parties agree, as Member States of the EU, to strengthen the economic pillar of the EMU by adopting a set of rules intended to foster budgetary discipline through a fiscal compact, to strengthen the co-ordination of their economic policies and to improve the governance of the euro area, thereby supporting the achievement of the EU's objectives for sustainable growth, employment, competitiveness and social cohesion. It introduced

imbalances in the euro area (O.J. 2011, L 306/8), available at: eur-lex.europa.eu/legal-content/EN/TXT/PDF/?uri=CELEX:32011R1174&from=EN; (3) Regulation (EU) 1175/2011 amending the surveillance procedures of budgetary positions (O.J. 2011, L 306/12), available at: eur-lex.europa.eu/legal-content/EN/TXT/PDF/?uri=CELEX:32011R1175&from=EN; (4) Regulation (EU) 1176/2011 on the prevention and correction of macroeconomic imbalances (O.J. 2011, L 306/25), available at: eur-lex.europa.eu/legal-content/EN/TXT/PDF/?uri=CELEX:32011R1176&from=EN; (5) Regulation (EU) 1177/2011 amending the procedure concerning excessive deficits (O.J. 2011, 306/33), available at: eur-lex.europa.eu/legal-content/EN/TXT/PDF/?uri=CELEX:32011R1177&from=EN; and (6) Directive on requirements for budgetary frameworks of the Member States (O.J. 2011, L 306/41), available at: eur-lex.europa.eu/legal-content/EN/TXT/PDF/?uri=CELEX:32011L0085&from=EN.

40 Regulation (EU) 1177/2011 amending the procedure concerning excessive deficits (O.J. 2011, 306/33), available at: eur-lex.europa.eu/legal-content/EN/TXT/PDF/?uri=CELEX:32011R1177&from=EN, Article 1 (2), emphasis added.

41 Available at: consilium.europa.eu/media/20399/st00tscg26_en12.pdf. It was signed by all Member States in the EU except for the Czech Republic, the UK and Croatia.

a stricter version of the Stability and Growth Pact aiming to tackle the structural shortcomings of economic and monetary integration by introducing an enforceable balanced budget rule for the contracting parties.[42] This so-called 'golden rule' obliges, in other words, government budgets to be balanced.[43] Despite its importance and a certain foundation on solidarity, there is no explicit use of the term.

In contrast, solidarity is mentioned in the so-called Four Presidents' Report, entitled 'Towards a Genuine Economic and Monetary Union', launched on 26 June 2012, and prepared by President of the European Council, Herman Van Rompuy, in close co-operation with the Presidents of the Commission, the Eurogroup and the ECB.[44] Its overall purpose is to set out a vision for the future of the EMU and how it can best contribute to growth, jobs and stability, and it proposes to move, over the next decade, towards a stronger EMU architecture, based on integrated frameworks for the financial sector, for budgetary matters and for economic policy.[45] It is in this context that there are several references to solidarity, among which one is of relevance here. Thus, in the context of the launched vision for a stable and prosperous EMU, one of its four essential 'building blocks' refers thereto in the following manner: 'Ensuring the necessary democratic legitimacy and accountability of decision-making within the EMU, based on the joint exercise of sovereignty for common policies and *solidarity*.'[46]

Since it came into force in October 2012, the European Stability Mechanism (ESM) has been the sole and also permanent mechanism responding to new requests for financial assistance by Eurozone Member States.[47] In this connection, Article 136 TFEU was amended to form the legal basis, although not initially, as first an intergovernmental treaty outside the formal TEU structures between the Eurozone Member States

[42] J. Lievens, S. van Hecke, S. Sottiaux and W. Wolfs, 'A social compact for a social union?', *Euroforum Policy Papers* (2014), 1–16, at 5, available at: kuleuven.be/euroforum/viewpic.php?LAN=ETABLE=DOCS&ID=940.

[43] M. Adams, F. Fabbrini and P. Laroche, 'Introduction. The constitutionalization of European budgetary constraints: effectiveness and legitimacy in comparative perspective', in M. Adams, F. Fabbrini and P. Laroche (eds.), *The Constitutionalization of European Budgetary Constraints* (London: Hart Publishing, 2014), pp. 1–15, at 1.

[44] Council, *Towards a Genuine Economic and Monetary Union. Report by: President of the European Council, Herman Van Rompuy – in close cooperation with the Presidents of the Commission, the Eurogroup and the European Central Bank*, 26 June 2012, available at: consilium.europa.eu/media/33785/131201.pdf.

[45] Ibid., p. 1.

[46] Ibid., p. 3, emphasis added.

[47] See generally esm.europa.eu/index.htm.

established the ESM as an international organisation.[48] The ESM Treaty itself refers once explicitly to solidarity as it in the Preamble is stated that: 'This Treaty and the TSCG are complementary in fostering fiscal responsibility and *solidarity* within the economic and monetary union.'[49] Thereby, an explicit commitment to solidarity is expressed.[50]

Shortly afterwards, in November 2012, the Commission published a Communication entitled *A Blueprint for a Deep and Genuine Economic and Monetary Union. Launching a European Debate.*[51] It is introduced by, among other things, emphasising that the EU 'shall promote economic, social and territorial cohesion, and *solidarity* among Member States'.[52] More importantly, the way forward is seen to consist of steps towards more responsibility and economic discipline, which should be combined with more solidarity and financial support.[53] In that regard, it is envisaged that in '. . . the long term (beyond 5 years), based on the progressive pooling of sovereignty and thus responsibility as well as *solidarity* competencies to the European level, the establishment of an autonomous euro area budget providing for a fiscal capacity for the EMU to support Member States in the absorption of shocks should become possible',[54] and importantly that:

> In view of these considerations, the existing framework for economic governance of the euro area should be strengthened further through ensuring greater ex-ante coordination of major reform projects and, following the decision on the next MFF, through the creation of a "Convergence and Competitiveness Instrument" to provide support for the timely implementation of structural reforms (see Annex 1 for a more detailed description of the intended setup). This instrument would combine deepening integration of economic policy with financial support, and thereby respect the principle according to which steps

[48] P. Craig and G. de Búrca, *EU Law. Text, Cases, and Materials* (Oxford: Oxford University Press, 2015), p. 738. It was signed on 2 February 2012. Also see Case C-370/12, *Pringle*, EU:C:2012:756, where the legality of the ESM is challenged.

[49] Available at: esm.europa.eu/sites/default/files/20150203 – esm treaty_-_en.pdf, emphasis added.

[50] See further e.g. G. Lo Schiavo, 'The European Stability Mechanism and the European Banking Union: promotion of organic financial solidarity from transient self-interest solidarity in Europe', in A. Biondi, E. Dagilytė and E. Küçük, *Solidarity in EU Law* (Cheltenham: Edward Elgar, 2018), pp. 161–90.

[51] Commission Communication, *A Blueprint for a Deep and Genuine Economic and Monetary Union. Launching a European Debate*, COM(2012)777 of 28 November 2012, available at: statewatch.org/news/2012/nov/eu-com-emu-blueprint.pdf.

[52] Ibid., p. 1, emphasis added.

[53] Ibid., p. 11.

[54] Ibid., p. 12, emphasis added.

> towards more responsibility and economic discipline are combined with more *solidarity*. The Commission will, in a forthcoming proposal, set out the precise terms for this instrument.[55]

Indeed, what is envisaged is in reality 'new EU rules on *solidarity* between Member States', which is rather new.[56]

The Two-Pack of measures was adopted in May 2013 and may be seen as supplementing the abovementioned Six-Pack.[57] Among others, it seeks to improve budgetary co-ordination. Its legal basis is Article 136 TFEU and it only applies to the Eurozone Member States. There is no mentioning of solidarity in the two measures.

The communication from the Commission launched in October 2013, entitled *Strengthening the Social Dimension of the Economic and Monetary Union*, is also worth mentioning.[58] It is a further contribution from the Commission to the debate on deepening the EMU, where a number of initiatives to strengthen the social dimension of it are proposed with a particular focus on three points, namely: (1) reinforced surveillance of employment and social challenges and policy co-ordination; (2) enhanced solidarity and action on employment and labour mobility; and (3) strengthened social dialogue.[59] Although solidarity here is mainly understood in the context of the social dimension of the EMU, as it is also connected with the abovementioned 'Blueprint' there are also references to solidarity in a more general understanding, including visions of solidarity competencies at European level:

> The Commission's Blueprint for a Deep and Genuine EMU provides a comprehensive vision conducive to a strong and stable architecture in the financial, fiscal, economic and political domains. It is also relevant for the development of the social dimension of the EMU. The blueprint sets out the actions the Commission believes must be taken in the short,

55 Ibid., p. 20, emphasis added.

56 Ibid., p. 35, emphasis added.

57 Regulation (EU) 473/2013, O.J. 2013, L 140/11, on common provisions for monitoring and assessing draft budgetary plans and ensuring the correction of excessive deficit of the Member States in the euro area available at: eur-lex.europa.eu/legal-content/EN/TXT/PDF/?uri=CELEX:32013R0473&from=EN; and Regulation (EU) 472/2013, O.J. 2013, L 140/1, on the strengthening of economic and budgetary surveillance of Member States in the euro area experiencing or threatened with serious difficulties with respect to their financial stability available at: eur-lex.europa.eu/legal-content/EN/TXT/PDF/?uri=CELEX:32013R0472&from=EN.

58 Commission Communication, *Strengthening the Social Dimension of the Economic and Monetary Union*, COM(2013)690 of 2 Oct. 2013 available at: eur-lex.europa.eu/LexUriServ/LexUriServ.do?uri=COM:2013:0690:FIN:EN:PDF.

59 Ibid., p. 1.

> medium and long term. On this path, steps towards more responsibility and economic discipline should be taken in parallel with *more solidarity* and financial support. Some of the required steps can be adopted within the limits of the current Treaties. Others will require modifying the current Treaties and giving new competences to the EU.[60]

To sum up with regard to this first phase, the initiatives to combat the crisis were introduced gradually. Generally, solidarity among Member States has been given substantive weight and seemingly increasingly so over time.

3.3 The Period Under the Juncker Commission

The next phase to be examined is timewise slightly shorter than the previous, as it only runs from 1 November 2014 until the end of September 2018, that is, ten years after the start of the crisis.[61] As before, examples of initiatives of importance will be briefly presented and analysed.[62]

Importantly, in relation to solidarity the phase may be seen as taking its point of departure in the Euro Summit of 24 October 2014, 'which called for work to continue to develop concrete mechanisms for stronger economic policy coordination, convergence and *solidarity*'.[63] In an analytical note of 12 February 2015 from Juncker in close cooperation with

[60] Ibid., p. 10, emphasis added. Also see p. 11, where it is stated that: 'Finally, in the long term, based on progressive pooling of sovereignty and thus responsibility and *solidarity competencies at European level*, it should become possible to establish an autonomous euro area budget providing the euro area with a fiscal capacity to support Member States absorb shocks. The central budget would provide for an EMU-level stabilisation tool to support adjustment to asymmetric shocks, increase economic integration and convergence and avoid setting-up long-term transfer flows. Overall, a shared instrument could deliver net gains in stabilising power, compared with current arrangements. The size of this fiscal capacity would ultimately depend on the depth of integration desired and on the willingness to enact accompanying political changes.' (emphasis added)

[61] The Juncker Commission's office runs in principle until 31 October 2019. However, it may be claimed that by now the economic crisis has already come to end; nevertheless, it is here assumed that even that being so, the consequences therefrom under all circumstances are still felt to this day, and that it is thus worthwhile examining also the most present years to get the full picture.

[62] Also as before, certain speeches, notes, etc. may be included.

[63] According to Juncker in close cooperation with Tusk, Dijsselbloem and Draghi, *Preparing for Next Steps on Better Economic Governance in the Euro Area, Informal Council*, 12 February 2015, available at: ec.europa.eu/commission/sites/beta-political/files/analytical_note_en.pdf, emphasis added.

Tusk, Dijsselbloem and Draghi, entitled *Preparing for Next Steps on Better Economic Governance in the Euro Area*, this call is clearly addressed, as it is stated: 'In view of the current weak economic environment in the euro area as a whole and the remaining vulnerabilities and rigidities in a number of individual countries, there is a need to move gradually towards "concrete mechanisms for stronger economic policy coordination, convergence and *solidarity*"'.[64] Later on in June 2015, the overall – far-reaching – proposal in the Five Presidents' Report was launched. It had been prepared by President of the European Commission, Juncker, in close cooperation with the presidents of the European Summit, the Eurogroup, the ECB and the European Parliament, and was entitled 'Completing Europe's Monetary and Economic Union'. It concerns how progress can be made – the purpose being to set a direction for deepening and completing the EMU.[65] In that context, an awareness of the need for solidarity is also clearly acknowledged as it is stated that:

> The euro is more than just a currency. It is a political and economic project. All members of our Monetary Union have given up their previous national currencies once and for all and permanently share monetary sovereignty with the other euro area countries. In return, countries gain the benefits of using a credible and stable currency within a large, competitive and powerful single market. This common destiny requires *solidarity* in times of crisis and respect for commonly agreed rules from all members.[66]

It may be added that in Vice-President of the European Commission, Dombrovskis' speech in September 2015 concerning 'The Euro and the Future of Europe', it is once again acknowledged that 'European *solidarity* and inclusiveness is particularly important within the Euro area.'[67]

[64] Available at: ec.europa.eu/commission/sites/beta-political/files/analytical_note_en.pdf, p. 7, emphasis added.

[65] Commission, *Completing Europe's Monetary and Economic Union. Report by: Jean-Claude Juncker in close cooperation with Donald Tusk Jeroen Dijsselbloem Mario Draghi and Martin Schulz*, 22 June 2015, available at: ec.europa.eu/priorities/economic-monetary-union/docs/5-presidents-report_en.pdf.

[66] Ibid., p. 4. Later on in the same year, President of the European Commission Juncker, held his significant speech on the *State of the Union 2015: Time for Honesty, Unity and Solidarity*, Speech/15/5614 of 9 September 2015, available at: europa.eu/rapid/press-release_SPEECH-15-5614_en.htm, emphasis added. Despite the reference to solidarity already in the title of the speech, it did not really concern solidarity in relation to the EMU.

[67] Speech/15/5687 of 21 September 2015, available at: europa.eu/rapid/press-release_SPEECH-15-5687_en.htm?locale=en, emphasis added.

From the following year, 2016, reference may be made to the President of the European Commission Juncker's State of the Union speech. Here solidarity in relation to the EMU is included in the following manner: 'Solidarity is the glue that keeps our Union together. The word "solidarity" appears 16 times in the treaties which all our Member States agreed and ratified. Our European budget is living proof of financial solidarity … The euro is an expression of solidarity.'[68]

The year of 2017 is in relation to the EMU of especial interest because several initiatives regarding the social dimension thereof – including the launching of the European Pillar of Social Rights – were taken. Although solidarity here is of importance, the context it is operating in is, nevertheless, different from the kind searched for here.[69] Therefore, the *White Paper on the Future of Europe*, which was launched in March 2017, may be considered to be of much more relevance as again solidarity, as well as the vision of a deepening of the EMU, feature strongly.[70] This is somehow already indicated by being introduced in the following quotation of French foreign minister Schuman on 9 May 1950, which still today shows a convincing degree of wisdom: 'Europe will not be made all at once, or according to a single plan. It will be built through concrete achievements which first create a de facto *solidarity*.'[71] It was later on to become followed up by various further initiatives. Also in 2017, yet another reflection paper worth mentioning was launched, namely the *Reflection Paper on*

[68] Juncker, *State of the Union 2016. Towards a Better Europe – A Europe that Protects, Empowers and Defends*, available at: publications.europa.eu/en/publication-detail/-/publication/c9ff4ff6-9a81-11e6-9bca-01aa75ed71a1/language-en/format-PDF/source-30945725, emphasis added.

[69] See in particular: European Commission, *Reflection Paper on the Social Dimension of Europe*, 26 April 2017, available at: ec.europa.eu/commission/sites/beta-political/files/reflection-paper-social-dimension-europe_en.pdf; *Social Scoreboard to monitor Member States' progress on social indicators* (operational on 26 April 2017 and embedded in the European Semester since November 2017), available at: composite-indicators.jrc.ec.europa.eu/social-scoreboard/; and *The European Pillar of Social Rights* (Commission policy initiative launched in 2015 (State of the Union speech) and resulting in booklet/text proclaimed by Parliament, Council and Commission in November 2017), available at: europa.eu/rapid/press-release_IP-17-1007_en.htm.

[70] European Commission, *White Paper on the Future of Europe. Reflections and Scenarios for the EU27 by 2025*, 1 March 2017, available at: ec.europa.eu/commission/sites/beta-political/files/white_paper_on_the_future_of_europe_en.pdf.

[71] Ibid., p. 4, emphasis added. The quotation originates from the famous Schuman Declaration, in which the creation of a European Coal and Steel Community, whose members would pool coal and steel production, was proposed; see europa.eu/european-union/about-eu/symbols/europe-day/schuman-declaration_en.

the Future of EU Finances.[72] Here, solidarity is also expressed as being essential and the understanding expressed is among other things that the 'EU budget should continue to make the European economy stronger and more resilient by promoting long-term competitiveness, sustainability and *solidarity*' and that by 'combining both internal and external policies, the EU and the Member States are developing a comprehensive approach grounded in mutual trust and *solidarity* among Member States and institutions'.[73]

In September in the same year, President of the European Commission Juncker again refers several times to solidarity in his State of the Union speech, however not in a context of real relevance here.[74] Following up on the various steps as described above, in particular the Five Presidents' Report and the two recent Reflection Papers of spring 2017, the Commission's roadmap for deepening Europe's EMU (including several concrete measures) launched by the end of year, has a certain degree of importance, as it is here emphasised that all 'reforms initiated so far have been driven by the need to combine *solidarity* and responsibility at all levels and this is also a central priority of today's package'.[75] The package in question includes the following four main initiatives, among which several are of interest here: (1) a proposal to establish a European Monetary Fund (EMF), anchored within the EU's legal framework and built on the well-established structure of the ESM; (2) a proposal to integrate the substance of the Treaty on Stability, Coordination and Governance into the Union legal framework, taking into account the appropriate flexibility built into the Stability and Growth Pact and identified by the commission since January 2015; (3) a communication on new budgetary instruments for a stable euro area within the Union framework setting out a vision of how certain budgetary functions

[72] European Commission, *Reflection Paper on the Future of EU Finances*, 28 June 2017, available at: ec.europa.eu/commission/sites/beta-political/files/reflection-paper-eu-finances_en.pdf.

[73] Ibid., pp. 13 and 19, emphasis added.

[74] Juncker, *State of the Union 2017. Catching the Wind in Our Sails*, 13 September 2017, available at: http://europa.eu/rapid/press-release_SPEECH-17-3165_en.htm.

[75] European Commission, *Commission sets out Roadmap for deepening Europe's Economic and Monetary Union*, 6 December 2017, available at: ec.europa.eu/commission/publications/completing-europes-economic-and-monetary-union-factsheets_en, emphasis added; and in particular European Commission, Further steps towards completing Europe's Economic and Monetary Union: a Roadmap, COM(2017) 821, available at: ec.europa.eu/transparency/regdoc/rep/1/2017/EN/COM-2017-821-F1-EN-MAIN-PART-1.PDF. For a general account and critique thereof, see 'Editorial comments', *Common Market Law Review* (2018), 709–18.

essential for the euro area and the EU as a whole can be developed within the framework of the EU's public finances of today and tomorrow; and (4) a communication spelling out the possible functions of a European Minister of Economy and Finance who could serve as Vice-President of the Commission and Chair the Eurogroup, as is possible under the current EU treaties.[76] Among these, in the present context, notably the proposal concerning the transformation of the ESM into a EMF is indeed very noteworthy.[77]

The final year to be taken into consideration here, 2018, is mainly characterised by a continuation of the attempts to make the initiatives already launched, especially in the year before, to become a reality. Therefore, it may just be noticed here that in the annual State of the Union speech by President of the European Commission Juncker, solidarity still plays a significant role. In that regard, it is of general interest that it is quite convincingly stated that 'We cannot continue to squabble to find ad-hoc solutions each time a new ship arrives. Temporary *solidarity* is not good enough. We need lasting *solidarity* – today and forever more. We need more *solidarity* not for *solidarity*'s sake but for the sake of efficiency.'[78]

To sum up in relation to this second phase, references to solidarity are at least apparent and perhaps even increasingly so, when compared to the first phase. This change may be explained by solidarity having become

[76] Ibid.

[77] See further European Commission, Proposal for a Council Regulation on the establishment of the European Monetary Fund, COM(2017) 827. It is explained at 4 that the proposal builds on the well-established structure of the European Stability Mechanism by creating a European Monetary Fund anchored within the EU's legal framework. L. Lionello, 'Prospects for completion of the economic and monetary union: community proposals and Franco-German pressure', *The Federalist* LX (2018), 36, adds to this that: 'On the one hand, the future EMF, as conceived in the Commission proposal, would become part of the EU's legal framework, but the Member States' resources would continue to be theirs alone. Indeed, as stated in article 8 of the draft statute of the EMF, "the liability of each EMF member shall be limited, in all circumstances, to its portion of the authorized capital stock at its issue price. No EMF member shall be liable, by reason of its membership, for obligations of the EMF." This is borne out by the fact that the rules governing activation of the EMF would be virtually the same as those currently governing activation of the ESM, i.e. the decisions almost always have to be adopted by unanimity or by reinforced qualified majority (the latter representing 85 per cent of the subscribed capital), which would give Germany, France and Italy the power of veto.'

[78] Juncker, *State of the Union 2018. The Hour of European Sovereignty*, available at: ec.europa.eu/commission/priorities/state-union-speeches/state-union-2018_en, emphasis added. Also see the 2018 Commission Work programme – key documents available at: ec.europa.eu/info/publications/2018-commission-work-programme-key-documents_en.

one of the new Commission's focal points, but also as playing a role as an essential 'selling argument'. Yet, the phase may mainly be characterised by political statements rather than by concretised legal action, although important legal proposals in that regard have been put forward.

4. Conclusions

Solidarity has become a very essential and unavoidable component in understanding and defining modern Europe – and thereby EU law as well – including the challenges, tensions and changes it faces during these years, not least in the context of the EMU. This chapter has analysed and compared the appearance of the concept solidarity in primary EU law and in the addressing thereof in reactions to the economic crisis in the context of the EMU over approximately a ten-year period. Regarding solidarity among (mainly) the Member States in the EMU – in both its early days and in particular in the period after the start of the crisis – it has been shown that although the emerging picture is rather complex, it can as a guiding mechanism at least be said to have become clearer over time.

Despite solidarity, in principle, having been present in primary EU law since the very beginning, those elements thereof dedicated to the EMU started out with hardly any explicit mentioning thereof, which is still the case of today. When also including the EU reactions to the economic crisis, the use thereof has intensified over time, however much more so as political rhetoric or wishful thinking, rather than representing a strong change of direction. However, although solidarity is often a concept without actual strength, in fact, it may in the area under scrutiny here be considered to some degree to have materialised in the shape of Member States' assistance of those in need by transfers of resources. This development has, first mainly been observed in relation to the launching of the EFSM and the EFSF, and later on most significantly in the ESM and the proposal of establishing a EMF. The Commission has recognised there is some way to go, which is, among other things, clear from the abovementioned references to the need of new EU rules on solidarity between Member States and legislative proposals for further changes.[79] Although already having moved far and having visions of more, there may still be some distance from an expression of promises

[79] Ibid., p. 35.

to actual deliveries, and therefore the impression is still – illustrated with reference to the following dialogue by Shakespeare:

POLONIUS (TO HAMLET)	: . . . What do you read, my lord?
HAMLET	: Words, words, words.[80]

In sum, Stiglitz, as quoted in the introduction, is justified in considering solidarity to be essential to the survival of the euro, and is not mistaken as to what could be referred to as a lack of strength in its materialisation. Nevertheless, as pointed out above, when looking at it from a more legal standpoint, certain nuances may be added giving a fuller picture of the situation.

[80] Shakespeare, *Hamlet*, Act II, Scene 2, available at: cs.cornell.edu/home/llee/talks/uai04 .pdf.

7

Negative Solidarity

The European Union and the Financial Crisis

GRAHAM BUTLER AND HOLLY SNAITH

1 Introduction

The European Union (EU) is cloaked in expressions of solidarity in a multitude of forms. Despite the fundamental role played by the solidarity in the EU, cracks have appeared and become more evident across Member States. The euro – a transnational single currency – was a bold endeavour when it was first established, and its adoption was expected to generate a leap forward for solidarity in the Union; by making European integration stronger, and more resilient. The prolonged battle of the sovereign debt crisis that emerged in 2009 tested the limits of solidarity across the EU: a confrontation waged on multiple levels, playing into constitutional frameworks and socio-economic divisions, and exacerbating the fault-lines between Member States. Yet despite frequent arguments made to the contrary, solidarity was a feature of the financial crisis, albeit of a particular kind. The legitimate expectation of what role different concepts of solidarity *ought* to have played (particularly where fiscal redistribution is concerned), compared to the role it actually served, ensured that an expectations deficit opened.

This chapter examines solidarity within the EU's legal framework in the context of the Eurozone crisis. It analyses the ramifications of the idea of solidarity, variously defined, and the implications it may have for the future direction of the Union as it faces ever-greater challenges. This contribution makes three important claims. First, the Eurozone crisis, rumbling on for the past decade, has seen instances of *negative* rather than *positive* solidarity being expressed transnationally across Europe. Second, that solidarity and its forms are – legally speaking – grossly misunderstood in an EU context. Third, it is argued that future crises, financial or otherwise, will continue to generate mixed attitudes towards solidarity in Europe, for the fault-lines that became evident in the past decade have not been fully paved over. Accordingly, true transnational solidarity across the EU will need significant time to develop before it can ever be considered 'organic' (to borrow Durkheim's concept).

1.1 The EU Financial Crisis

If one had not paid close attention to Europe over the past fifteen years, it would be hard to spot the difference in the legal make-up of the Union. A treaty change – with renumbered provisions, and no field greatly simplified – generates little to remark upon. However, constitutional arrangements put in place at the periphery of the treaty framework created have involved change and even transformation: the sovereign debt crisis originated in the financial services sector in a subset of Member States, which in turn generated a political and *legal* crisis among Member States themselves, and the entirety of the EU itself. The evolving Eurozone governance arrangements, put in place out of necessity, in turn played a significant role in de-escalating the sovereign debt crisis. Part of this process saw some of the Union's underlying values being downplayed in the name of expediency. This makes the sovereign debt crisis and EU law a fine example of solidarity in action.

Financial turmoil initially shook the globe over a decade ago. While Europe – no stranger to the integrated world of global financial markets – experienced many of the same convulsions as the Anglosphere, the political and economic centrality of the euro (embedded within the institutional framework of the European System of Central Banks [ESCB]) entailed that the crisis would always be filtered through a different political lens. The institutional nexus of the euro entailed that two crises became intertwined – a banking crisis and a sovereign debt crisis – as the initial banking crisis led to capital flight and the opening of large spreads in the bond yields between core and periphery economies, which in turn threatened the ability of those Member States to finance their debt,[1] a mechanism exacerbated by the strictures of a common currency. (These two elements will collectively be labelled the 'Eurozone crisis' in the argument that follows.) Together, they have led to the increased centralisation of pan-European governance arrangements over financial regulation (with the creation of the European

[1] See Carmen M. Reinhart and Kenneth S. Rogoff, *This Time Is Different: Eight Centuries of Financial Folly* (Princeton, NJ: Princeton University Press, 2009).

Supervisory Agencies and a range of new market regulations) and fiscal matters (with the inauguration of the European Semester process), which curtailed the power of Member States to run economic policy unilaterally, as a means of insuring against the emergence of future risks. Collectively, these changed the nature of the EU as a socio-legal construct, and opened rifts between richer and poorer Member States that – until that point – had been participating within the euro project on nominally equal terms.

The Eurozone crisis was arguably one of the tensest and most difficult periods during the entirety of the EU's existence. Given the tremendous difficulty it posed in terms of law, politics and economics, the financial crisis is an excellent demonstration of what happens to the understanding of solidarity when emergency responses are needed. This chapter is not focused on the causality of the financial crisis, or about proposing any solution for how future shocks to the financial system could be managed. Instead, the aim is simply to elucidate the place of solidarity within considerations of the crisis and within the political economy and the law of the EU more broadly.

1.2 Solidarity and the EU

The concept of solidarity has long been the subject of rigorous scholarly analysis.[2] The classical definition of solidarity is a bind of some form with other creatures within a group – often those of similar characteristics. It encompasses an abundance of meanings and an array of forms: it includes duties towards others within a similar group, notions of the group striving to achieve common aims and objectives, as well as a means of facilitating cohesion and enabling trust. Legally and sociologically, it is a complex expression, for understandings vary to the extent that expectations weighing upon the term can be diametrically opposed (for example, with different parties placing different demands upon what a 'solidaristic' response might be, particularly where interpretations of the justification for fiscal redistribution are concerned). In the context of the EU, and particularly the euro, this inherent conceptual complexity is layered upon an institutional framework that redefines the national boundaries of solidarity: as Wim Duisenberg, first President of the European Central Bank (ECB), famously declared:

[2] For one of the more recent and prominent works, see Kurt Bayertz (ed.), *Solidarity* (Dordrecht: Kluwer Academic Publishers, 1999).

'the euro is the first currency that has not only severed its link to gold, but also its link to the nation-state'.[3]

EU solidarity is therefore encoded not only within the treaty framework, but also exists outside this stringent legal sphere in popular understandings of justice and fairness. This *inside–outside* dynamic can be represented in the case of the Eurozone crisis, where the response partly took place *inside* the EU treaties, as well as *outside* the EU legal framework in the realm of politics – ultimately recasting the legal dimensions of the EU itself. Rightly or wrongly, there is the expectation that solidarity ought to play an oversized role in all Union actions and policies. This level of confidence and trust in such an elusive idea – as will be argued – is misplaced, for while solidarity has been present during the financial crisis, it has been in the form of *negative* solidarity.

Positive solidarity involves acting genuinely in the interests of the whole out a sense of duty (in the manner, for example, of an act of self-sacrifice with little immediate or potential upside, such as volunteering for military service). This is the most typically understood form of solidarity and is implicitly *unconditional*, for nothing is expected in return. There could be cause for Member States in a stronger financial position to be able to recognise another Member State's difficulty, and act in an enlightened, altruistic fashion, for the communal benefit of a stronger, collective Union. *Negative solidarity* by contrast involves acting in a way that may be superficially aligned with the interests of the whole, while being primarily and self-evidently driven by a self-interest. A Member State could provide financial or other forms of assistance to another Member State, merely because they themselves may one day require the same form of assistance from others, or because they could envisage compensatory short-term political gains from doing so. In addition, a Member State may choose to act in such a way because ultimately, in a Union where there are some forms of economic integration, that contagion of crises will occur.[4] Negative solidarity is responsive and reactionary,[5] and is much less understood.

This distinction between *positive* and *negative* solidarity is important, for when solidarity is discussed in the context of the financial crises, it is more usually understood as a manifestation of the negative form (which,

[3] Speech at Charlemagne prize ceremony, Aachen, 9 May 2002.

[4] Jean Tirole, 'Country solidarity in sovereign crises', *American Economic Review*, 105 (2015), 2354.

[5] Graham Butler, 'Solidarity and its limits for economic integration in the European Union's internal market', *Maastricht Journal of European and Comparative Law*, 25 (2018), 313.

indeed, coheres with the classic economic view of the rationally self-interested actor). In the Eurozone crisis, it will be demonstrated that Member States acted in such a manner that put negative solidarity on full display. In an EU context, this is premised on the understanding that Member States are self-interested actors.

The question of where solidarity with strangers begins and ends has been historically much contemplated in the context of the EU.[6] The basis of European integration – the 'ever closer union' – was a sense that the horrors of war could be avoided in future by making European states economically, and legally, dependent on one another.[7] It was not French Foreign Minister Robert Schuman – who famously stated in 1950 that '[Europe] . . . will be built through concrete achievements which first create a de facto solidarity' – who can claim credit for being the first to map out a vision for future integration. In fact, two years beforehand in 1948, the Belgian Prime Minister Paul-Henri Spaak had delivered a speech on the need for European solidarity.[8] Spaak invoked ideas of commonality (and the threat of communist Russia) when he stated that: 'it is necessary to practice between a certain number of countries, which have arrived at the same intellectual and moral development, which have the same legal conceptions and policies with comparable levels of civilization, above all, collaboration and solidarity'.[9] Thus, the founding intellectual principles of the EU were derived directly from expressions of commonality.

Within the European legal sphere, solidarity fulfils the function of being simultaneously a principle, a value, a concept and even an objective. It is a robust, classic principle of EU integration for some,[10] but yet fuzzy for others.[11] It is a principle that is 'operational and functional', and

[6] Suvi Sankari and Sabine Frerichs, 'From resource to burden: rescaling solidarity with strangers in the single market', *European Law Journal*, 22 (2016), 808.

[7] See, for example, Desmond Dinan, *Ever Closer Union* (Basingstoke: Palgrave, 2010)

[8] Paul-Henri Spaak, 'La nécessité d'une solidarité européenne (The need for European solidarity)', Luxembourg, 13 March 1948.

[9] 'Et dès lors, pour résister à cela et pour bâtir dans ce monde troublé quelque chose de constructif, il faut, à mon avis, et avant tout, pratiquer entre un certain nombre de pays, qui sont arrivés au même développement intellectuel et moral, qui ont les mêmes conceptions juridiques et politiques et qui ont des niveaux de civilisation comparables, il faut avant tout arriver à la collaboration et à la solidarité.'

[10] Armin Von Bogdandy, 'Founding principles', in Armin Von Bogdandy and Jürgen Bast (eds.), *Principles of European Constitutional Law*, 2nd edition (Oxford: Hart Publishing, 2009), p. 53.

[11] Andrea Ott, 'A flexible future for the European Union: the way forward or a way out?', in Steven Blockmans and Sacha Prechal (eds.), *Reconciling the Deepening and Widening of the European Union* (The Hague: TMC Asser Press, 2007), p. 153.

one used as a compass for 'value orientation'.[12] The spread of sources in which the term appears proves that the concept has enduring importance as both a driver and a tool of the law, but also a political and economic aspiration. Transnational solidarity can be viewed through three prisms – market solidarity, communitarian solidarity and aspirational solidarity[13] – all of which contribute to the cohesiveness of the EU polity as a means of governance beyond the state. But solidarity has to be balanced between 'the virtues of uniformity ... and the virtues of variation'[14] – and uniformity may be an increasingly alien concept when levels of migration into, and within, the EU have risen substantially since 1957.[15] Furthermore, differences between the levels of social capital in various European states broadly increased between 1990 and 2012.[16]

Despite the EU treaties being heavy on rhetoric of solidarity, they fail to define it, and thus its substance outcomes are intangible. Solidarity is contained in the language of the treaties to a significant degree (for example, the infamous Treaty of Rome declaration that the then-EEC served 'to lay the foundations of an ever closer union among the peoples of Europe', not least through 'a continuous and balanced expansion, an increase in stability, an accelerated raising of the standard of living and closer relations between the States belonging to it'). Within the contemporary EU treaties themselves, solidarity finds an explicit location in a number of both general and specific terms.[17] While the values in the treaties, including solidarity, may appear lofty,[18] they nonetheless do serve as a guide for which all action related to Union policies may be conducted. Explicitly, Article 4(3) Treaty on European Union (TEU), states that '[p]ursuant to the principle of sincere cooperation, the Union

[12] Jenö Czuczai, 'The principle of solidarity in the EU legal order – some practical examples after Lisbon', in Jenö Czuczai and Frederik Naert (eds.), *The EU as a Global Actor – Bridging Legal Theory and Practice: Liber Amicorum in Honour of Ricardo Gosalbo Bono* (Leiden: Brill, 2016), p. 164.

[13] See, Floris De Witte, 'Transnational solidarity and the mediation of conflicts of justice in Europe', *European Law Journal*, 18 (2012), 694.

[14] Stephen Weatherill, *Law and Values in the European Union* (Oxford: Oxford University Press, 2016), pp. 258–9.

[15] See https://ec.europa.eu/eurostat/statistics-explained/index.php/Migration_and_migrant_population_statistics.

[16] See Francesco Sarracino and Małgorzata Mikucka, 'Social capital in Europe from 1990 to 2012: trends and convergence', *Social Indicators Research*, 131 (2017), 407.

[17] TEU: Article 2, 3(3), (5), 21(1), 24(2), 24(3), 31)1), 32, and TFEU: 67(2), 78(1), 78(3), 80, 107(2)(b), 107(3)(a), 107(3)(b), 122(1), 194(1), 222.

[18] René Smits, *The European Central Bank: Institutional Aspects* (The Hague: Kluwer Law International, 1997), p. 190.

and the Member States shall, in full mutual respect, assist each other in carrying out tasks which flow from the Treaties'. This horizontal reach of the treaties could generously be read that provision of solidarity from one Member State to another is an obligation. However, given its absolute generality, it is questionable how far it could be applied specifically to cases where Member States are in financial difficulty.

To understand solidarity in the context of the financial crisis, solidarity needs to be broken down into two further categories to elucidate their fuller meaning, and how it was active during that period. To illustrate, one way is that if a Member State is facing difficulties in financing a public deficit,[19] an onus might exist upon other Member States, particularly those in the Eurozone, to come to the assistance of that Member State with its short-term difficulties, as a demonstrable means of solidarity. Viewed another way, however, that same understanding of solidarity could mean that all Member States ought to have only spent what was within their means, and being subject to strict conditionality in a debt assistance programme would be the only means that assistance would be provided. Neither vision is compatible with one another,[20] and so, when a crisis hits, the two concepts must be adjudicated, and one vision must prevail over the other. In the context of the EU, both approaches must be set within concern for the good of the whole. From an economic perspective, solidarity in the EU has been 'driven by the fear that spillovers from the distressed [Member State]'s default negatively affect the rescuer'.[21]

1.3 EMU and the Eurozone

The financial crisis in Europe made for a lethal cocktail of trauma. There has been no shortage of commentary on the pitfalls of the euro currency; its flaws; and how it *ought* to have been designed and rolled-out. However, such analysis has often shied from considering the financial crisis through a prism of a solidarity-orientated Union – and

[19] Which may exist because of profligacy and excessive spending, but may also arise due to an unexpected shortfall in receipts, or an excessive reliance on the part of the private sector on outside sources of short-term finance, which then dry up and requires public intervention. For a consideration of a classic case, see Paul Blustein, *The Chastening: Inside the Crisis That Rocked the Global Financial System and Humbled the IMF* (New York: Public Affairs, 2001).

[20] For a summary of the moral determinants of austere policies, see Mark Blyth, *Austerity* (Oxford: Oxford University Press, 2015).

[21] Tirole, 'Country solidarity in sovereign crises', p. 2354.

doing so reveals that the seeds of the Eurozone crisis were sown much earlier. The financial crisis starting in the 2007–8 period was by no means the first that the Union faced, as events of the late 1960s, during the final convulsions of Bretton Woods, bear comparison. In August 1969, in anticipation of floating exchange rates, the French government devalued the franc by 11 per cent,[22] and the same year, the German government revalued the mark by just over 9 per cent.[23] The subsequent collapse of the European 'snake in the tunnel' system of pegged exchange rates (which created closer bands of alignment within the Bretton Woods system) cemented for many European elites an idea of the benefits of fully integrated monetary policies; but while the Werner Report – which in 1970 set out a three-stage plan for monetary union – laid much of the groundwork,[24] the operationalisation of European Monetary Union (EMU) was still far off in the distance. It spoke of solidarity,[25] but for political reasons, and with other (largely economic) events consuming political attention at the time,[26] the report was not acted upon.

The Treaty of Maastricht, which committed to a three-stage process for the creation of the euro, heralded fresh ground for the newly formed EU, and was a stepping-stone for stronger economic integration when it came to the market freedoms – goods, services, workers and capital. It has been the closest the bloc has ever come to a 'constitutional moment',[27] and

[22] See Bertrand Blancheton and Christian Bordes, 'Débats monétaires autour de la dévaluation du franc de 1969', *Revue européenne des sciences sociales. European Journal of Social Sciences* (2007), 213. This had wider effects well beyond Europe. See Richard N. Cooper, *Currency Devaluation in Developing Countries* (Princeton, NJ: Princeton University Press, 1971), p. 24.

[23] Hans J. Stueck, 'The mark, a year later', *New York Times*, 25 October 1970.

[24] 'Report to the Council and the Commission on the Realisation by Stages of Economic and Monetary Union in the Community (Werner Report)' (Council of the European Union and the European Commission 1970) 16.956/II/70-F.

[25] Ibid. 'It is desirable that the *solidarity* of the member countries in the determination of their exchange parities should be supported by a reinforcement of the consultation procedures in the matter', p. 22, emphasis added; and, 'To reinforce *solidarity* within the Community in the matter of foreign exchange, the central banks are invited, from the beginning of the first stage, to restrict on an experimental basis the fluctuations of rates between Community currencies within narrower bands than those resulting from the application of the margins in force in relation to the dollar', p. 28, emphasis added.

[26] Alexander Mackenzie Stuart, *The European Communities and the Rule of Law* (London: Stevens and Sons, 1977), pp. 89–90.

[27] See Joseph H.H. Weiler, *The Constitution of Europe: 'Do the New Clothes Have an Emperor?' And Other Essays on European Integration* (Cambridge: Cambridge University Press, 1999).

brought about major institutional and structural changes more generally, which continue, to a large extent, to provide the legal framework for the Union twenty-five years on. The Treaty of Maastricht did not fully envisage what was to come – a majority of Member States becoming ever more interdependent. It was believed that monetary union would contribute towards a greater sense of overall stability of the Union, but the euro currency, stipulated by Article 3(3) TEU, accelerated the level of differentiated integration in the Union – in both conceptual and practical terms, with multi-speed integration on various levels.[28] The Eurozone itself is quite disparate in composition, and prior to the creation of the euro, was not – in so far as making such a judgment is possible[29] – an optimal currency area according to economic analyses. At the moment of the currency's creation, there were wide divergences between the fiscal positions of various Member States, with the Commission being forced to fudge the so-called 'convergence criteria' in order to allow countries such as Belgium and Italy to make the cut (the Commission argued that their debt ratios, which greatly exceeded the notional 60 per cent cut off, were on a 'sustainable downward path').[30]

Upon EMU's establishment, it was far from clear whether 'in existential crisis – the bonds of political solidarity would prove strong enough to hold the construction together' given the pathologies in the fiscal structure.[31] The design of the euro – according with an approach often called the 'monetarist' or 'coronation' position, whereby convergence prior to the creation of the single currency was emphasised[32] – did not develop terribly extensive mechanisms to encourage ongoing convergence towards a low-debt regime, beyond the Stability and Growth Pact (SGP), which made Member State debt and budget deficits a regulated matter at EU level, but provided few

[28] See, Kenneth Dyson and Martin Marcussen, 'Transverse integration in European economic governance: between unitary and differentiated integration', *Journal of European Integration*, 32 (2010), 17.

[29] See Holly Snaith, 'Narratives of optimum currency area theory and Eurozone governance', New Political Economy, 19 (2014), 183.

[30] Greece was the only country that was initially denied entry on this basis, it subsequently joined in 2001 – using fiscal data that Eurostat determined in 2014 to be false. Available at: http://ec.europa.eu/economy_finance/publications/pages/publication8013_en.pdf.

[31] Kenneth Dyson and Ivo Maes, 'Intellectuals as policy-makers', in Kenneth Dyson and Ivo Maes (eds.), *Architects of the Euro: Intellectuals in the Making of European Monetary Union* (Oxford: Oxford University Press, 2017), p. 6.

[32] See Wayne Sandholtz, 'Monetary bargains: the treaty on EMU', in Alan W. Cafruny and Glenda G. Rosenthal (eds.), *The State of the European Community, Vol. 2: The Maastricht Debates and Beyond* (Harlow: Longman, 1993).

tools for enforcement.[33] Furthermore, private debt was excluded from the target figures, which created an incentive for public debt to be masked as private debt. This meant that there would be continued national burdens of adjustment, or implicit expectations of redistribution, if convergence were to be facilitated post-EMU – and there was initially no advance institutional blueprint for how this ought to be achieved.

Similar snags were present on the monetary side of the euro's design. Monetary policy, with all the trade-offs it involves, was to be centralised in one institution, independent of Member States, in the form of the ECB, with the newly independent national central banks (NCBs) to participate via the ESCB and Eurosystem. But as observed, although it 'has become fashionable to talk about the "science" of monetary policy',[34] best practices are constantly in flux, and the legitimacy of a central bank is at least in part dependent on its public accountability.[35] The uniformity and delegation inherent in the new structure deviated from the norm dynamics of national public policy, and placed the ECB in an alternative value-laden realm where principles, values and concepts like solidarity would conjure a very different meaning. Furthermore, the structure of the single currency made it more likely that shocks would result in asymmetric adjustments. One of the intellectual founders of the optimum currency area theory argued: 'the main cost of monetary union may not derive, as we once thought, from forgoing reliance on exchange rate changes to offset expenditure-switching shocks. It may instead derive from forgoing reliance on national monetary policies to offset expenditure-changing shocks, wherever they originate and partaking instead of a monetary policy that can never be perfectly optimal for any single member.'[36] In other words: demands on solidarity among EU Member States were made more likely by the construction of the single currency.

[33] See Martin Heipertz and Amy Verdun, *Ruling Europe: The Politics of the Stability and Growth Pact* (Cambridge: Cambridge University Press, 2010).

[34] Sheri Berman and Kathleen R. McNamara 'Bank on democracy: why central banks need public oversight', *Foreign Affairs*, 78 (1999), 2.

[35] William R. White, 'Is monetary policy a science? The interaction of theory and practice over the last 50 years', Federal Reserve Bank of Dallas Globalization and Monetary Policy Institute, Working Paper No. 155 (2013).

[36] Peter Kenen, 'Five years of the ECB', LSE Centre for Economic Performance, CentrePiece, Summer (2003).

1.4 Obligations Regarding Solidarity

When the 2007–8 financial crisis hit, the EU legal framework was not fit to withstand it, for it exceeded the limits of EMU's constitutional design. The financial crisis ended up in several 'rescue operations' that came up against such limits; first, the legal limits of EU law; and second, the worth of solidarity contained within the EU legal sphere. And yet, the fact that such rescue operations were executed at all – hesitant and imperfect though they may be – demonstrated some aspect of solidarity at work.

European integration, and the advent of the Eurozone, was meant to do more. Abstractly, it was supposed to ensure that markets *between* Member States would become more intertwined through trade, and thus make national economies more interdependent than they already were.[37] Article 3(3) TEU requires the promotion of solidarity between Member States. According to one reading, this necessitated that from the outset of EMU, both EU institutions and Member States should have been taking a proactive approach to ensuring they all strive for common objectives derived under the treaties.[38] While this proposal is extreme, it demonstrates that, fundamentally, the legal structure fell short of being able to successful implement financial crisis measures.

Indeed, long before the financial crisis, the Eurozone was considered a 'solidarity compact',[39] by which there existed a potential obligation for providing financial assistance to Member States who adopted the single currency to be supported in times of need. Article 122(2) Treaty on the Functioning of the European Union (TFEU) grants Member States wide latitude to decide if the 'exceptional occurrences' threshold is met,[40] and the Court of Justice of the European Union (Court) determined long ago that failure to fulfil obligations flowing from EU law represented a Member State 'fail[ing] in the duty of solidarity' to other Member

[37] Andrew K. Rose, 'One money, one market: estimating the effect of common currencies on trade', *Economic Policy, CEPR*, 15 (2000), 7.

[38] Roland Bieber, 'The economic and monetary union', in Dennis Patterson and Anna Södersten (eds.), *A Companion to European Union Law and International Law* (Chichester: John Wiley & Sons, 2016), p. 299.

[39] Matthias J. Herdegen, 'Price stability and budgetary restraints in the economic and monetary union: the law as guardian of economic wisdom', *Common Market Law Review*, 35 (1998), 22.

[40] Alberto de Gregorio Merino, 'Legal developments in the economic and monetary union during the debt crisis: the mechanisms of financial assistance', *Common Market Law Review*, 49 (2012), 1634.

States.[41] That may have meant that Member States ought to bail out Member States in financial distress, but this is not a prevalent perspective that has been followed during the financial crisis.[42] Redistributive (which is to say positive) solidarity between Member States, especially ones who adopted the euro, gained little traction as a palliative action, because it has not been seen as a legal imperative to come to the rescue of such states. Rather, it has been voluntary, in the name of negative solidarity.

Fiscal solidarity, if it were to exist, 'would most likely encompass some sort of transfer or automatic equali[s]ation mechanism between euro members'.[43] This would have a number of consequences, and face obstacles. First, it would increase the divergence that exists between euro and non-euro Member States. Second, it would breach several legal prohibitions, to be discussed below. Third, there is little conceivable probability that Member States will ever adopt such an instrument to allow centralised decision making to use their contributed funds to bail out other Member States that have been less-than-diligent in their public finances, as the continued failure of the Commission's 'Eurobonds' idea demonstrates.

2 Navigating EMU's Legal Prohibitions

The provisions covering EMU are mostly absent of theoretical or practical applications of solidarity. It has been left out of Title VIII (Economic and Monetary Policy), in contrast to other areas of the EU treaties. Article 119(1) TFEU ensures that economic policy is the preserve of Member States, in comparison to Article 127(1) TFEU, which specifies that monetary policy is for the ECB and NCBs. The restrictions of, and potential overlap between, these two sets of competencies set the scene for conflict during the Eurozone crisis, where expectations of what actors *should* be able to do collided with what they *could* do.[44] As the financial

[41] Case C-39/72, *Commission of the European Communities v. Italian Republic*, ECLI:EU:C:1973:13, paragraph 25.

[42] [I]t cannot be inferred from the concept of solidarity that there exists a duty to provide financial assistance of the kind that is to be provided by the ESM'. View of Advocate General Kokott, Case C-370/12, *Thomas Pringle v. Government of Ireland and Others*, ECLI:EU:C:2012:675, paragraph 143.

[43] Alicia Hinarejos, *The Euro Area Crisis in Constitutional Perspective* (Oxford: Oxford University Press, 2015), p. 166.

[44] Roland Bieber, 'The allocation of economic policy competences in the European Union', in Loïc Azoulai (ed.), *The Question of Competence in the European Union* (Oxford: Oxford University Press, 2014), p. 88.

crisis told hold, Member States had to first look after domestic matters (by, for example, taking action to address risks in their domestic banking infrastructure). The spillover effects of these actions generated both short- and longer-term pressures for change (leading eventually, for example, to the creation of the Single Supervisory Mechanism (SSM)). But the most immediate need was to find solutions for those Member States that were proving to be unable to help themselves. Here, the overarching treaty framework provided little by way of firm guidance.

The legal structure of EMU provides for three key 'guiding principles', as per Article 119(3) TFEU. The first is *stable prices*; the second *sound public finances and monetary conditions*; and the third *a sustainable balance of payments. Price stability* also exists elsewhere in the treaties,[45] and in that context references to duties upon 'the Union' appear as a shared goal, underwritten by a sense of European solidarity. However, references to price stability in some ways militate against assumptions of solidarity: partially because 'the stability of the euro area as a whole – rather than euro area solidarity – is the central objective for the granting of financial assistance'[46] to a Member State; and partially because the construction of the SGP is very much predicated on the assumption that public spending is inflationary. Moreover, the treaties were framed so that troubled Member States would not be able to expect direct aid, save for 'exceptional occurrences beyond its control' (such as natural disasters) where the Council, upon a proposal by the Commission, may agree to financial assistance being provided to Member States.[47]

For all the aspirational solidarity that the EU as a legal text appears to muster, there is also the sharp edge and limits to solidarity, apparent in the EMU provisions. Indeed, so robustly structured around neo- or ordoliberal ideas of prudence was EMU, that it contained reference to four explicit prohibitions designed to prevent 'bail-outs' by EU institutions.

[45] The wording of Article 119(3) TFEU ('stable prices') conflicts with Article 3(3) TEU, Article 119(2) TFEU, Article 127(1) TFEU, Article 140(1) TFEU, Article 141(2) TFEU, Article 219(1) TFEU, Article 219(2) TFEU, and Article 282(2) TFEU, and Article 2 of Protocol (No 4) on the Statute of the European System of Central Banks and of the European Central Bank ('price stability').

[46] Gianni Lo Schiavo, 'The European stability mechanism and the European banking union: promotion of organic financial solidarity from transient self-interest solidarity in Europe?', in Andrea Biondi, Egle Dagilyte and Esin Küçük (eds.), *Solidarity in EU Law: Legal Principle in the Making* (Cheltenham: Edward Elgar, 2018), pp. 170–1.

[47] Article 122(2) TFEU. There is also a parallel with the original drafting of the SGP, which provided a get-out clause for member states unable to meet the 3 per cent budget target.

During the crisis, the construction of the Eurozone collided with Member State self-interest (negative solidarity) when it became apparent that the preventative measures that had been designed to avert the incidence of moral hazard (such as strictures on public spending) had failed, and that the consequences could sink the entire project.

2.1 *Articles 123 and 124 TFEU (No monetary financing or privileged access)*

Collectively, the four prohibitions imply nothing more than conditional solidarity, or none at all. A conservative reading would suggest that the financing of Member States was designed to be conducted solely by means of the financial markets – with a Member State to be left alone,[48] without any form of EU-led rescue package, regardless of the risk of sovereign default. The first two prohibitions cover monetary financing and access to credit. Article 123 TFEU specifies that '[o]verdraft facilities or any other type of credit facility with the European Central Bank or with the central banks of the Member States ... shall be prohibited'. Furthermore, it also prohibits overdraft facilities 'purchase[d] directly ... by the European Central Bank or national central banks of debt instruments.' This dual objective prevents the direct allocation of credit by the ECB and NCBs. It attempts to ensure that Member States are financed in the same manner as private corporations – on open markets – on the same terms and conditions as if they were any other entity, under both business as usual and crisis conditions.

Specifically, Article 123(1) TFEU prevents the ECB from intervening directly in primary sovereign bond markets. Read generously, the provision does not appear to exclude the purchase of sovereign bonds on secondary markets[49] (which is indeed how the ECB has since interpreted the provision, via the Securities Markets Programme and later Outright Monetary Transactions – on which, see below – although interestingly

[48] Stefaan Van den Bogaert and Vestert Borger, 'Differentiated integration in EMU', in Bruno De Witte, Andrea Ott and Ellen Vos (eds.), *Between Flexibility and Disintegration: The Trajectory of Differentiation in EU Law* (Cheltenham: Edward Elgar, 2017), p. 217.

[49] At the time of writing, this issue is currently being challenged before the Court. Case C-493/17, *Weiss and Others*, pending. Notably, in the Opinion of the Advocate General, he said 'I am of the opinion that the purchase of government bonds on secondary markets authorised by the PSPP does not have an effect equivalent to that of a direct purchase of that type of bond from the public authorities and bodies of the Member States'. Opinion of Advocate General Wathelet, Case C-493/17, *Weiss and Others*, ECLI:EU:C:2018:815, paragraph 84.

the ECB has not made public the denominations of the bonds it holds[50]). Next, Article 124 TFEU seeks to prohibit any measure 'establishing privileged access', which it 'not based on prudential considerations', by EU or Member State authorities to financial institutions.

2.2 *Articles 125 and 126 TFEU (No bail-outs, or excessive deficits and debts)*

Coupled with Articles 123 and 124 TFEU, are two further equally important clauses in the EU treaties – a prohibition on bail-outs, save for certain reading of its contents; and general rules on running excessive deficits and incurring debts. Given the lack of EU-level control over national budgets (with fiscal policies being a devolved competence), there was a keenness among the core Member States to ensure that some (mostly peripheral) Member States would not free-ride on the budgetary discipline of others, although any such goals have been enforced with questionable efficacy in practice.[51] Nor is fiscal policy the end of the story: core banks benefitted during the 'NICE' decade (non-inflationary continuous expansion) from their unfettered ability to invest in peripheral bubbles while being assured of implicit support from their sovereigns.[52] Nonetheless, the goal in both cases was for Member States to contribute to the good of the whole by taking responsibility for their own policies, in order to prevent any recourse to positive redistributive actions.

Article 125 TFEU is the infamous 'no bail-out' prohibition. The Article has gone unchanged since the formal establishment of EMU with the Treaty of Maastricht, and is an attempt to build a wall between national finance ministries. As put, neither the Union, nor Member States 'shall not be liable for or assume the commitments of . . . Member State[s], without prejudice to mutual financial guarantees for the joint execution of a specific project'.[53] There is an enabling provision,[54] clarifying the

[50] Christoph Trebesch and Jeromin Zettlemeyer, 'ECB interventions in distressed sovereign debt market: the case of Greek Bonds', CESifo Working Paper Series No. 4731, January 2018.

[51] Charlotte Rommerskirchen, *EU Fiscal Policy Coordination in Hard Times* (Oxford: Oxford University Press, 2019).

[52] Mark Blyth, *Austerity* (Oxford: Oxford University Press, 2015).

[53] Article 125(1) TFEU.

[54] Article 125(2) TFEU: 'The Council, on a proposal from the Commission and after consulting the European Parliament, may, as required, specify definitions for the application of the prohibitions referred to in Articles 123 and 124 and in this Article'.

rules, but in its simplest form, the clause ensures that Member States' public finances are their own respective constitutional responsibility. For some, the no bail-out provision is the most essential element accompanying the price stability principle of EMU,[55] but it also shows the true limits of any sense of European solidarity[56] by preventing any co-responsibility for national debt. Despite all the treaties' posturing on solidarity, this provision attempts to try and exclude fiscal (redistributive and positive) solidarity. Read critically, the no bail-out clause contradicts the broader principles contained in Article 3(3) TEU on solidarity,[57] as it implies that this EMU provision was a carve-out from such values (although notably it applies to 'the Union' more generally and not merely to Eurozone members). Yet a construal of this Article that emphasises the wider framing of solidarity expressed elsewhere in the treaties means that the no bail-out clause does not necessary prohibit financial assistance at all. The narrowness of the practical reach of the no bail-out clause can be seen in subsequent legal challenges, which are discussed at length below.

Next, the longest of the four prohibitions, Article 126 TFEU, seeks to ensure that Member States do not run up unsustainable deficits in their public finances, nor accrue debts that they are unable to bear. It was inserted at Maastricht as the former Article 104c, and subsequently bolstered by the SGP in 1997 (revised in 2005 and amended post-crisis by the European Semester process). Article 126(1) TFEU has language mimicking Article 119(3) TFEU,[58] but the former appears to be more stringent than the latter. Notably, the provision is addressed to Member States individually, and not the EU or the Eurozone collectively – the imposition of individual order for them to each manage their own affairs. Member States can be addressed notices for running excessive deficits,[59]

[55] Jean-Victor Louis, 'The No-bailout clause and rescue packages', *Common Market Law Review*, 47 (2010), 977.

[56] Päivi Leino and Tuomas Saarenheimo, 'Fiscal stabilisation for EMU: managing incompleteness', *European Law Review*, 43 (2018), 628.

[57] Phoebus Athanassiou, 'Of past measures and future plans for Europe's exit from the sovereign debt crisis: what is legally possible (and what is not)', *European Law Review*, 36 (2011), 562.

[58] Article 126(1) TFEU: 'Member States shall avoid excessive government deficits'. Article 119(3) TFEU: 'These activities of the Member States and the Union shall entail compliance with the following guiding principles: stable prices, sound public finances and monetary conditions and a sustainable balance of payments'.

[59] As per Article 126(9) TFEU. This has included member states who have (programme countries), and have not received financial assistance. For the former, 'L 145/6. Council Decision of 10 May 2010 Addressed to Greece with a View to Reinforcing and Deepening Fiscal Surveillance and Giving Notice to Greece to Take Measures for the Deficit

but the sanction power for the Council contained in Article 126(11) TFEU has never been exercised against Member States for not addressing such deficits (it was first abrogated by the Council in a decision against France and Germany in 2003). In addition, Article 126(10) TFEU bars any form of infringement procedure being taken by the Commission for failure to correct excessive deficits and debts.

2.3 The Prohibitions Caveat

The articles of the EU treaties cannot be looked at in isolation, but must be read alongside one another to grasp the entirety of the objectives and aims of EU primary law. Article 122(2) TFEU – on exceptional occurrences – immediately precedes the atomistic no bail-out clause from Article 125 TFEU and suggests that a strict reading is not correct. Article 122(2) TFEU has existed in various forms since the founding treaties. In the most recent iteration, an attempt to foster horizontal solidarity is made through the inclusion of the provision 'in a spirit of solidarity between Member States',[60] as if it was not implicit already.[61] This is a rare existence of positive solidarity in the law of EMU. Reading Article 122(2) TFEU and Article 125(1) TFEU together, and not in isolation, suggests that bail-outs may be permitted – but only under rare, exogenous circumstances.

Article 122(2) TFEU is a solidarity measure, even if this is not explicitly stated.[62] Yet despite the possibility that this may provide for financial assistance to struggling Member States, its remit is limited, for it allows only for assistance – temporarily – and not much more. That is despite

Reduction Judged Necessary to Remedy the Situation of Excessive Deficit (2010/320/EU)'.; and for the latter, 'L 135/19. Council Decision of 27 April 2009 on the Existence of an Excessive Deficit in France (2009/414/EC)'.

60 Article 122(1) TFEU.

61 The amendments made to the Article at the Treaty of Maastricht, read one way, implied it was linked to the understanding of solidarity from the treaties as a whole. Jörn Pipkorn, 'Legal arrangements in the Treaty of Maastricht for the effectiveness of the economic and monetary union', *Common Market Law Review*, 31 (1994), 274.

62 This reading is supported in Jean-Paul Keppenne, 'Institutional report', in Ulla Neergaard, Catherine Jacqueson and Jens Hartig Danielsen (eds.), *The XXVI FIDE Congress in Copenhagen, 2014: Congress Publications: The Economic and Monetary Union: Constitutional and Institutional Aspects of the Economic Governance within the EU*, vol. 1 (Copenhagen: Djøf Publishing, 2014), p. 185, and Article 122(2) TFEU has been overstated as a 'solidarity clause'. Dariusz Adamski, 'National power games and structural failures in the European macroeconomic governance' *Common Market Law Review*, 49 (2012), 1329.

the *Pringle* judgment on the legal basis of the European Stability Mechanism (ESM) (discussed in section 3.2 below) being absent of any form of discussion on how solidarity were to apply in the provision of financial assistance. Instead, the judgment of the Court focused on the risk to the Eurozone. *Pringle* has also been criticised for the way it reasoned, overcoming Article 125 TFEU's no bail-out clause – arguably the objection that had the strongest legal claim. As put, the Court 'through the combination of an absurdly narrow, ostensibly literal but unnatural interpretation of [Article 125] TFEU with a contestable purposive reading of the "market logic" ... ignores the disincentives and contagion risk flowing from "socialising" the debts of individual Member States through common guarantees given by all [Eurozone] governments'.[63] While this is an exaggerated claim, it is true that any attempt to engage in redistribution under the circumstances envisaged under Article 122 TFEU would have to respect some of Article 125 TFEU's basic premise.

3 The Rescue Instruments and Solidarity

Solidarity is no mere political notion, for it too is in part driven by legal impetus. When it became clear that some Member States were going to need financial assistance, it was soon decided that this would consist of the Eurozone Member States taking 'determined and coordinated action, if needed, to safeguard financial stability in *the euro area as a whole*'.[64] The key interest, therefore, was in protecting the collective security of the Eurozone as an entity, rather than in safeguarding individual members. This allowed for a means of squaring the circle of the contradictory elements of the TFEU – by working for the good of the whole, rather than bailing out individual Member States.

In 2010, the ECB launched the Securities Markets Programme (SMP),[65] which was the formal outlining of the ECB's intention, if it deemed necessary, in public and private debt markets – essentially, bond purchases (although using a sterilisation method, such that the corresponding liability to the commercial banks selling their sovereign bonds were compelled

[63] Gunnar Beck, 'The Court of Justice, legal reasoning, and the Pringle case – law as the continuation of politics by other means', *European Law Review*, 39 (2014), 239.

[64] 'Statement by the Heads of State or Government of the European Union (11 February 2010)' (European Council 2010), emphasis added.

[65] 'L 124/8. Decision of the European Central Bank of 14 May 2010 Establishing a Securities Markets Programme (ECB/2010/5) (2010/281/EU)'.

to hold fixed deposits with the ECB in exchange, in order to restrict any inflationary effect). This policy found its legitimacy in Article 127(2) TFEU, a general legal basis to allow the ECB to 'define and implement the monetary policy of the Union'. Its compliance was dependent upon a narrow construal of Article 123 TFEU's prohibition on monetary financing, which was dubious at best. The Outright Monetary Transactions (OMT) programme (Draghi's 'bazooka') replaced it in 2014, to allow for hypothetically unlimited purchases in the secondary markets of the bonds of distressed economies already subject to Troika 'programmes'. Thus, solidarity was embedded in conditionality.

3.1 *The Temporary Solutions – the EFSM and the EFSF*

One of the features of the financial crisis were the instances of the legal responses to it taking place both *inside* and *outside* the EU legal order. The European Financial Stabilisation Mechanism (EFSM) was established on the basis of Article 122(2) TFEU.[66] Given that Article 122(2) TFEU is confined to 'exceptional occurrences', it is questionable how the EFSM as a legal instrument was, in fact, legal. Based on Article 122(2) TFEU, the Regulation itself was an instrument of secondary EU law, and did not mention solidarity – and indeed came with a huge caveat. It did not include financial assistance in itself, but rather, laid the groundwork for specific financial assistance programmes when permitted by the Council, as per Article 3(2) of the Regulation,[67] thus reinforcing negative solidarity by leaving the final decision to the self-interest of Member States. Moreover, as per Article 3(3) of the Regulation, the granting of financial assistance was predicated on 're-establishing a sound economic or financial situation in the beneficiary Member State and to restoring its capacity to finance itself on the financial markets', firmly in line with the market orientation of the EMU provisions of the treaties.

In some instances, international agreements were utilised on an intergovernmental basis. Outside the EU legal framework, the European Financial Stability Facility (EFSF) was established as a special purpose vehicle (SPV) in the law of one Member State – Luxembourg. EU resources facilitated the EFSM, but the EFSF was to be ultimately financed by

[66] 'L 118/1. Council Regulation (EU) No 407/2010 of 11 May 2010 Establishing a European Financial Stabilisation Mechanism'.

[67] Article 3(2): 'Union financial assistance shall be granted by a decision adopted by the Council, acting by a qualified majority on a proposal from the Commission.'

Member State resources. The two were needed because of the budget implications of the former – for the EU's own resources. Reforms to Member States' economic policy were subject to negotiated conditionality.[68] It has been argued that the establishment of the EFSF was in violation of Article 125 TFEU,[69] taking a strict reading of 'shall not be liable for or assume the commitments' of another Member State. Given what had to be done immediately during the height of the financial crisis, the EFSM and the EFSF were seen as best placed in the absence of a longer-term solution, and without greater regard for the Union's underlying values. The EFSM and EFSF were put to use in order to assist a number of Member States.[70] Together, they were temporary rescue operations designed as dual-track facilities, and formed the early stages of what appeared to be a form of a European Monetary Fund (EMF). However, the EFSM and EFSF were only operating on borrowed time,[71] and a more sure-footed legal response would be needed.

3.2 *The Permanent Solution – the ESM*

In recognition of the fact that the EFSM and EFSF would only be interim solutions, a longer-term mechanism was sought to sustain the financial assistance to Member States that was expected to be necessary in the future. The ESM was established in September 2012. Like the EFSF, the ESM was to be established outside the EU legal framework, and upon its establishment, its authorised capital stock was over €700 billion (although with called-up capital of only €80 billion, the rest being generated via leverage),[72] putting it in a position to provide loans, purchase bonds, and recapitalise banks – all in the name of price stability.

[68] The paradox being that the Court in *Pringle* said that 'the ESM is not concerned with the coordination of the economic policies of the Member States, but rather constitutes a financing mechanism'. Case C-370/12, *Thomas Pringle v. Government of Ireland and Others*, ECLI:EU:C:2012:756, paragraph 110.

[69] Matthias Ruffert, 'The European debt crisis and European Union law', *Common Market Law Review*, 48 (2011), 1785.

[70] For example, through the EFSM, Ireland, 'L 30/34. Council Implementing Decision of 7 December 2010 on Granting Union Financial Assistance to Ireland (2011/77/EU)'; and also through the EFSM, Portugal, 'L 159/88. Council Implementing Decision of 30 May 2011 on Granting Union Financial Assistance to Portugal (2011/344/EU)'.

[71] Articles 2(11) and 11(2) of the EFSF Framework Agreement specified agreements could only be entered into up to 30 June 2013.

[72] Article 8(1) of the ESM Treaty.

The ESM, while making little explicit mention of any dimensions of solidarity,[73] was de facto a 'fiscal solidarity mechanism',[74] but only among members of the Eurozone – and it was itself created to bypass the anti-solidarity no bail-out clause of Article 125 TFEU. With Article 122(2) TFEU being designed to cover situations of a temporary nature,[75] it was decided that a new legal basis was needed.[76] Accordingly, an amendment to Article 136 TFEU was made, adding an additional paragraph. The inserted Article 136(3) TFEU specified that '[t]he Member States whose currency is the euro may establish a stability mechanism to be activated if indispensable to safeguard the stability of the euro area as a whole. The granting of any required financial assistance under the mechanism will be made subject to strict conditionality.' The negative solidarity visible here is therefore linked to the self-interest of the Eurozone 'as a whole', and not individual Member States (although their fear of the systemic consequences of a default may also have played a role).[77]

Thus, the ESM addressed the transience of the EFSM's and EFSF's legal bases, and their subsequent longer-term incompatibility with the treaties. The ESM was designed to provide loans to Member States, but does not assume a Member State's debt – an important legal distinction – so that its actions would not fall foul of the Article 125 TFEU no bail-out clause. Indeed, the treaties might appear to have flatly contradictory statements – Article 125 TFEU's no bail-out clause, and the new Article 136(3) TFEU on allowing a bail-out mechanism. This qualified form of negative solidarity sought to ensure that any claim that Article

[73] Barring a brief passing mention in the Preamble, the ESM Treaty itself and the TSCG were to be 'complementary in fostering fiscal responsibility and solidarity within the economic and monetary union'.

[74] Jean-Victor Louis, 'The EMU after the Gauweiler Judgment and the Juncker Report', *Maastricht Journal of European and Comparative Law*, 23 (2016), 68.

[75] This appears to have been confirmed by the Pringle judgment, which stated: '[a]dmittedly, Article 122(2) TFEU confers on the Union the power to grant *ad hoc* financial assistance to a Member State which is in difficulties or is seriously threatened with severe difficulties . . . [h]owever . . . Article 122(2) TFEU does not constitute an appropriate legal basis for the establishment of a [permanent] stability mechanism . . .'. Case C-370/12, *Thomas Pringle v. Government of Ireland and Others*, ECLI:EU:C:2012:756, paragraph 65.

[76] However, there have also been other arguments to suggest that Article 136(3) TFEU only has 'declaratory value'. Rainer Palmstorfer, 'To bail out or not to bail out? The current framework of financial assistance for euro area member states measured against the requirements of EU primary law', *European Law Review*, 37 (2012), 784.

[77] Jean Tirole, 'Country solidarity in sovereign crises', *American Economic Review*, 105 (2015), 2354.

136(3) TFEU significantly departs from Article 125 TFEU would not legally hold. However, problematically, the ESM was able to come into operation before the amendment to the treaties – the insertion of Article 136(3) TFEU – was completed. This is a demonstrable failure, and a challenge for the rule of law,[78] meaning that the ESM was instituted before due consideration could be given to EU principles and values.

Unsurprisingly, the ESM was subjected to legal challenge. The Court in its *Pringle* judgment managed to resolve the conundrum that was before it by reasoning that the new Article 136(3) TFEU did not actually confer any new competence upon the Union,[79] on the premise that the ESM would still remain within the control of the Eurozone Member States. Further in the Court's reasoning, it said that any financial assistance stemming from the ESM was compatible with the no bail-out clause, so long as two conditions are met. First, that such assistance is 'indispensable for the safeguarding of the financial stability of the euro area as a whole'; and, second, that the granting of such assistance would be 'subject to strict conditions'.[80] For financial assistance under the ESM to be triggered, the financial situation must be sufficiently serious as to meet the threshold that it would jeopardise financial stability. Otherwise, Article 125 TFEU's no bail-out clause prevails. The Court in *Pringle* actually read-in *financial* stability, for the term appears nowhere in the EU treaties. In effect, it confirmed that the solidaristic financial assistance provided to a Member State was prohibited, unless it put the entire Eurozone at risk.

It is often argued that solidarity in all its aspects is stronger when action to combat crisis is taken within the EU framework. As a non-Union measure upon establishment, the ESM thus lacked the character of being covered by the concepts, values and principles that were inherent in legislation that is adopted within the EU framework. The permanency of the ESM means it will later have to be incorporated into

[78] Jonathan Tomkin, 'Contradiction, circumvention and conceptual gymnastics: the impact of the adoption of the ESM treaty on the state of European democracy', in Bruno De Witte, Adrienne Héritier and Alexander H Trechsel (eds.), *The Euro Crisis and the State of European Democracy* (Fiesole: European University Institute, 2013), p. 81.

[79] Case C-370/12, *Thomas Pringle v. Government of Ireland and Others*, ECLI:EU:C:2012:756, paragraph 73.

[80] Case C-370/12, *Thomas Pringle v. Government of Ireland and Others*, ECLI:EU:C:2012:756, paragraph 136.

the EU treaties,[81] and there is an outstanding Commission proposal to incorporate it into EU law via a Regulation.[82] This will rebalance the interests of the individual states, and the collective interests of the Union as a whole. While bringing a newly renamed EMF into line with the Union and its value-laden operation, it might be questioned as to whether 'the adaptation [. . .] would be sufficient to achieve the desired improvements in the effectiveness ... of the stability mechanism'.[83]

3.3 *Ex Post Legal Challenges*

Solidarity has also come before the Court before in previous crises.[84] In the past, the Court had used colloquial language such as '[the] absence of appropriate rules . . . reveal a neglect of the principle of [Union] solidarity which is one of the foundations of the [Union].'[85] Yet the Court's language during the financial crisis case demonstrated a striking feature – it did not speak the language of solidarity. For example, when questions arose about the Memorandum of Understanding signed with Cyprus, deriving from the ESM, the Court confined itself to saying the action pursued 'corresponds to an objective of general interest pursued by the [EU], namely the objective of ensuring the stability of the banking system of the euro area as a whole'.[86] The Court has rightly refrained from passing judgment on any form of policy choice with respect to the rescue assistance programmes,[87] and instead focused on the legality of such measures. It is thus unclear whether the Court sees solidarity as a relevant principle for the financial assistance programmes.

[81] Through the EU's flexibility clause in Article 352 TFEU. See, Graham Butler, 'The EU flexibility clause is dead, long live the EU flexibility clause', in Antonina Bakardjieva Engelbrekt and Xavier Groussot (eds.), *The Future of Europe: Political and Legal Integration Beyond Brexit* (Oxford: Hart Publishing, 2019).

[82] 'Proposal for a Council Regulation on the Establishment of the European Monetary Fund (COM(2017) 827 Final 2017/0333 (APP))'.

[83] Julio Baquero Cruz, *What's Left of the Law of Integration? Decay and Resistance in European Union Law* (Oxford: Oxford University Press, 2018), p. 196.

[84] Butler, 'Solidarity and its limits for economic integration', pp. 321–3.

[85] Case C-77/77, *Benzine en Petroleum Handelsmaatschappij BV and others v. Commission of the European Communities*, ECLI:EU:C:1978:141, paragraph 15. s

[86] Joined Cases C-8/15 P to C10/15 P, *Ledra Advertising Ltd and Others v. European Commission and European Central Bank (ECB)*, ECLI:EU:C:2016:701, paragraph 71.

[87] This is prudent. On policy choices that the Court is faced with, see, Graham Butler, 'In search of the political question doctrine in EU law', *Legal Issues of Economic Integration*, 45 (2018), 329.

It would only be a matter of time, given the new intervention both inside and outside the EU legal order, that such actions would be challenged. In the light of the OMT programme that the ECB had put in place,[88] monetary policy was subjected to judicial review within the EU legal order. In the *Gauweiler* case, the Court confirmed the legality of the conditionality requirements of the rescue programmes.[89] However, there was one striking element of the Court's judgment. It said that '[the] ECB . . . is obliged to take decisions which, like open market operations, inevitably expose it to a risk of losses . . . without specifically delimiting the risks which the [ECB] may take in order to achieve the objectives of monetary policy.'[90] In short, the OMT programme was seen not to breach Article 123 TFEU's prohibition on monetary financing – thus emptying the prohibition of some of its value. In the same case, the Court had the opportunity to elaborate on what it meant by *financial* solidarity from its *Pringle* prior, but it chose not to. Thus, the *Gauweiler* judgment affirmed the legality of OMT, while the ECB was busy preparing the next stage of intervention through quantitative easing – the Public Sector Asset Purchase Programme (PSPP)[91] – whose legality is presently being challenged before the Court.[92] A colossal programme of purchases bonds of Eurozone Member States,[93] PSPP is in effect a solidarity programme, running very close to breaking the EU's prohibition on monetary financing under Article 123 TFEU, given that the ECB is in effect providing *indirect* financial assistance through government bond purchases in the secondary markets.

4 Fiscal Responsibility and Solidarity

A dichotomy exists between the idealised notion of European solidarity, and the hard reality of fiscal responsibility. Measures have been taken,

[88] Albeit provisionally, and announced by a press release on the ECB's website. See Announced in a press release by the ECB. 'Press Release: Technical Features of Outright Monetary Transactions', available at: www.ecb.europa.eu/press/pr/date/2012/html/pr120906_1.en.html.

[89] Case C-62/14, *Peter Gauweiler and Others v. Deutscher Bundestag*, ECLI:EU:C:2015:400, paragraph 60.

[90] Ibid., paragraph 125.

[91] 'L 121/20. Decision (EU) 2015/774 of the European Central Bank of 4 March 2015 on a Secondary Markets Public Sector Asset Purchase Programme (ECB/2015/10)'.

[92] At the time of writing, Case C-493/17, *Weiss and Others*, pending.

[93] Klaus Tuori, 'Has euro area monetary policy become redistribution by monetary means? "Unconventional" monetary policy as a hidden transfer mechanism', *European Law Journal*, 22 (2016), 862.

implicitly, to avoid the expectation that solidarity of any kind be provided should any fiscal need occur again. Technocracy is typically associated with the functioning and operation of EMU on a mundane day-to-day level. The technicalities of economic governance have not been a highly politically salient manner – that was, until the sovereign debt crisis struck. This put the matter of economic coordination onto the political agenda in the way it had not been previously. This in turn raised questions of the how far fiscal solidarity could be stretched, when monetary policy is essentially centralised, while economic policy is decentralised to the Member States.

With the advent of the euro, financial markets would come to see lesser risk in the holding of bonds issued by periphery Eurozone Member States. The logic behind the advantages of forming a single currency was twofold. First was the economic assumption that it would lower cross-border transaction costs by removing exchange rate friction, and therefore increase distributional efficiency and promote trade.[94] Second, there was a genuine belief that by enhancing the single market, EMU would afford average Europeans greater benefits from economic integration.[95] Yet there remain major weaknesses in the economic governance arrangements of EMU that arise from the paradox of combining centralisation with domestic autonomy (and free capital markets), and which have yet to be fully addressed two decades on.

While it is by no means an uncontroversial assessment, the finger of blame for the sovereign debt crisis is often pointed towards the Member States who suddenly found themselves with unserviceable debt–GDP ratios.[96] This is not least because the economic pathologies incumbent in the cruelly monikered 'PIGS' economies (Portugal, Italy, Greece and Spain) were largely different, and encompassed a range of problems generated by both public and private sectors.[97] However, attention at the EU level was principally focused on the question of how to resolve national debt burdens, and how to develop a narrative surrounding their emergence. The dissuasion effect of the EU treaties – attempting to ensure solid budgetary discipline by preventing opportunities for moral

[94] Robert Mundell, 'A theory of optimum currency areas', *The American Economic Review*, 51(4) (1961), 509–17.

[95] See for example the Commission's 2005 tract 'Europe on the move, Better off in Europe: How the EU's Single Market Benefits You' (DG Press and Communication, November 2005).

[96] Mark Blyth, *Austerity* (Oxford: Oxford University Press, 2015).

[97] Neil Dooley, *The European Periphery and the Eurozone Crisis: Capitalist Diversity and Europeanisation* (Abingdon: Routledge, 2018).

hazard – did not work, and new tools had to be created. Given that some national banks in the Eurozone – particularly the larger ones – are now subject to direct oversight of the ECB via the SSM and Single Resolution Mechanism (SRM), the 'doom loop' between Eurozone Member States and some of their systemically important banks has been weakened.[98] Furthermore, decision making by Member States has been curtailed, or at least its outer parameters drawn, with a stronger role for European bodies to make determinations on national budgetary matters post-crisis.

National fiscal discipline is supposed to be at the heart of EMU. Ideally, a successful EMU would contain '[w]ell-designed numerical rules ensuring discipline and flexibility, coupled with judicious multilateral surveillance and peer pressure.'[99] Strictly speaking, fiscal policy is still the responsibility of Member States post-crisis, as the EU treaties still put Member States in charge of their own agenda for meeting the targets set down,[100] but initiatives such as the European Semester, Six-Pack and Two-Pack have all provided economic governance means for the EU to more attentively monitor the budgetary adherence of Member States. Moreover, measures were also taken to encode the principle of balanced budgets into national law. The Treaty on Stability, Coordination and Governance (TSCG), otherwise known as the Fiscal Compact, signed in 2012, responded to the failure of Member States to adhere to the EU's pre-existing fiscal governance rules by doubling down. The TSCG, another measure taking place outside of the EU treaties, was designed to ensure that Member States could not circumvent balanced budget requirements – even, presumably, in the interests of supporting other Member States.[101] Solidarity is not mentioned in it substantively, and while the preamble demonstrates its ties

[98] For the SSM, 'L 287/63. Council Regulation(EU) No 1024/2013 of 15 October 2013 Conferring Specific Tasks on the European Central Bank Concerning Policies Relating to the Prudential Supervision of Credit Institutions'; and for the SRM, 'L 225/1. Regulation (EU) No 806/2014 of the European Parliament and of the Council of 15 July 2014 Establishing Uniform Rules and a Uniform Procedure for the Resolution of Credit Institutions and Certain Investment Firms in the Framework of a Single Resolution Mechanism and a Single Resolution Fund and Amending Regulation (EU) No 1093/2010'.

[99] Marco Buti and Gabriele Giudice, 'EMU fiscal rules: what can and cannot be exported', in George Kopits (ed.), *Rules-Based Fiscal Policy in Emerging Markets: Background, Analysis, and Prospects* (Basingstoke: Palgrave Macmillan, 2004), p. 107.

[100] Marco Buti and Gabriele Giudice, 'Maastricht's fiscal rules at ten: an assessment', *Journal of Common Market Studies*, 40 (2002), 844.

[101] Vaughne Miller, 'The Treaty on Stability, Coordination and Governance in the Economic and Monetary Union: political issues', House of Commons Library Research Paper 12/14, 27 March 2012.

with EU law, it is a distant link. This is notable, given that this is a treaty that is operable in non-crisis periods, and does nothing to foster any solidarity-bound ideals of the Union.

While national political bodies are designed in a democratic society to be responsive to the demands raised by their respective electorates; *independent* bodies and agencies, be they national or transnational, are more insulated from political winds and demands – a benefit often deemed particularly necessary in the case of central banks.[102] The ECB has had a critical role to play in the response to the financial crisis, with its independence secured through the EU treaties, collectively addressing interests across the entirety of the Eurozone. It was said that the ECB in its early life may not have acted so boldly, for wanting to avert any form of constitutional crises.[103] Its role has been 'efficiency-orientated' embedding 'price stability ... in an economic constitution'.[104] Owing to the ECB's independence, it has been argued that a direct obligation cannot be placed upon it to meet all of the objectives of the Union set out in the treaties.[105] Instead, the ECB's mission is more firmly tied to that of its overarching institutional aim – price stability. At the same time however, that does not mean that concepts such as solidarity are entirely removed from the ECB's vision, but rather, they can only be considered without prejudice to the ECB's treaty-defined 'primary objective ... [which] ... shall be to maintain price stability',[106] meaning the broader aims of the EU treaties fall to the wayside.

4.1 *The Potential of Solidarity in the EU*

Solidarity is not all-encompassing in EU law: regardless of whether it is a principle, value or concept, it has stated limits for its role in European integration.[107] According to one reading, it can be 'difficult to derive

[102] See, for example, J.B. Goodman, 'The politics of central bank independence', Comparative Politics, 23(3) (1991), 329–49.

[103] Paul Beaumont and Neil Walker, 'The Euro and European legal order', in Paul Beaumont and Neil Walker (eds.), *Legal Framework of the Single European Currency* (Oxford: Hart Publishing, 1999), p. 184.

[104] Philip Brentford, 'Constitutional aspects of the independence of the European Central Bank', *International and Comparative Law Quarterly*, 47 (1998), 110.

[105] Chiara Zilioli and Martin Selmayr, *The Law of the European Central Bank* (Oxford: Hart Publishing, 2001), p. 35.

[106] Article 127(1) TFEU.

[107] See Butler, 'Solidarity and its limits for economic integration'.

exact legal consequences in individual legal doctrinal issues',[108] which has a bearing on interpretations of solidarity, which must be drawn from a very small range of worked examples. The financial crisis therefore exposed what had not been practically obvious beforehand – that genuine solidarity towards other Member States was thin. Positive solidarity in the Union during the financial crisis was particularly absent. Economic and monetary union is not a transfer union: solidarity, therefore, is not an end in itself, or it is but a guide to decision-making at political and administrative levels. Furthermore, it is not a licence for any particular form of competence, and nor is it meant to provide authorisation for EU legal acts. This underlines solidarity's weakness as a legal form. As a result of the financial crisis and the ramifications of the rescue programmes that were put in place, blame was naturally apportioned to different actors. However, it should not be forgotten that it is the Member States themselves that established EMU the way they did, and thus, must bear some of the responsibility for that very design. Solidarity as a principle in the EU has to be balanced against Member States' own responsibilities,[109] and the running of excessive deficits by Member States in the early days of the SGP was not treated as seriously as it (arguably) ought to have been, particularly by the Council.[110]

Not all of the pathologies of the Eurozone crisis can be attributed exclusively to the institutional design of the euro. Insofar as the origins of the global financial crisis can be laid at the doors of the financial services sector, then the previous failures to successfully manage risk in the system were equally visible on the other side of the Atlantic.[111] Given the lack of centralisation in the fiscal space, Member States can also be held responsible for weaknesses in structural policy that may have enhanced the budgetary crises that began to emerge – and the need for focused attention at the national level undoubtedly contributed to the

[108] Kaarlo Tuori and Klaus Tuori, *The Eurozone Crisis: A Constitutional Analysis* (Cambridge: Cambridge University Press, 2014), p. 135.

[109] Alison McDonnell, 'Solidarity, flexibility, and the Euro-crisis: where do principles fit in?', in Lucia Serena Rossi and Federico Casolari (eds.), *The EU after Lisbon: Amending or Coping with the Existing Treaties?* (Heidelberg: Springer, 2014), p. 67.

[110] Albeit the institutional battleground for how financial discipline was enforced was subject to litigation. For example, Case C-27/04, *Commission of the European Communities v. Council of the European Union*, ECLI:EU:C:2004:436. See Imelda Maher, 'Economic policy coordination and the European Court: excessive deficits and ECOFIN discretion', *European Law Review*, 29 (2004), 831.

[111] See Eric A. Posner, *Last Resort: The Financial Crisis and the Future of Bailouts* (Chicago, IL: University of Chicago Press, 2018).

overall lack of political inclination towards positive solidarity. Simply put, responsibility cannot be 'offloaded' from the Member States to the EU.[112] For any future reforms or rescue packages, it will again be ultimately in the hands of the Member States through the Council and European Council to drive them forward, as the Commission and Parliament possess neither command of the policy agenda, nor the legal or policy tools (particularly in terms of the EU budget) to work autonomously.

Despite transnational solidarity being of the negative kind, there has also been evidence of bilateral positive solidarity during the financial crisis. It was not just EU solutions, as, for example, the UK, albeit not a Eurozone Member State, provided bilateral financial assistance in the form of a loan to Ireland of €3.84 billion.[113] This action was reaffirmed in *Pringle*, which the Court said 'it is apparent from the wording used in Article 125 TFEU . . . that that article is not intended to prohibit either the Union or the Member States from granting any form of financial assistance whatever to another Member State'.[114] However, bilateral solidarity could certainly not be relied upon to arrest the Eurozone crisis, and indeed the effect of this loan pales into insignificance in comparison to the activity of the European stabilisation mechanisms, or the activities of the ECB.

However, despite this rarity, solidarity between the Member States during the financial crisis was put deeply under strain. The EU has prided itself on an apparent cohesiveness, built up over decades with, for example, the evolution and growth of the Structural and Cohesion Funds (principally the ERDF and ESF), which now consume the largest part of the EU budget. However, the limits of this cohesion became apparent with the profound reluctance exhibited by the better-off economies to consider direct assistance for the lesser-off when financial crisis struck: despite the interdependence of Member States, support was not fully leveraged for those in the most distress. Greece, the most hard-hit by the economic shock, had sold a large amount of its public debt to banks in other Member States. Indeed, the first Greek bail-out programme was designed largely to recapitalise the financial system, and significant

[112] Paul Craig, 'The financial crisis, the European Union institutional order and constitutional responsibility', *Indiana Journal of Global Legal Studies*, 22 (2015), 253.

[113] Loans to Ireland Act 2010 (2010 c 41)., passed by the Houses of Parliament of the United Kingdom in December 2010.

[114] Case C-370/12, *Thomas Pringle v. Government of Ireland and Others*, ECLI:EU:C:2012:756, paragraph 130.

amounts were allocated to reimburse bondholders outside of Greece (according to a 2016 study, less than 5 per cent of the overall sums provided in the first two bail-outs landed in the Greek Treasury).[115] In order for solidarity to truly take hold in Europe, it must continue to transform. One of these renovations has to entail a denationalisation of solidarity in order for it to have real effect during future financial crisis, as it seems inevitable that EU economies will experience testing times again in future.[116]

According to one observer, the financial crisis saw a transition from negative solidarity, as demonstrated, to positive solidarity.[117] This is, as we have argued, a generous reading of past events. It is true that a deliberately broad reading of Article 122(2) TFEU was provided to allow the ESFM to be established, and an equally deliberate narrow reading of Article 125 TFEU and its no bail-out clause had been construed. If solidarity was not on offer, it would not take the most articulate lawyer to reach the opposite conclusion – that Article 122(2) TFEU was insufficient to assist Member States, and that Article 125 TFEU's no bail-out clause was absolute. Instead, pragmatism ruled. That said, the expressions of solidarity that resulted were certainly not unconditional, and issues of moral hazard were always at the fore – exemplified for example in the construction of the ESM to avoid taking on Member States' debt, and the consistent opposition to Eurobonds. Any future efforts on this score would not be unequivocally positive for solidarity across the EU as a whole, as it would deepen the distinction between Eurozone and non-Eurozone Member States, and require amendments to the treaties – involving unanimity of all Member States and national ratification procedures. This would imply that expressions of positive solidarity in this context may, in fact, take on the properties of a zero-sum game.

Nonetheless, the mechanisms that have already been put in place may pave the way for the emergence of greater institutionalised solidarity in future. The current Commission proposal to incorporate the various extra-legal mechanisms of the crisis into EU law via a Regulation may provide one means of developing such a framework.[118] It may however

[115] Jörg Rocholl and Axel Stahmer (2016), 'Where did the Greek bailout money go?', EMST White Paper No. WP-16-02.

[116] See Reinhart and Rogoff, *This Time Is Different*.

[117] See Vestert Borger, 'How the debt crisis exposes the development of solidarity in the euro area', *European Constitutional Law Review*, 9 (2013), 7.

[118] 'Proposal for a Council Regulation on the Establishment of the European Monetary Fund (COM(2017) 827 Final 2017/0333 (APP))'.

be difficult to engender further solidarity through legal arrangements: during the Eurozone crisis, a judicialisation of solidarity did not occur, despite some of the rescue programmes being challenged on the grounds of legality. Indeed, the delineation between economic policy (the domain of Member States) and monetary policy (determined at the EU level) has become more difficult to discern in the financial crisis. This is particularly so given the role that the ECB has played in intervening, and assisting with solutions when called upon.[119] It has long been predicted that the Court would eventually have to draw a distinction between economic and monetary policy,[120] in effect, drawing demarcation lines. It has yet to fully do so, and would likely be reluctant to engage in such an exercise to limit the fluidity of governance arrangements in EMU, and its ability to adapt to changing circumstances. While the judiciary have helped to shape understandings of the limits of the new financial assistance mechanisms, they have done little to decisively alter our understanding of solidarity in the EU.

4.2 *Future EU Financial Crises*

The conflict between solidarity and monetary union was well foreseen.[121] Reconciling the two is no easy feat: Member States have taken divergent political positions on whether they should indeed provide support for the rescue programmes, and where support has been agreed, it has been subject to thorough conditionality. The claim that 'crises may act as an incentive for solidarity'[122] was first made over thirty years ago, but does not appear to have been decisively proven to date. The financial crisis was a difficult affair for Europe. The way in which the financial crisis was

[119] Fabian Amtenbrink, 'General report', in Ulla Neergaard, Catherine Jacqueson and Jens Hartig Danielsen (eds.), *The XXVI FIDE Congress in Copenhagen, 2014: Congress Publications: The Economic and Monetary Union: Constitutional and Institutional Aspects of the Economic Governance within the EU*, vol. 1 (Copenhagen: Djøf Publishing, 2014), p.176.

[120] Paul Craig, 'EMU, the European Central Bank, and judicial review', in Paul Beaumont and Neil Walker (eds.), *Legal Framework of the Single European Currency* (Oxford: Hart Publishing, 1999), p. 115.

[121] Opinion of Advocate General Cruz Villalón, Case C-62/14, *Peter Gauweiler and Others v. Deutscher Bundestag*, ECLI:EU:C:2015:7, paragraph 131.

[122] Daniel J Elazar and Ilan Greilsammer, 'Federal democracy: The U.S.A. and Europe compared: a political science perspective', in Mauro Cappelletti, Monica Seccombe and Joseph HH Weiler (eds.), *Integration Through Law: Volume 1: Methods, Tools and Institutions, Book 1: A Political, Legal and Economic Overview* (Berlin: De Gruyter, 1986), p.117.

handled has been the subject of scathing critique, both academic and otherwise.[123] As put, the rescue programmes have been 'inconsistently applied', and that 'purely cosmetic moves have been taken to addressing the legality and fundamental rights issues' that arose in the course of implementing the programmes during the financial crisis.[124] Ultimately however, no Member State defaulted on major amounts of financial obligations; and nor did any Eurozone state leave the single currency. This is a testament to the strength of EMU, the willingness of its political and economic masters to do 'whatever it takes',[125] and ultimately to the limited concept of solidarity that underwrites the EU.

In legal terms, the financial crisis manifested itself within the existing primary law framework, which, as turned out, was grossly inadequate for handling the scale of the problems. Given this questionable viability,[126] non-Union instruments outside of EU law were used, and thus, were not governed by the EU's broader principles and values – such as solidarity. Nonetheless, the emergence of mechanisms such as the ESM suggests that Eurozone Member States are willing to engage in redistributive efforts in extremis, but if, and only if, their own self-interest would be threatened if intervention did not occur. This suggests that a pattern of negative solidarity is equally likely to govern future crises, although the institutionalisation of the ESM (and potentially, ESF) may pave the way for greater positive solidarity by virtue of their incorporation into the pantheon of EU law.

The solutions conjured up during the financial crisis had a number of aims in mind: for the banking crisis, ensuring that financial institutions were shored up for longer-term sustainability, and for the sovereign debt crisis, guaranteeing that the affected Member States would be in a position to return to international financial markets. Both these aims are not, per se, rooted in instincts of solidarity. Rather, they were matters of economic and political expedience. The limits to the amount of the EU's own resources (set at a maximum of 1.23 per cent of gross national income), coupled with the lack of direct taxation powers, will continue to

[123] See, Claire Kilpatrick, 'On the rule of law and economic emergency: the degradation of basic legal values in Europe's bailouts', *Oxford Journal of Legal Studies*, 35 (2015), 325.

[124] Claire Kilpatrick, 'The EU and its sovereign debt programmes: the challenges of liminal legality', *Current Legal Problems*, 70 (2017), 363.

[125] Mario Draghi, 'Verbatim of the remarks: speech by the President of the European Central Bank', Global Investment Conference, London, 26 July 2012.

[126] Fabian Amtenbrink, 'The metamorphosis of European economic and monetary union', in Damian Chalmers and Anthony Arnull (eds.), *The Oxford Handbook of European Union Law* (Oxford: Oxford University Press, 2015), p. 752.

mean that any EU contributions to rescue programmes will continue to be much more marginal that those of Member States. This generates challenges for the future of EMU,[127] as further reforms to shore up and build upon the existing mechanisms for better financial governance are uncertain.

However, while taking measures outside the EU legal order was pragmatic, it did not come without consequences. For example, the EU institution that has been historically most supportive of transnational solidarity – the European Parliament – was largely left by the wayside. So, too, were national legal and political actors. This would suggest that any future efforts to foster solidarity may be undermined by a lack of organic support from political and civil society. Indeed, during the sovereign debt crisis, it has been in national courts where the outer limit of solidarity with respect to the rescue programmes provided to other Member States has been tested. The claims they have been hearing from litigants concern the conditionality requirements, and the budgetary power held by national parliaments.[128]

It has been argued that the changes undertaken to EU law during the financial crisis provide a 'new framework of economic adjustment' to ensure compliance with conditions.[129] Any financial assistance granted to Member States under the ESM is conditional on the Member State signing the TSCG, and implementing it within its national legal order. Without such conditionality, there would have likely been greater consequences. For example, there would be a legitimate fear that recipient states would 'take excessive risks and free ride on the greater fiscal rectitude practised by others'.[130] Furthermore, it is uncertain that structural reforms to Member States in receipt of financial assistance would have been carried out if conditionality was not present.

[127] See, Federico Fabbrini, 'Taxing and spending in the Eurozone: legal and political challenges related to the adoption of the financial transaction tax', *European Law Review*, 39 (2014), 155.

[128] Christian Joerges, 'Pereat justitia, fiat mundus: what is left of the European economic constitution after the Gauweiler Litigation?', *Maastricht Journal of European and Comparative Law*, 23 (2016), 105.

[129] Federico Fabbrini, *Economic Governance in Europe: Comparative Paradoxes and Constitutional Challenges* (Oxford: Oxford University Press, 2016), p. 8.

[130] Paul Craig, 'Economic governance and the Euro crisis: constitutional architecture and constitutional implications', in Maurice Adams, Federico Fabbrini and Pierre Larouche (eds.), *The Constitutionalization of European Budgetary Constraints* (Oxford: Hart Publishing, 2014), p. 31.

There is therefore a distinction to be made between forward-looking solidarity and ad hoc emergency responses. A key feature of the Eurozone's original design was a desire to prevent free-riding and moral hazard emerging, by avoiding the institution of any guarantees to intervene in national-level fiscal crises. Although measures have been taken to address the crises that have already crystallised, the desire to avoid future-facing commitments persists. Grounding financial assistance programme too strenuously in solidarity may therefore put those financial assistance programmes, and thus the Eurozone, at risk, by compromising support. This reading would suggest that the anti-solidarity no bail-out clause remains vital for the full support of EMU across the Member States. Therefore, while a strict reading of Article 125 TFEU might have condemned the Eurozone to disaster, abrogating it entirely would likely have proven problematic in other ways. Ad hoc measures guided by notions of negative solidarity therefore provided a middle way through the crisis.

The speed of the necessary response meant that matters such as underpinning principles and values were at best given secondary consideration, and this may yet come to hamper future attempts to use the architecture that has been created. For strengthened solidarity of all kinds in the Union, the reduction of state power through intergovernmental and EU frameworks would have to be achieved – and the EU's own legal framework would need to be clarified in order to determine whether EU institutions would themselves be able to act. There is currently no such thoroughgoing appetite for change shot through all the strata of the EU polis. In consequence, the operation of financial assistance to Member States in the future is uncertain, despite the existence of model assistance programmes that have now been tested. This not least because the rescue programmes imposed constraints upon public policy choices of the recipient states, which has affected public confidence in the EU in these states.[131] The fundamental paradox of EMU – uniting centralised monetary policy with national-level fiscal controls – has yet to be resolved. The last crisis may have been largely overcome, but that is no guarantee that

[131] As recently as June 2018, only 2 per cent of Greeks polled as part of the Eurobarometer survey considered the situation of their national economy to be good. This compares to an EU average of 49 per cent and a high of 93 per cent in the Netherlands and Luxembourg. Only in Greece and the UK were a minority of citizens pessimistic about the future of the EU. See European Commission press release, 'Spring 2018 Standard Eurobarometer: one year ahead of the European elections, trust in the Union and optimism about the future is growing' (14 June 2018).

the next will be. The Eurozone crisis created no groundswell of support for European integration, or Euro-wide solidarity as would be understood by the demos.[132] While the Eurozone crisis is never far from memory, the subsequent emergence of UK withdrawal from the Union and the migrant crisis have turned attention away from fixing the Eurozone, and towards how to improve the Union as a whole as a large Member State departs. And it is these processes that are instead shoring up support for Europe-wide solutions to the issues that citizens take an interest in.

4.3 The Prevalence of Negative Solidarity

Europeans – eastern and western, north and south, young and old – have come to understand a prosperous way of life. Underpinning this has to be an architecture for EMU that works, a well-functioning financial system, and a legal system designed to ensure that the destabilisation of the achievements of integration does not come about. Demonstrations of positive solidarity during the crisis – namely, selfless and unconditional acts – appeared to materialise within the national political and fiscal systems of individual Member States, whereas European-level action, mired as it was in conditionality, was much more clearly evident of negative solidarity. The claim that solidarity in EU law is an 'indivisible, universal value' therefore holds,[133] but comes with a large qualification: that it is negative solidarity. This is perhaps unsurprising, given that there are always competing values and principles within the EU that also warrant attention and consideration (in the case of the EU, this includes the terms of Article 125 TFEU).

Moreover, it should be noted that solidarity is not present at all in classical public international law. Indeed, the rescue programmes implemented by the EU were not just a financial project of the EU's alone. It also involved the efforts to bring the relevant Member States' fiscal position back onto a sustainable footing with the assistance of the International Monetary Fund (IMF), which, unlike the EU, does not

[132] For some, for the fact that the financial crisis did not see solidarity expressed strongly means that the Euro has not met a standards test. Ashoka Mody, *EuroTragedy: A Drama in Nine Acts* (Oxford: Oxford University Press, 2018), p. 264.

[133] Ulla Neergaard, 'In search of the role of "solidarity" in primary law and the case law of the European Court of Justice', in Ulla Neergaard, Ruth Nielsen and Lynn Roseberry (eds.), *The Role of Courts in Developing a European Social Model – Theoretical and Methodological Perspectives* (Copenhagen, Djøf Publishing, 2010), p. 115.

have a have any solidarity-related reference values or principles in its founding Articles of Agreement – and indeed, severe disagreements have emerged between the IMF, the Commission and the ECB (collectively, the Troika) over the most effective means of intervening,[134] as the reference points of the institutions differ. Whereas the IMF was mandated to intervene on request, the EU had to work around contradictory legal bases that could have been read as a mandate *not* to intervene. Therefore, even hints of merely negative solidarity in the EU – a transnational and supranational context – make the EU a remarkable polity in the study of solidarity.

All the talk of solidarity in the Union by its leaders across the political spectrum do not entirely match the hard facts. While some redistributive measures were ultimately instituted, these were so heavily caveated that they can only be regarded as a marker of negative solidarity. It can be argued that there were good political and economic reasons for this – namely, the desire to avoid generating future problems of moral hazard – it remains the case that none of the events of the past decade represent anything close to what Durkheim labelled 'organic' solidarity. And so, if such solidarity is ever to be used as a basis for further integration, it must be accompanied by more robust political support. Crises come and go in vicious cycles. Whether enough has been done in the context of the post-2007–8 financial crisis was enough to thwart future similar crises is uncertain.

5 Conclusion

This chapter began by outlining three claims. First, that responses by both Member States and the EU itself to the Eurozone crisis represent instances of *negative* rather than *positive* solidarity. Second, that understanding solidarity as a legal principle of the EU involves navigating a range of potentially contradictory provisions in the EU institutions' various frameworks. Third, it has been suggested that while there have been practical demonstrations of (conditional) solidarity during the crisis, they have been explicitly set up to provide retrospective solutions rather than a future base. Whatever their legal status, as they lack any accompanying measure of public support across the EU demos, they do not provide a solid base for future redistributive action.

[134] IMF Independent Evaluation Office, 'The IMF and the Crises in Greece, Ireland and Portugal: an Evaluation by the Independent Evaluation office', 8 July 2016.

The place of solidarity within the EU legal order remains uncertain, for sometimes during the Eurozone crisis it has been referenced and served as guidance, and sometimes not. This points to the reality that solidarity is a relatively weak, and contested, concept. While solidarity continues to be a component of EU law, no politically accepted interpretation of its meaning has permeated from its legal status. What happens when the next financial crisis occurs can only be speculated upon. The old east/west divide in Europe is still present, but the north/south divergence has also grown. Common ownership of Eurozone has prevailed without any permanent established leadership – beyond perhaps the ECB. Empathy and identification towards other Europeans, states, and citizens takes time to bring about – and may come to be crucial in the future as a glue to hold the current patchwork of ad hoc institutional responses together in the event of future crises.

8

Refugee Protection as a Public Good

How to Make Responsibility-Sharing Initiatives More Effective

EIKO THIELEMANN

1 Introduction

Europe has faced strong criticism for not providing more protection for asylum seekers and refugees during the biggest forced migration crisis since the Second World War, with over 68.5 million people displaced worldwide at the end of 2017.[1] It has also been criticised for not addressing the highly unequal distribution of asylum responsibilities across EU Member States. In 2015, at the height of the Syrian crisis, the EU with its population of over 500 million people hosted roughly the same number of Syrians as Lebanon, which has a population size of 4.5 million and about half the number hosted by Turkey (population size of about 80 million). In Europe, Germany received more than one-third of all asylum applications lodged by Syrians in the EU in 2015. The focus of this article is on intra-EU responsibility-sharing as the lack of agreement on the internal sharing of responsibilities among the Member States constitutes a significant obstacle to any efforts that seek to develop collective EU policies in support of refugee-hosting countries outside Europe.

Concerns over the unequal distribution of refugee responsibilities in Europe are not new.[2] The existing literature offers three main reasons to account for the highly unequal distribution of responsibilities

[1] UNHCR (2018) Global Trends: Forced Displacement in 2017, Geneva.

[2] M. Barutciski andA. Suhrke, 'Lessons from the Kosovo Refugee Crisis: innovations in protection and burden-sharing', *Journal of Refugee Studies*, 14(2) (2001), 95–115; G. Noll, 'Prisoner's dilemma in fortress Europe: on the prospects for equitable burden-sharing in the European Union', *German Yearbook of International Law*, 40 (1997), 405–37; E. Thielemann (ed.), 'European burden-sharing and forced migration', *Journal of Refugee Studies*, 16(3) (2003), Special Issue, 225–358.

among EU Member States.[3] First, the literature points to the role of structural pull-factors, such as existing migrant networks, geographic location, historic or language ties, which have been shown to have a large influence on asylum seekers' choice of destination country. Second, there is the role of policy-related pull-factors. Countries with less restrictive immigration policy regimes are expected to be more attractive to migrants. And third, there is the effect of EU policy measures such as the Dublin Regulation,[4] which allocates responsibilities for the processing of asylum seekers and allows Member States to return applicants to the EU country deemed to be the one responsible under Dublin rules, usually the one through which they first entered the EU.

These explanations, however, do not fully account for the fact that unequal refugee responsibilities arise from countries unilaterally agreeing to voluntarily shoulder increased responsibilities (as Germany did in 2015 when it opened its borders to Syrian refugees and suspended Dublin transfers). Nor do they satisfactorily explain why European efforts to develop effective responsibility-sharing mechanisms at the EU level have remained so elusive.

This chapter seeks to address these two questions by applying the literature on public goods to the analysis of refugee protection dynamics in Europe. Earlier works that applied public goods theory to refugee protection dynamics[5] have not always been very clear on what specific dimension of refugee protection constitutes a 'public good' as many of the benefits of refugee protection to protection seekers and countries are private, rather than public, in nature. This article argues that public goods theory is likely to provide the greatest insights in the context of large-scale refugee crises, such as that triggered by the conflict in Syria. During such crises, when one observes large-scale migratory movement across borders, refugee protection

[3] T.J. Hatton, 'European asylum policy', *National Institute Economic Review*, 194(1) (2005), 106–19; T.J. Hatton, 'Asylum policy in the EU: the case for deeper integration', *CESifo Economic Studies*, 61(3–4) (2015), 605–37; E. Neumayer, 'Asylum destination choice: what makes some West European countries more attractive than others?', *European Union Politics*, 5(2) (2004), pp. 155–80; E.R. Thielemann, 'Why European policy harmonization undermines refugee burden-sharing', *European Journal of Migration and Law*, 6(3) (2004), 43–61.

[4] Regulation 604/2013/EU of 26 June 2013 (Dublin III).

[5] A. Betts, 'Public goods theory and the provision of refugee protection: the role of the joint-product model in burden-sharing theory', *Journal of Refugee Studies*, 16(3) (2003), 274–96; A. Suhrke, 'Burden-sharing during refugee emergencies: the logic of collective versus national action', *Journal of Refugee Studies*, 11(4) (1998), 396–415; E. Thielemann and T. Dewan, 'The myth of free-riding: refugee protection and implicit burden-sharing', *West European Politics*, 29(2) (2006), 351–69.

efforts produce non-excludable and indivisible benefits (public goods), largely in the form of enhanced stability and increased security. Large states are in a unique position in such a situation of mass displacement to unilaterally make a significant contribution to the provision of public goods, such as internal security, by accepting a significantly large number of asylum seekers into their territory.[6] In doing so, they can help to reduce the scale of unregulated movement and stabilise a highly volatile situation. Smaller states in turn have an incentive to free ride on the protection efforts of larger states. Insights from the public goods literature also suggest that in order to overcome such free-riding dynamics, responsibility-sharing initiatives require effective international co-operation. It will be argued that in particular in situations of mass displacement, viewing refugee responsibility-sharing through the lens of public goods theory can provide significant insights about refugee protection dynamics, in particular in the EU context. By highlighting how free-riding undermines the provision of public goods, such as EU internal security, a public goods framework helps to explain why some countries voluntarily accept higher responsibilities during large-scale refugee crises. By demonstrating the insufficiency of symbolic and non-binding co-operation efforts of the past, this chapter also points to ways in which refugee responsibility-sharing initiatives could be made more effective in the future.

The chapter will start by reviewing the literature on migration pull-factors before seeking to apply some of the principal hypotheses developed by public goods scholars to the European refugee context in relation to predictions made about the distributional dynamics in the provision of public goods. It then applies those insights to the EU policy environment in an attempt to categorise different types of responsibility-sharing initiative. The final two sections analyse the effectiveness of the various refugee responsibility-sharing initiatives that have been developed by the EU and propose some principles for future policy reform.

2 Conceptualising Responsibility-Distribution and Responsibility-Sharing Initiatives

2.1 *Why Have Responsibilities Remained Unequal?*

When trying to explain the distribution of refugee responsibilities, it is useful to start with the analysis of the various factors that influence the

[6] The reference to 'large' states is most frequently made in relation to GDP but also with regard to population size (which is strongly correlated with GDP in OECD countries).

relative attractiveness of different host states to asylum seekers and refugees. A useful distinction in the discussion of pull-factors is the distinction between structural and policy-related pull-factors.[7] Structural factors refer to factors such as geography, the economy or historic ties. Ease of access, in particular geographic proximity, between a country of origin and a country of destination can be expected to constitute an important consideration for an asylum seeker's choice of host country. Similarly, economic considerations are likely to matter. Neo-classical economic migration theory[8] expects that any choice in the selection of a particular host country a migrant might have will be influenced by considerations of income maximisation and risk minimisation. Historical ties between countries of origin and destination countries also make some countries more likely destination countries. Language ties, communication links and cultural networks can be responsible for channelling international migration to particular destination countries.[9] Moreover, the fact that migrant or refugee communities have been established in certain destination countries as a result of historic ties, will often lead to the growth of migrant networks that may foster future migration flows. Such ties can significantly reduce the costs and risks of migration, thus channelling migration flows in the direction of earlier migration flows. Once migration connections have been established, the presence of relatives, friends and/or others from the same community of origin may form a strong incentive to choose a particular destination. In contrast to structural pull-factors, policy-related pull-factors are those that relate to policy-differentials between potential host countries. States often regard asylum responsibilities as a 'zero sum' phenomenon, in which a reduction of one country's responsibility will result in increasing responsibilities for the others. This means that policymakers will try to use restrictive migration policy instruments to make sure that their country will not be seen as a 'soft touch', that is, an overly attractive destination country.

[7] E.R. Thielemann, 'The effectiveness of governments' attempts to control unwanted migration', in C.A. Parsons and T.M. Smeeding (eds.), *Immigration and the Transformation of Europe* (Cambridge: Cambridge University Press, 2006).

[8] G. Ranis and J.C.H. Fei, 'A theory of economic development', *American Economic Review*, 51(4) (1961), 533–65.

[9] D.S. Massey, J. Arango, G. Hugo, A. Kouaouci, A. Pellegrino and J.E. Taylor, 'Theories of international migration: review and appraisal', *Population and Development Review*, 19(3) (1993), 431–66, at 446–7.

However, the analysis of factors such as the ones discussed so far, is of only limited help when trying to understand why states (in particularly large, powerful ones) appear to sometimes adopt policies through which they voluntarily accept higher responsibilities. This is where the literature on collective action and public goods provides useful insights. Public goods are assumed to have the following two characteristics: (1) non-excludability: if the collective good is provided for, everyone automatically benefits (in others words, non-contributors cannot be kept from benefiting from that good), and (2) non-rivalry: if the good is available to any one person/state, it is available to others at little or no additional cost.

There are two prominent predictions that flow from this. First, the literature predicts the under-provision of public goods. Given the 'non-excludability characteristics' of public goods, that is the fact that non-providers cannot be excluded from their consumption (see below), the reasons for this under-provision are clear. As countries have an incentive to rely on positive spill-ins, they try to conceal their true preferences for the particular good in question in the hope of being able to free ride on the efforts of others. Contributions to public goods are therefore expected to be provided at inefficient or suboptimal levels. Owing to their particular characteristics, public goods lead to actions that are rational from an individual's perspective, but that can be suboptimal (or even disastrous) from a collective viewpoint.[10] The other prominent prediction of the public goods literature is about the distributional consequences of free-riding. Responsibilities are expected to be shared unevenly among states, with large countries predicted to shoulder a disproportionate share of the contribution effort (relative to size and capacity) relative to smaller states. Non-excludability leads some nations using positive externalities/spill-ins, to rely on the provision of their neighbours to satisfy their demand for public goods through free-riding.[11] Contribution decisions made by states 'are such that the "larger" nation – the one that places the higher absolute value on the alliance goodwill – bears a disproportionately large share of the common burden'.[12] This has come to be known as the so-called *exploitation hypothesis*. As larger states have potentially more to lose (in absolute terms) from the non-provision of the particular good in question and are also the ones who are in

[10] A. Rapoport and A.M. Chammah, *Prisoner's Dilemma: A Study in Conflict and Cooperation* (Ann Arbor, MI: University of Michigan Press, 1965).

[11] M. Olson and R. Zeckhauser, 'An economic theory of alliances', *Review of Economics and Statistics*, 48 (1966), 266–79, at p. 268.

[12] Olson and Zeckhauser, 'An economic theory of alliances', p. 269.

a position to unilaterally make a significant difference in its provision, they will have less of a free-riding incentive than smaller states.

Responsibility-sharing discussions that have made references to the particular challenges that the provision of public goods entail have long been prevalent in matters related to international security, defence and peacekeeping, and have also become increasingly important in areas such as climate change and refugee protection.[13] While references to the public goods concept in the discussion of refugee policy are therefore not new, much of that literature has remained somewhat vague as to what the public goods are that refugee protection efforts are expected to provide. A number of the 'goods' produced by refugee protection clearly do not fulfil the essential requirements to qualify as public goods, namely those of non-excludability and non-rivalry. Protection provided to individuals fleeing persecution is above all a private good for the individuals concerned. Similarly, the reputational benefits that accrue to states that engage in humanitarian efforts to protect refugees, also do not qualify as public goods.

There are though some examples of much more clear-cut 'public goods' produced by refugee protection, for example, the greater stability and security that states 'create' when allowing forced migrants to enter and remain in their territory. Providing protection reduces the incentives and/or necessity to engage in onward (secondary) movement for asylum seekers. It therefore limits the destabilising effects that such movements can entail. A state's refusal to protect refugees or efforts to divert refugee flows onto other countries can be expected to lead to increased instability and heightened insecurity as a result of tensions at the border, irregular onward movements and tensions with other states, which might end up being the new target countries for such migrants as a result of such restrictive policies by other states. What makes refugee protection a public good therefore, is the fact that the enhanced stability and security provided by one country's refugee protection efforts will not

[13] Betts, 'Public goods theory'; Olson and Zeckhauser, 'An economic theory of alliances'; J.R. Oneal, 'Testing the theory of collective action: NATO defence burden, 1950–84', *Journal of Conflict Resolution*, 43 (1990), 426–48; J.R. Oneal, 'The theory of collective action and burden sharing in NATO', *International Organization*, 44 (1990), 379–402; S.D. Roper and L.A. Barria, 'Burden sharing in the funding of the UNHCR: refugee protection as an impure public good', *Journal of Conflict Resolution*, 54(4) (2010), 616–37; T. Sandler, *Collective Action – Theory and Applications* (Ann Arbor, MI: University of Michigan Press, 1992); T. Sandler and D. Arce, 'Pure public goods versus commons: benefit–Cost duality', *Land Economics*, 79 (2004), 355–68; Suhrke, 'Burden-sharing during refugee emergencies'; Thielemann and Dewan, 'The myth of free-riding'.

only benefit the country that is providing such protection but such benefits will accrue to all countries in the region, no matter whether those other countries have themselves engaged in costly protection efforts or not. Stability and security benefits produced by refugee protection efforts are in this sense indivisible and non-excludable.

It would seem reasonable to expect that in low-level refugee inflow situations (with small numbers of arrivals), the stability and security implications of such flows are likely to be limited and private goods produced by refugee protection efforts are likely to shape political responses to such inflows. However, in large-scale, 'mass-influx' situations during a major refugee crisis, one would expect the stability and security dynamics induced by such flows to be much more prominent. It is in such contexts that the insights and predictions provided by public goods theories are likely to be most relevant.

2.2 *What Can Be Done to Address Unequal Responsibilities?*

When thinking about different ways to address unequal distributions of responsibilities, it is useful to distinguish between three broad types of initiative:[14] (1) harmonising laws (sharing policy); (2) resource sharing (sharing money); and (3) physical responsibility-sharing (sharing people). On top of that it is crucial, in particular if one is concerned about free-riding dynamics, to distinguish between initiatives that are voluntary or discretionary and those that are binding and automatic (see Table 8.1).

In regard to the first sharing category, it is reasonable to assume that while structural pull-factors are often beyond the reach of refugee policymakers, policies that aim at changing the incentives of potential asylum seekers when making destination choice decisions can be expected to have an influence on the distribution of responsibilities among states. Traditionally, national policymakers have engaged in regulatory competition by adopting deterrence policies in order to make sure that their country is not perceived as a soft touch. They will try to have more restrictive policies on access to their territory (for example, through restrictive visa and border-control policies), on access to protection (for example, through the restrictive interpretation about who can access the refugee determination process and be awarded protection status) and access to the labour market, healthcare and welfare system.

[14] G. Noll, *Negotiating Asylum* (The Hague: Nijhoff, 2000).

Table 8.1 *Types of responsibility-sharing mechanisms I*

		Sharing category		
		Sharing policies	Sharing resources	Sharing people
Sharing rule	**Voluntary**	Recommendations, declarations, best practice, etc.	Practical co-operation	Pledging
	Binding	Binding laws	Automatic budget transfers	Quotas

In other words, states often seek to establish more restrictive refugee policies than their neighbours in an attempt to shift responsibilities onto other states. Common rules or minimum standards can therefore help to address responsibility inequalities that are the result of policy differentials. We would, however, only expect policy harmonisation to be effective in addressing responsibility inequalities if there is a credible commitment to implementing common rules (that they are legally binding and enforceable) and to the extent that such inequalities are indeed the result of policy-related rather than structural pull-factors.

Second, in relation to the sharing of resources, financial or otherwise (personnel, hardware and so on), it is useful to distinguish between voluntary and discretionary instruments and those that constitute binding legal obligations on states and are automatic and non-discretionary.

One would expect the former to be normally less effective than the latter. If resource sharing is subject to negotiations on a case-by-case basis, we can expect delays and great uncertainty in the provision of such resources. Moreover, while resource-sharing initiatives can certainly help to address inequalities, not all costs that arise out of the unequal distribution of refugees (say political costs) can be effectively addressed by resources or financial responsibility-sharing initiatives.

The third category of responsibility-sharing initiatives (people-sharing) refers to the physical relocation of asylum seekers and refugees from one state to another. This type of responsibility-sharing addresses some of the limitations that other instruments suffer from (while also raising a set of wider ethical and political issues). If the principal concern of refugee responsibility-sharing is with the disproportionate number of protection seekers in a particular state, relocation initiatives can address such concerns head on. Again, voluntary (non-binding) distribution schemes, while less controversial, can be expected to be less effective than binding and automatic ones, such as those that are automatically triggered once a certain threshold of inequality or disproportionate responsibility is reached. Similarly, initiatives that are based on voluntary pledging of relocation places rather than based on legal quota-based commitments should also be expected to be less effective in addressing responsibility inequalities. Given the high cost implications of asylum seekers (in terms of the determination process and the potential costs of removing those from the territory who are not successful in their claim), asylum responsibility-sharing initiatives can be assumed to be more effective than those schemes that solely target the relocation of already recognised refugees.

Another useful way of categorising different types of responsibility-sharing initiative is presented in Table 8.2 which again builds on the crucial distinction between binding and non-binding measures but which also distinguishes between one-dimensional and multi-dimensional responsibility-sharing regimes.

First, there are one-dimensional responsibility-sharing regimes that aim to equalise the efforts of states on one particular contribution dimension, usually by seeking to equalise the number of asylum seekers and refugees that states have to deal with. This can be done in two ways – through voluntary pledging mechanisms or through binding rules. If states cannot agree on a binding distribution key, countries faced with high responsibilities can appeal to states with smaller responsibilities and ask them to alleviate some of their responsibility. Redistributive quotas are an example of a binding mechanism, that seeks to equalise observed imbalances or inequities in responsibilities through an agreed

Table 8.2 *Types of responsibility-sharing mechanisms II*

		Sharing dimensions	
		One-dimensional	Multi-dimensional
Sharing rule	**Voluntary**	Pledging	Implicit compensation/trade
	Binding	Quotas	Explicit compensation/trade

distribution key (which is usually based on one or several fairness principles such as responsibility, capacity, benefit or cost).

Multi-dimensional responsibility-sharing regimes are those that do not seek to equalise responsibilities or responsibilities on one particular contribution dimension alone, but instead operate across several contribution dimensions. A first type of multi-dimensional responsibility-sharing mechanisms is based on an implicit trading logic, which recognises that states can contribute to international collective goods in different ways.[15] In the refugee context, these include what might be called pro-active measures, which attempt to halt the escalation of potential refugee problems by, for instance, sending peacekeeping troops to a region in order to prevent or contain forced migration. Another set of contributions are those which can be called reactive measures. This last set of measures deal with the consequences of refugee problems once they have occurred, in particular by admitting protection seekers to a host country's territory. Another type of multi-dimensional regime is based on an explicit compensation logic. In these cases, a country's disproportionate efforts in one contribution dimension are recognised and that country gets compensated (through benefits or cost reductions) in other dimensions, for example through resources received from a financial compensation fund. In the following section, the conceptual discussion above will inform the analysis of strengths and limitations of existing and proposed EU responsibility-sharing initiatives.

3 Responding to Crises: EU Responsibility-Sharing Initiatives and Their Effectiveness

In response to concern about overall responsibilities and their unequal distribution, the EU has developed a number of policies. These measures have included restrictive visa policies for asylum-sending countries,[16] safe third country and safe third country of origin provisions;[17] measures to reduce the numbers of individuals arriving irregularly without a visa (such as carrier sanction policies); joint border-control operations

[15] Thielemann and Dewan, 'The myth of free-riding'.

[16] M. Czaika and M. Hobolth, 'Do restrictive asylum and visa policies increase irregular migration into Europe?', *European Union Politics*, 17(3) (2016), 345–65.

[17] A. Achermann and M. Gattiker, 'Safe third countries: European developments', *International Journal of Refugee Law*, 7(1) (1995), 19–38; M.T. Gil-Bazo, 'The practice of Mediterranean states in the context of the European Union's justice and home affairs external dimension. the safe third country concept revisited', *International Journal of Refugee Law*, 18(3–4) (2006), 571–600.

(through the European Border and Coast Guard Agency [FRONTEX] for example) and increasing use of return agreements (like the recent EU–Turkey agreement). At the same time, there have been some limited initiatives to channel additional resources into non-EU countries that are close to refugee producing conflicts and to relieve these countries of some of their responsibilities (for example through the work towards a greater EU-wide resettlement scheme). These initiatives notwithstanding, the EU has continued to face criticism by third countries and human rights organisations for prioritising external border control over responsibility-sharing with third countries.[18] Many observers would agree that in terms of concrete responsibility-sharing initiatives, the focus of EU polices has been on internal responsibility-sharing and solidarity initiatives to help the most affected Member States.[19] It is on these initiatives that this chapter will therefore focus in the subsequent analysis.

Following the typologies developed earlier in this chapter, this section will briefly analyse 'internal' EU responsibility-sharing initiatives across three types of responsibility-sharing: sharing policies, sharing money/ resources and sharing people. The focus will be on initiatives that have been developed in response to the refugee crises in the former Yugoslavia, Iraq, Afghanistan and particularly Syria.

3.1 Policy Harmonisation (Sharing Policy)

One way to achieve a more equitable distribution of asylum responsibilities is to take a common policy approach through the harmonisation of domestic refugee legislation, creating legally *binding* obligations aimed at preventing Member States from deflecting asylum seekers to other Member States through particularly restrictive unilateral policy measures. The EU has worked towards the convergence of Member States' laws on forced migration since the mid-1980s, a process spurred on by the adoption of the 'Dublin system'.

18 T. Gammeltoft-Hansen and J.C. Hathaway, 'Non-refoulement in a world of cooperative deterrence', *Columbia Journal of Transnational Law*, 53 (2014), 235–84; T. Spijkerboer, 'Moving migrants, states, and rights human rights and border deaths', *The Law & Ethics of Human Rights*, 7(2) (2013), 213–42.

19 Internal responsibility-sharing initiatives in the refugee context are usually based on Articles 67 and 80 of the Lisbon Treaty. According to Article 80, the policies of the Union and their implementation 'shall be governed by the principle of solidarity and fair sharing of responsibility, including its financial implications, between the Member States'.

To reduce the incentives for secondary movement, the Dublin rules make it clear that the adoption of effective common EU-wide standards on reception conditions, qualification rules, procedural rights and safeguards in the process of returning those who do not qualify for protection,[20] should be regarded as a necessary complement to the implementation of the Dublin transfer mechanism that allows Member States to return asylum seekers to the 'country of first entry' (the Member State through which the asylum seeker first entered the EU).

The Commission summarises the underlying logic of EU policy harmonisation as a responsibility-sharing instrument as follows:

> Further approximation of national asylum procedures, legal standards and reception conditions, as envisaged in creating a Common European Asylum System, is bound to reduce those secondary movements of asylum seekers which are mainly due to the diversity of applicable rules, and could thus result in a more fair [*sic*] overall distribution of asylum applications between Member States.[21]

The effectiveness of this approach has been challenged. Even the European Commission now accepts that the establishment of common asylum rules will not completely change the fact that asylum seekers will find some Member States more attractive than others for reasons that have to do with structural rather than policy-related pull-factors.[22] Policy harmonisation can only address imbalances due to differences in domestic legislation in the first place. It is well established that policy differences are only one of several determinants for a protection-seeker's choice of host country, with structural factors such as historic networks, employment opportunities, geography or a host country's reputation being at least equally, if not more, important. The Commission's trust in the equalising effect of policy harmonisation was always going to be at least partly misplaced. If structural pull-factors are indeed crucial for the scale of a country's asylum and refugee responsibilities, then policy harmonisation might actually make it more difficult to achieve a more equitable distribution of asylum seekers across the Member States, as states can no longer counterbalance particular pull-factors with their own specific policy approach. This is why policy harmonisation might in fact undermine rather than facilitate efforts to achieve

[20] Directive 2013/33/EU of 26 June 2013 (Reception recast); Directive 2011/95/EU of 13 December 2011 (Qualification recast); Directive 2013/32/EU of 26 June 2013 (Procedures recast); Directive 2008/115/EC of 16 December 2008 (Return).

[21] European Commission (2007) 'Green Paper on the Future of the Common European Asylum System', COM (2007) 301 final, Brussels, 6 June 2007.

[22] European Commission (2007:11)

more equitable responsibility-sharing.[23] In practice, however, convergence on the ground has remained limited. The United Nations High Commission for Refugees (UNHCR) notes that 'asylum legislation and practice still vary widely from country to country, and as a result, asylum seekers receive different treatment from one Dublin State to another'.[24]

There is an increasing recognition within the EU that in order to achieve greater convergence in implementation, more effective monitoring and enforcement mechanisms are needed. In response, Member States expanded the Court of Justice of the European Union's (CJEU) jurisdiction over Justice and Home Affairs (JHA) matters with the Lisbon Treaty and the Commission intensified its infringement scrutiny. Moreover, in its recent proposals to complete the reform of the Common European Asylum System of 13 July 2016,[25] the Commission proposed replacing some of the EU's principal directives with a set of new regulations, a move that is clearly aimed at limiting the discretion of Member States when implementing EU rules in this area.[26]

The renewed focus on achieving a greater convergence in the implementation of common rules was also reiterated by the Commission proposals of 4 May 2016, which aim to transform the existing European Asylum Support Office (EASO) into a fully fledged EU agency for asylum. One of the core objectives of the new agency is to ensure 'a greater convergence in the assessment of applications for international protection across the Union, strengthening the practical cooperation and information exchange between Member States and promoting Union law and operational standards regarding asylum procedures, reception conditions and protection needs'.[27] These new initiatives that strengthen the 'binding' character of EU 'policy-sharing' are a step in the right direction in terms of efforts to achieve greater policy convergence, even though some differences in policy

[23] Thielemann, 'Why European policy harmonization undermines refugee burden-sharing'.

[24] UNHCR, *Response to the European Commission's Green Paper on the Future Common European Asylum System* (Geneva: UNHCR, 2007), p. 38.

[25] European Commission (2016) 'Completing the reform of the Common European Asylum System: towards an efficient, fair and humane asylum policy', Press Release, Brussels, 13 July 2016.

[26] For a theoretical discussion see F. Franchino, 'Delegating powers in the European community', *British Journal of Political Science*, 34(2) (2004), 269–93; M. Scipioni, 'Delegation to the European Commission in EU migration policy: expertise, credibility, and efficiency', doctoral dissertation, Birkbeck, University of London, 2015.

[27] European Commission (2016) 'Towards a sustainable and fair Common European Asylum System', Press release, 4 May 2016.

outcomes will continue to exist due to the nature of the asylum determination process[28] and the variation of structural pull-factors across the Member States.[29]

3.2 EU Migration Funds (Sharing Money/Resources)

The EU has also started to introduce multi-dimensional responsibility-sharing elements in order to address existing disparities. It has done so through the payment of financial compensation to the most popular destination countries for asylum seekers. This kind of explicit financial responsibility-sharing has been taking place since the establishment of the European Refugee Fund (ERF), which was put in place to support and encourage efforts of the Member States in bearing the consequences of receiving refugees and displaced persons. Its rationale is 'to demonstrate solidarity between Member States by achieving a balance in the efforts made by those Member States'. The decision's text states as its rationale that 'it is fair to allocate [EU] resources proportionately to the burden on each Member State by reason of its efforts in receiving refugees and displaced persons'.[30] The ERF was incorporated into the new EU Asylum, Migration and Integration Fund (AMIF), which was set up for the period 2014–20 with a total budget of just over EUR 3 billion over seven years. Under the two 2016 emergency relocation schemes,[31] Italy and Greece receive funding through their AMIF national programmes to support their efforts on relocation. AMIF assistance is also provided to the Member States in that they receive a lump sum of EUR 6,000 for each person relocated from Italy and Greece. A total of 1,040 million EUR has been earmarked for the relocation of 160,000 persons.[32] Recent responses to the Syrian crisis have strengthened earlier efforts in the area of non-financial resource sharing, in particular through practical co-operation

[28] J. Ramji-Nogales, A.I. Schoenholtz and P.G. Schrag, 'Refugee roulette: disparities in asylum adjudication', *Stanford Law Review*, 60(2) (2007), 295–411.

[29] Thielemann, 'Why European policy harmonization undermines refugee burden-sharing'.

[30] Council of the European Union (2000) 'Council Decision 2000/596/EC of 28 September 2000 establishing a European Refugee Fund', OJ L 252, 6 October 2000.

[31] Council of the European Union (2015a) 'Council Decision (EU) 2015/1523 of 14 September 2015 establishing provisional measures in the area of international protection for the benefit of Italy and of Greece'; Council of the European Union (2015b) 'Council Decision (EU) 2015/1601 of 22 September 2015 establishing provisional measures in the area of international protection for the benefit of Italy and Greece'.

[32] European Commission (2016c) 'First Report on Relocation and Resettlement', COM (2016) 165 final, 16 March, at p. 7.

initiatives such as the sharing of expert personnel. The EU's 'Hotspot Approach' of 2015 is a prominent example of such initiatives and aims to assist frontline Member States such as Greece and Italy in coping with sudden dramatic increases in migrants at their external border by offering resources to help with their identification, registration, fingerprinting and security checks.[33]

However, one should not put too much trust in the effectiveness of such resource-sharing measures as they do not address one crucial issue, namely that such instruments generally have failed to provide for effective incentives that would make states with smaller asylum and refugee responsibilities accept greater responsibilities. The fact remains that despite the welcome increase in EU financial and other resources to Member States that have been most affected by large-scale inflows, EU resources remain and are likely to remain, small in comparison to domestic spending in the Member States and unlikely to provide credible incentives for those less affected to make significantly greater protection contributions on the basis of the EU resource incentives on offer. Given the limitations of policy-sharing and resource-sharing initiatives, interest in 'people-sharing' has grown significantly in recent years.

3.3 EU People-Sharing Initiatives

The idea of 'people-sharing', or the physical transfer of protection seekers from one host territory to another on the basis of a capacity-based distribution key, is perhaps the most obvious *one-dimensional* responsibility-sharing method to address disparities in refugee responsibilities. In the EU context, one of the first explicit references to such responsibility-sharing ambitions was made by EU ministers in 1992 in response to the refugee crisis in the Balkans. These deliberations led to a German Presidency Draft Council Resolution on Burden-Sharing in July 1994.[34] This proposal foresaw the legally binding sharing of refugees according to a distribution key that was based on three criteria: population size, size of Member State territory and gross domestic product. The centrepiece of the German draft foresaw the introduction of a compulsory relocation mechanism. The text of the proposal stated:

[33] European Parliament, *On the Frontline: The Hotspot Approach to Managing Migration* (Brussels: Policy Department for Citizen's Rights and Constitutional Affairs, 2016).

[34] Council of the European Union (1994) 'Draft Council Resolution on Burden-sharing in July 1994', Council Document 7773/94 ASIM 124.

> Where the numbers admitted by a Member State exceed its indicative figure . . . other Member States which have not yet reached their indicative figure . . . will accept persons from the first State.

However, this proposal did not find the necessary support in the Council. Instead, Member States developed a number of voluntary initiatives, which were based on pledging rather than binding and automatic quota-based relocation. One of those initiatives was the 2001 Council Directive on Temporary Protection in the Case of Mass Influx.[35] The Directive develops a range of non-binding mechanisms based on the principle of 'double voluntarism', which meant that the agreement of both the recipient state and the individual protection-seeker is required before individual asylum seekers can be transferred from an 'over-burdened' Member State to another. Under this instrument, Member States are expected, in the spirit of 'European solidarity', to indicate their reception capacity and to justify their offers. These pledges are to be made in public, to allow for mechanisms of peer pressure or 'naming and shaming'. However, the directive has no automatic trigger but instead needs to be explicitly launched by a decision in the Council. The instrument has never been operational and remained unused during the migration crises triggered by the Arab Spring and the ongoing Syrian crisis. Similar, non-binding, instruments were used in some pilot projects for the intra-EU relocation of refugees, such as EUREMA (EU Relocation Malta). In addition, there have been a number of small-scale ad hoc bilateral relocation projects between individual Member States, which have also been aimed at sharing refugee responsibilities among the Member States.[36] However, these initiatives have resulted in the transfer of only a few hundred individuals overall.

Consequently, the Commission promoted a new approach at the height of the Syrian crisis. In 2015, the Commission proposed a new emergency response mechanism to assist Italy and Greece,[37] which originated through the use of Article 78(3) of the Treaty on the Functioning of the European Union. A total of 40,000 persons were to be relocated from Italy and Greece to other EU Member States based on

[35] Council of the European Union (2001) 'Council Directive 2001/55/EC of 20 July 2001 on minimum standards for giving temporary protection in the event of a mass influx of displaced persons and on measures promoting a balance of efforts between Member States in receiving such persons and bearing the consequences thereof', OJ L.212/12–212/23, 7 August 2001.

[36] European Commission (2010).

[37] Council of the European Union (2015a).

a capacity-based distribution key. This scheme was extended by the September 2015 emergency relocation decision for 120,000 refugees from Greece, Hungary and Italy, following the sharp increase in border crossings in the central and eastern Mediterranean, but also on the western Balkans route.[38] While the first scheme was still based on voluntary pledges, the relocation for the second was to be done on the basis of a mandatory distribution key using objective and quantifiable criteria (40 per cent of the size of the population, 40 per cent of the GDP, 10 per cent of the average number of past asylum applications, 10 per cent of the unemployment rate). The May 2016 'Dublin+' proposal contained a permanent quota-based relocation mechanism.[39] The Dublin+ proposal envisages complementing the traditional Dublin system's rules in determining the Member States responsible for a particular asylum seeker (such as the country of first entry principle) with a corrective allocation tool (the so-called 'fairness mechanism'), which could ultimately replace the earlier proposal for a permanent relocation scheme. The proposed new mechanism automatically establishes when a country is handling a disproportionate number of asylum applications. It does this with reference to a country's size and wealth. If one country is receiving disproportionate numbers above and beyond that reference (over 150 per cent of the reference number), all further new applicants in that country will be relocated after an admissibility verification of their application, across the EU until the number of applications is back below that level. If a Member State decides not to take part in the reallocation, it will be expected to make a 'solidarity contribution' of €250,000 for each applicant for whom it would otherwise have been responsible under the fairness mechanism, to the Member State that is reallocated the person instead. When analysing newly adopted and recently proposed EU people-sharing initiatives a number of contentious issues can be identified.

First, binding new relocation initiatives adopted as a response to the Syrian crisis constitute a significant departure from earlier voluntary relocation initiatives in that they are all quota-based rather than reliant on ad hoc pledging mechanisms that have proven so ineffective in the past. While there are likely to be different views about which particular

[38] Council of the European Union (2015b).

[39] European Commission (2016d) 'Proposal for a Regulation establishing the criteria and mechanisms for determining the Member State responsible for examining an application for international protection lodged in one of the Member States by a third-country national or a stateless person (recast)'. Brussels, 4.5.2016. COM (2016) 270 final. 2016/0133 (COD) (Dublin+ Proposal).

distribution key will produce the fairest outcomes, the principle of basing responsibility on capacity is to be strongly welcomed (even though one has to question the wisdom of continuing with the highly problematic Dublin rules for the initial allocation of responsibilities). The decision to replace voluntary mechanisms with binding ones has been resisted by some Member States as shown by the attempt of some eastern European Member States to block the adoption of the September emergency relocation instrument.[40] Such opposition is also reflected in the very slow implementation record of the two emergency instruments to date.[41]

The move away from the principle of 'double voluntarism' has also been controversial from the perspective of asylum seekers who are subject to relocation. For individual protection seekers, the key issue is about whether they can refuse to relocate to a country deemed responsible under a quota-based scheme and if not, whether their preferences will be taken into account when their asylum case is allocated to a particular Member State. There are strong humanitarian reasons for preference matching to support family unification but preference matching could also be considered as being more cost effective from an integration perspective (allowing for support from established communities, facilitating labour market integration and so on). However, variations in pull-factors mean that perfect preference matching cannot be an absolute requirement in all cases as such a mechanism would undermine effective responsibility-sharing efforts. A second related issue is the question about accompanying instruments. What accompanying measures could make constraints on an individual's choice of processing country acceptable? Mandatory relocation would not only necessitate a much greater harmonisation of the ways in which Member States interpret their protection obligations with the Common European Asylum System, for instance it would require more similar outcomes for similar cases across the Member States. Moreover, free movement rights after a minimum period of legal residence should be extended to those that have been offered protection status and this should be done more quickly than after

[40] Eastern European governments had severely criticised what they regarded as a reckless unilateral decision by Germany, when it decided to open its borders to Syrian refugees, creating significant costs for transit countries in the process. Under the Slovakian Council presidency, the Slovak government tabled an alternative proposal based on the concept of 'effective solidarity', see J. Barigazzi, 'Slovakia outlines alternative migration plan', *Politico*, 16 June (2016).

[41] European Commission (2016e) Eighth report on relocation and resettlement. Communication from the Commission to the European Parliament, the European Council and the Council, Brussels, 8.12.2016 COM (2016) 791 final.

five years as currently stipulated in the EU's 'Long Term Residence Directive'.[42] Third, any distribution key mechanism would have to be complemented by financial and practical support mechanisms for countries with less developed asylum systems.

Some have suggested going one step further and have proposed increasing the efficiency of relocation by allowing for multi-dimensional quota trading among the Member States under the new system.[43] From a theoretical perspective it is easy to see how quota trading could enhance efficiency and promote 'buy-in' in the face of strong domestic opposition. However, through the de facto attaching of a price tag to a country's asylum quota, such proposals run the risk of being perceived as 'treating refugees as commodities in inter-state transactions'.[44] Even non-financial trading, such as allowing states to engage in resettlement efforts instead of contributing to the sharing of responsibilities towards asylum seekers is problematic from both a legal and a political point of view and might undermine efforts to establish more effective responsibility-sharing mechanisms for asylum seekers. Having said that, financial penalties like the 'solidarity contribution' in the Dublin+ proposal, which could also be criticised on commodification grounds, might nevertheless be necessary in order to strengthen compliance. In sum, moves towards more binding instruments, better monitoring and less discretion can be regarded as steps towards the kind of substantive co-operation that the public goods literature calls for in order to overcome collective action dilemmas. Building on this discussion of the relative strengths and limitations of different responsibility-sharing options, the final section seeks to summarise some of the wider implications for future policy development.

4 Beyond Symbolic Responsibility-Sharing? Lessons for Future Reform

While push–pull models of international migration continue to be useful when trying to explain forced migration flows, insights from the public

[42] European Parliament and Council (2011) 'Directive 2011/51/EU of 11 May 2011 amending Council Directive 2003/109/EC to extend its scope to beneficiaries of international protection', OJ L.132/1-132/4, 19 May 2011.

[43] R. Bauböck, 'Refugee protection and burden-sharing in the European Union', *JCMS*, 56 (1_ (2017), 141–56; J.F.H. Moraga and H. Rapoport, 'Tradable refugee-admission quotas and EU asylum policy', *CESifo Economic Studies*, 61(3–4) (2015), 638–72.

[44] D. Anker, J. Fitzpatrick and A. Shacknove, 'Crisis and cure: a reply to Hathaway/Neve and Schuck', *Harvard Human Rights Journal*, 11 (1998), 295.

goods literature can contribute to our understanding of the highly unequal and often highly inequitable distribution of asylum and refugee responsibilities. This chapter has sought to demonstrate that particularly in crisis situations that trigger mass border crossings of protection seekers and consequently wider security concerns, the analysis of free-riding dynamics enhances our understanding of protection dynamics and helps us to better account for disproportional contributions made by some countries like those that stemmed from policy choices made by the German government at the height of the Syrian crisis. Moreover, it has been demonstrated how the choice of particular sets of non-binding responsibility-sharing mechanisms do not live up to requirement of effective co-operation that the public goods literature calls for in order to curb free-riding dynamics. It is therefore unsurprising that EU responsibility-sharing initiatives have largely remained ineffective. From the analysis in this chapter, three key lessons can be drawn with a view to informing future policy reforms. First, while it is clear that EU Member States will always be different with regard to their structural attractiveness, the typology of responsibility-sharing mechanisms and their application to existing and proposed EU initiatives has demonstrated that more can, and should, be done to manage policy-related pull-factors and counter free-riding dynamics that are often linked to the non-implementation of commonly agreed standards and rules. Moreover, the analysis of the cornerstone of the EU's asylum system, the Dublin Regulation, with its core principle of designating the country of first entry as the responsible Member State for a particular asylum seeker, goes squarely against the type of substantive co-operation that the public goods literature calls for in order to curb free-riding incentives. Instead, the deterrence objectives of the Dublin system, aimed at discouraging irregular migrants and at strengthening the border controls of EU external border countries continue to undermine responsibility-sharing efforts and instead legitimise responsibility-shifting practices.

Second, while implicit responsibility-sharing[45] might be all that is possible in a global context that lacks the necessary institutions for the promotion of effective responsibility-sharing, Europe can be more ambitious. The EU's highly developed institutional environment is much more conducive to overcoming collective action problems and free-riding in the provision of public goods. Responsibility-sharing initiatives that involve more than one contribution dimension and which allow

[45] Thielemann and Dewan, 'The myth of free-riding'.

Member States to make choices regarding the type of contributions to certain public goods they want to make, can help efficiency and to overcome political deadlock. Financial incentives or sanctions with a quota system, for example, can help to create buy-in and help implementation. However, any system that is perceived as allowing rich states to buy themselves out, enabling them to shift non-financial responsibilities onto poorer countries might be counter-productive to a collective responsibility-sharing effort. Similarly, attempts to allow states to escape their obligations to asylum seekers, by allowing them to contribute exclusively through resettlement initiatives, should be resisted.[46]

Finally, the insights of the public goods literature suggest that the key to tackling free-riding in the provision of public goods is the need for substantive co-operation and more credible commitments, in particular with regard to effective monitoring and enforcement when it comes to the implementation of joint agreements. Developing a more effective Common European Asylum System ultimately is about accepting joint responsibilities in a spirit of European solidarity. However, it can be all too easy to agree that there is a need for solidarity while remaining vague about what kind of solidarity one is referring to. Clearly symbolic solidarity measures that so far have dominated in this area are insufficient and do not satisfy the requirement for what might be called 'substantive co-operation' that, as the public goods analysis in this chapter demonstrates, is necessary for the achievement of effective and equitable responsibility-sharing outcomes. Binding quota-based refugee responsibility-sharing initiatives and efforts to create more credible oversight over implementation through agencies, such as EASO, are a step in the right direction of increasing the credibility of EU actions in this area. If anything, the analysis in this chapter suggests that in order to address the limited effectiveness of the European asylum system, which was so evident during the Syrian crisis, Europe needs to strengthen co-operation and move beyond the mere demonstration of symbolic solidarity. Ultimately, the future development of the EU refugee protection system is a critical test of Europe's collective

[46] Any quota system would need to be embedded in a wider, comprehensive, EU protection regime that strengthens protection capacities of states and safeguards the rights of asylum seekers who are subject to relocation. While asylum seekers put forward for relocation should not have an absolute veto in this process as this would potentially undermine the original responsibility-sharing objective, their preferences should be taken into account to the greatest extent possible to minimise secondary movements and promote long-term integration.

identity,[47] its commitment to human rights and its relationship with third countries. If it fails this test, the result will entail more harm for refugees, increased tensions between Member States and the risk of undermining some of the core principles and achievements of the European integration process.

[47] A. Wendt, 'Collective identity formation and the international state', *American Political Science Review*, 88(2) (1994), 384–96.

9

The Brexit Crisis

Challenges for Cross-Border Solidarity

ALISON L. YOUNG

On 23 June 2016, the UK held a referendum on its continued membership of the European Union (EU). The outcome of that referendum is well-known. Of those who participated, 51.9 per cent voted in favour of leaving, with 48.1 per cent voting in favour of remaining in the EU. The outcome sent a shockwave through the UK and the EU, whose consequences continue to be felt. Not only does this challenge cross-border solidarity between the UK and the EU, but it has also caused further challenges to solidarity within the union between England, Wales, Scotland and Northern Ireland, particularly as Scotland and Northern Ireland both voted to remain in the EU.

This chapter will discuss the ramifications of this decision. There still remains great uncertainty as to the UK's future relationship with the EU. So much so that any text written on Brexit runs the risk of becoming obsolete almost before it is completed, let alone published. At the time of writing, the European Council had agreed to three extensions to Article 50. The last deadline was 31 January 2020. Following the outcome of the general election, held on 12 December 2019, it is extremely likely that the UK will leave the EU on that date. The Conservative government, with Boris Johnson as prime minister, has a large majority. The Queen's Speech, which sets out the legislative agenda for the government, includes a commitment to enact the European Union (Withdrawal Agreement) Bill 2019–20 in time for the 31 January deadline. At the time of writing, the Bill had completed its passage through the House of Commons and was progressing through the House of Lords. The current provisions of this Bill state that a minister of the Crown 'may not agree in the Joint Committee to an extension of the implementation period'. [1] As things stand, the implementation period will end on

[1] European Union (Withdrawal Agreement) Bill 2019–20, clause 33, inserting section 15A into the European Union (Withdrawal) Act 2018.

31 December 2020, regardless of whether the UK leaves with or without a future deal. An extension could only be agreed to by the UK if future legislation were enacted empowering a minister to agree to an extension of the implementation period.

Regardless of the UK's future position, it is impossible to deny that Brexit has posed a strong challenge to cross-border and intra-border solidarity. However, it is also hard to deny that the UK's membership of the EU will continue to have an impact on the UK's constitution and its legal and political culture. The chapter will explore these issues, first, giving an account of recent events, in order to explain how Brexit was motivated, at least in part, by concerns over cross-border solidarity. It will then evaluate the extent to which the Brexit crisis poses a threat to cross-border solidarity, focusing in particular on citizens' rights. Then the chapter will set out the extent to which some of the fruits of cross-border solidarity may continue to have influence in a post-Brexit UK. It will argue that learning lessons from EU membership may help to prevent a possible erosion to intra-border solidarity between the component nations of the UK.

1 Mapping the Brexit Crisis

It is important to recognise the political pressures in the UK that led to the holding of the Brexit referendum. Given the legal framework under which the referendum was held, it was difficult for political campaigns, legal checks, public debate or parliamentary debate to place a check on the swell of emotions and public opinion behind Brexit. This both explains the UK's current situation and the large impact of Brexit on trans-national solidarity.

From 2010 to 2015, the UK was governed by a coalition government composed of the Conservative Party and the Liberal Democrats, with David Cameron, the then leader of the Conservative Party, as the prime minister and Nick Clegg, the then leader of the Liberal Democrats, as the deputy prime minister. During the coalition government, tensions continued to rise in the Conservative Party concerning the UK's continued membership of the EU. While some factions in the Conservative Party were strongly in favour of remaining in Europe, others were deeply distrustful of the EU and wished to leave. Moreover, there was growing support for UKIP – the United Kingdom Independence Party – whose main aim was to seek the UK's independence through an exit from its membership of the EU. A lot of these concerns – valid or otherwise – stemmed from fears over immigration rights. Particularly in areas of the UK affected by adversity, there were concerns that too many immigrants from other EU countries were using scarce social services, meaning that UK citizens were unable to have access to these services.[2]

In the face of these divisions in the Conservative Party and the growing support for UKIP, the Conservative Party manifesto included a promise to hold a referendum on the UK's continued membership of the EU.[3] Following the success of the Conservative Party in the 2015 general election, David Cameron, returning as prime minister of a Conservative majority government, announced that measures would be put in place to hold the referendum on EU membership.

The referendum campaign of Vote Leave – one of the groups campaigning to leave the EU – focused predominantly on the need for Britain to remain independent and regain its sovereignty, taking back control of its borders against a perceived flood of immigrants.[4] This message of the need to leave the EU in order to control immigration was then used by more mainstream politicians – for example, Boris Johnson and Michael Gove – in their pro-leave campaigning prior to the referendum. These sentiments were also echoed in pro-leave newspapers. Those in the Remain campaign, however, focused predominantly on the economy, setting out the way in which leaving the EU would cause economic damage. The use of slogans, and the general lack of education in the UK as to how the EU works, meant that it was easy for political campaigns to focus more on emotion than reason. Despite later evidence of the Electoral Commission as to spending irregularities in some of those groups campaigning in favour of the UK leaving the EU,[5] there was no role of the Electoral Commission during the campaign to act as a fact-checker for information. The emotive campaigns and slogans of some of the campaign groups meant that normal political processes were less able to provide a range of views from which voters could discern the relevant facts and arguments. Emotion frequently replaced reason, undermining cross-border solidarity.

[2] See the manifesto of UKIP, available at: https://d3n8a8pro7vhmx.cloudfront.net/ukipdev/pages/1103/attachments/original/1429295050/UKIPManifesto2015.pdf?1429295050.

[3] See the manifesto of the Conservative Party, available at: www.conservatives.com/manifesto2015.

[4] The Why Vote Leave campaign, available at: www.voteleavetakecontrol.org/why_vote_leave.html.

[5] 'Vote Leave Fined and Referred to the Police for Breaking Electoral Law', The Electoral Commission, 17 July 2018, available at: www.electoralcommission.org.uk/i-am-a/journalist/electoral-commission-media-centre/party-and-election-finance-to-keep/vote-leave-fined-and-referred-to-the-police-for-breaking-electoral-law.

This was exacerbated by the European Union Referendum Act 2015. Crucially, in contrast to other recent referendums and referendum requirements, the 2015 Act did not create a legally enforceable obligation on the government in response to the referendum outcome.[6] The outcome of the referendum was only 'politically advisory'.[7] The high turnout for the referendum led politicians to view the referendum as almost constitutionally binding. It imposed such a high political obligation on MPs that many believed they needed to achieve the outcome of the referendum to leave the EU, even if they had voted to remain in the EU in their personal capacity as a voter in the Brexit referendum, or their constituency had voted in favour of remain. This belief was expressed in a series of motions in the House of Commons.[8] Consequently, politicians were swept up in this potential undermining of cross-border solidarity.

The European Union Referendum Act was also silent on a further point – it did not provide the prime minister, or any other minister of the Crown, with a legal power to contact the European Council, notifying it of the UK's intention to withdraw from the EU under Article 50 Treaty on European Union (TEU). This gave rise to litigation challenging whether prerogative powers could be used to trigger the UK's notification of its intention to withdraw from the EU under Article 50. The question came before the UK High Court and the Supreme Court in the *Miller* case. Both the High Court,[9] and the Supreme Court,[10] concluded that the broad prerogative power to enter into and withdraw from treaties did not extend to include a power to modify the law, remove rights or frustrate legislation. As such, legislation would be required to empower the prime minister to withdraw from the EU. However, despite focusing on purely legal arguments, the judiciary faced criticism for reaching this conclusion. The three members of the High Court in *Miller* were infamously

[6] This can be contrasted with the provisions of the Northern Ireland Act 1998, Section 1, the Local Government Act 2000, Sections 34 to 36 and the Parliamentary Voting System and Constituencies Act 2011, Section 8.

[7] *R. (Miller)* v. *Secretary of State for Exiting the European Union* [2017] UKSC 5, [2017] 2 WLR 583.

[8] See, in particular, the Opposition Day motions on 12 October 2016, Hansard HC vol 615, cols, 313–415, available at: https://hansard.parliament.uk/commons/2016-10-12/debates/F327EC64-3777-4D40-A98D-BEC2E11763A2/ParliamentaryScrutinyOfLeavingTheEU and the 7 December 2016, Hansard HC vol 618, cols 220–336 available at: https://hansard.parliament.uk/commons/2016-12-07/debates/CA09D9B2-9634-41C8-8979-8B9CD82DBB8F/TheGovernmentSPlanForBrexit.

[9] *R. (Miller)* v. *Secretary of State for Exiting the European Union* [2016] EWHC 2768 (Admin).

[10] *R. (Miller)* v. *Secretary of State for Exiting the European Union* (n 10).

pilloried as 'Enemies of the People' by the *Daily Mail* newspaper.[11] While the media were more restrained in their reaction to the decision of the Supreme Court,[12] there was still a strong feeling that as 'the people had spoken', the referendum outcome had to be implemented, further undermining any ability to challenge the outcome of the Brexit referendum and exacerbating the harm to cross-border solidarity.

Following the *Miller* decision, Parliament enacted the European Union (Notification of Withdrawal) Act 2017, section 1 of which states that '[t]he Prime Minister may notify, under Article 50(2) of the Treaty on European Union, the United Kingdom's intention to withdraw from the EU'. The legislation was introduced to the House of Commons two days after the Supreme Court's decision in *Miller*.[13] It was agreed to in the House of Commons without amendment, by 494 votes to 122.[14] Nevertheless, a political assurance was given that:

> the Government will bring forward a motion on the final agreement, to be approved by both Houses of Parliament before it is concluded. [The Government] expect and intend that this will happen before the European Parliament debates and votes on the final agreement.[15]

The Bill became law without amendment, receiving royal assent on 16 March 2017.[16] However, section 13 of the European Union (Withdrawal) Act 2018 replicates some of the failed amendments of the House of Lords and implements the political assurance given to the House of Commons. It requires a vote of the House of Commons on the Framework for the Future Relationship, as well as on the Withdrawal Agreement. There are also provisions for a neutral vote in the House of Commons, with a debate in the House of Lords to take note of this vote, should the UK be in a position where it would leave the EU without an agreement. However, these provisions fall short of

[11] C. Phipps, 'British newspapers react to judges' Brexit ruling: "enemies of the people"', *The Guardian*, 4 November 2016, available at: www.theguardian.com/politics/2016/nov/04/enemies-of-the-people-british-newspapers-react-judges-brexit-ruling.

[12] R. Greenslade, 'How the press reacted to the Article 50 verdict', *The Guardian*, 24 January 2017, available at: www.theguardian.com/politics/2017/jan/24/article-50-how-press-front-page-supreme-court-verdict.

[13] HC Deb vol 620, col. 472, 26 January 2017.

[14] HC Deb vol 621, cols 557–560, 8 February 2017.

[15] HC Deb vol 621, col. 264, 7 February 2017.

[16] https://publications.parliament.uk/pa/ld201617/minutes/170320/ldordpap.htm#minproc.

the Parliamentary approval required in the original amendment of the House of Lords.

A common theme is the extent to which the referendum outcome effectively silenced political debate. The policy decision having been taken by the British people, there was no room for further deliberation. Attempts to challenge the facts on which the referendum campaign was based faced criticism; again, undermining any ability to provide a balanced account of how the Brexit referendum could undermine cross-border solidarity, or how the UK benefitted from EU membership. Nor were governmental and political institutions able to further deliberative democracy to help mitigate this potential damaging impact.

2 Undermining Cross-Border Solidarity

The largest impact of Brexit on cross-border solidarity would occur were the UK to leave with no deal. Although revocation of Article 50 may appear to have the smallest impact on trans-national solidarity, if this were not accompanied by a large swing of public opinion behind continued EU membership, it may fail to repair the damage already done and could further exacerbate tensions between the UK and the rest of the EU. Leaving the EU under the terms of the current Withdrawal Agreement may have the least damaging impact on trans-national solidarity if the UK were to continue to remain almost equally divided between those wishing to leave and those wishing to remain in the EU.

While it would still be possible for the UK to trade with the EU if the UK were to leave with no deal, this would no longer be according to the provisions of the free movement of goods, services, capital and persons guaranteed under the provisions of EU law. It would also be possible for the EU to impose visa requirements or quotas on UK citizens travelling to the EU, and vice versa. Moreover, the UK would no longer participate in the decision-making processes of the EU. UK citizens would no longer elect Members of the European Parliament and EU nationals living in the UK would be unable to stand for and vote in local elections, the same right derived from EU law being removed from UK citizens living in other EU Member States.

Should the UK leave with no deal, the impact on cross-border solidarity would be devastating. Not only would this undermine freedom to travel, work and reside in other EU countries, damaging cultural exchange and understanding, but also the impact on trade would undermine the connections between businesses across Europe. Many manufacturers rely on components manufactured in a range of EU countries. These supply chains foster relations between companies across Europe, enabling developments through cross-border collaboration. These collaborations would be made more difficult in a post-Brexit UK were the UK to leave with no deal.

Even if, as now seems impossible given the December general election result, the UK were to unilaterally revoke Article 50, thus preserving its status as a Member State of the EU, the whole process of triggering Article 50 has, in and of itself, damaged cross-border solidarity. The Court of Justice of the European Union (CJEU) in *Wightman* required that any unilateral revocation of Article 50 must follow a democratic process.[17] But there is no requirement for this democratic process to include a referendum. Nor would a referendum be required as part of the UK constitutional requirements – at least not in terms of a legal requirement. Consequently, it would be possible for the UK to unilaterally revoke Article 50, while it is still the case that the last time the UK held a referendum on its continued membership of the EU, the majority of those who voted wished to leave the EU. This may make it difficult for the UK to rebuild relationships with its EU neighbours. These difficulties may be exacerbated by the negative media coverage of the negotiations between the EU and the UK for the purposes of Article 50 TEU. Some media coverage has persistently referred to the EU as 'bullies', regarding the aim of the EU as being to ensure that the UK gets a bad deal.[18] Moreover, were the UK to unilaterally revoke Article 50, even with a referendum, if the division between those wishing to leave and those wishing to remain in the EU were as finely balanced as it currently appears to be, concerns would still remain as to whether the UK would later seek to trigger Article 50 again were there to continue to be calls for the UK to leave the EU.

Brexit has also had repercussions for the EU beyond the UK's membership. Other Member States whose populations or even political leaders have begun to question the role of the EU have been watching Brexit closely. Were the UK to leave relatively easily, this might trigger other Member States to follow the same path. Even if the UK were to leave with no deal, were this to lead to a situation in which the UK's economy were not as adversely affected as even the current forecasts of the UK

[17] C-621/18 *Wightman* v. *Secretary of State for Exiting the European Union* [2019] 1 CMLR 973.

[18] See, for example, *The Sun*, available at: www.thesun.co.uk/news/7319766/sun-says-theresa-may-freedom-brexit/ and the *Daily Express*, available at: www.express.co.uk/news/politics/1030962/brexit-news-latest-theresa-may-EU-summit-arlene-foster-northern-ireland-border and at www.express.co.uk/news/uk/1045303/Brexit-news-UK-fishing-video-EU-bully-Brexit-punish-British-fishing-Theresa-May.

government predict,[19] then other Member States may also be tempted to trigger Article 50. The mere fact that one Member State has used Article 50 may mean that other Member States may be tempted to trigger Article 50 in order to start the process of leaving the EU. It is hard to gauge the extent to which this may occur. However, it is important to recognise this further indirect impact on cross-border solidarity.

The impact on cross-border solidarity if the UK were to leave with a Withdrawal Agreement is harder to predict. This is because the Withdrawal Agreement provides predominantly for the nature of the relationship between the UK and the EU during the transition period from EU membership towards the future relationship between the UK and the EU. This future relationship is currently set out in the Framework for a Future Relationship, a non-legally binding statement of general provisions and aspirations, rather than a detailed document setting out a clear future relationship. The only element that is set out in the Withdrawal Agreement concerns the revised protocol on Northern Ireland. Under the revised protocol, Northern Ireland will remain part of the customs territory of Great Britain. However, Northern Ireland will continue to apply EU customs rules and to apply EU VAT rules as well as following EU rules on the trade in goods. This means that tariffs will be imposed on goods moving from GB to Northern Ireland when these goods are at risk of entering the EU.[20]

The most damaging impact on cross-border solidarity stems from the impact of the Withdrawal Agreement on the UK's participation in the EU law-making process, both in terms of its institutions and of UK nationals. During the transition period, the UK will not participate in the 'nomination, appointment or election of members of the institutions, bodies, offices and agencies of the Union'[21] and also will not

[19] HM Government, 'EU Exit. Long-Term Economic Analysis. November 2018' Cm 9742, available at: https://assets.publishing.service.gov.uk/government/uploads/system/uploads/attachment_data/file/760484/28_November_EU_Exit_-_Long-term_economic_analysis__1_.pdf.

[20] Draft Agreement on the Withdrawal of the United Kingdom of Great Britain and Northern Ireland from the European Union and the European Union Atomic Agency, Revised Protocol on Ireland/Northern Ireland, available at: https://ec.europa.eu/commission/sites/beta-political/files/revised_withdrawal_agreement_including_protocol_on_ireland_and_nothern_ireland.pdf

[21] Agreement on the withdrawal of the United Kingdom of Great Britain and Northern Ireland from the European Union and the European Atomic Energy Committee, 19 October 2019, available at: https://assets.publishing.service.gov.uk/government/uploads/system/uploads/attachment_data/file/840655/Agreement on the withdrawal of the United Kingdom of Great Britain and Northern Ireland from the European Union and the European Atomic Energy Community.pdf, Article 7(1)(a).

participate in 'the decision-making and the attendance in the meetings of the institutions'.[22] Nor will the UK participate in the 'decision-making and governance of the bodies, offices and agencies of the Union'.[23] Nor can the UK attend 'meetings of the committees ... of the European Parliament and of the Council, of the Commission expert groups or of other similar entities, or in the meetings of expert groups or similar entities of bodies, offices, and agencies of the Union, unless otherwise provided in this Agreement'.[24] The Withdrawal Agreement provides for the EU to invite the UK to attend these meetings. [25] This removal of the UK from the vast majority of decision-making procedures undermines cross-border solidarity through removing opportunities for the UK to participate in decision making and law creation in the EU. This removes both an aspect of cross-border deliberation on contemporary issues, in addition to the development of solidarity in achieving common objectives.

However, this impact may be mitigated by the creation of a Joint Committee responsible for the implementation and application of the Withdrawal Agreement.[26] The Joint Committee is co-chaired by the EU and the UK, supplemented by a Secretariat consisting of an official of the European Commission and an official of the UK government.[27] Its meetings would normally alternate between Brussels and London.[28] The Joint Committee is to meet at least once a year, and can make decisions and recommendations by mutual consent,[29] as well as adopting amendments to the Withdrawal Agreement when permitted by the Withdrawal Agreement.[30] The Withdrawal Agreement also establishes specialised committees on: citizens' rights; on other separation provisions; on the issues related to the implementation of the Protocol on Ireland/Northern Ireland; on the issues related to the implementation of the Protocol relating to the Sovereign Base Areas in Cyprus; on the implementation of the Protocol on Gibraltar; and on the financial provisions.[31] Each of these specialised committees is composed of

22 Ibid, Article 7(1)(a).
23 Ibid., Article 7(1)(b).
24 Ibid., Article 7(1)(c).
25 Ibid., Article 128.
26 Ibid., Article 164.
27 Ibid., Annex VIII, Rules 1 and 2.
28 Ibid., Annex VIII, rule 4.
29 Ibid., Article 164.
30 Ibid., Article 164.
31 Ibid., Article 165.

representatives of the UK and of the EU and is under the supervision of the Joint Committee.[32] The meetings of these committees provide a means of maintaining cross-border solidarity between the UK and the EU, albeit in a more reduced manner than those found under the current EU Treaties.

The Withdrawal Agreement also provides for the settlement of disputes over its meaning and implementation in a manner which may maintain cross-border solidarity. The Withdrawal Agreement includes a principle of co-operation, requiring that the UK and the European Union 'shall at all times endeavour to agree on the interpretation and application' of the Withdrawal Agreement and 'shall make every attempt, through cooperation and consultations, to arrive at a mutually satisfactory resolution of any matter that might affect its operation'.[33] Where no mutually satisfactory resolution can be agreed within three months, the Withdrawal Agreement establishes an arbitration procedure.[34] Any arbitration panel is composed from a list of twenty-five members, ten members proposed by the EU, ten by the UK and a further five possible chairs of a panel jointly proposed by the EU and the UK. Each panel is composed of five members: two from the EU list, two from the UK list and a chair from the jointly appointed list of chairs.[35] The arbitration procedure aims to facilitate cross-border solidarity by ensuring equal participation by both the EU and the UK, as well as aiming to further cooperation, consultation and dialogue rather than more adversarial or confrontational means of dispute resolution.

The Withdrawal Agreement also preserves citizens' rights both during the implementation period and beyond. The Withdrawal Agreement preserves all citizens' rights during the implementation period, ensuring that these are also extended to family members of EU citizens as per the current requirements of EU law.[36] These provisions include the right of non-discrimination on the grounds of nationality and the provision of equal treatment. Moreover, EU nationals accrue citizens' rights during the transition period. In addition, the Member States and the UK 'shall disseminate information' about citizens' rights and obligations.[37] This protection extends to workers and

[32] Ibid., Articles 164 and 165.
[33] Ibid., Article 167.
[34] Ibid., Article 170.
[35] Ibid., Article 171.
[36] Ibid., Articles 9 to 39.
[37] Ibid., Article 37.

self-employed workers and includes the recognition of professional qualifications as well as provisions relating to frontier workers. However, a derogation is allowed with regard to entitlements to social assistance, in addition to the provision of maintenance grants or vocational training to those who have not yet acquired permanent status, save as is required for workers, the self-employed, those who retain this status or members of their families.[38]

These provisions apply beyond the end of the transition period – with citizens' rights triggered up to the end of the transition period extending for life, unless an individual loses their status under the Withdrawal Agreement.[39] Those who have acquired rights of permanent residence can lose them if they reside outside of the host state for a period exceeding five consecutive years.[40] The Withdrawal Agreement also regulates possible visa requirements that may be imposed by the UK or the EU after the end of the transition period. Where host states require family members joining EU citizens to have an entry visa after the end of the transition period, these visas 'must be issued free of charge as soon as possible, and on the basis of an accelerated procedure'.[41] All of these measures mitigate the impact of Brexit on citizens' rights, thereby mitigating the impact of Brexit on cross-border solidarity.

However, it is hard to predict how far these measures may alleviate the tensions already caused. For some who voted to leave the EU, the retention of citizens' rights in this manner may merely fuel their distrust of the EU, regarding any such long-term retention of rights as 'bullying', further undermining the relations between UK and EU nationals. This negative reaction may be exacerbated if EU nationals enter the UK in larger numbers during the transition period in order to commence their ability to obtain long-term citizens' rights. The hope is that this negative reaction will only be present in a small minority of the population and the continuance of citizens' rights in the Withdrawal Agreement, both for EU citizens in the UK and for UK citizens residing in Member States of the EU, will mitigate the impact of Brexit on cross-border solidarity through providing a means of continued cultural exchanges and relations between the UK and the EU.

[38] Ibid., Article 23(2).
[39] Ibid., Article 39.
[40] Ibid., Article 15(2).
[41] Ibid., Article 14(2).

3 The Enduring Influence of Cross-Border Solidarity from EU Membership Post Brexit

Despite the potential mitigating effects if the UK is to leave the EU under the terms of the current Withdrawal Agreement, it is hard to deny that Brexit will have a negative impact on cross-border solidarity. Nevertheless, it is equally hard to deny that the UK's membership of the EU has had an influence on the UK above and beyond the cultural exchanges between the UK and the other 27 EU Member States. We can see this influence, for example, in the way in which EU membership has had an impact on the UK's constitution. Membership of the EU, combined with other features – particularly the Human Rights Act 1998 and its incorporation of Convention rights into UK law – have led to an increasing judicialisation and constitutionalisation of the UK's legal system. Judicialisation occurs as the courts are being used more frequently as the means through which to resolve constitutional issues, with citizens of the UK being more willing to use judicial as opposed to political means to resolve these issues. Constitutionalisation occurs as the UK is beginning to develop a hierarchy between constitutional and ordinary statutes and other measures. This cultural exchange has given rise to a transformation that is being reinforced through the Brexit process and which is likely to remain post Brexit. A further change has been less fruitful. The UK's membership of the EU meant that the UK began to understand cross-border solidarity through means of multi-layered government. This was reinforced through greater devolution of power from Westminster to Scotland, Wales and Northern Ireland. However, the UK government's lack of understanding of the cultural reality of devolution has created tension between the UK's component nation states. Unless the UK is willing to build on this legacy of cross-border solidarity, the UK runs the risk of alienating its component nation states, leading to potential threats to the union.

3.1 Judicialisation

It is easy to track the progress of judicialisation of the UK constitution, triggered at least in part by the UK's membership of the EU, and experience of applying EU law in the UK. EU law requires that directly effective provisions of EU law have supremacy. To the extent that there is a conflict between UK law and directly effective EU law, EU law requires that UK courts apply the directly effective provision of EU law.[42] This is the case even if this means that UK courts should disapply UK legislation. The nature of this relationship was incorporated into UK law through the provisions of the European Communities Act 1972, in particular sections 2(1) and sections 2(4). However, the true nature of this relationship, and in particular the ability to grant an injunction to suspend the application of UK legislation, or to disapply UK legislation, was developed in a series of pivotal UK cases. It was not until the series of cases in the *Factortame* litigation, particularly *Factortame II*, that it became clear that UK courts could grant an injunction to suspend the application of UK legislation to Spanish fishermen to the extent that this contradicted their directly effective rights in EU law.[43] Moreover, it was not until a recent series of cases concerning the application of EU human rights, particularly the EU's Charter of Fundamental Rights and Freedoms, that UK courts developed the ability to disapply legislation. The first Supreme Court case in which legislation was disapplied was *Benkharbouche*, in which the Supreme Court disapplied provisions of the State Immunity Act 1978 to the extent that they contradicted Article 47 of the Charter through denying Ms Benkharbouche her ability to protect rights under EU law before UK courts.[44]

Of particular importance is the decision of the High Court in *Thoburn*.[45] Laws LJ concluded that the reason that the UK courts had been able to suspend the application of legislation in *Factortame* was not because of principles of EU law, but because of a development of the common law. The common law determined the content of parliamentary sovereignty and, as such, the courts were able to modify its content. This recognition elevates the role of the judiciary. According to Laws LJ, if, and to the extent that, courts recognise and protect the sovereignty of Parliament it is because this is a principle of the common law. As such, courts, through their control of the common law, play a larger role in the constitution than was previously believed to be the case. This recognition of the role of the court suggests that courts are not subservient to Parliament; rather Parliament itself is governed by principles of the common law as established by the courts.

[42] C-6/64 *Costa* v. *ENEL* [1964] ECR 595 and C-106/77 *Amministrazione delle Finanze dello Stato* v. *Simmenthal SpA* [1978] ECR 629.

[43] *R. (Factortame Ltd)* v. *Secretary of State for Transport* [1990] 2 AC 85.

[44] *Benkharbouche* v. *Secretary of State for Foreign and Commonwealth Affairs* [2017] UKSC 62, [2017] 3 WLR 957.

[45] *Thoburn* v. *Sunderland City Council* [2002] EWHC 195 (Admin), [2003] QB 151 and *H* v. *Lord Advocate* [2012] UKSC 24, [2013] 1 AC 413.

This judicialisation of the constitution has been evident through the Brexit process, which has seen a series of cases challenging Brexit. Two notable cases will suffice to illustrate this trend. The first is the pivotal case of *Miller*, mentioned above.[46] What is important is the way in which this case came before the court. Normally, judicial review challenges occur in response to a particular decision or action of an administrative body. Here, however, the challenge was brought in response to the government's statement of its intention to use the prerogative to trigger Article 50. This statement was in response to statements of claim sent to the government by the litigants in *Miller*.[47] Challenges to draft decisions, or statements of government policy had been made before *Miller*.[48] However, *Miller* started a trend for initiating judicial review claims in relation to Brexit, not all of them successful. In addition, the approach of both the High Court and the Supreme Court in *Miller* was much more 'constitutional' in nature; focusing on broader themes, developing new constitutional principles and thinking more in terms of 'top-down' as opposed to 'bottom-up' reasoning.[49]

The second example is *Wightman*, before the Scottish courts.[50] *Wightman* also did not involve a challenge to a decision of the UK government or any other public body. Andy Wightman, a Member of the Scottish Parliament, and others brought an action requesting the Scottish courts to make a preliminary reference to the CJEU under Article 267 Treaty on the Functioning of the European Union (TFEU) to determine whether the UK could unilaterally revoke Article 50. Difficulties arose given that, the government had not taken a decision to revoke Article 50. Moreover, the government had made it clear that it had no plans to revoke Article 50. Consequently, the issue of whether this was legally possible was moot. The Outer House originally concluded that the issue was hypothetical, given that revocation of the Article 50 notification would require a change in governmental policy and a change in political will; neither of which looked likely to happen in

[46] *R. (Miller)* v. *Secretary of State for Exiting the European Union* (n 10).

[47] M. Elliott, J. Williams and A.L. Young, 'The Miller tale: an introduction', in M. Elliott, J. Williams and A.L. Young (eds.), *The UK Constitution after Miller: Brexit and Beyond* (Oxford: Hart Publishing, 2018).

[48] *R. (Public Law Project)* v. *Lord Chancellor* [2016] UKSC 39, [2016] AC 1531.

[49] A.L. Young, '*Miller* and the future of constitutional adjudication', in Elliott, Williams and Young, *The UK Constitution after Miller*.

[50] *Andy Wightman MSP* v. *The Advocate General* [2018] CSIH 18, 2018 SLT 356, [2018] CSOH 61, and *Andy Wightman MSP* v. *Secretary of State for Exiting the European Union* [2018] CSIH 62.

the near future. Nevertheless, following an appeal to the Inner House, permission was confirmed and a reference was sent to the Court of Justice of the European Union. The different outcome was influenced by two factors. First, Wightman and others had now been joined by members of the Westminster Parliament. Second, section 13 of the European Union (Withdrawal) Act 2018 had come into force. This section, inter alia, provides the criteria for the ratification of the Withdrawal Agreement establishing the terms of the UK's withdrawal from the EU. It includes the approval of the Withdrawal Agreement and the Political Statement on the Framework for the Future Relationship by a resolution of the House of Commons.[51] Information as to whether it was legally possible for the UK to unilaterally revoke Article 50 and to remain a member of the EU would be relevant to MPs when exercising their right to vote. As such, the court concluded that a reference could be made.[52]

Again, what is interesting about these decisions is the extent to which UK courts are being asked to determine key constitutional issues. Individuals and MPs are turning to the courts as opposed to political mechanisms to resolve constitutional questions. This trend is exacerbated by the growth in crowdfunding for judicial review applications – *Miller* marked the first case in which a partially crowdfunded judicial review application reached the Supreme Court. There is no sign of this trend abating as the Brexit process draws to a close. Indeed, in the face of the broadly worded provisions of the European Union (Withdrawal) Act 2018 – in particular section 8 which contains a Henry VIII clause empowering ministers to modify or amend primary legislation by delegated legislation – such litigation is likely to increase as challenges are brought to delegated legislation enacted under these provisions.[53] There may also be legal challenges brought to clarify the status of EU-derived law post exit day, particularly given the complex nature of Section 7 of the European Union (Withdrawal) Act 2018 and the way in which it focuses predominantly on how EU-derived law can be repealed or modified, but provides little information as to how to resolve conflicts between different types of EU-derived law, or EU-derived law and legislation and regulations enacted

[51] European Union (Withdrawal) Act 2018, Section 13(1)(b).

[52] The Court of Justice concluded that it was possible for the UK to unilaterally revoke Article 50 (n 4).

[53] Henry VIII clauses empower the executive to enact delegated legislation to modify or amend primary legislation.

after exit day, save as regards its status for the Human Rights Act 1998.[54]

3.2 *Constitutionalisation*

A second impact of the UK's membership of the EU on the UK's constitution has been an increasing constitutionalisation of the UK. The traditional understanding of parliamentary sovereignty is that there is no hierarchy between ordinary legislation and constitutional legislation. The UK's membership of the EU, again, provided a catalyst for change. When reaching his conclusion in *Thoburn*, Laws LJ developed the concept of constitutional statutes. While ordinary statutes can be impliedly repealed, this is not the case for constitutional statutes.[55] According to Laws LJ:

> For the repeal of a constitutional Act or the abrogation of a fundamental right to be affected by statute, the court would apply this test: is it shown that the legislature's *actual* – not imputed, constructive or presumed – intention was to affect the repeal or abrogation? I think the test could only be met by express words in the later statute, or by words so specific that the inference of an actual determination to the effect the result contended for was irresistible. The ordinary rule of implied repeal does not satisfy this test. Accordingly, it has no application to constitutional statutes.[56]

Laws LJ classified this development as beneficial given that it allows the UK the advantages of a written constitution through preserving fundamental rights, while preserving the sovereignty of the legislature and the flexible nature of the UK constitution.[57] Similar statements can be found in other cases concerning the principle of legality. The principle of legality has two components. First, that broad or general words found in legislation would not be read so as to abrogate or reduce fundamental common law rights. Legislation must be clear, precise and specific to restrict or remove fundamental common law rights.[58] Second, even if there are clear and precise words to enable the restriction of fundamental rights, any restriction of the right must be necessary in order to achieve the aim of the legislation.[59] As

[54] European Union (Withdrawal) Act 2018, Schedule 8, part 2, para 30.
[55] *Thoburn* v. *Sunderland City Council* (n 50), [60]-[63].
[56] Ibid., [63], emphasis in the original.
[57] Ibid., [64].
[58] See *R.* v. *Secretary of State for the Home Department, ex parte Leech* [1994] QB 198, *R.* v. *Lord Chancellor ex parte Witham* [1998] QB 575, *R.* v. *Secretary of State for the Home Department, ex parte Pierson* [1998] AC 539.
[59] See *R.* v. *Secretary of State for the Home Department, ex parte Daly* [2001] UKHL 26, [2001] 2 AC 532 and *R. (Unison)* v. *Lord Chancellor* [2017] UKSC 51, [2017] 3 WLR 409.

explained by Lord Hoffmann in *R.* v. *Secretary of State for the Home Department, ex parte Simms*,

> Parliamentary sovereignty means that Parliament can, if it chooses, legislate contrary to fundamental principles of human rights. The Human Rights Act 1998 will not detract from this power. The constraints upon its exercise by Parliament are ultimately political, not legal. But the principle of legality means that Parliament must squarely confront what it is doing and accept the political cost. Fundamental rights cannot be overridden by general or ambiguous words. This is because there is too great a risk that the full implications of their unqualified meaning may have passed unnoticed in the democratic process. In the absence of express language or necessary implication to the contrary, the courts therefore presume that even the most general words were intended to be subject to the basic rights of the individual. In this way the courts of the United Kingdom, though acknowledging the sovereignty of Parliament, apply principles of constitutionality little different from those which exist in countries where the power of the legislature is expressly limited by a constitutional document.[60]

This constitutionalisation was also evident in the way in which the UK constitution ensured the primacy of directly effective EU law, as discussed above.

The development of constitutionalisation is evident in the Brexit process and will likely continue to develop post Brexit. The most obvious example of constitutionalisation through the Brexit process is the *Miller* decision. Not only did the case refer to the principle of legality, but in addition the case also developed a further principle of the UK constitution.[61] The judgment of the majority asserted a 'long-standing and fundamental principle' of the UK constitution that it was unconstitutional for a 'far-reaching change to the UK constitutional arrangements to be brought about by a ministerial decision or ministerial action alone'.[62] In addition, the Withdrawal Agreement refers to the need for the UK to ensure that it disapplies legislation that is either inconsistent or incompatible with the provisions of EU law which continue to apply in the UK through the Withdrawal Agreement during the transition period.[63] The Act preserves the supremacy of EU law post exit day

[60] [2000] 2 AC 115, 131.

[61] *R. (Miller)* v. *Secretary of State for Exiting the European Union* (n 10), [87].

[62] Ibid., [81].

[63] Draft Agreement on the Withdrawal of the United Kingdom of Great Britain and Northern Ireland from the European Union and the European Union Atomic Agency, (n 23), Article 4(2).

'so far as relevant to the interpretation, disapplication or quashing of any enactment or rule of law passed or made before exit day'.[64]

While the UK's membership of the EU may have been the catalyst for these developments, they form part of a growing influence of cross-border solidarity; providing evidence of the UK benefitting from its experience both of applying EU law and of interacting with other legal systems that provide for a strong protection of fundamental rights. The UK has been influenced by its membership of the European Convention on Human Rights (ECHR) in addition to its membership of the EU. The lasting changes that this membership has created for the UK constitution will continue post Brexit.

3.3 *Multi-layered Constitutionalism*

The UK's experience of multi-layered constitutionalism has had less of an influence, although it may be that this experience will help the UK moving forward post Brexit. These difficulties can best be explained by revisiting the European Union (Withdrawal) Act 2018. Under the Sewel convention, the UK government normally obtains the consent of the devolved legislatures when enacting legislation in a devolved area, or which modifies the powers of the devolved nations. Accordingly, a legislative consent motion was sought from both Scotland and Wales for the European Union (Withdrawal) Bill. However, given their disagreement with some of the provisions of the Bill, in particular Section 12, both the Scottish Parliament and the Welsh Assembly enacted their own legislation to provide for the continuity of EU law in Scotland and Wales, respectively.[65]

After the legislation had passed through the relevant procedures of the Scottish Parliament and the Welsh Assembly, but before royal assent had been granted, the UK government proposed amendments to Section 12 of the European Union (Withdrawal) Bill. The original version of Section 12 did not allow for repatriated powers from the EU to be transferred to Scotland and Wales when such powers were within the scope of the Scottish Parliament and the Welsh Assembly. Rather, these powers would be transferred on a temporary basis to the Westminster Parliament. The modifications to Section 12 provided that the powers

[64] European Union (Withdrawal) Act 2018, Section 5(2).

[65] The European Union (Legal Continuity) Scotland Bill 2018 and the Law Derived from the European Union (Wales) Act 2018.

repatriated from the EU which fell within the scope of the devolved legislatures would return to Scotland and Wales. However, it also empowered UK ministers to enact regulations to return some of these powers to Westminster on a temporary basis. These regulations required a consent motion from the devolved legislatures – in a similar manner to the Sewel convention only applying to devolved legislation which was placed on a statutory as opposed to a convention basis. However, although the UK minister needed to obtain a consent motion, a motion from a devolved legislature refusing consent would satisfy this requirement.

The Welsh Assembly accepted this solution and voted in favour of a legislative consent motion for the European Union (Withdrawal) Bill. The Law Derived from the European Union (Wales) Act 2018 came into force on 6 June 2018.[66] However, following negotiations between the devolved Governments and the Westminster government, assurances were received that no Section 12 orders would be enacted at this time.[67] Following these assurances, the Welsh government exercised its power under Section 22 of the Act to repeal the legislation. Consequently, the Act is no longer in force.[68]

The situation in Scotland was more complicated. Scotland refused to grant a legislative consent motion to the European Union (Withdrawal) Bill. Following the passing of the European Union (Legal Continuity) Scotland Bill 2018, but prior to it receiving royal assent, the UK government challenged the validity of the legislation through a reference of the attorney general under Section 33 of the Scotland Act 1998. The Supreme Court concluded that, although the challenge to the legislation as a whole failed, nevertheless provisions of the European Union (Legal Continuity) Scotland Bill 2018 were beyond the law-making capacity of the Scottish Parliament.[69] In particular, Section 17 was beyond the legislative capacity of the Scottish Parliament. This section would have required Westminster ministers to obtain the consent of the Scottish Parliament prior to enacting a regulation transferring power from Scotland to Westminster. In addition, although provisions of the European Union

66 www.thegazette.co.uk/notice/3048643.

67 Cabinet Office, 'The European Union (Withdrawal) Act and Common Frameworks: 26 June 2018 to 25 September 2018', November 2018, available at: www.assembly.wales/laid%20documents/pri-ld11578/pri-ld11578-e.pdf.

68 The Law Derived from the European Union (Wales) Act 2018 (Repeal) Regulations 2018, available at: www.legislation.gov.uk/wsi/2018/1211/pdfs/wsi_20181211_mi.pdf.

69 *The UK Withdrawal from the European Union (Legal Continuity) Scotland Bill: A Reference by the Attorney General and the Advocate General of Scotland* [2018] UKSC 64, [2019] 2 WLR 1.

(Legal Continuity) Scotland Bill were valid were enacted, since their enactment, the UK European Union (Withdrawal) Bill had received royal assent. It placed a further restriction on the Scottish Parliament – it was not able to legislate contrary to the provisions of the European Union (Withdrawal) Act 2018.[70] Therefore, provisions of the European Union (Legal Continuity) Scotland Bill which contradicted this Act, though valid when enacted, were beyond the legislative capacity of Scotland at the time when the legislation would have come into force. This included, for example, the preservation of the Charter as an aspect of Scots law, given that the European Union (Withdrawal) Act clearly states that the Charter will not be part of domestic law on or after exit day.[71]

The tension between Scotland and Westminster over legislation to retain EU law in domestic law post exit day demonstrates a further failure in cross-border solidarity, understood in terms of the relationship between two nations within the same state. It is to be hoped that lessons can be learnt from the UK's membership of the EU to repair these relations, drawing on the different models of cross-border solidarity between governments found within the EU. For example, the UK could learn from developing a better understanding of shared competences between Westminster and the devolved legislatures, creating inter-governmental committees to work together to produce legislation based on forming a consensus across the nation states. To this end, the UK may benefit from adopting inter-governmental structures similar to the Joint Committee structure found in the Withdrawal Agreement.

4 Conclusion

It is difficult to see Brexit as anything other than a major challenge to cross-border solidarity. Although disputes remain as to the key motivation for those who voted to leave the EU, it is hard to deny that this was due, at least in part, to issues arising from immigration. Rather than seeing the EU as an opportunity to forge relations with our neighbours and to work together to achieve common goals, the EU was perceived as harming the sovereignty of the UK and of preventing the UK from controlling its borders. There was a swing away from reaching out towards closing off relations with our closest neighbours. This reaction has persisted in some of the media outlets during the Brexit negotiations,

[70] European Union (Withdrawal) Act 2018, Schedule 3, paragraph 21.
[71] European Union (Withdrawal) Act 2018, Section 5(4).

particularly the more right-wing section of the tabloid press that has consistently portrayed the EU as bullies. Negotiations are not seen as a means of reaching common agreement, but as a battle of 'red lines', standing firm and refusing to give in to pressure from the other side on the negotiation table. As Brexit becomes increasingly likely in the face of the new strong Conservative majority, with the strong possibility that the UK could leave the EU with no future trade deal given the UK ministerial inability to agree to an extension of the negotiation period under the Withdrawal Agreement beyond 31 December 2020, it is difficult not to fear that cross-border solidarity will be further eroded.

However, it is also important to remember the legacy of cross-border solidarity that will remain even if the UK were to leave with no future trade deal. The UK's membership of the EU has been a catalyst for constitutional change. This has been added to through the Brexit process. It is unlikely that this constitutionalisation and judicialisation of the UK constitution will be reversed. Moreover, if the UK were to leave the EU under the terms and conditions of the current Withdrawal Agreement on 31 January 2020, the UK constitution may be required to change even further in order to enable the UK to make long-term legally binding commitments to protect citizens' rights and to ensure non-regression of environmental protection and social and labour rights. However, the terms of the current European Union (Withdrawal Agreement) Bill 2019–20 have not taken this option, with no provisions for legal entrenchment. More fundamentally, it is to be hoped that a longer-lasting legacy of trans-border solidarity will remain, enabling the UK to address tensions that have arisen between the component nations of the UK through the Brexit process as well as with regard to the future relationship between the UK and her European neighbours.

10

Transnational Claims in the European Union and the Founding Principle of Solidarity

ANTONI ABAT I NINET

1 Introduction

To define solidarity is not an easy task for a number of reasons, such as the complexity and forms of solidarity (horizontal, vertical, organic, mechanical), the lack of a precise legal definition, the effects of the process of juridification to the normative definition of the principle of solidarity, the link solidarity has with other principles and values (loyalty, cooperation, cohesion, subsidiarity), and its material implications for internal and external policies. The starting point of this chapter is an analysis of the concepts of secession and solidarity. That is followed by an investigation of the significance of solidarity in the European Union (EU) and the effects of its inclusion in Article 2 of the Treaty on European Union (TEU). The legal perspective is completed with an analysis of other EU legal instruments, decisions of the European Court of Justice (ECJ) and other acquis communautaire related with this founding principle of the EU.

This chapter provides an empirical case scenario, the secessionist claim of Catalonia, to put into practice and perspective the theoretical aspects under analysis. This empirical example is analysed within the framework, principles, values and aims of the EU. To build up this theoretical exercise, the paper enters into a critical dialogue with J.H.H. Weiler's approach to this research question on the relations between secessionism and solidarity in the EU context. The chapter ends with a reflection on the various forms of solidarity, and a proposal on how to solve potential conflicts between them, and the implications of this topic in the EU integration project.

2 Secession and Solidarity

For the purpose of this chapter, secession is understood in a classical sense, that is, a group in a portion of the territory of a state attempting to create a new state through a secessionist attempt to exit thereby leaving the original state behind in a reduced form.[1] Although the way in which the process of secession is conducted can have effects on the required solidarity among the Member States of the EU, this chapter does not deal with the withdrawal process. It does not differentiate between secession that is consensual (when secession results from a negotiated agreement between the state and the secessionists), through constitutional processes (as the Supreme Court of Canada recently envisioned for the secession of Quebec), or undertaken unilaterally (in the sense of having a liberty-right and establishing that the group has a moral claim-right to secede).[2] The claim of secession is equated with the claim of the external dimension of self-determination in international law.

As Closa correctly points out, the June 2016 referendum in the UK forced the EU and its stakeholders to reflect on an unknown and unexplored situation for which there had been little preparation in the EU.[3] The result of the 2016 UK referendum, which was unpredicted and unwanted by Euro-bureaucrats, lobbies, stakeholders and those in charge of the EU, has suddenly introduced the potential withdrawal from the EU of a Member State, and the parallel secession of a territory of that Member State which wishes to remain a part of the EU. This lack of political concreteness and legal anomia in the EU has several causes but none of them seem to be legal.

The legal penumbra shows not only that the whole EU project is a work in process, but also a very complex, diverse and plural political system with twenty-seven sovereigns exposed to strong structural challenges. The EU has proved incapable of predicting a co-ordinated, reasonable and shared response to these kinds of challenges. Only when the threat materialises and produces effects does the response seem to come, and (in many cases) then appears precipitated, uncoordinated and conditioned by the different interests of the Member States and the polycephaly.

[1] A. Buchanan, 'Secession', in E. N. Zalta (ed.), *The Stanford Encyclopedia of Philosophy* (Fall 2017 Edition), available at: https://plato.stanford.edu/archives/fall2017/entries/secession/ (accessed 13 May 2019). See also W. Kymlicka, *Liberalism, Community and Culture* (Oxford: Oxford University Press, 1989).

[2] Buchanan, 'Secession'.

[3] C. Closa, 'Troubled membership: secession and withdrawal', in C. Closa (ed.), *Secession of a Member State and Withdrawal from the European Union* (Cambridge: Cambridge University Press, 2017), p. 6.

Following the definition of 'emergency' that Closa uses, it would be appropriate that the EU applies a rational preventive action, a sort of white paper, so as not to be moved to react by urgency or the political pressure of being the centre of attention in the media, to be able to politically predict a response to the secessionist claim or to legally accommodate a procedure of secession within the EU that prepares the EU to face ensuing fears (domino effect, contagious effect, an incentive to new or dormant secessionist claims, excessive fragmentation of the EU a weaker and more complicated integration process, etc.).

A preventive response will also confront other kinds of 'inner' difficulties related to the unclear political nature and evolution of the EU. This indeterminacy creates an impediment to a potential autonomous institutional response from the EU to that of the Member States. A second pitfall consists in the difficulties of achieving a common response to this sort of challenge when it affects a Member State (for example, the hitches that imply the enforcement of the measures of Article 7 TEU against Poland, Hungary or Spain). Finally, a third obstacle, which is not a systemic EU case but related to any constitutional system, comes into effect when two fundamental constitutional values conflict. A conflict of founding values is a constitutional antinomy, a dilemma that typically involves two elements and requires a choice between two fundamental constitutional rights that always causes the loss of a good protected by a fundamental right, no matter what the decision involves.[4]

The claim for Catalan secession is not new or sudden, quite to the contrary. In the Catalan case, the declaration of independence passed by the Parliament of Catalonia (10 October 2017) formulised the challenge. However, the Decision of the Spanish Constitutional Court, 8045–2006 of June 2010,[5] on the statute of Autonomy of Catalonia has been widely considered as the trigger for the current constitutional and political conflict between Catalonia and Spain. The political and constitutional disagreements are long-standing and originate from the founding moment, the War of Spanish Succession (1701–14), when the Crown of Catalonia and Aragon lost its political, legal and economic independence in favour of that of Castile. From that date forward, Spaniards have attempted, unsuccessfully, to accommodate their

[4] L. Zucca, 'Conflicts of fundamental rights as constitutional dilemmas', in E. Brems (ed.), *Conflicts Between Fundamental Rights* (Cambridge: Intersentia Publishers, 2008), p. 20.

[5] Decision of the Spanish Constitutional Court, 8045–2006 of 16 June 2010.

political communities and national vision. The EU has had years to prepare a response to this kind of claim, and the secessionist claims cannot be brushed under the carpet.

The absence of a response or procedure to attend these claims has been covered under the principle of neutrality. In legal terms, EU neutrality refers not only to the absence of explicit treaty provisions but also to the silent attitude, which authorities have largely maintained in the contexts of Scotland and Catalonia.[6] The principle of neutrality is premised on the fact that there are no legal grounds for the EU to take sides in the internal processes of the Member States that could potentially lead to their territorial reconfiguration and even eventual secessions of their parts, resulting in the articulation of new statehood on the European continent.[7] Importantly, such neutrality necessarily implies assisting both parties – while of course acting strictly within the sphere of competences of the EU – to come as close as possible to the attainment of the EU objectives of peace, prosperity and democratic development, values which the EU and its Member States draw upon.[8] Weiler also considers neutrality, and non-indulgence of the independence claims of unoppressed sub-state nations in the EU, as the proper response of the EU.[9] He considers that secessionist claims betray the very ethos of integration, reconciliation and continental solidarity.[10]

Neutrality is a basic principle of liberal theory. According to Bruce Ackerman, it is the one that should rule modern liberal societies, and for Ronald Dworkin, the liberal theory of neutrality is the one that analyses questions related to justice with total independence of any human excellence or a good life. Thus, all discussions about the legitimisation of the relations of powers have to be submitted to the principle of neutrality.[11]

Neutrality does not necessarily mean non-intervention or inaction. In ancient Greece, as in modern international law, neutrality was a legal position involving a wide range of specific rights and obligations,[12] and

[6] Closa, *Secession of a Member State*, p. 4.

[7] D. Kochenov and M. Brink, 'Secessions from EU Member States: the imperative of Union's neutrality', University of Edinburgh School of Law Research Paper, 2006, p. 6.

[8] Ibid.

[9] J. H. H. Weiler, 'Catalonian independence and the European Union', *European Journal of International Law*, 23 (2012), 909–13.

[10] Ibid.

[11] B. Ackerman, 'What Is neutral about neutrality?' Ethics, 93(2) (1983), 372–90; R. Dworkin, 'Liberalism', in S. Hampshire (ed.), *Public and Private Morality* (Cambridge: Cambridge University Press, 1978).

[12] R. A. Bauslaugh, *The Concept of Neutrality in Classical Greece* (Berkeley, CA: University of California Press, 1991), p. xi.

the topic appears explicitly in legal references (for instance, in Solon and Cicero's laws, which promote and penalise neutrality in time of stasis).[13]

Neutrality, as such, is a focus on objectivity and reality under a recognised norm, as seen in the action of a judge when determining a case or issue through the application of a recognised norm.[14] Subjection to the concrete obligations of law is what first enables objectivity and, as a consequence, this sort of neutrality which, with the independence of the magistrates, leads to a decision.[15]

The principle of neutrality can be respected or even reinforced by following a legal procedure. Neil Walker proposes the drafting of an explicit treaty provision to overcome the situation of anomia or legal penumbra that the Scottish and Catalan claims gave rise to. Among the advantages of an express legal accommodation in the TEU, Walker remarks that a general, procedure-centred approach would be much better equipped to discriminate between very different scenarios than the treatment of individual cases on an ad hoc basis as they arise.[16]

An express accommodation will provide legal certainty and can provide the relevant data to evaluate whether a concrete secessionist claim breaches the principle of solidarity and institutional loyalty as established in the EU.

3 Definition of Solidarity

As it has previously been mentioned, it is not an easy task to define solidarity because the concept has had various meanings, synonyms and conceptualisations, and is still indeterminate today. Solidarity is a universal concept that is affected by a strong eurocentrism even though it is co-substantial to the fundamental Confucian concept of harmony or to the Islamic concepts of *Zakat* (زكاة, 'that which purifies') and *Ummah* (امة, 'the community of believers'). Solidarity is also a gendered concept in its history, practice and theoretical presentation. This gendered epistemological construction has horrific consequences in the narratives and challenges that necessary comprehensive protection measures against

[13] P. E. V. Wout, 'Solon's law on stasis: promoting active neutrality', The Classical Quarterly, 60(2) (2010), 290.

[14] C. Schmitt, *Der Begriff des Politischen* (Berlin: Duncker and Humblot, 1963), p. 100.

[15] Ibid.

[16] Neil Walker, 'Internal enlargement in the European Union: beyond legalism and political expediency', in C. Closa (ed.), *Troubled Membership in the European Union* (Cambridge: Cambridge University Press, 2017), p. 42.

gender-based violence are facing in countries such as Spain, Italy or Greece.

Solidarity, 'an agreement between and support for the members of a group, especially a political group',[17] is relatively new in the Anglo-Saxon world. Etymologically, the term solidarity comes from the Latin word *in solidum*. As its terminological root (the Latin word *solidum*) implies, the notion of solidarity connotes a shared responsibility for the whole common objective, not just the provision of care for an individual.[18]Roman civil law institutionalised the 'obligation *in solidum*' (obligation of several persons each held responsible towards the creditor for the entire amount of a loan) that is still used by civil continental systems. The notion was also considered as a cornerstone of Christian ethics. Solidarity is considered a social virtue and has transcended political systems throughout history despite the casuistry and other particularities of each political system and concrete age.

It is disputed whether the modern political concept of solidarity has its origins in the French utopic revolutionary principle of *fraternité*. Irrespective, the principle of solidarity was not much coined in legal terms as the principle of *fraternité*[19] and the signifier *fraternité* did not transmute later to that of *solidarité*. However, fraternity is a political and anthropological principle that can be a means with which look at the articulation between the individual and the community.[20] The Dictionary of the French Academy proposes the definition: 'relationship of brother to brother ... it signifies also fraternal union, fraternal friendship. ... it also said of the close connection that those who, without being brothers do not fail to treat each other as brothers'.[21]

It is evident that the concepts of solidarity and fraternity share substantive elements and telos, and thus some authors (see Hawkins, Waheed Hussain, Campanelli, Dann, Brunkhorst, Forrest) also link the epistemological conceptualisation of solidarity with other notions, for

[17] Entry of solidarity for Cambridge Dictionary, available at: https://dictionary.cambridge.org/dictionary/english/solidarity (accessed 25 October 2018).

[18] H. Brunkhorst, *Solidarität: Von der Bürgerfreundschaft zur globalen Rechtsgenossenschaft* (Berlin: Surhkamp, 2002), see note 2, p. 127; C. Taylor, 'Aneinander vorbei', in A. Honneth (ed.), *Kommunitarismus Eine Debatte über die moralischen Grundlagen moderner Gesellschaften* (Frankfurt: Campus Verlag, 1993), p. 122.

[19] P. Cot, *Les Procès de la République* (Paris: La Maison française, 1944).

[20] Brunkhorst, *Solidarität*; K.H. Metz, 'Solidarität und Geschichte', in K. Bayertz (ed.), *Solidarität: Begriff und Problem* (Berlin: Surhkamp, 2002), pp. 172 et seq.

[21] A. Rozenn-Morel, 'Le principe de fraternité dans les fictions utopiques de la Révolution française', *Dix-huitième siècle*, 41(1) (2009), 120.

instance, Aristotle's elements of the classification of governments. As Campanelli remarks, Kant made an invaluable contribution to the development of the notion of solidarity at the international level. For Kant, the sentiment of international solidarity stems from the concept of *allgemeiner Menschenstaat*, a worldwide peaceful community composed of all existing peoples where individuals are mutually interdependent (*Wechselwirkung*).[22]

The utopic revolutionary concept of fraternity is *inter pares* (among equals), horizontal requiring mutual recognition. Fraternity is an epitome value of the French revolutionary political engineering to idealise the French nation. This ideal version of fraternity, as a universal value, is related with solidarity in a *vertical sense.* Solidarity with moral connotation and a cosmopolitan sense. Vertical solidarity is succeeded by charity, which Durkheim defines as *mechanical solidarity* or solidarity by similarities. Some authors criticised this kind of solidarity, exercised from top to bottom, because it humiliates those who receive it and never alters the power relations.[23]

This kind of social solidarity comes from a number of states of consciousness common to all the members of a society. It lies in the social cohesion, a psychic type of the society.[24]

Social assistance, charity and other forms of vertical solidarity imply co-operation of those who have more economic resources with those who have fewer opportunities. An emergent phenomenon, the social factor consists of commonalities, similitudes and likenesses. It is what individuals share, what they have in common. *Mechanical solidarity* derives from, and is proportional to, the strength of the collective conscience.[25]Vertical solidarity is also the basis of the modern conceptualisation of solidarity as a form of social link related to democracy because of the concept of the democratic equality of citizens.[26]

The ethical dimension of solidarity is a fundamental value and, as a principle enshrined in the Charter itself, has been articulated in recent times by the General Assembly of the United Nations and other

[22] D. Campanelli, 'Principle of solidarity', in *Encyclopedia Oxford Public of International Law* (Oxford: Oxford University Press, 2011).

[23] E. Galeano, *Patas Arribas, la escuela del mundo al Revés* (Madrid: Siglo XXI editores, 2005).

[24] E. Durkheim, *La división du travail sociale* (Paris: Presses Universitaires de France, 2013).

[25] W. Pope and B. D. Johnson, 'Inside organic solidarity', *American Sociological Review*, 48 (5) (1983), 681.

[26] P. Leroux, *Du Christianisme et de son origine démocratique* (Paris: Forgotten Books, 2018).

international treaties[27] The principle of solidarity is explicitly referred to in some treaties, such as in Article 3 of the Convention to Combat Desertification in Those Countries Experiencing Serious Drought and Desertification, particularly in Africa. Other treaties and international instruments implicitly refer to solidarity.[28]

The UN Millennium Declaration, in paragraph 6, defines 'solidarity' as one of the 'fundamental values to be essential to international relations in the twenty-first century'. It is defined in the following words: '[g]lobal challenges must be managed in a way that distributes the costs and burdens fairly in accordance with basic principles of equity and social justice. Those who suffer or who benefit least deserve help from those who benefit most.'[29] It can be said that in the international sphere, the concept of solidarity stresses a vertical and cosmopolitan perspective.

Some of the elements in the evolution of the juridification of the principle of solidarity in the EU have evolved analogically with the codification and context in international law. In international law, solidarity plays a very similar role as its role in the EU, primarily in relation to international disaster relief and humanitarian, international and state responsibility.[30]

At the domestic level, constitutional texts have had different ways to constitutionalise this fundamental value, the principle of solidarity is one of the 'common constitutional characteristics'.[31] Constitutional texts have accommodated solidarity as a basic social right (Article 25 of the Constitution of Greece of 1975); as a fundamental principle (Article 2 of the Italian Constitution of 1947); as a social right and duty (Chapter 2 of the Portuguese Constitution of 1976); or as an inter-territorial obligation (Articles 2 and 138 of the Spanish Constitution of 1975). In other constitutional texts, the mention is ordinary (such as in Article 87 French Constitution of 1958, or Article 104a of the German Constitution of

[27] K. Wellens, 'Revisiting solidarity as a (re-)emerging constitutional principle: some further reflections', in R. Wolfrum and C. Kojima (eds.), *Solidarity: A Structural Principle of International Law* (Berlin: Springer, 2010), p. 3.

[28] D. Campanelli, 'Principle of solidarity'.

[29] D. Phillip, 'Solidarity and the law of development cooperation', in R. Wolfrum and C. Kojima (eds.), *Solidarity: A Structural Principle of International Law* (Berlin: Springer, 2010), p. 64.

[30] M. Klamert, 'Solidarität als Rechtsprinzip der Europäischen Union', in M. Knodt and A. Tews (eds.), *Solidarität in der EU* (Baden-Baden: Nomos, 2014), p. 25.

[31] C. Walter, 'International law in a process of constitutionalization', in J. Nijman and A. Nollkaemper (eds.), *New Perspectives on the Divide between National and International Law'* (Oxford: Oxford University Press, 2007), p. 191.

1949) and some constitutions do not even mention the term solidarity (for example, the Constitution of Denmark of 1953, the Constitution of Sweden of 1974 and the Constitution of Finland of 1999).

The lack of explicit reference to the concept in the Nordic constitutions is partially due to the main elements of Scandinavian constitutionalism, a mixed continental-based system but with elements of common law and, in some cases, with old constitutions (Norway and Denmark). This constitutional silence has not prevented the Nordic countries from being among the most solidary countries in the world. Constitutionalisation is 'not intrinsically good, but is instrumental to the achievement of other values'.[32]

Explicit reference to the term seems to be a post-Second Word War constitutional response aiming to provide a rationalisation of the principle to allow for its enforcement, at least on a domestic level. A different debate is whether it would be pertinent to include an express mention in constitutional texts for symbolic and programmatic reasons, or to update constitutions to meet legal developments and needs. In this sense, and it is analysed later in this piece, the EU opted for a preeminent accommodation as a founding and constitutive principle aiming to stress not only the descriptive sense of EU constitutional founding values but also their prescriptive one.

There is another form of solidarity, *Horizontal solidarity,* which is exercised between equals and differs from charity. Durkheim defined this kind of solidarity as organic and it is the origin of the modern political and legal principle. Horizontal solidarity presupposes co-operation between a more egalitarian society or a society in which individuals have comparable situations of opportunity available to them.

This sort of solidarity also has its parallel version in fraternity, the core value of the French revolutionary political project to idealise the French nation. Fraternity among '*les enfants de la Patrie*' who sacrifice their 'bare life' (Giorgio Agamben) following the mother (*la Marianne*) who guides them, with the French flag in the hand, to liberty, as Lacroix magnificently painted. Fraternity, therefore, is understood as mutual assistance between and only between brothers, *frater.*

Durkheim describes *organic solidarity* as resembling the co-operation we observe among the higher social animals. Each organ has its special physiognomy, its autonomy, and yet the unity of the organism is

[32] J. Trachtman, 'The constitutions of the WTO', *European Journal of International Law*, 17 (2006), 623.

strengthened as the individuation of the parts is more marked. Because of this analogy, we propose to call the solidarity which is due to the division of labour, organic.[33]

4 Solidarity in the EU

4.1 Solidarity in the Communitarian Geist and Acquis

Solidarity as a fundamental principle of European integration was mentioned for the first time in the 1950 Schuman Declaration and was subsequently incorporated into the Preamble of the 1951 treaty establishing the European Coal and Steel Community.[34] The Preamble of the Treaty of Maastricht (1992) served as a sort of 'birth certificate' providing a constitutional 'home' and 'identity' for the concept.[35] The inclusion of a provision in a Preamble not only has political significance but is also an authoritative recital of the Treaty's purposes, which are understood to play a role in constitutional interpretation.[36] The reference to solidarity in the Preamble is a reflection of the progressive political integration envisioned by the EU. The Preamble of the Maastricht Treaty not only has an important interpretive principle, but also makes a declarative statement on the purpose that explicates principles of positive law.

The Treaty of Lisbon strengthens the concept of solidarity and Article 2 TEU includes solidarity among the common values of the Member States that must prevail. Its inclusion in this article has strong political and legal implications. A breach of the value of solidarity can trigger the application of the measures prescripted by Article 7 TEU. This special protection aims to give a real applicability and aversive sense to the value that prevent it from being simply aspirational.[37] This conceptualisation also determines objectives (*Zielbestimmung*).

[33] W. Pope and B. D. Johnson, 'Inside organic solidarity', *American Sociological* Review, 48 (5) (1983), 682.

[34] A. Giannapoulos, 'Introduction solidarity: sociological, legal and ethical aspects of a fundamental EU-principle', in A. Giannapoulos (ed.), *Solidarity in the EU: Challenges and Perspectives*, research paper 9 (Tel Aviv, 2017).

[35] G. J. Jacobsohn, *Constitutional Identity* (Harvard, MA: Harvard University Press, 2010).

[36] B. Leiter, C. E. Handler and M. Handler, 'A reconsideration of the relevance and materiality of the Preamble in constitutional interpretation', *Cardozo Law Review*, 12 (1990), 117.

[37] K. L. Scheppele, 'Aspirational and aversive constitutionalism: the case for studying cross-constitutional influence through negative models', *International Journal of Constitutional Law*, 1(2) (2003), 296.

Solidarity is now a general legal principle of law in the EU. In this sense, it is not only a value in the abstract but also a feature of the EU constitutional identity. The prominence of solidarity in the Charter of Fundamental Rights of the European Union also demonstrates its fundamental importance in the EU.[38]

Other primary EU law that accommodates the principle of solidarity is the Preamble and Chapter IV of the Charter of Fundamental Rights of the European Union, and the 'solidarity clause' established by Article 222 of the Treaty on the Functioning of the European Union (TFEU). Solidarity is mentioned in the TEU as a common value and mission of the EU with regard to the mutual relations of Member States, their relations with third countries, and relations among all citizens of the EU. Moreover, it is incorporated in articles of primary European law establishing specific guarantees, full rights and equally full obligations.[39] Some examples in EU secondary law that come from the principle of solidarity are the Declaration (No 37) on Article 222 TFEU, the Council Decision of 24 June 2014 on the arrangements for the implementation by the EU of the solidarity clause.

The European Court of Justice (ECJ) has applied the principle of solidarity in a case concerning complaints made by self-employed workers against compulsory contributions to the mutual fund established to provide social protection. The court has also cited the solidarity clause to defend certain welfare schemes from the application of competition law, to validate obstacles to free movement, and to justify requiring state authorities to provide temporary financial support to immigrant citizens. Regarding citizens' rights within the framework of EU solidarity principles, the ECJ has become a highly influential[40]

The ECJ has had to interpret the principle of solidarity in relation to the principles of sovereignty and autonomy of the Member State. Simultaneously, the Court has dealt with different concepts of solidarity pertaining to different actors, peoples of the EU, the Member State and non-EU actors.[41] The classic concept of solidarity focuses on closer communities and the state-nation context does not seem to be flexible enough to fit the EU political reality. The problem seems to be that in the

[38] Klamert, 'Solidarität als Rechtsprinzip der Europäischen Union'.

[39] Giannapoulos, 'Introduction solidarity', p. 5.

[40] Ibid.

[41] M. Knodt and A. Tews, 'Einleitung: Solidarität im europäischen Mehrebenen-system', in M. Knodt and A. Tews (eds.), *Solidarität in der EU* (Baden-Baden: Nomos, 2014), p. 8.

EU, it is not only the individual level that is a bearer of solidarity, but also Member States as collective actors.[42]

EU law defines the concept of solidarity imprecisely and with heterogeneity. The EU conceptualisation has an ethical dimension and is also related with the concept of identity. The context of solidarity is linked with other principles such as integration, subsidiarity and loyalty.[43] Even in the case of the principle of loyalty with respect for national identities, the principle of solidarity is subject to a tension. A union of states, without solidarity, will inevitably breach the principle of loyalty and cooperation when the particular interest of one Member State collides with the interests of another.

Solidarity in EU law is the expression of a variety of financial obligations and political support which are essential for the functioning of an organisation whose raison d'être has long been limited exclusively to the economic dimensions of cooperation.[44] The principle of solidarity represents a high political goal that compels the Member States to support each other mutually and to prosecute a common political goal, as well as to be integrated into the EU.[45]

There are different forms of solidarity within the EU. In this sense, and following the classification of Knodt and Tews, the horizontal principle of solidarity in the EU has two scopes, the first of which is a transnational solidarity based on the national systems at the level of individual Member States. Transnational solidarity builds on ideas and values that transcend national boundaries[46] and encompasses the reception of the Catholic solidarity discourse in the Catholic Church.[47] The second scope of horizontal solidarity based as collective actors is international solidarity, where the solidary action takes place outside the borders of the EU.

The vertical dimension also has an individual scope related to supranational solidarity. The vertical nature of supranational solidarity shows that vertical solidarity is not exclusive to the European level, it also has a character that complements or even overrides the lower levels by becoming the guarantor of the EU, which also entitles the citizens of the Member States to additional rights over their national

[42] Ibid.
[43] Klamert, 'Solidarität als Rechtsprinzip der Europäischen Union'.
[44] Ibid., p. 35.
[45] Ibid.
[46] Knodt and Tews, Einleitung: Solidarität im europäischen Mehrebenen-system', p. 12.
[47] Ibid.

territory.[48] Vertical solidarity is defined in a collective sense as intergovernmental solidarity. This kind of solidarity makes the EU a collective solidary actor and fluctuates between the principles of action of autonomy, conservation and community support, as well as subsidiarity.[49]

4.2 *The Paradox of Secession*

Weiler brilliantly considers some of the main points of this chapter in his 'Secessionism and its discontents'.[50] One of the topics that Weiler addresses in that piece are trends that he considers contradictory (internal secessionism as Europhilic and external secession as Euroscepticism). He advocates for a sort of relativism in order to analyse both trends saying that neither claim can be so simplified.[51]He is right; there are different tones and exceptions, contexts and particular casuistry matters.

Weiler's piece goes further by examining interesting aspects of the morality of the secessionist claims and their effects on national identities. Although these are not within the scope of this chapter, I consider that some of Weiler's statements are not accurate. There can be arguments to disqualify the secessionist claims of Scotland and Catalonia, but to state that the Catalan self-determination claim is based on Francoist grievances is not precise and seems to oversimplify the question. Spain is a normal imperfect democracy (as all democracies are) that has recently experienced some episodes that are denigrating the quality of the young Spanish democracy dramatically.

Weiler states that the secessionist claims of these sub-state entities breach the idea of solidarity that the founding fathers of European integration had in mind. Concretely, 'the commanding moral authority rooted in the Christian ethic of forgiveness coupled with an enlightened political wisdom which understood that it is better to look forward to a future of reconciliation and integration rather than wallow in a past, which was infinitely worse than the worst excesses, of say, the execrable

48 M. Knodt and A. Tews 'Einleitung: Solidarität im europäischen Mehrebenen-system', p. 13.

49 Ibid., p. 14.

50 J. H. H. Weiler, 'Secessionism and its discontents', in C. Closa (ed.), *Secession of a Member State and Withdrawal from the European Union* (Cambridge: Cambridge University Press, 2017), p. 12. The piece follows an argument that the author introduces previously in J. H. H. Weiler, 'Slouching towards the Cool War; Catalonian Independence and the European Union; Roll of Honour; In this Issue; A Personal Statement' (2012) 23/4 909.

51 Ibid., p 13.

Franco'.[52] True, but pardon and forgiveness in the Christian ethic require two very basic things, repentance (Peter 3:9, 'He is patient with you, not wanting anyone to perish, but everyone to come to repentance'; Jeremiah 15:19, 'If you repent, I will restore you that you may serve me') and confession (1 John 1:9, 'If we confess our sins, he is faithful and just and will forgive us our sins and purify us from all unrighteousness').

In Spain, there is neither repentance nor confession. The Spanish transitional period from the death of the dictator Francisco Franco in 1975 until democratic elections were held in 1982, has been exalted by theorists and academics and even used as a model for other transitions to democracy.[53] However, the bargained route to democracy left important legacies on the democratic system in Spain. These burdens are only visible after a period of time and are now reappearing after forty years of democratic regime. The Spanish state ranks second in the world, only surpassed by Cambodia, in an index of the number of mass graves containing disappeared victims.[54] None of the political leaders, or members of the military and police forces of the Francoist regime have been prosecuted for alleged universal crimes against humanity.

To the present day in Spain, there are more than three hundred streets with Francoist and fascist names,[55] dozens of monoliths and monuments exalting Franco and fascist generals (such as *el Valle de los Caídos* [the Valley of the fallen], *Sa Feixina* or the Monument to Franco) and relics of the Nazi Condor Legion.[56] In 2013, there was a public recognition of the Blue Division, a Spanish military expeditionary unit integrated in the Nazi *Wermacht* as the 250 Division. A final example of lack of repentance and therefore impossible eschatological expiation of the 'sin' was the Spanish Parliament's refusal in May 2018 to withdraw the award granted

52 Ibid., p 17.

53 See: J. J. Linz and A. Stepan, *Problems of Democratic Transitions and Consolidation: Southern Europe, South America, and Post-Communist Europe* (Baltimore, MD: Johns Hopkins University Press, 1996).

54 It is estimated at 140,000 the number of missing victims of the Spanish civil war and the subsequent Franco dictatorship whose bodies have neither been recovered nor identified. In 2008, the judge Baltasar Garzon received a list with the names of 143,353 missing in the Civil War and dictatorship, delivered by the Platform for Victims of Enforced Disappearances by the Franco regime.

55 www.elconfidencial.com/espana/2015-12-26/calles-franquistas-espana-ley-memoria-historica_1126620/ (accessed 25 October 2018).

56 www.politico.eu/article/spain-franco-history-valle-de-los-caidos-fascism/ (accessed 25 October 2018), see also http://cadenaser.com/ser/2015/02/11/album/1423676472_686767.html#1423676472_686767_1423677319 (accessed 25 October 2018).

to the torturer Juan Antonio González Pacheco, inspector of the Social Political Brigade, in 1977.

The self-determination claim in Catalonia calls upon these issues. As evidence of this fact, the Catalan Parliament recently passed the Law 11/2017 of 14 July 2017, that annuls all the summary trials that occurred in Catalonia between 1939 and 1980.[57] Previously, in 2009, the Parliament had also passed the Law 10/2009 on the location and identification of disappeared people during the Civil War and the Francoist dictatorship, and the dignifying of the common graves.[58]

The Catalan self-determination claim is based on a principle of democracy and the right of self-determination. No serious self-determination claim made in Catalonia or the Basque country is based on the 'Franco card', as Weiler says, but they harken to the effects of a political transaction that perpetuated political and economic castes. The lack of a real democratic transition, of repentance and pardon, burdens the Spanish political system and conditions the possibilities of enabling a referendum in Catalonia (as happened in Quebec, Scotland and as it will happen in the Faroe Islands). In the Faroese case, a territory under the sovereignty of the Kingdom of Denmark, a transatlantic community with partners of very different sizes and (fluid) legal status, with limited forms of sovereignty-all of them, the consultation will be held even in the light of the ambivalence towards referenda in the Faroese constitution.

Weiler then anchors the secessionist claims in Scotland and Catalonia in: 'an outdated sense of the collective self but for seriously misdirected social and economic egoism, cultural and national hubris and often naked ambition of local politicians'.[59] For the object of this chapter, I will focus my attention on the alleged 'economic egoism'.

As Dietrich explains:

> Although hardly anyone denies that economic incentives may fuel separatist demands, most researchers deem a more complex explanation necessary, for at least two reasons. First, the existence of a strong national or ethnic identity appears to be a precondition for the emergence of separatist aspirations. Usually, shared economic interests do not lead to a desire for political independence if a deeper sense of community is lacking. Second, the occurrence of economically disadvantageous secessions, such as Slovakia or Kosovo, suggests that other factors can play an

[57] http://anc.gencat.cat/web/.content/anc/noticies/Documents/20170707_PC_Llei_11_reparacio_juridica_victimes_franquisme.pdf (in Catalan) (accessed 20 July 2017).

[58] www.parlament.cat/document/nom/TL092.pdf (in Catalan) (accessed 20 July 2017).

[59] Ibid., p. 17.

> important role. Simply assuming that the inhabitants of these regions miscalculate the economic consequences of their political independence would be unsatisfactory.[60]

In the Catalan context, it is generally acknowledged that Catalonia played a key role in the democratisation of Spain by heavily endorsing EU membership, providing economic and industrial leadership, and being committed to solidarity towards Spain. Vitally, Catalan nationalism was instrumental in overcoming the 1993 crisis and strongly supported Spanish fulfilment of the conditions to join the euro.[61] The label of selfishness affixed to the Catalan claim of self-determination presupposes that Catalonia (or Scotland) would end their moral duties towards their fellow state citizens once they secede. However, this will not necessarily be the case, particularly if the dissolution of the political union is conducted fairly and by accepting responsibility for some share of public debts.[62]

Additionally, it is disputed whether independence will be economically beneficious for Catalonia. The economic motivation is not among the main reasons for the secessionist claim and is, in fact, often cited as a strong argument against secession. In this sense, since the independence vote in Catalonia, 2,700 business have moved their headquarters to other regions of Spain.[63] However, secessionist support among the Catalan population has not significantly decreased.[64]

The stereotype 'secessionism and economic egoism' fails because the claim of self-determination in Catalonia is very transversal and includes a wide range of political and economic options including an anarchist youth group, a conservative party of free marketers and a left-wing party committed to enhancing the welfare state.[65] Solidarity in Catalonia has not been limited to other regions of Spain but has also been developed by

60 F. Dietrich, 'Secession of the rich, a qualified defence', *Politics, Philosophy & Economics*, 13(1) (2014), 63.

61 M. Gimbernau, 'The rise of secessionism in Catalonia has emerged out of the will to decide the region's political destiny as a nation', available at: http://blogs.lse.ac.uk/europpblog/2012/05/29/catalonia-secession/ (accessed 25 October 2018).

62 Dietrich, 'Secession of the rich, a qualified defence'.

63 www.washingtonpost.com/news/worldviews/wp/2017/11/30/since-catalonias-independence-vote-2700-businesses-have-moved-their-headquarters/?noredirect=on&utm_term=.a211bfd38539 (accessed 25 October 2018).

64 http://upceo.ceo.gencat.cat/wsceop/6668/Abstract%20in%20English%20-885.pdf (accessed 25 October 2018).

65 www.nytimes.com/2017/10/09/world/europe/catalonia-independence-spain.html (accessed 25 October 2018).

local movements on a basis of neighbourhood and not nationhood. Some of the social and solidary measures, led by secessionist forces, of the Catalan Government also evidence that the claim of lack of support for secessionism needs to be revisited.

Catalan Secessionist governments passed, and Spanish governments subsequently banned: the Decree 6/2013 by which families in need are protected from their household electricity and gas being cut off by energy supply companies; the Legislative Decree 1/2015 on extraordinary and urgent measures to mobilise housing resulting from mortgage execution processes; Act 14/2015 on taxing unoccupied housing and Act 24/2015 on urgent measures to address the housing emergency and energy poverty; the Law 4/2016 of Effective Equality between Women and Men and the Law 21/2017 of the Agency of Social protection; and Law 9/2107 for the universalisation of sanitary assistance.

Other examples that challenge the general assumption of secessionism as egoist are the Catalan Government's request to the European Commissioner for Immigration, Interior and Citizenship, to convey Catalonia´s willingness to receive and host 4,500 refugees, a claim that was blocked by Spain,[66] or the Catalan Parliament Resolution 1156/X of 23 July 2015 demanding that the Spanish government close the detention facilities for aliens because of their continuous breaching of the human rights of internees.

Weiler is not thinking in terms of this sort of solidarity, neither in the Christian or the Kantian ethics sense, but in a vertical way seeing solidarity as an intergovernmental solidarity, the kind of solidarity created among the Member States by the social contract that Leroux criticised.[67] A kind of solidarity that requires recognition (in the Hegel or Honneth sense). According to Weiler, Catalonia and Scotland cannot claim this kind of solidarity because neither is a *unus,* as in the Swiss motto '*unus pro omnibus, omnes pro uno*', the EU is a '*domaine réservée*' of the Member State, nor regions but neither individuals.

Some further questions might arise, such as; what happens when different forms of solidarity collide? Which form prevails? That which protects founding values such as democracy, the rule of law and human rights or the solidarity that protects memberships? As it was previously mentioned, we may be in front of a constitutional antinomy.

[66] www.ara.cat/en/Puigdemont-Brussels-Catalonia-take-refugees_0_1543045869.html (accessed 25 October 2018).

[67] Leroux, *Du Christianisme et de son origine démocratique.*

5 Conclusion

The proper way to reassert the nature of the project of European integration is to base the EU position on its own principles; fairness, non-discrimination and sincere co-operation.[68] It is also necessary to include respect for the founding values of the EU enshrined in Article 2 of the TEU. This kind of reassertion, based on general principles and values, has at least three functional pitfalls that are difficult to avoid in the current situation, with a EU that places sovereignty in its Member States and not in the EU by itself, a kind of USA without federal government. Solidarity plays a major role in aspects of central importance in the EU. Solidarity facilitates integration and generates EU identity. In this sense, the principle of solidarity in the EU is also connected with the intersubjective recognition and, by analogy to Honneth's solidarity among individuals, Member States must not only be concerned with the collective defence of interests or political integration of other Member States, but rather the existence of an open and pluralist framework within which social respect is recognised.[69]

A conceptual limitation of the founding principle and EU value of solidarity in its intergovernmental form contravenes an original interpretation of the communitarian acquis and the intents of the EU founding fathers; it does not provide the necessary pluralist framework to offer recognition and social respect, and denies a cosmopolitan and anthropocentric project for the EU. Unless you accept that, the EU founding conception of solidarity, that some link with Christian theology, is exclusionary and only applicable to Member States, and contrarily, as Pelagius remarked in relation to salvation, that you do not need to be a Christian to be saved because God has conceded his grace to all the human race.[70] In our context, the alleged idealised version of solidarity in the EU cannot be restricted to a relationship between Member States.

[68] Closa, 'Troubled membership: secession and withdrawal', p. 6.

[69] A. Honneth, *Kampf um Anerkennung, Zur moralischen Grammatik sozialer Konflikte* (Berlin: Suhrkamp, 1994).

[70] T. Todorov, *Les enemies intimes de la democratie* (Paris: Biblio essais, 2012).

PART III

(Re)Establishing Transnational Solidarity Within Existing European Institutions and Political Settings

11

Postnational European Democracy

Aristotelian Caveats

ALEXANDER SOMEK

1 Trigger Warning

The claim made and defended in this chapter may strike some readers as archconservative, if not outright reactionary. It says that the type of postnational democracy envisaged by its most outspoken advocates amounts to pouring new wine into old bottles. In order to be sufficiently lively and socially significant, such a postnational democracy would have to draw precisely on the type of cultural resources that also feed into national solidarity.[1] In this understanding, a postnational democracy would be different from national democracy only in name. A *truly* postnational democracy, by contrast, would not be bolstered by a sense of community. We should not be surprised to encounter phenomena such as apathy, disengagement, distrust or even cynicism.

2 Desperate Radicalism

The defence of the European Union (EU) has recently become more assertive and even somewhat aggressive. Indeed, in lieu of understating the Union's long-term significance by characterising supranational integration as a means of reining in nation states and stripping them of their adverse effects,[2] the Union is now cast as the vehicle designed to

1 German scholars have pointed out, in this vein, that democracies have to avail of 'relative homogeneity'. See Hermann Heller, 'Demokratie und soziale Homogenität', in Ch. Müller *(ed.), Gesammelte Schriften*, vol. 2 (Leiden: Nijmhof, 1971), pp. 423–33; Ernst-Wolfgang Böckenförde, *Constitutional and Political Theory: Selected Writings*, ed. M. Künkler and T. Stein (Oxford: Oxford University Press, 2017), pp. 331–2.

2 See J. H. H. Weiler, *The Constitution of Europe: 'Do the New Clothes Have an Emperor?' and Other Essays on European Integration* (Cambridge: Cambridge University Press, 1999), pp. 249–51, 340–2.

overcome nation and nationalism *tout court*. Unsurprisingly, the resolute apologists of European integration try to come up with a new narrative that attributes to the members of the founding generation – Adenauer, de Gaspari and Monnet? – the intention to extirpate once and for all the scourge of the nation.[3] If European integration were to be ever successful, then the nation state would disappear from the face of the continent.

Two authors publishing in German have relatively recently taken this apparently radical turn: The German political scientist Ulrike Guérot, for one, and the Austrian writer Robert Menasse, the other. In 2013, they published a joint manifesto advocating the creation of a European republic.[4] The new pro-European radicalism shares two central themes.

The first theme is that the Union ought to be transformed into a European republic. Oddly enough, the republic is showcased as the genuinely European idea and sharply distinguished from the old-fashioned dream of a United States of Europe. The latter is now dismissed as being out of step with the necessities of our time. According to Menasse, modelling integration on the American example would merely emulate a precedent that is deeply steeped in the aggressive, imperialist and nationalist thinking of the nineteenth century.[5] According to both Menasse and Guérot, the creation of a republic would, by contrast, not be burdened with the legacy of violence and exclusion. This claim must come as a surprise to those familiar with Renaissance history that abounds in bloodshed and destruction.

The second theme is that the EU can, as it were, only reach its full potential if it fundamentally alters its structure. It should develop, indeed, into a 'Europe of regions'.[6] Powers ought to be reallocated between the central and the regional levels. This would spell the end for the nation state. Menasse bolsters this claim with the observation that regional

[3] See Robert Menasse, *Der euroäpische Landbote: Die Wut der Bürger und der Friede Europas*, 2nd edition (Herder: Freiburg, 2015), pp. 76, 93, 114–15. Guérot is more nuanced, since she claims that owing to the exigencies of the cold war the founding generations 'stumbled' into adopting a national federalist project. See Ulrike Guérot, *Der neue Bürgerkrieg: Das offene Europa und seine Feinde* (Berlin: Ullstein, 2017), p. 68.

[4] Ulrike Guérot and Robert Menasse, 'Manifest für die Begründung einer Europäischen Republik', *Die Presse*, 23 March 2013.

[5] See Menasse, *Der euroäpische Landbote*, pp. 100, 117. Menasse claims the European integration has never had the USA as its model and the latter stands for the old (violent, colonialist) European project.

[6] See Menasse, *Der euroäpische Landbote*, pp. 67, 84–5, 87–8, 118. Guérot, *Der neue Bürgerkrieg*, p. 67. I am translating from Menasse (page 67): 'Europe truly is a Europe of regions. It would have to be the task of European politics, to transform Europe politically into what it factually is.'

identity is real and genuine, whereas national identity is fictitious and fake.[7] A Europe of regions would be a truly authentic Europe.

Interestingly, the institutional means to kill off the nation would be the elimination of the Council of the European Union (it is never quite clear whether Menasse is talking about the European Council or the Council of the European Union). With the elimination of the Council the nation state would lose its significance. And if the nation state no longer served as the vehicle of political control the nation itself would 'wither away'.[8] The causal chain of destruction – Council, nation state, nation – evidently takes aim at 'the nation' as its final target. The reason is that the nation is believed to be the source of all social evils—a communitarian Pandora's box based on a dangerous fiction. Nothing good is ever to come from it, for it is, at the end of the day, a betrayal by means of which the better off instil into the worse off the readiness to incur great sacrifices.[9] The belief in a national social bond is characteristic of those who live in a fool's paradise. One should not be tricked into believing that its good features could be preserved and the bad avoided. The nation is a 'shabby ideology' that eventually and necessarily turns ordinary people into belligerent monsters perpetrating crimes against humanity.[10]

In Menasse's view, the EU should embark on the unheard of, unprecedented, 'totally new', innovative and bold vanguard project of creating a postnational democracy.[11] The European people are supposed to be equally represented[12] in the European Parliament, which is, according to Menasse, expected to co-operate with the 'enlightened' bureaucracy of the Commission.[13] In a similar vein, Guérot adopts the motto of 'one market – one currency – one democracy'.[14] Her republic would realise

[7] See Menasse, *Der euroäpische Landbote*, pp. 88, 118.

[8] Ibid., p. 115. Yes, Menasse has a penchant for mustering Marxist rhetoric in support of his cause. He goes so far as to claim that a new subject of history has emerged in Europe, a subject that could play the role that had been originally accorded to the proletariat (Ibid., 105–6).

[9] Ibid., pp. 59, 85

[10] Ibid., pp. 64, 114.

[11] Ibid., pp. 95, 100.

[12] That is a major point in Guérot's work. See Guérot, *Der neue Bürgerkrieg*, pp. 63, 72.

[13] Ironically, Menasse's post-nationalism is very Austrian in that it is based upon the admiration of Josephinism, which is a variety of administrative elitism that developed in the late eighteenth century under the enlightened absolutism of emperor Joseph II. The motto was, everything for the people, but nothing by the people. See Menasse, *Der euroäpische Landbote*, pp. 41, 70–1.

[14] See Guérot, *Der neue Bürgerkrieg*, pp. 60, 80, 88.

the 'one person, one vote' principle and hence make an end to the unequal representation of Europeans in the European Parliament.[15]

The postnational democracy envisaged by its advocates may well be a democracy as we have known with regard to its institutional set-up. It is not unlikely to assign a central role to a representative assembly the members that are elected by the citizenry at large. Substantially, it would embrace strong social policies, however, without drawing on the common sympathies among fellow nationals. At any rate, this is what authors such as Guérot and Menasse really seem to have in mind. This is clear in the case of Menasse, who is all for the creation of a European social welfare state, and even more so for Guérot. She actually believes that a common European system of unemployment benefits and some form of basic European social welfare guarantee (or small basic income amounting to €400) would help to garner the loyalty of the people.[16]

The major question is, of course, whether a democracy of this type could be either sufficiently socially significant or even lively without availing itself of an equivalent to the national bond mediating the connection between democracy and solidarity.[17] Postnationalists take the non-legal conditions of democracy lightly and pay no heed to matters such as a common language, shared media of mass communication or common sympathies.[18] Neither author considers any of the notorious cultural preconditions necessary for its success, in particular not even a common language, for any such condition would, in their view, merely replicate and perpetuate the mindset of the nationalist project.[19] Unsurprisingly, therefore, they combine a thin and rather formal approach to democracy, which basically equates democracy with the election and the working of a representative body with the ambitious project of turning the EU into something resembling a European welfare state. The obstacles notwithstanding that many political scientists perceive to be placed along this path – obstacles stemming from the diversity of existing welfare regimes[20] – the advocates of postnational Europe present their project with a boldness that has to make us suspicious as

15 Ibid., pp. 69, 72–4.

16 Ibid., pp. 80–1.

17 For a by now classical account on the positive role played by nationality, see David Miller, *On Nationality* (Oxford: Clarendon Press, 1995), pp. 184–5.

18 See John Stuart Mill, *Considerations on Representative Government* (reprint, Buffalo, NY: Prometheus Books, 1991), pp. 310–11.

19 See Menasse, *Der euroäpische Landbote*, p. 119.

20 See Fritz W. Scharpf, 'Legitimate diversity: the new challenge of European integration', in T. Börzel and R. Cichowski (eds.), *The State of the European Union* (Oxford: Oxford

to whether they have taken into account the conditions that would make it possible.

3 Liveliness and Social Significance

At this point one encounters, indeed, two questions in one. The first question concerns the conditions under which a democratic process can be sufficiently *lively* and draw on the energy that originates from public debate and civic vigilance.[21] The second concerns the conditions under which the adoption of *significant* social policies seems possible and realistic within a democratic regime. Such 'significance' means that there is a reciprocal readiness to come to the aid of others experiencing adversity. It is relative to how far social policies exceed the residual level of means-tested support that is calibrated towards subsistence and the prevention of criminal activity (such as robbery, theft or public unrest). For consistently liberal societies all social policy is part and parcel of policing the population and sustaining public tranquillity. This is not what we have in mind when we speak of *significant* social policy.

It is submitted that both conditions, even though realistically intertwined, have to be kept distinct.

A democracy is likely to be sufficiently *lively* if the readiness on the part of the people to share their fate with one another is routinely on the agenda of the political process. This is the case if matters such as the allocation of responsibility in the relation of individual and community or the equitable sharing of burdens become a focus of public debate. Democracies are lively to the extent that the scope and design of mutual sacrifices are a topic of debate, for they are then concerned with the core question of solidarity. The question is, of course, how far this liveliness extends. The more recent debate in Austria whether child rearing allowances should be paid out at an adjusted lower rate to European citizens whose children do not reside in

University Press, 2003), pp. 79–104; Fritz W. Scharpf, 'The European social model: coping with the challenges of diversity', *Journal of Common Market Studies*, 40 (2002), 645–70.

21 I am, admittedly, of a mind with Crouch who also believes that democracy is strong and vigorous as long as ordinary people – the working class – takes an interest in political processes with the confidence that politics will advance their interests. See Colin Crouch, *Post-Democracy* (Cambridge: Polity Press, 2004), p. 7. Crouch also usefully distinguishes between positive and negative citizenship. Whereas in the former case citizens join forces in order to assert their interests in the latter case the political climate is poisoned by 'an activism of blame on complain, where the main aim of political controversy is to see politicians held to account, their heads placed in blocks, and their public and private integrity held up to intimate scrutiny' (Crouch, *Post-Democracy*, p. 13).

Austria – an adjustment that would be arguably contrary to existing EU law – was moderately lively. Many people in Austria were paying attention, but the engagement did not extend to include the political processes and publics of the countries whose nationals would be affected by cuts. While there were voices of protest in the central European countries affected, within Austria it remained a rather Austrian debate. This demonstrates that the liveliness of the debate does not automatically translate into significant advances of social policies. Rather, it can even reinforce and entrench the egoism of contending groups. It also shows that even though an externality was at stake, the democratic process did not attain the transnational dimension that would have led to mutual engagement. It was still possible to contain it in the national realm and, of course, to play national democratic resistance off against 'Europe'.[22]

Nevertheless, the condition of liveliness points to a deep – and not at all contingent – connection between democracy and solidarity. A democracy that is merely concerned with matters of product safety or custom tariffs is in all likelihood not going to be lively. By contrast, a democracy that looks at issues such as compulsory military service or how the health care system ought to be funded is more likely to see citizen engagement, for it addresses the core question of whether and how people ought to be 'willing to see other's misfortune as giving [them] reason to come to their aid'.[23] If this willingness exists people are sharing their fate with one another. If the country is attacked we have to put our life at risk in order to defend it. If others fall ill we have to pick up the bill. If others are laid off we need to support them. Whatever happens to them affects us. Their fate is our fate. Indirectly, what they have to go through engages our responsibility.

Of the many conditions on which this readiness depends – such as reciprocity, playing by the rules[24] or a long-term commitment to a shared place[25] – the following discussion focuses exclusively on the importance of

22 Admittedly, it is Austria's right-wing government that is to blame for this. More liberal governments may have handled the matter differently or not even take the initiative in the first place.

23 Andrea Sangiovanni, 'Solidarity as joint action', *Journal of Applied Philosophy*, 1 (2015), 340–59, at 348.

24 On fair play as a condition of solidarity, see Claus Offe, 'Pflichten versus Kosten: Typen und Kontexte solidarischen Handelns', in J. Beckert et al. (eds.), *Transnationale Solidarität: Chancen und Grenzen* (Frankfurt aM: Campus, 2004), pp. 35–50, at 42.

25 A transitory form of solidarity is activated if someone is affected by sudden and undeserved hardship of catastrophic proportions. Moderately goodhearted people who avail of the means to help will immediately experience a mechanical impulse to come to their aid. In Durkheimian terms, this means that any form of cosmopolitan compassion with the

what readers of Aristotle's ethics call 'civic friendship'.[26] This narrow focus is chosen for the reason that the somewhat embarrassing fact is often unaccounted for that solidarity presupposes regarding others as 'good people'. Nevertheless, it is this fact that explains one of the conditions of significant *social* policy.

4 Civic Friendship

As is well known, Aristotle introduces readers of his *Nicomachean Ethics* to three different reasons for loving a friend. Friendship[27] can be motivated[28] by pleasure, utility or the good.[29] The pleasure to be obtained from friends can lie in their sheer presence or in sexual satisfaction.[30] Utility is the basis of friendship among those exchanging commodities or services.[31] Friendship that is based on the good can mean, possibly, two things. Either the friends delight in the same activities, a matter that likens this friendship somewhat to the two other versions, for they then obtain pleasure from doing things together (such as playing table tennis or attending operatic performances) and are pleased or pained by the same things;[32] or, in the case of 'complete' friendship,[33] the friends regard

suffering is a mechanical form of solidarity because it does not arise organically from the division of labour. See Émile Durkheim, *The Division of Labour in Society*, trans. W.D. Hall (New York: Free Press, 2014), pp. 133, 316. This impulse is, however, short-lived, in particular if there is no sense of a pre-existing connection between benefactors and beneficiaries.

26 Friends will do whatever they can do to help. See Aristotle, *Nicomachean Ethics*, trans. R. C. Bartlett and S. D. Collins (Chicago, IL: University of Chicago Press, 2011), 1163b 15, at 186.

27 Note that friendship designates the relation of one person to another. Whether it is sustained, however, depends on its being reciprocated. The friendship of the father for the son is not the same as that of the son for the father, for in each case a different virtue is involved. The reasons for loving the other also differ. Ibid., 1158b 15, 18.

28 It is the greatness of the type of ancient political philosophy that one encounters in Aristotle that it does not require drawing a distinction between reasons and motives.

29 See Aristotle, *Nicomachean Ethics*, 1155b 20.

30 Actually, Aristotle points out quite adamantly that friends do not necessarily have to share the same ground of friendship and can be quite heterogeneous. While in a homoerotic relation with a young boy the grown up man seeks pleasure from the boy, the boy wants to have something useful in return. Aristotle's views on friendship are, indeed, rather sobering. Ibid., 1163b 34–6, 1164a 8–9.

31 Ibid., 1156a 30–2.

32 Ibid., 1167a 10–12.

33 Ibid., 1156b 7–8. In contrast to the friendship that is based upon loving the character of the friend the friendships based upon pleasure and utility are friendship only in semblance (ibid., 1157a 31).

the other as a specimen of a good person, that is as someone whom they believe to be *successful at being human*.[34] Admiration or spontaneous goodwill, of course, are not sufficient for friendship[35]. Friendship requires enduring mutual benevolence, and this benevolence has to be explicit.[36] As Aristotle puts it, '. . . those who are friends on account of their virtue are eager to benefit each other'.[37] He expresses this eagerness also by saying that friendship consists more in loving than in being loved.[38] To love means to wish for the other, and for his or her sake, those things that one believes to be good and to work actively towards this end.[39] Friends actively want to do each other good.

Aristotle's account is, in spite of the very particular circumstances of polis life for which it had been developed, still illuminating. First, Aristotle does not draw sharp lines between the types of friendship. Rather he explains that one can move from one to the other and possibly back again.[40] Second, he is perceptive enough to identify benevolence in the sense of wishing others well, even in what must seem to be entirely instrumental relationships.[41] Even if others are means to one's own end, 'friendly' persons are interested in seeing their business partners happy with what they receive. Hence, friendship is involved in what we would likely call 'fair dealings' with one another. There must be, evidently, some kind of 'likemindedness'[42] involved in this, for each has to perceive the deal in the same way. This bridge between the instrumental and the non-instrumental explains how we can make friends even though we first establish contact with others perhaps only on account

[34] This is usually referred to as 'character friendship'. See Sibyl A. Schwarzenbach, 'On civic friendship', *Ethics*, 107 (1997), 97–128, at 100. See also Paul Schollmeier, *Other Selves: Aristotle on Personal and Political Friendship* (Albany, NY: SUNY Press, 1994), pp. 44–5.

[35] See Aristotle, *Nicomachean Ethics*, 1166b 30.

[36] See Ursula Wolf, *Aristoteles' 'Nikomachische Ethik'* (Darmstadt: Wissenschaftliche Buchgesellschaft, 2002), p. 215.

[37] See Aristotle, *Nicomachean Ethics*, 1162b 5–7.

[38] Ibid., 1159a 27, 11591 34–35.

[39] See Aristotle, *Rhetoric* 1381a 1–2 (London: Collins Classic, 2012), p. 89.

[40] See Aristotle, *Nicomachean Ethics*, 1157a 10–13, 1158a 1–2.

[41] Friendship based on utility appears to be quite instrumental and therefore also potentially not very durable. See Aristotle, *Nicomachean Ethics*, 1156a 10–11: 'Those who love each other on account of utility, then, do not love each other in themselves, but only insofar as they come to have something good from the other.' The same is true of those who are loved because of the pleasure they provide. Ibid., 1156a 10–11.

[42] 'Likemindedness is a mark of true friendship, not only because of a likeness of opinions but because of a shared readiness to do something.' Ibid., 1167a 23. Evidently, this is relevant for civic friendship.

of utility. We make friends if we begin to like them for who they are, namely, good people.[43] Third, the concept is so broad as to include intimate[44] as well as public relations. It reminds us of the pervasiveness not only of morality, but of affection in our life. Aristotle is quite outspoken about the fact that political communities seem to exist for the mutual benefit of the participants[45] (other communities have their advantage too), yet he quickly adds that these benefits amount to the good life as a whole.[46] Friendship is superior to justice, for friends do not have to reason about justice and are obviously ready to do more than what they owe, even though observing reciprocity is essential to sustaining friendships in the long run.[47] Justice, however, in order to be effective, requires friendship. Apparently, we are disinclined to give those whom we dislike their due.[48] It is also the case that the type of friendship determines the principles of justice that are relevant to it.[49]

The friendship that holds the city together is manifest in the relation between the ruler and the ruled. Intriguingly, it extends the basic make-up of relations in the private sphere to the public domain.[50] The friendship prevalent in a city always bears a semblance to some form of family relation.[51] Accordingly, different family relations provide the lens for conceiving of the political relation. In the case of a kingdom,[52] it is the relation between the father and his sons, the relation of husband and wife in the case of aristocracy,[53] and the relation of brothers in the case of a republic (which is referred to as 'timocracy' in the *Nicomachean Ethics*).[54] The friendship in the case of kingship is asymmetrical[55]. It is based on the superiority of the 'shepherd of the people' taking care of his flock. What the king is given in return is reverence and honour. His rule is entirely discretionary. Aristocracy mirrors the relation between

[43] Ibid., 1157a 19.
[44] Ibid., 1159a 27–31, 1166a 6, 1168a 28 on unilateral and unconditional maternal love.
[45] See Schwarzenbach, 'On civic friendship', p. 105.
[46] See Aristotle, *Nicomachean Ethics,* 1160a 12, 20.
[47] Ibid., 1163b 11.
[48] Ibid., 1155a 23, 26, 1159a 25–7.
[49] Ibid., 1162a 32.
[50] See the remark, ibid., 1162a 17, where Aristotle says that man is more a coupling being than a political one.
[51] Ibid., 1160b 25.
[52] Ibid., 1161a 11.
[53] Ibid., 1161a 22–23.
[54] Ibid., 1160b 26.
[55] Asymmetrical friendships are not unusual, but when differences of wealth become too big than it becomes difficult to sustain them. Ibid., 1158b 31–3.

husband and wife, which accords with virtue. Each of them is playing their role.[56] Finally, comrades and equal citizens behave like brothers who are of a similar age. In the context of an ancient democracy, they take turns in ruling one another.[57]

According to Aristotle, it is important for the civic friendship of a free society that the rulers and the ruled have something 'in common'.[58] In a democracy, there is friendship 'to a greater degree' than somewhere else because those who are equal have many things in common.[59] The matter is somewhat puzzling when Aristotle explains what 'in common' means with regard to natural pedigree.[60] Parents feel affection for their children for these literally are their offspring; children feel attached because they are something that has come from their parents.[61] Brothers have the same relation to their parents in common. And they are 'the same thing' residing in different bodies.[62]

The cue that we take from Aristotle's political psychology is that it is essential for the existence of civic friendship that the citizens believe that they share something. The frequent references to natural pedigree in case of children suggest that what they share is supposedly a common inheritance that accounts for who they are and why they belong together. More generally, perhaps, it is the perception of equality that matters. Brothers share 'being the son of X'. That is what they are in virtue of being brothers. Democratic citizens simply share 'being citizens of X' and are not divided by markers of social class or inherited status.

Of course, the friendship among citizens does not have to be intimate at all and not comprise the person's character fully.[63] What we can take from Aristotle for our modern conditions, which are no longer those of the ancient city state, is that the lives of persons with whom we are friendly, even though we do not know them, have to *look good* from a distance. That is, the doings of others have to exhibit features of the type

[56] It is, of course, totally unacceptable for us that Aristotle believes that husbands deserve more of the good because of their greater virtue. Ibid., 1164a 22–23.

[57] Ibid., 1160b 26.

[58] Schwarzenbach, 'On civic friendship', p. 104, reminds us that 'community' (*koinonia*) comes from 'sharing' (*koinoneo*).

[59] See Aristotle, *Nicomachean Ethics*, 1161a 32, where this is denied for tyranny.

[60] See Anthony W. Price, 'Friendship (VIII und IX)', in O. Höffe (ed.), *Aristoteles' Nikomachische Ethik*, 3rd edition (Berlin: Akademie Verlag, 2010), pp. 229–51, at 232–3.

[61] See Aristotle, *Nicomachean Ethics*, 1161b 18–21, 28.

[62] Ibid., 1161b 31, 33.

[63] See Schwarzenbach, 'On civic friendship', p. 109.

of life that we mutually recognise because it is good in the sense of being ordinary, respectable or even admirable.[64] Those whose lives pass, from a distance, as ordinary, respectable or admirable are those whom we regard as 'good people'. We say that they are good people and hence worthy of our support if they need it. It is with them that we share, owing to the mutuality of our views, an outlook on life. We are likeminded.[65]

This seemingly trivial point deserves to be highlighted because it strongly suggests the relevance of character friendship to socially significant democracy. It is the friendship among those who know very little of one another except that they share an outlook on life. Thus understood, our friends are people to whom we are not embarrassed to refer as 'our own'.[66]

5 The Noble Lie: From Recognition to National Legacy

Aristotle's social psychology of friendship provides us with a straightforward explanation for the existence and significance of associative obligations. If in the course of dealing with other people we begin to like them in virtue of their good character, we befriend them. It is a mark of friendship that the well-being of friends by default has to have priority over the interest of strangers. In a like manner, Aristotle adds, the demands of justice increase with friendship, for it would be more terrible not to aid a brother or a comrade than a stranger.[67]

[64] This point is explained more fully in my article, Alexander Somek, 'The European concept of transnational democracy', *German Law Journal*, 19 (2018), 435–59, at 440–1.

[65] See Aristotle, *Nicomachean Ethics*, 1167a 23.

[66] It should be noted that the group that one would be ready to embrace as one's own is perhaps *not* primarily composed of fellow nationals. Rather, it is most likely to consist of those enacting various life styles that one considers to be 'cool' or 'normal'. An urban lifestyle, whatever this may precisely be, is not tied to one particular culture. Only secondarily and indirectly becomes the urban lifestyle a national affair if a people develops the ability, or at least the desire, to control its existence for reasons having to do with what they believe to be their historical legacy. It is not the case that cultures 'are' national, as though this were a given social fact; rather, the collective ambition to sustain practices and beliefs for a group of people is what bestows upon various elements of culture a national imprint. National cultures emerge from intermittent endorsements of various cultural fragments. Thus understood, culture becomes an 'object of collective preferences'. For this expression, see Andreas Cassee, *Globale Bewegungsfreiheit: Ein philosophisches Plädoyer für offene Grenzen* (Berlin: Suhrkamp, 2016), p. 155. For a discussion of this problem see Jeremy Waldron, 'Minority cultures and the cosmopolitan alternative', in W. Kymlicka (ed.) *The Rights of Minority Cultures*, Oxford: Oxford University Press, 1995), pp. 93–119; Will Kymlicka, *Multicultural Citizenship* (Oxford: Oxford University Press, 1995), pp. 85–7.

[67] See Aristotle, *Nicomachean Ethics*, 1160a 5, 1165b 35.

The perception of the good character involves culturally specific evaluations that account for what merits recognition and what does not.[68] The existence of a cultural semantics also, however, does not explain why modern civic friendship within a nation state extends beyond the circle of people with whom one is personally acquainted and why, once the circle has been extended, it usually does not include all good people. Puzzlingly, solidarity is engaged only if the good people are regarded as *my* good people even though I do not know them at all. Already Plato understood that something must intervene in order to establish the relevance of a particular group and that the requisite intervention amounts to a 'noble lie'.[69]

Nevertheless, the explanation for the bounded nature of civic friendship has to begin with recognising that culturally particular evaluations of human life are an integral to making sense of one's life. For reasons that have been explained elsewhere,[70] people cannot want to see their cultural horizon disappear since this would diminish the significance of their lives and erode a very important condition for sharing their fates. Since culture exists only if it is mutually sustained, they have to help one another to address this risk. This explains why the background conditions of meaningful choices are routinely turned into an object of collective preferences.[71] They become cast as a shared legacy.

This is the point at which, in the modern age, nationhood plays an important role. Constructing a nation evidently springs from a desire to be powerful,[72] and its emergence is empowering for those getting under its shelter.[73] Protecting cultural contexts against erosion – or, alternatively, rekindling lost traditions – requires collective agency. The most powerful vehicle of collective agency is the sovereign state. It is not by accident, hence, that efforts to sustain the purportedly unconditional that

[68] Hence, systems of solidarity have a significant propensity for cultural intolerance. This is particularly true for the slippage from recognising ordinary lives to recognising people as ordinary. This slippage can be reversed and result in exclusion. For no fault of their own, migrants from distant and culturally foreign places, in particular if they are not well educated, easily fail to pass as ordinary, respectable or admirable people.

[69] The noble lie is necessary in order to make people loyal to a particular city. See Plato, *The Republic*, trans. A. Bloom (New York, Basic Books 1991), p. 414d.

[70] For a further elaboration of this point see Somek, 'The European concept of transnational democracy', pp. 441–2.

[71] Schwarzenbach, 'On civic friendship'.

[72] See below note 91 and accompanying text.

[73] See, generally, Eric Hobsbawn, *Nations and Nationalism since 1780* (Cambridge: Cambridge University Press, 1990).

is taken to give value to life[74] relies on the state or wish to attain, at any rate, that level of self-control that we associate with statehood.

The exigency of co-operating within the confines of a territorially bounded unit gives rise to a twofold phenomenon: *abstraction*, on the one hand, and *haphazard association*, on the other. It is this phenomenon, in addition to the priority of statehood over the nation, that explains why nationhood is 'a noble lie'. We shall see below (see pp. 242–245) that the ploy is complete once irresponsible believing has been added.

The participants that co-operate in order to protect their cultural contexts need to refer to certain cultural artefacts as their common heritage. They therefore have to find for various ways of life some anchor that invisibilises the differences that set them apart. The construction of a national consciousness is an elite effort that involves the forging of coalitions and hammering out a semantics that does not exclude some participants. It is among the most insightful observations made by Bernard Yack[75] that nations use a common inheritance to assert mutual loyalty and concern among its members, but less so actual cultural practices (think merely of adjurations of 'Christian Europe'). The inheritance can be entirely detached from how people live and what they really care about. Austrian national identity, for example, rests in no small part on linking the present with the ambivalent legacy of the Habsburg monarchy; but this is not, of course, directly relevant to how Austrians live their lives today or what their political ambitions are. The inheritance just signifies that there is some historical pedigree that nationals share, however removed it may be from their actual experience. It is the medium for claiming that 'we belong together'. The shared cultural inheritance serves as the means with which nationals affirm a legacy as a source of mutual concern and loyalty.[76] Collective memories provide them also with some orientation. Evoking them hints at where a people is supposed to move to owing to either past proven accomplishments (for example, the New Deal) or the felt need to overcome shameful experiences (for example, 'Jim Crow' laws). The evaluative import of national memories is most contested when it comes to this. It will often reflect political partisanship.

At the same time, however, abstraction opens the door to haphazard association. Once a narrative concerning inheritance is in place, everyone

[74] For an explanation, see The European concept of transnational democracy', pp. 441–2.

[75] See Bernard Yack, *Nationalism and the Moral Psychology of Community* (Chicago, IL: University of Chicago Press, 2012), p. 69.

[76] Ibid., p. 82. We will see below why it can serve as such a medium.

is free to seek shelter for his or her own cultural way in order to have it shielded by the nation. It is through this latter process that relatively free-floating ways of life become aggregated, even if only loosely, into one bounded 'national' culture. There is no nation that does not bear the imprint of collective action (as is manifest, for example, in education) or at least the anticipation of it (the writing of a national narrative). This explains why nationhood is so weird. There is, on the one hand, a permanent contest about how to 'read' the official story concerning the national inheritance with an eye to the future; on the other hand, the nation is a patchwork quilt because nationhood attracts an assemblage of various forms of life that become haphazardly and somewhat strangely solidified under the guise of one tradition.[77] All of a sudden, the widespread habit of consuming alcoholic beverages at a relatively excessive level, the desire to sustain cattle farms in mountain regions and the appreciation of classical music become merged into elements of one Austrian culture. The result is, undeniably, a hodgepodge, and one should expect to see tensions between and among the various elements.

6 Irresponsible Believing

The construction of a shared legacy and the haphazard association of ways of life with this relatively more abstract legacy do not yet explain why people feel that they share a responsibility for their nationals. This responsibility concerns both liabilities and accomplishments. At this point the noble lie of nationhood extends an invitation to believe irresponsibly in the existence of a social bond. This, to be sure, is its most intriguing feature.

Responsible beliefs are those for which a reason can be offered as a warrant.[78] If I am happy about the publication of my latest book sympathetic observers may say that I have reason to be proud of my 'output'. If, by contrast, it is making me both happy and proud that Marcel Hirscher has won another slalom competition, I have no reason

[77] Throughout my life I have benefited from hailing from a country that lays claim to at least two original recipes of the *Sachertorte* and features the Imperial Riding School. I have done nothing to deserve the international standing that flows from the recognition of these facts. Fragmentary cultural elements become synthesised for the simple and rather contingent reason that they are eligible to receive the agent's attention and protection. On this basis, however elusive as it may be, the significance and value of life forms becomes mutually reinforced.

[78] See Stephen Toulmin, *The Uses of Arguments*, updated edition (Cambridge, Cambridge University Press, 2003), pp. 111–20.

for feeling happy and proud other than the fact that he is a fellow national. But this reason clearly begs the question. Hirscher has all the reason in the world to be happy for, and proud of, himself. But why should the fact that the same country has issued our passports give me reason to feel in a like manner? While my belonging to a nation may *cause* the contagion of sentiments, this fact does not, in and of itself, give me any *reason* to endorse its soundness.

In order to elucidate the issue, it is helpful to compare this case to a situation among family members. Parents, siblings and children also have no reason to be proud of the accomplishment of their loved one's other than the fact that they happen to be close relatives. We accept it as true, however, that being a close relative makes one disposed to take a special interest in their well-being. One cares about them. This disposition is rooted in regular personal contact and, more importantly, in the unconditional acceptance that lends expression to familial affection. This acceptance is not least manifest in identification vis-à-vis the outside world. Whatever harm may be done to a family member affects all others and gives rise to reactive attitudes; whatever is accomplished by one of them is taken to reflect well on all kin. Individual accomplishments show who everyone else is or at least demonstrate their potential.

Put very briefly and simply, members of a family are *close* to one another. The closeness is the reason for being happy for, and proud of, one another. We do not reproach a father boasting about the scholarly accomplishments of his child by saying that he should not bask in the glory of another person; rather, we are ready to confirm that he has reason to feel proud. By contrast, Marcel Hirscher and I are not close. My reaction to his win is the same as though we were close, while we actually are not. We have never met. Taking pride, on my part, in his extraordinary stamina and skills is very similar to how a family feels about successful kin. And yet, being close is not the warrant giving me a reason. Viewed from that angle, my joy and pride appear to be *unwarranted*. They are based upon an *irresponsible belief*.

Irresponsible believing is, nonetheless, different from believing falsely or believing something that is entirely fictitious. It involves a certain structure and teleology. Beliefs of this type do not involve deontic commitments that require one to come forward with explanations or reasons.[79] Rather, they use placeholders of reasons – proxies, as it were.

[79] See Robert Brandom, *Articulating Reasons: An Introduction to Inferentialism* (Cambridge, MA: Harvard University Press, 2000), pp. 47–52.

For example, the reason for buying a book is that one would like to read it, or at least a part of it, in the future. Those, however, hoarding copies of works in gargantuan quantities in spite of their want of time and discipline to read even a small fraction of these have substituted this reason for the proxy reason that collecting books equals reading. A similar observation could be made about photocopying, in which case the light of the machine screening the text serves even as a quite visible analogue to the reader's gaze. Of course, no reasonable person could believe, responsibly, that hoarding or photocopying books is tantamount to reading. But one can cope with the frustration stemming from the lack of opportunities for reading interesting books. Hence, one can live with this frustration by relying on a proxy reason that is based upon the equation of collecting with reading. Of course, such reliance does not give you the real satisfaction, but it helps you to *forget* your own limitations.

The example demonstrates that irresponsible believing is facilitated by a belief in *substitutability*.[80] Taking buying and photocopying to be tantamount to reading is what gives rise to the proxy reason for buying and copying books. Of course, nobody who is not completely out of his mind could ever endorse the soundness of a belief that is warranted by a proxy reason.

Irresponsible believing has to be mediated, accordingly, by delegating the belief to someone else. The irresponsible believer has to be in the position to yield to the authority of someone whose beliefs are such that no rational person could ever find them believable. This someone cannot be someone in particular. No reasonable person could ever believe a belief that is underwritten by a proxy reason. Hence, the believers can only be other people, but no one in particular.

Other people whom you never encounter live in a different orbit. They inhabit the unconscious. The belief in substitutability that gives rise to a proxy reason is an unconsciously held belief. Actually, a great deal of what has come down upon us as *neurotic symptoms* is based upon the belief that one action can substitute another and thereby reconcile an inner conflict. Hence, practices that are based upon unconscious beliefs in substitutability are the equivalent of symptoms that attempt to resolve conflicts. And it is indeed possible that people share their unconsciously held beliefs by acting upon them while simultaneously disavowing any conscious commitment to their soundness.

[80] I am indebted, on this point, to Robert Pfaller, *Die Illusionen der anderen. Über das Lustprinzip in der Kultur* (Frankfurt: Suhrkamp, 2002).

This explains why it is not uncommon that pronounced postnationalists would never miss watching a game of their national soccer team. If asked how they are able to reconcile the apparent inconsistency they would presumably reply, 'Yeah, I know, but, you know, it's not serious . . ..'

7 The Imagined Community Reconsidered

The relevance of irresponsible believing for nationality is quite straightforward. Those relying on state power or any other form of collective agency in order to assert particular cultural mores as though they expressed unconditional demands presuppose that the state is preceded by the nation qua equivalent to the family or a family writ large.[81] This equivalence is revealed in phenomena such as taking pride in the *grandezza* of significant figures in national history or, for that matter, the solidarity among members. It is not by accident that solidarity among members of the nation is first spelled out in terms of 'fraternity', which is, in a sense, almost a Freudian slip. We had better take 'fraternity' or 'brotherhood' literally in this context.[82] Imagining the nation as a substitute for a family gives rise to the proxy reason for taking pride in the accomplishments of fellow nationals and for treating them with special concern.[83]

In his celebrated book on nationalism, Benedict Anderson characterises the nation as an 'imagined community' on the ground of the fact that '. . . members of even the smallest nation will never know most of their fellow-members, meet them, or even hear of them, yet in the minds of each lives the image of their communion'.[84] Alas, Anderson did not explore more deeply what this image really is, for all that he meant to capture was the fact that compatriots hardly ever meet.[85] Had he

[81] Clearly, the proposal made here is similar to George Lakoff's claim about the moral psychology of nations. See George Lakoff, *Moral Politics: How Liberals and Conservatives Think*, 3rd edition (Chicago: University of Chicago Press, 2015); George Lakoff, *Thinking Points: Communicating Our American Values and Vision* (New York: Farrar, Straus & Giroux, 2006), pp. 49–50. Quite perceptive observations regarding the relevance of historical pedigree and the mediation of horizontal mutual concern by vertical 'relatedness' are made by Yack, *Nationalism and the Moral Psychology*, p. 76.

[82] See already on Aristotle, *Nicomachean Ethics*.

[83] The family also provides the background explaining why ethno-nationalism has had so much appeal. A natural connection is a connection that cannot be changed, it is written, as is were, into our genes. See on this also Yack, above note 74 at 64–65.

[84] See Benedict Anderson, *Imagined Communities: Reflections on the Origin and Spread of Nationalism* (London: Verso, 1983) at 15.

[85] For a similar critique, see Yack, *Nationalism and the Moral Psychology*, pp. 59–60.

ventured into the social psychology of nationhood it may have occurred to him what is imagined is the nation as a substitute family and that this imaginary is adhered to in an irresponsible fashion.

Much more fine-grained than Anderson's account is Bernhard Yack's magisterial exploration of the field.[86] Yack emphasises that nations are communities of special obligation ('social friendship').[87] Its members affirm something that they share as a source for their connection. What members of a nation believe to be sharing is, according to Yack, their cultural inheritance.[88] If Yack is right about this, namely, that artefacts rather than practices matter, then he captures accurately that members of a nation transform culture into an object of preference. This is how they communicate – and construct – their connectedness.

8 Nationhood qua Symptom

However, if acting on the proxy reason underlying the nation is some kind of a resolution of conflict, one must wonder what this conflict might be. Not by accident, belief in nationality and national ties, which had been around for ages, turns into *nationalism* once people realise that the emancipation from feudal ties and the loyalties of inherited status has left them to their own devices.[89] Belief in the nation is then experienced as empowering, for it helps to overcome 'existential aloneness'[90] and spells out what it is that accounts for the people's power to create governments. Nationalism, thus understood, is a way of resolving the conflict between the quest for individual independence and the increasing individual dependence on sovereign power to make such independence not only possible, but also a relatively safe bet. Your nation showers you with the blessings of unconditional acceptance that Emerson conjured up in *Self-reliance* when he spoke of the nonchalance of a boy that is always sure of a dinner.[91] What makes nationalism into a *symptom*, and hence into a failed attempt at resolving the conflict, is that it is ruthlessly concerned with insiders.

86 Ibid.

87 Ibid., p. 51.

88 Ibid., p. 82.

89 See Ernest Gellner, 'The coming of nationalism and its interpretation: the myths of nation and class', in G. Balakrishnan (ed.), *Mapping the Nation* (London: Verso, 1996), pp. 98–145.

90 See Weiler, *The Constitution of Europe*, pp. 247, 338.

91 See Ralph Waldo Emerson, 'Self-reliance', in D. Crase (ed.), *Essays: First and Second Series* (New York: Vintage Books, 1990), pp. 29–52, at 31.

Would a postnational democracy provide the cure? Is it possible to imagine the blessings of solidarity among strangers to flow from a manner of imagining a mode of connection that would not involve construing an inheritance, bringing local narratives under its shelter and modelling mutual responsibility on the irresponsible belief of being a family writ large?

The record of the EU casts this prospect into doubt. Where the Union tries to steer clear of developing narratives it loses sight of the lure of particularity and embraces the universal. Where, by contrast, the Union puts itself into the context of a particular historical narrative it is not easy for all participating countries to relate to this narrative as their own.

9 Values and Narratives

The Union, qua stabilising agent of a transnational civil society[92] has already attempted to assist us in imagining the connection by pointing out what it is that we share. It has ventured to do so without appeal to heroes, imposing examples or stories evoking the deeds of 'great men'. The Union did not emulate nationalist narratives that talk of struggles and victories or of humiliation followed by victory; rather, it decided to dwell on abstractions. As a starry-eyed adaptor of constitutional patriotism, the Union has incorporated into the EU treaties a long list of values for which it claims to stand: human dignity, equality – in particular between men and women – freedom, the rule of law and a number of other great things. If you lack imagination – if you do not know how to tell a story of how 'we' have become who we are – that is exactly what you put into the inventory of what you stand for. The problem with these values is that they belong to humankind, and someone who rejects speciesism could even include a few animals into the set. One cannot create awareness of a particular community on the basis of values that supposedly encompass all. They do not provide people with a social home to which they can return after they have been to foreign places. They turn the whole world into a world inhabited by foreigners. This is not the type of community we find it easy to care about.

From this seems to follow, that a functional equivalent to shared national legacy is next to impossible to imagine. Unsurprisingly, therefore, one encounters traces of cautious nation building in the Union.

[92] On effectiveness as the traditional legitimating factor of the EU, see Jan Zielonka, *Is the EU Doomed?* (Cambridge: Polity, 2014), p. 41.

Yack has taught us that the process of building a nation can use two entries. One can either begin with a shared cultural inheritance and affirm it as a source of connection or begin with inchoate sentiments of civic friendship and then feel out their cultural roots:[93]

> In the first case, the what leads to the who: the sense of sharing some good or practice or purpose leads us to imagine ourselves connected to a particular group of individuals. In the second case the who leads to the what: the sense of connection to others leads us to try to specify what it is that we share with them. In other words, community involves imagining connections to those with whom we share things as well as imagining the things that we share with those with whom we feel connected. The first process creates communities as objects of imagination; the second leads to their development.

The first path consists of developing some particular narrative. Honestly, this has been going on in the European Union all the while. The Union is cast as originating from a negative constitutional moment, namely, the Second World War, if not even the Holocaust. We are told that we owe its design to towering founding figures, such as Jean Monnet. Now and then, it is seen as tied to a way of life that appeals to all Europeans alike. It is presented as embracing a European social model or – using current EU treaties language – the social market economy. The old nation states are not supposed to disappear. Indeed, but this merely shows that the Union is a federal project.

Hence, we have seen attempts to create awareness of a common European inheritance that is not universal, but indeed exceptional. Those efforts are not at all dissimilar to constructing a common inheritance qua medium to affirm the special social bond uniting the members of a nation. One can find, therefore, indications of timid nation building in Europe. But it is unlikely to be very successful under current conditions, owing to the fact that people increasingly retreat to their particular national legacies as though they offered them a safe place.[94] Moreover, the enlargement of 2004 and its aftermath appear to have resulted in an ever growing divide between Eastern and Western Europe.[95] It makes one wonder whether Eastern Europeans do not suspect the European social model to amount to a fraud presented in order to blunt their

[93] Yack, *Nationalism and the Moral Psychology*, p. 60.

[94] See Jan Zielonka, *Counterrevolution: Liberal Europe in Retreat* (Oxford: Oxford University Press, 2018).

[95] For an interesting contrast, see Ivan Krastev, *After Europe* (Philadelphia, PA: University of Pennsylvania Press, 2017).

competitive edge.[96] The 'refugee crisis' has done a great deal to aggravate this problem. The crosscutting cleavages produced by recurring Eurozone safeguard measures work to reinforce highly moralised divisions among Europeans.[97] Not only have they given rise to various questions concerning the rule of law and subsidiarity in Europe, they have also raised the spectre of a European *Großraum* in which Germany occupies the position of the hegemon.[98] It is impossible to build a common European inheritance if many are under the impression that one old nation state is pulling the strings in the Union.

If Yack is correct, however, the process could also work in the opposite direction. One could begin with common sympathies or some inchoate feeling of belonging together. And, indeed, Europeans seem to share, within a range of variations, a certain work ethic and seem to have similar outlooks with regard to what counts as an ordinary, respectable or admirable life. Admittedly, there are differences concerning the lifestyle of Northern and Southern Europeans, but not only is there mutual respect, it is also to be expected that competitive pressures are going to even these increasingly out in the future. Nevertheless, it is difficult to imagine how a historically relatively heterogeneous Union could possibly arrive at a shared narrative. Viewing the Union as originating from one major mistake to which all countries in one way or another contributed – the Second World War – presupposes taking a critical stance towards one's own national history. It is not so clear that all countries or nations are ready to take this step. Some may be inclined to view their country or their nation, for that matter, in the role of a victim. Nevertheless, overcoming common mistakes – mistakes made in the light of high aspirations – would perhaps be the most plausible focus for a narrative anchoring European identity.

[96] See Damjan Kukovec, 'Law and the periphery', *European Law Journal*, 21 (2014), 406–28.

[97] See Zielonka, *Is the EU Doomed?*, pp. 21–2.

[98] For the exposition of the concept of the *Großraum*, see Carl Schmitt, *Völkerrechtliche Großraumordnung mit Interventionsverbot für raumfremde Mächte. Ein Beitrag zum Reichsbegriff im Völkerrecht*, 4th edition (Berlin: Deutscher Rechtsverlag, 1941), p. 49. For a reconstruction of the idea and the controversy to which it had given rise, see Christian Joerges, 'Europe a Großraum? Shifting legal conceptualisations of the integration project', in C. Joerges and N. Ghaleigh (eds.), *Darker Legacies of Law in Europe. The Shadow of National Socialism and Fascism over Europe and Its Legal Traditions* (Oxford: Hart Publishing, 2003), 167–91, at 173–7. On the role of Germany in the current EU see, notably, Ulrich K. Beck, *Das deutsche Europa: Neue Machtlandschaften im Zeichen der Krise*, 2nd edition (Berlin: Suhrkamp, 2012).

The partial reluctance to accept a story that, again, is likely to find more resonance in Western Europe is one factor explaining why an equivalent to the traditional national narratives is unlikely to take roots. Another factor is that the Union is still driven by its imperial desire to grow. In many respects, Europe behaves like an empire.[99] It expands and recognises limits only to transcend them; it has jagged boundaries at which participation in the Union becomes a matter of more or less involvement and more or less voice; and the Union does not seem to worry about its multi-national composition for the reason that there is a hegemonic culture – modern capitalism – and the motives for staying together are peace and prosperity. One could even add, in a Schmittian vein, that it performs this 'katechontic' role of preventing the apocalypse.[100] If it were not for the Union, Europe would relapse to old barbarian ways. This is at least what we keep telling ourselves all the time.

10 Conclusion

The conclusions that follow are simple und unsurprising.

Presumably, European democracy can be lively without giving rise to significant social policies. Perhaps it already is, and if it is it concerns the nation states involved in negotiating various forms of retreating from sharing responsibilities. It is to be expected, however, that the eye of the public will be fixated upon debates in the national arena and vigilant with regard to how governments position themselves in the Council. This is not, however, what advocates of European postnational democracy wish for, but it is a form of democracy that matches situations in which contending social groups – for example, ethnicities or social classes – negotiate various deals in order to keep out of each other's way. They may also agree to delegate certain tasks to administrative bodies that are in charge of levelling a playing field and managing risks. The liveliness of European democracy is then, however, in all likelihood derivative of the liveliness of national democratic processes.

It is not terribly likely that we are going to see democratic politics that is heavily invested in social policy for the simple reason that Europe lacks the requisite relative homogeneity. Such homogeneity depends on viewing others as good people and, equally important, as likeminded on

[99] See Jan Zielonka, 'Europe as a global actor: empire by example?', *International Affairs*, 84 (2008), 471–84.

[100] See Carl Schmitt, *Der Nomos der Erde im Völkerrecht des Jus Publicum Europaeum*, 3rd edition (Berlin: Duncker & Humblot, 1988), pp. 28–30.

matters such as reciprocity and fairness. We cannot have solidarity in the EU if the Germans are under the impression that solidarity means that Germany has to pick up the bill while the Greeks evade taxes. We cannot have solidarity in the EU when the Eastern Europeans feel exploited by Western businesses and Western Europeans believe that Eastern Europeans shirk when it comes to doing their bit.

A postnational European democracy may be lively, but not socially significant. Indeed, there is no reason to believe that we still have to engage in an effort to build a postnational democracy. We may already have it. And possibly, the alternative to move Europe more towards creating a nation would come at a high cost. National identity is quick when it comes to drawing a line towards the other. Turkey and Russia would end up being on the other side. Would that be an unequivocally desirable result?

12

Solidarity in the Case Law of the European Court of Justice

Opportunities Missed?

DAGMAR SCHIEK

1 Introduction

Achieving and maintaining solidarity in the European Union (EU) increasingly seems challenging: political projects prioritising individual nation states and renouncing any solidarity beyond national borders are gaining in momentum. The 2016 'Brexit' vote in the UK epitomises these tendencies, though scepticism of any form of transnational solidarity is certainly shared by more Europeans than those English voters supporting 'LEAVE'. Can the EU survive as a project of a community based on law that promotes transnational solidarity? The EU Treaties at least express that solidarity is one of the EU's fundamental values (Articles 2, 3 (2) Treaty on European Union [TEU]). In a community of law, the validity of this value would depend on its capacity as a legal principle. This chapter explores whether and how far the case law of the Court of Justice (ECJ) supports solidarity as an EU constitutional law principle.

This chapter does not endeavour to compete with the expansive discussion on what solidarity may mean.[1] Instead, it focuses on the question

[1] Recently see, with a focus on EU perspectives, A. Biondi, E. Dagilyte andE. Kucuk, *Solidarity in EU Law: Legal Principle in the Making* (Cheltenham: Edward Elgar, 2018); G. Butler, 'Solidarity and its limits for economic integration in the European Union's internal market', *Maastricht Journal of European and Comparative Law*, 25(3) (2018), 310–31; I. Ciornei andE. Recchi, 'At the source of European solidarity: assessing the effects of cross-border practices and political attitudes', *Journal of Common Market Studies*, 55(3) (2017), 468–85; C. Lahusen and M. Grasso (eds.), *Solidarity in Europe. Citizens' Responses in Times of Crisis* (London: Palgrave Macmillan, 2018); D. Schiek, 'Perspectives on social citizenship in the EU: from status positivus to status socialis activus via two forms of transnational solidarity', in D. Kochenov (ed.), *EU Citizenship and Federalism* (Cambridge: Cambridge University Press, 2017); S. Sciarra, *Solidarity and Conflicts.*

of what solidarity signifies as a constitutional concept of EU law. Since the EU's integration project ultimately aims at linking societies of Member States,[2] it is not surprising that solidarity emerges as a central EU value in the Treaties' norms and preambles. Linking societies of Member States through the integration project ultimately presupposes that the interaction of citizens eventually leads to solidarity bonds beyond the nation states, through a re-orientation of both Member States and citizens towards transnational solidarity. Citizens need to be prepared to regard citizens of other Member States as equally worthy of inclusion.[3] Member states should support such developments by embracing solidarity as a value of the EU that is common to the Member States. Nevertheless, a number of authors continue to promote the limitation of practical solidarity to the national level,[4] possibly supported by a 'holding environment' at EU level.[5] There are reasons to doubt whether the implicit separation of economic integration at EU level and social integration at national levels can succeed.[6] More likely, if solidarity is not enacted at EU level, EU policies pursued may well result in social deprivation in citizens' lives, especially in Member States whose economy does not yield a constant export surplus.

Instead of developing a definition of solidarity, this chapter asks what, if anything, the case law of the ECJ[7] contributes to the discursive exegesis of solidarity as a principle of EU law. In order to answer this question, it offers an empirical analysis of the Court's case law framing the notion of

European Social Law in Crisis (Cambridge: Cambridge University Press,2018); as well as the contributions in this edited collection.

[2] D. Schiek, *Economic and Social Integration. The Challenge for EU Constitutional Law* (Cheltenham: Edward Elgar, 2012).

[3] See on this perspective: J. Gerhards and H. Lengfeld, *Citizenship and Social Integration in the European Union* (Abingdon: Routledge, 2015).

[4] E.g. under the heading of 'conflicts law constitutionalism' by C. Joerges, 'Social justice in an ever more diverse union', in F. Vandenbroucke, C. Barnard and G. D. Baere (eds.), *A European Social Union after the Crisis* (Cambridge: Cambridge University Press, 2017), pp. 105–7.

[5] F. Vandenbroucke, 'The idea of a European social union', in Vandenbroucke, Barnard and Baere (eds.), *A European Social Union after the Crisis*, pp. 3–46.

[6] Schiek, *Economic and Social Integration*, pp. 215–43; Schiek, Perspectives on social citizenship in the EU, pp. 345–54.

[7] The Court of Justice of the European Union (CJEU) consists of the Court of Justice (still abbreviated to ECJ), the General Court (GC) and special courts, whose number can be expanded (see Article 19 TEU). Our analysis is confined to ECJ cases, because it reviews the case law of the GC, hears all national references (Article 267 TFEU) and thus has the best opportunity to elaborate how EU law should interact with national law and socio-economic reality.

solidarity. The analysis is not limited to cases which have gained the status of key cases in a largely undisclosed process of peer consensus. Instead, we use a method suitable to identify all cases in which the concept of solidarity was not only mentioned, but also relevant. Thus, we analyse the full extent of the Court's discourse on solidarity, rather than adding to the literature on those cases which have long been identified as key cases in the area.

The next section introduces the methodology used for identifying and analysing the case law sample, and explains what this methodology seeks to achieve. Though this chapter is not on the concept of solidarity from a philosophical, sociological or legal theory perspective, it is necessary to introduce the main content of solidarity as a concept in EU (Constitutional) Law, in order to identify the dimensions and types of solidarity we expect to find in the analysis. We distinguish four dimensions (solidarity between citizens, between Member States and the EU, between Member States and citizens, and international solidarity) and altogether six types of solidarity within the subcategories categorial definition (solidarity as charity, solidarity as mutual obligation, solidarity as risk mitigation) and functionalities (embedding individual rights, embedding the Internal Market, rejecting limiting effects of national solidarity). The third section presents the results of a content analysis of ECJ case law using the term 'solidarity'. The conclusion identifies a number of missed opportunities, in particular in recent years and in response to events perceived as critical junctures for the future of EU integration. The judicial response to Brexit constitutes one prime example for this: when the Court enabled the UK to revoke the notice of its intention to withdraw from the Union, it emphasised EU citizenship as fundamental status of the EU without any reference to the solidarity dimension of EU citizenship.[8] We conclude that there is much space for solidarity becoming more relevant to the Court's case law.

2 Analysing the Court's Discourse on Solidarity – Why and How

In analysing the Court's case law on solidarity, this chapter exposes the textual discourses of the Court's case law through an empirical analysis.[9] The purpose of this investigation is both explanatory and normative.

[8] This is discussed in more detail below, in the text around note 83.

[9] On this see already D. Schiek, 'Is there a social ideal of the European Court of Justice?', in: U. Neergaard, R. Nielsen and L. Roseberry (eds.), *The Role of Courts in Developing a European Social Model* (Copenhagen: DJØF Publishing, 2010), pp. 63–96; D. Schiek, 'Social ideals of the Court of Justice of the European Union', in: T. Evas, U. Liebert and

In so far as it is explanatory, the chapter contributes to understanding how judges deal with law's indeterminacy, as well as uncovering judges' ideas on adequate organisation of society represented in case law, which will be influential on the Court's future case law and on EU law- and policy-making more generally.[10] There is little doubt that the ECJ relies on more than positive law in its rulings. This is a logical consequence of law's principled indeterminacy, which requires any court to produce rules and participate in governance of society by making law, alongside parliaments and government.[11] As a consequence, no court can be but a political and social actor in deciding which aspects of an indeterminate norm to stress.[12]

For the EU judiciary, this role is compounded by its character as a constitutional court, whose tasks extend beyond mere interpretation of positive law. Article 19 Treaty on European Union (TEU) requires the Court to 'ensure that in interpretation and application of the Treaties the law is observed'. This phrase distinguishes between the positive law of the Treaties and the law elsewhere, referring to the difference between *lex*

C. Lord (eds.), *Multilayered Representation in the European Union: Parliaments, Courts and the Public Sphere* (Baden-Baden: Nomos, 2012), pp. 157–82.

10 E. Achtsioglou and M. Doherty, 'There must be some way out of here: the crisis, labour rights and member states in the eye of the storm', *European Law Journal*, 20(2) 2014, 219–40, at 233–5.

11 Aside from profound differences in detail, there is agreement in so far between linguists, positivists and different jurisprudential schools. Linguists agree on the existence of imbued meaning and the necessity of drawing on circumstantial knowledge when understanding textual language, which is also the starting point of critical discourse analysis, see T. v Leeuwen, 'Discourse as recontextualisation of social practice: a guide', in R. Wodak and M. Meyer (eds.), *Methods of Critical Discourse Analysis*, 2nd edition (London: Sage, 2009), p. 147. Positivist legal theorists acknowledge the open texture of law as described above, see L. Hart, *The Concept of Law (with a postscript by Penelope Bulloch and Joseph Raz)*, 2nd edition (Oxford: Oxford University Press, 1997), pp. 118, 123–26, but may prefer other terms, including 'uncertainty' (Hart) or judicial discretion or choice, see D. Leczykiewicz, 'Why do the European Court of Justice judges need legal concepts?', *European Law Journal*, 14(6) 2008, 773–86, at 774.

12 This is upheld widely for the ECJ, see for example A. Stone Sweet, 'The European Court of Justice and the judicialization of EU governance', *Living Reviews in European Governance*, 5(2) 2010, 7–9; see also J. Bengoetxea, N. MacCormick and L. Moral Soriano, 'Integration and integrity in the legal reasoning of the European Court of Justice', in G. d. Búrca and J. H. Weiler (eds.), *The European Court of Justice* (Oxford: Oxford University Press, 2001), p. 43, who question the concept of a clear line between law and politics underlying the critique of the Court, suggesting that the challenge is to manage the inevitable overlap between law and politics in constitutional adjudication. The EU's highest judge accepts the necessity of 'non-deductive' arguments, i.e. reasoning not reliant on the text of EU norms, as a reality in the Court's daily work. K. Lenaerts, 'Discovering the law of the EU: the European Court of Justice and the comparative method', in T. Perisin and S. Rodin (eds.), The Transformation or Reconstitution of Europe (Oxford: Hart, 2018), p. 61.

and *ius*, which is acknowledged by most European languages.[13] The Court is thus charged with ensuring the congruence of positive law with justice derived from supra-positive law.[14] Contrary to a popular critique, fulfilling a constitutional court's task of deriving general principles of law from supra-positive sources does not constitute any illegitimate usurpation of parliamentary or government functions.

The question remains how the Court discharges with the task of finding justice beyond the positive law – and this is the question the selected method sets out to answer. It starts where the traditional methods of interpreting the positive law end, exploring how judges use their 'imagination'[15] through a systematic analysis of the Court's paradigmatic engagement with discourses in national societies and the emerging European society. It thus complements the academic works on the Court as a political actor.[16] In doing so, it shares some common ground with legal realism, a school which in the USA has seen a revival as New Legal Realism from 2005,[17] and is closely linked to empirical legal studies dedicated to either predicting future case law or to analysing interaction of societies with courts from.[18] New European Legal Realism[19] relates to this school as well as to Scandinavian Realism

[13] See also F. Jacobs, *The Sovereignty of Law. The European Way* (Cambridge: Cambridge University Press, 2007).

[14] See also T. Tridimas, 'The Court of Justice of the European Union', in R. Schütze and T. Tridimas (eds.), *Oxford Principles of European Union Law, Volume 1: The European Union Legal Order* (Oxford: Oxford University Press, 2018), p. 583.

[15] L. Azoulai, 'The Court of Justice and the social market economy', *Common Market Law Review*, 45(5) 2008, 1335–46, at 1339–40.

[16] See for example K. Alter, *The European Court's Political Power* (Oxford: Oxford University Press, 2009); D. Sindbjerg Martinsen, *An Ever More Powerful Court? The Political Constraints of Legal Integration in the European Union* (Oxford: Oxford University Press, 2015); Stone Sweet, 'The European Court of Justice and the judicialization of EU governance'.

[17] See H. Erlanger et al., 'Is it time for a new legal realism?', *Wisconsin Law Review*, 2005(2) (2005), 353–63; V.Nourse and G. Shaffer, 'Varieties of new legal realism: can a new world order prompt a new legal theory?', *Cornell Law Review*, 95(1) (2010), 61–138.

[18] N. Barber, 'Legal realism, pluralism and their challengers', in U. Neegard and R. Nielsen (eds.), *European Legal Method – Towards a New European Legal Realism?* (Copenhagen: DJØF Publishing, 2013), pp. 189–209; M. C. Suchman and E. Mertz, 'Towards an new legal empiricism: empirical legal studies and new legal realism', *Annual Review of Law and Society*, 6(2010), 555–79; for a European example of new legal empirics attempting to predict ECJ case law see M. Malecki, 'Do ECJ judges all speak with the same voice? Evidence of divergent preferences from the judgments of the chambers', *Journal of European Public Policy*, 19(1) (2012), 59–75.

[19] H. Koch, K. Hagel-Sørensen, U. Haltern and J.Weiler (eds.), *Europe. The New Legal Realism* (Copenhagen: DJØF Publishing, 2010); U. Neergaard and R. Nielsen (eds.),

a jurisprudential school seeking to derive the content of the law from observation of its operation, distancing itself from any normative theory.[20] A pragmatist approach led to observing the use of a variety of sources, including ideologies and the Zeitgeist.[21] The approach taken here takes on board the numerical dimension of empirical legal realism, though it is not concerned with judicial behaviour.[22]

The point of social ideal analysis is to identify the ideational and zeitgeisty elements of case law. Presupposing that law as a whole is a social practice,[23] the textual analysis addresses the discursive practice of courts. A court's discourse, though inherently authoritative, is not independent from other discursive practices in society. Law while endowed with its own internal logic, is at best semi-autonomous, but never fully self-referential.[24]

European Legal Method – Towards a New European Legal Realism? (Copenhagen: DJØF Publishing, 2013).

20 R. Nielsen, 'Legal realism and EU law', in H. Koch, K. Hagel-Sørensen, U. Haltern and J. Weiler (eds.), *Europe. The New Legal Realism* (Copenhagen: DJØF Publishing, 2010), pp. 545–63; R. Nielsen, 'New European legal realism – new problems, new solutions?', in U. Neeergaard and R. Nielsen (eds.), *European Legal Method – Towards a New European Legal Realism?* (Copenhagen: DJØF Publishing, 2013), pp. 75–124.

21 The latter is perceived as the base of Hjalte Rasmussen's European legal realism, see M. R. Madsen, 'Scandinavian (neo-)realism and European courts', in H. Koch, K. Hagel-Sørensen, U. Haltern and J. H. Weiler (eds.), *Europe: The New Legal Realism* (Copenhagen: DJØF Publishing, 2010), pp. 437–55.

22 As are some of the legal realists from both sides of the Atlantic do: the US new legal realists Leiter describes analysing what courts do as the main interest of new and old legal realists, B. Leiter, 'Legal realisms, old and new', *Valparaiso Law Review*, 47(4) (2013), 949–963, while Nourse and Shaffer see judicial behaviour studies as only one of three strands of new legal realism, V. Nourse and G. Shaffer, 'Varieties of new legal realism: can a new world order prompt a new legal theory?', *Cornell Law Review*, 95(1) (2010), 61–138. For Scandinavian legal realists, courts are an important, if not the most important site of exploration, as law only becomes real when it is applied, Nielsen, 'New European legal realism – new problems, new solutions?', pp. 95–9).

23 As a social practice, law only maintains a relative autonomy from socio-economic reality in which it develops, for Bourdieu the main distinction of his approach to law from Luhmann's systems theory, P. Bordieu, 'The force of law: towards a sociology of the juridical field', *The Hastings Law Journal*, 38 (1987), 805–53, at 816–53). For a more recent summary of law as a social practice see A. Marmor, 'The nature of law', in E. N. Zalta (ed.), *The Stanford Encyclopedia of Philosophy* (Stanford, CA: Stanford University, 2011).

24 Tuori suggests that systems theory might be usefully applied to the relation between law and politics, but loses its value in relating law to societies, K. Tuori, 'The relationality of European constitution(s). Justifying a new research programme for European constitutional scholarship', in U. Neergaard and R. Nielsen (eds.), *European Legal Method: Towards a New Legal Realism?* (Copenhagen: DJØF Publishing, 2013), pp. 26–30, with references to Luhman and Teubner. By contrast, Grimmel suggests that law relates to 'political realities', A. Grimmel, 'The uniting of Europe by transclusion: understanding

The normative dimension of the analysis is based on the assumption that case law as a discourse is constitutive of the EU's constitutional practice as well as conditioned by its normative foundations. Thus, the content of the Court's discourse matters, in that it conveys the finer granules of grand constitutional principles such as solidarity. In other words, we contend that what matters is not merely the Court's reaction to the increasing media coverage of its case law,[25] but also the Court's contribution to shaping the discourses on the content of central EU constitutional principles. It is the Court's privilege and opportunity to communicate to the public the content of those principles applied to everyday cases on the ground. The increasingly thorough press coverage of the Court's case law is only one indication of its relevance for the emerging European public sphere, and the EU's perception as a community of values. In times where solidarity of the Union with its Member States and its citizens is frequently doubted, nothing could be more important than a careful discourse of the Court filling solidarity as a central legal value of the EU[26] with life.

Conceiving EU case law as discourse that is socially constitutive and conditioned at the same time requires certain methodological choices. The assumption that the authority of case law is imbued in the text of the judgments, rather than in the persons of the judges, is a central tenet of social ideal analysis: its chosen method is a critical textual analysis. This textual approach is particularly adequate to the ECJ with its predominantly document-based procedure,[27] which also has engendered the habit of repeating

the contextual conditions of integration through law', *Journal of European Integration*, 36 (6) (2014), pp. 549–66, at 555, while having indicated earlier that it is autonomous from societal impact. A. Grimmel, 'Judicial interpretation or judicial activism? The legacy of rationalism in the studies of the European Court of Justice', *European Law Journal*, 18(4) (2012), 518–35, at 519.

25 M. Blauberger et al., 'The ECJ Judges read the morning papers. Explaining the turnaround of European citizenship jurisprudence', *Journal of European Public Policy*, 25(10) (2018), 1422–41.

26 As impressively presented by AG Bot in his opinion in case C-643/15 Slovakia v Council EU:C:2017:618, paragraphs 18, 'Solidarity is among the cardinal values of the Union and is even among the foundations of the Union. How would it be possible to deepen the solidarity between the peoples of Europe and to envisage ever closer union between those people, as advocated in the Preamble to the EU Treaty, without solidarity between the Member States when one of them is faced with an emergency situation? I am referring here to the quintessence of what is both the raison d'être and the objective of the European project.'

27 Tridimas, 'The Court of Justice of the European Union', pp. 599–601, pointing to the influence of English judges, which nudges the Court towards appreciating the oral elements of the procedure. This influence will decrease, though.

certain formulas verbatim in long lines of judgments.[28] The texts of these judgments are enunciated as collective decisions, much to the dismay of authors based in common law legal cultures with a more rhetorical tradition of adjudication.[29] This further supports the argument that at least for the ECJ it is adequate to evaluate the discourse transported by the texts themselves, rather than investigating the judges' motives.[30] The suggested research method thus utilises the abilities for hermeneutic analysis engendered by a legal education, and honed in legal scholarship.[31] It also goes well beyond classical legal method in its ambition to uncover ideals hidden in legal texts written by courts. This excludes following the conventional legal research method, which would focus on key cases that are identified as key cases through a process of peer conformity.[32] If we aim to capture the potential impact of judicial texts, we need to consider the totality of a certain case law section. Treating case law as empirical data in this way enhances the potential to generate new knowledge by establishing unique databases of case law. For the CJEU, this kind of analysis is eased by the existence of a searchable text data base, which enables researchers to use their own search terms and thus to capture the full extent of case law relevant to certain key concepts.

3 Solidarity as a Concept in EU Constitutional Law

This section establishes the conceptual matrix against which the notion of solidarity in ECJ case law will be analysed. To this end, it first sketches

[28] On the dominance of civil law traditions in the Court's procedure and practice see V. Perju, 'Reason and authority in the European Court of Justice', *Virginia Journal of International Law*, 49(2) (2009), 307–77, at 357.

[29] Malecki, 'Do ECJ judges all speak with the same voice?'; Perju, V., 'Reason and authority in the European Court of Justice'.

[30] M. Everson and J. Eisner, *The Making of a European Constitution: Judes and Law Beyond Constitutive Power* (Abingdon: Routledge, 2007), aim at unearthing those motives by interviewing judges. Similar aims can be pursued by combining case law analysis with experiments involving non-judicial actors, K. J. Bybee, 'Paying attention to what judges say: new directions in the study of judicial decisionmaking', *Annual Review of Law and Social Science*, 8(2012), 69–84, at 74.

[31] US Legal Realism has been criticised for not applying social science methodology consistently: realists, it is suggested, only do what lawyers do best: reading and analysing and systematising case law, B. Leiter, 'Legal realisms, old and new', *Valparaiso Law Review*, 47 (4) (2013), 949–63.

[32] For a traditional defence of this for EU law see G. Conway, *The Limits of Legal Reasoning and the European Court of Justice* (Cambridge: Cambridge University Press, 2012). From a more critical perspective, referring to the common law see J. Morison, 'What makes an important case? A research agenda', *Legal Information Management*, 12(4) (2012), 251–61.

solidarity as a concept, and then turns to it specification as an EU legal principle. Finally, dimensions and types of solidarity in EU constitutional law are identified, to serve as a coding system for analysing the Court's case law, alongside the policy fields in which solidarity can be expected to be used.

3.1 Solidarity as a Concept

Solidarity as a concept is not inherently legal. It originated as a fundamental concept in sociology and philosophy. The dualism proposed by Durkheim seems relatively modest today: he distinguished between mechanic solidarity, which is based on ties developed in small, closed groups (for example, by kinship), and organic solidarity, which emerges in industrial societies dependant on exchange between their individual members. Mechanic solidarity appears as a condition experienced as natural obligation, perhaps experienced as inescapable fate, or obligation.[33] Organic solidarity requires effort by a developed society, and the concept has been considered as unrealistic by critical voices.[34] Solidarity as a Weberian concept has been characterised as special type of social relationship established by the organising power of a polity.[35] Habermas' concept implicitly builds on the latter, in that Habermas characterises solidarity as emerging from a 'social context ... created through politics',[36] in which the concept of fraternity and solidarity were initially used synonymously to capture the bond emanating from common humaneness in a 'secular religion of humanity'.[37] From a Weberian and/or Habermasian perspective, solidarity is congruent with the organic interrelation of members of the same social class after industrialisation. Solidarity also succeeded charity as a social institution offering relief to the poor: instead of hoping for gaining income from altruistic activities of the better off, the expansion of the non-possessing classes also enabled them to mutually support each other. Solidarity as risk mitigation through mutual obligation was born in the mutual societies in the early industrial age in Europe.[38] This element of solidarity is not always

[33] See on the latter A. Somek, 'Solidarity decomposed: being and time in European citizenship', *European Law Review*, 36(6) (2007), 787–818.

[34] F. d. Witte, 'The end of EU citizenship and the means of non-discrimination', *Maastricht Journal of Comparative and European Law*, 18(1–2) (2011), 86–108.

[35] M. Ross, 'Solidarity – a new constitutional paradigm for the EU?', in *Promoting Solidarity in the European Union* (Oxford: Oxford University Press, 2010), p. 26.

[36] J. Habermas, *The Lure of Technocracy* (London: Polity Press, 2015), p. 26.

[37] Habermas, *The Lure of Technocracy*, p. 27

[38] See for example J. Zeitlin, 'From labour history to the history of industrial relations', *The Economic Historic Review*, 40(2) (1987), 159–84.

recognised, in particular by writers who use solidarity as an overarching term encompassing altruistic activities as well as activities based on mutuality, that is, collective interest. For example, Stjernø's[39] conceptual matrix proposes a continuum from solidarity based on homogeneity, with a strong collective orientation, over solidarity through shared interests towards a universal solidarity towards the whole of humankind, with the latter category building on the more compassionate and altruistic motives of caring for humanity.

Understanding solidarity not as a feeling, or orientation, but rather as a set of potential courses of actions shaped by institutional environments, we can distinguish between participative and receptive solidarity.[40] The former is expressed by collective or common action of those connected by common interests, while the latter is experienced in receiving benefits or other payments. As expanded before, both forms of solidarity move beyond solidarity as charity or spontaneous emotion in that they are organised on the basis of principles and norms, frequently enshrined in law. This corresponds to the fact that solidarity in post-mechanic societies in the Durkheimian sense depends on institutions, such as rights guarantees. These presuppose interaction with fellow citizens for creation and enforcement, as well as a constituted polity. Those interactions are not necessarily constrained within the boundaries of nation states. They could potentially encompass the world, or in our case transcend borders within the transnational entity constituted by the EU.

3.2 Solidarity in the EU Treaties

The EU since the Treaty of Lisbon, has enhanced its statutory commitment to solidarity, giving rise to solidarity as a new constitutional principle.[41] According to the TEU preamble, the Union is motivated by the desire to deepen solidarity between the Member States' peoples, while the preamble to the TFEU adds solidarity between the EU and the overseas countries, as already contained in the preamble to the Treaty on European Economic Community (EEC Treaty).[42]

[39] S. Stjernø, *Solidarity in Europe: The History of an Idea* (Cambridge: Cambridge University Press, 2009).

[40] Schiek, 'Perspectives on social citizenship in the EU'.

[41] See Ross, 'Solidarity – a new constitutional paradigm for the EU?'.

[42] U. Neergaard, 'In search of the role of solidarity in primary law and the case law of the European Court of Justice', in U. Neergaard, R. Nielsen and L. Roseberry (eds.), *The Role*

The first mentioning of solidarity in the Treaties appears in the TEU provision of values of the Union, which links the concept to the society:

> The Union is founded on the values of respect for human dignity, freedom, democracy, equality, the rule of law and respect for human rights, including the rights of persons belonging to minorities. These values are common to the Member States in a society in which pluralism, non-discrimination, tolerance, justice, solidarity and equality between women and men prevail. (Article 2 TEU)

The fact that solidarity is only mentioned in the second sentence may be read as incorporating a certain scepticism towards solidarity as a European value. Such scepticism would be based on the idea that activities epitomising solidarity, such as asset distribution and community building, require a pre-legal and pre-constitutional bond between peoples that does not exist beyond the boundaries of nation states. In this narrative, any dense constitution rooted in societies can only prevail in Member States, while the EU can never hope to proceed beyond mere formal or 'international' ties between Member States.[43] However, taking Article 2 TEU seriously, we suggest that the long process of constructing this provision[44] did purposely result in a clause which conceptually links Member States and the Union through the value of solidarity. It is correct that the provision lists the ingredients of liberalist constitutionalism in its first sentence, which may conjure the image of an abstentionist Union neither actively safeguarding human rights nor promoting their factual relevance. However, even that first sentence lists human dignity as a value, which constitutes a reference to the humane beyond liberal notions.[45] The first sentence also refers to equality, which again limits a mere liberal constitutional stance in that equal freedom demands an equitable distribution of assets.[46] Finally, the link between the first and the second sentence and the contents of

of Courts in Developing a European Social Model (Copenhagen: DJOV Publishing, 2010), pp. 97–138, reproduces specifications of solidarity in the EEC and EC treaties.

[43] See, for example, D. Grimm, *The Constitution of European Democracy* (Oxford: Oxford University Press, 2017), pp. 164–5.

[44] Article 2 TEU was originally drafted in the Constitutional Convention.

[45] On this see D. Kostakopoulou and N. Ferreira, *The Human Face of the European Union: Are EU Law and Policy Humane Enough?* (Cambridge: Cambridge University Press, 2015).

[46] U. Steinvorth, *Gleiche Freiheit. Politische Philosophie der Verteilungsgerechtigkeit* (Berlin: Akademie Verlag, 1999).

the second sentence matter. The second sentence links the values to the Member States, these are their common values. It also links them to the society (singular), instead of using the grammatical plural (societies). Article 2 TEU second sentence does thus not refer to national societies, conceiving these as distinct entities in each Member State. Instead, the provision presupposes that one European (or EUropean) society is emerging through the medium of European integration. Article 2 TEU posits normatively that this European society is informed by solidarity among other principles. It also relates to the Member States, thus paying tribute to the multi-level nature of the EU. Solidarity thus becomes a precondition for the existence of the EU's values.

3.3 *Identifying Dimensions and Types of Solidarity for Coding Case Law Analysis*

Even in the absence of a specific definition of solidarity as a constitutional key concept, the Treaties provide some orientation in that they specify relational dimensions of solidarity:[47] solidarity between the Union and Member States, solidarity between Member States, solidarity between Member States and citizens (of other Member States) and solidarity between individuals (for example, between generations). While it may seem counterintuitive that institutions such as the Member States or the EU as such can engage in solidarity, solidarity between the Union and the Member States, as well as mutual solidarity of Member States ultimately serves the ever closer union of peoples (Article 1 TEU), and thus also citizens, albeit indirectly. If Member States are required to exercise solidarity towards citizens of other Member States, this constitutes indirect solidarity of their citizens with those EU foreigners: after all the exercise in solidarity diminishes the funds available for national citizens. Similarly, solidarity between Member States can be viewed as indirect solidarity between their citizens as well. With this qualification, we arrive at four dimensions of solidarity, as indicated in the graph below.

Regarding the different notions of solidarity as they may emerge from the historical origin of the concept and different ideational approaches to

[47] See also I. Domurath, The three dimensions of solidarity in the EU legal order: limits of the judicial and legal approach', *Journal of European Integration*, 35(4) (2013), 459–475; P. Hilpold, 'Understanding solidarity within EU law: an analysis of the "islands of solidarity" with particular regard to monetary union', *Yearbook of European Law*, 34(1) (2015), 257–85.

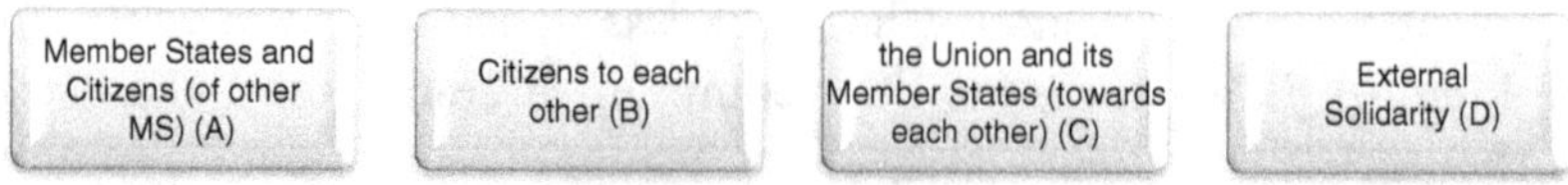

Figure 12.1 Dimensions of solidarity

its use, the Treaties do not offer any orientation. Thus, we would expect that the Court (alongside national courts, whose case law on solidarity under EU law is beyond the confines of this chapter) interprets and specifies solidarity. Deriving from the cursory overview of different approaches to solidarity, we would expect the case law to move between five types of solidarity, which on the one hand categorise solidarity and on the other hands allocate functions to solidarity specific for EU constitutional law.

We can distinguish three categorial types of solidarity. First, there is the option that solidarity is defined as the continuity of charity from premodern times. This form of solidarity would be characterised by a voluntary activity based on entirely altruistic motives, where the actor may follow an ethical or moral impetus, but which is beyond the realm of legal obligation. Second, if embracing the conceptual shift from charitable care for the poor to self-government of those who can only rely on their own work to sustain themselves, the notion of solidarity changes fundamentally. Solidarity is not a noble act based on potentially condescending altruism, but rather in principle based on mutual support. Instead, the contribution to a solidarity system are undertaken in the understanding that standing together individuals can shoulder risks they would be unable to bear individually. Even for the lucky ones who never need to rely on the activation of solidarity, being part of the system of mutual contributions grants the trust that they could rely on the collective. This leads to the third categorial type of solidarity, in which solidarity mitigates risks emanating from a fundamentally risky economic process governed not by plan and structure, but instead by market forces. In order to mitigate these market-driven risks, it is necessary to combine forces – even though there is no guarantee that each contribution (whether monetary or in kind) will be valued by actual support.

The categorial types of solidarity imply the functional types, which identify for which purpose (within the EU integration project) solidarity can be used. Here we expected two different types. Solidarity requires the obligation to contribute to a system even if an individual may not gain from his or her contributions. In a way solidarity thus defies individual

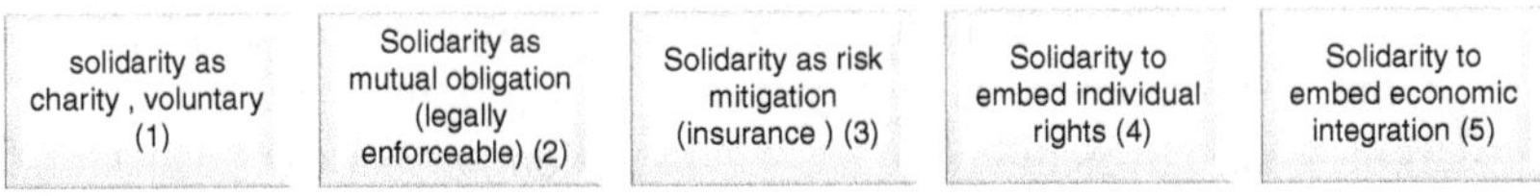

Figure 12.2 Categorial and functional types of solidarity

rights, which would demand that relinquishing property is rewarded in proportion to the contribution made. This means that the existence of solidarity bonds can also be used to justify limiting individual rights. Expressed differently, solidarity as a legal principle reminds us of the relational character of rights guarantees: rights can only be enjoyed in association with others, by an individual embedded in society. Solidarity thus serves to embed individual rights in society, or in the transnational integration of societies within the EU. While the fourth type of solidarity serves to embed individual rights, a fifth type is to be expected in the European Union as an entity integrating markets through legally enforceable institutions such as the economic freedoms and competition law. Those institutions frequently clash with national institutions established to engender that risk mitigation which is addressed by the second dimension of solidarity. Organising processes at national, subnational or perhaps even transnational level on the basis of solidarity can thus serve to justify restrictions of economic freedoms or the non-applicability of EU competition law because the entity acting on a market cannot be considered as an undertaking due to its solidarity-based constitution.

The categorial and functional types of solidarity are conceptually distinguished, though we must expect some overlap in the case law analysis: as stated, the limitation of individual rights as well as EU market-integrating concepts such as economic freedoms and competition rules is closely related to the function of solidarity as creating mutual obligations and as enabling the mitigation of risks. Case law categorisation will thus have to identify which type is most relevant to the case at hand.

4 Analysing CJEU Case Law in the Field

4.1 *Identifying relevant cases*

In order to identify all the cases using solidarity, the search function on case law on the CJEU web page was utilised. The search was limited to closed cases, and to those decided by the ECJ. The search for the term 'solidarity' for the period from the beginning of records in 1958 to March 2019 brought up 348 cases. For the evaluation, cases were excluded where 'solidarity' is cited from the name of parties, national institutions, national or EU legislation, although neither the EU Commission, any of the parties, the advocate general (AG) or the Court engaged substantively with the concept. These exclusions left 122 cases for evaluation.[48]

4.2 *Analysis Step One: Overall Picture*

The use of solidarity increases considerably over time, as can be established by grouping the analysis into five periods, separated by treaty reforms.

As the Figure 12.3 demonstrates, the ECJ did not depend on explicit treaty provisions on solidarity to develop the concept. The first case to mention solidarity was decided in December 1969,[49] and twelve more cases followed until the Single European Act was adopted. The notion of solidarity was used in a variety of areas, including value added tax, accession of the UK, staff regulations, agriculture and fisheries, as well as the fields identified as particularly relevant from today's perspective. Nevertheless, the use of solidarity in the Court's case law remained comparatively infrequent after the first treaty reform, the Single European Act 1987 and even after the Treaty of

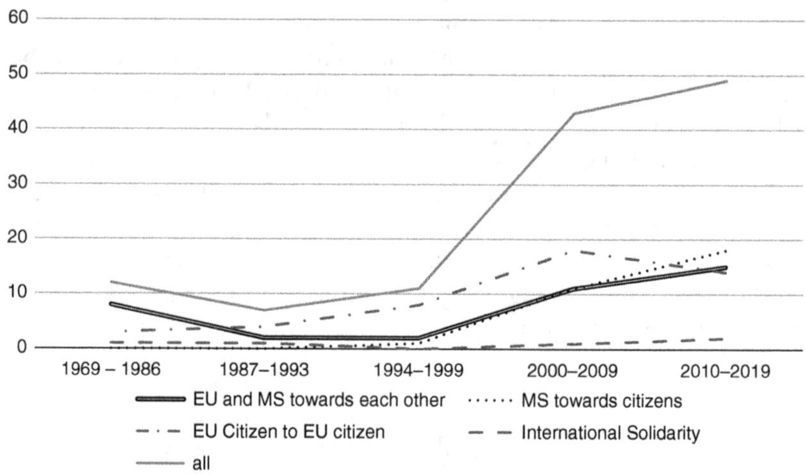

Figure 12.3 Frequency of dimensions of solidarity in ECJ case law over time

[48] Tables 12.1–5 listing the 122 cases chronologically and identifying which dimension and type of solidarity they were categorised under are available at the end of the chapter.

[49] Case 6/69 *COM* v. *France* EU:C:1969:68.

Table 12.1 *Phase 5: 2010–19 (eight years three months, forty-nine cases – about six annually)*

No.	Case no.	Ruling	Date	Parties	Area (courts category)	Category
1	C-216/18 PPU	Opinion ECLI:EU:C:2018:517 Judgment ECLI:EU: C:2018:586 Grand Chamber	28/06/2018 25/07/2018	Minister for Justice and Equality (Défaillances du système judiciaire)	area of freedom, security and justice – judicial cooperation in criminal matters	**2 C c**
2	C-412/17	Opinion ECLI:EU:C:2018:671	06/09/2018	Touring Tours und Travel	area of freedom, security and justice	**2 c C**
03	C-221/17	Opinion ECLI:EU: C:2018:572; Judgment ECLI:EU:C:2019:189	12/07/2018 12/03/2019	Tjebbes and Others	Citizenship of the Union	**4 a A**
04	C-163/17	Opinion ECLI:EU:C:2018:613 Judgment ECLI:EU: C:2019:218	25/07/2018 10/03/2019	Jawo	area of freedom, security and justice – asylum policy	**2 c C**
05	C-651/16	Judgment ECLI:EU:C:2018:162	07/03/2018	DW	Freedom of movement for workers	**6 g A**
06	C-646/16	Opinion ECLI:EU:C:2017:443; Judgment ECLI:EU:C:2017:586	08/06/2017ö 26/ 07/2017	Jafari	area of freedom, security and justice – asylum policy	**3 c C**

Table 12.1 (*cont.*)

No.	Case no.	Ruling	Date	Parties	Area (courts category)	Category
07	C-490/16	Opinion ECLI:EU:C:2017:443 Judgment (GC) ECLI:EU: C:2017:585	08/06/2017 26/07/2017	A.S.	area of freedom, security and justice – asylum policy	**2a c C**
08	C-442/16	Opinion ECLI:EU:C:2017:607 Judgment (GC) ECLI:EU: C:2017:1004	26/07/2017 20/12/2017	Gusa	Social security	**3 g A**
9	C-367/16	Opinion ECLI:EU:C:2017:636 Judgment (GC) ECLI:EU: C:2018:27	06/09/2017 23/01/2018	Piotrowski	area of freedom, security and justice – judicial cooperation in criminal matters	**2 c A**
10	C-259/16	Opinion ECLI:EU:C:2017:910 Judgment ECLI:EU: C:2018:370	28/11/2017 23/05/2018	Confetra and Others	Freedom of establishment	**5 b B**
11	C-226/16	Opinion ECLI:EU:C:2017:616 Judgment ECLI:EU: C:2017:1005	26/07/201720/12/ 2017	Eni and Others	Energy	**3 e C**

12	C-643/15	Opinion ECLI:EU:C:2017:618, Judgment ECLI:EU:C:2017:631	26/07/2017, 6 /09/ 2007 GRAND CHAMBER	Slovakia v Council	area of freedom, security and justice	**3 c C**
13	C-589/15 P	Opinion ECLI:EU:C:2017:175, Judgment ECLI: EU:C:2017:663 GRAND CHAMBER	07/03/2017, 12/09/ 2017	Anagnostakis v Commission	Economic and monetary policy	**2 d C**
14	C-638/16 PPU	Opinion ECLI:EU:C:2017:93 Judgment ECLI:EU: C:2017:173	07/02/2017 07/03/2017	X and X	Fundamental rights – Charter of Fundamental Rights	**2 c C**
15	C-404/15, 659/ 15 PPU	Judgment ECLI :EU : C :2016 :198 Opinion Bot ECLI:EU:C:2016:140	5 April 2016 3 March 2016	Pál Aranyosi (C-404/15) and Robert Căldăraru	European arrest warrant – Grounds for refusal to execute – Charter of Fundamental Rights of the European Union – Article 4 – Prohibition of inhuman or degrading treatment	**1 D c**

Table 12.1 (*cont.*)

No.	Case no.	Ruling	Date	Parties	Area (courts category)	Category
16	C-296/15	Judgment ECLI:EU:C:2017:431	08/06/2017	Medisanus	Approximation of laws	**3 b A**
17	Avis 3/15	Opinion Court (GC) ECLI:EU:C:2016:657 Opinion AG Wahl	March 2017 – not accessible 08/09/2016	Avis rendu en vertu de l'article 218, paragraphe 11, TFUE	Provisions governing the institutions	**6 f D**
18	C-201/15	Judgment (op) ECLI:EU:C:2016:972 (Grand Chamber)	21/12/2016	AGET Iraklis	Approximation of laws	**6 g B**
19	C-431/14 P	Judgment ECLI:EU:C:2016:145	08/03/2016	Greece v Commission	Competition – State aid	**6 b B**
20	C-346/14	Judgment ECLI:EU:C:2016:322	04/05/2016	Commission v Austria	Environment	**5 (environmental) C**
21	C-185/14	Judgment (Sum) ECLI:EU:C:2015:716	22/10/2015	EasyPay and Finance Engineering	Competition – state aid – services of general economic interest (wrong classification as tax)	**5 b C**

22	C-179/14	Judgment ECLI:EU:C:2016:108	23/02/2016	Commission v Hungary	Freedom of establishment	**6 b A**
23	C-50/14	Judgment ECLI:EU:C:2016:56	28/01/2016	Časta and Others	Principles, objectives and tasks of the Treaties	**5 b B**
24	C-25/14	Judgment (op) ECLI:EU:C:2015:821	17/12/2015	UNIS	Freedom to provide services	**6 b B**
25	C-543/13	Judgment (op) ECLI:EU:C:2015:359	04/06/2015	Fischer-Lintjens	Social security	**6 g B**
26	C-361/13	Judgment ECLI:EU:C:2015:601	16/09/2015	Commission v Slovakia	Freedom of movement for workers	**5 b A**
27	C-268/13	Judgment ECLI:EU: C:2014:2271	09/10/2014	Petru	Social security	**6 g A**
28	C-113/13	Judgment (op) ECLI:EU: C:2014:2440	11/12/2014	Azienda sanitaria locale n. 5 «Spezzino» and Others	Freedom of establishment	**5 b B**
29	C-574/12	Judgment (op, sum) ECLI:EU: C:2014:2004 5th chamber	19/06/2014	Centro Hospitalar de Setúbal and SUCH	Freedom of establishment	**6 b B**

Table 12.1 (*cont.*)

No.	Case no.	Ruling	Date	Parties	Area (courts category)	Category
30	C-507/12	Opinion ECLI:EU: C:2013:841	12/12/2013	St Prix	Citizenship of the Union – right of Entry and Residence	**3 a A**
31	C-370/12	Judgment (View) ECLI:EU:C:2012:756	27/11/2012	Pringle	Economic and monetary policy	**1 d C**
32	C-166/12	Judgment ECLI:EU:C:2013:792	05/12/2013	Časta	Staff Regulations of officials and Conditions of Employment of other servants	**4 g A**
33	C-140/12	Judgment (op) ECLI:EU:C:2013:565 Third	19/09/2013	Brey	Citizenship of the Union – Right of entry and residence	**2 a A**
34	C-136/12	Judgment ECLI:EU:C:2013:489 (fourth chamber)	18/07/2013	Consiglio nazionale dei geologi and Autorità garante della concorrenza e del mercato	Principles, objectives and tasks of the Treaties	**5 b B**

35	C-57/12	Judgment (op) ECLI:EU:C:2013:517 First Chamber	11/07/2013	Femarbel	Freedom to provide services	**1 b A**
36	C-433/11	Opinion EU :C :213 :6	10/01/2013	Jeltes and Others	Social Security	**2, g, A**
37	C-179/11	Judgment (op, SUM) ECLI:EU:C:2012:594	27/09/2012	Cimade and GISTI	area of freedom, security and justice – asylum policy	**3 c C**
38	C-75/11	Judgment (OP) ECLI:EU:C:2012:605	04/10/2012	Commission v Austria	non-discrimination – Non-discrimination on grounds of nationality (Citizenship)	**2 a A**
39	C-606/10	Judgment ECLI:EU:C:2012:348	14/06/2012	ANAFE	area of freedom, security and justice – Border checks	**2a c C**
40	C-562/10	Judgment ECLI:EU:C:2012:442	12/07/2012	Commission v Germany	Freedom to provide services	**5 b A**

Table 12.1 (*cont.*)

No.	Case no.	Ruling	Date	Parties	Area (courts category)	Category
41	C-411/10	Judgment (op) ECLI:EU:C:2011:865 Grand chamber	21/12/2011	N. S.	Principles, objectives and tasks of the Treaties	**2 c C**
42	C-149/10	Judgment ECLI:EU:C:2010:534	16/09/2010	Chatzi	Social policy	**1 g B**
43	C-490/09	Judgment ECLI:EU:C:2011:34	27/01/2011	Commission v Luxembourg	Freedom to provide services	**6 b A**
44	C-437/09	Judgment (op, SUM) ECLI:EU:C:2011:112	03/03/2011	AG2 R Prévoyance	Competition – Agreements, decisions and concerted practices	**5 b B**
45	C-345/09	Judgment (op, SUM) ECLI:EU:C:2010:610	14/10/2010	van Delft and Others	Social security	**4 g B**
46	C-492/08	Judgment (op) ECLI:EU:C:2010:348	17/06/2010	Commission v France	Taxation – Value added tax	**6 b B**

47	C-271/08	Judgment ECLI:EU:C:2010:426 (Grand Chamber)	15/07/2010	Commission v Germany	Freedom of establishment	**6 b B**
48	C-135/08	Judgment (SUM) ECLI:EU:C:2010:104	02/03/2010	Rottmann	Citizenship of the Union	**4 A**
49	C-51/08	Judgment ECLI:EU:C:2011:336	24/05/2011	Commission v Luxembourg	Freedom of establishment – AG	**6 b A**

Table 12.2 *Phase 4: Treaty of Amsterdam to Treaty of Lisbon (2000–10) forty-three cases, more than four annually*

No.	Case no.	Ruling	Date	Parties	Area (courts category)	Category
50	C-350/07	Judgment (op, SUM) ECLI:EU:C:2009:127	05/03/2009	Kattner Stahlbau	Competition – Agreements, decisions and concerted practices Social insurance and solidarity	**3 b B**
51	C-300/07	Judgment (op) ECLI:EU:C:2009:358	11/06/2009	Hans & Christophorus Oymanns	Freedom of establishment [solidarity and social insurance bodies]	**6 b B**
52	C-166/07	Judgment (op) ECLI:EU:C:2009:499	03/09/2009	Parliament v Council	Provisions governing the institutions – Acts of the institutions	**1 d A**
53	C-158/07	Judgment (op) ECLI:EU:C:2008:630	18/11/2008	Förster	Freedom of movement for workers	**2 a A**
54	C-499/06	Judgment (op) ECLI:EU:C:2008:300	22/05/2008	Nerkowska	Citizenship of the Union – Right of entry and residence	**6 a A**
55	C-428, 429, 430, 431, 432, 434/06	Judgment (op) ECLI:EU:C:2006:757	11/09/2008	Comunidad Autónoma de Castilla y León	Competition – State aid	**6 b A**

56	C-120 – 121/06 P	Judgment ECLI:EU:C:2007:212	09/09/2008	Fedon & Figli and Fedon America v Council and Commission, FIAMM	Agriculture and Fisheries – Fruit and vegetables	**6 h C**
57	C-461/05	Judgment (GS) ECLI:EU:C:2009:783	15/12/2009	Commission v Denmark	Financial provisions – Own resources	**2a b C**
58	C-351/05	Judgment ECLI:EU:C:2007:809 OpinionECLI:EU:C:2007:291	18 Dec 2007 23May 2007	Laval en partneri	Freedom to provide services	**6 b B**
59	C-438/05	Judgment (op) ECLI:EU:C:2007:772	11/12/2007	International Transport Workers' Federation and Finnish Seamen's Union	Freedom of establishment	**6 b B**
60	C-372/05	Judgment ECLI:EU:C:2009:780	15/12/2009	Commission v Germany	Financial provisions – Own resources	**2a b C**
61	C-303/05	Judgment (SUM) GC ECLI:EU:C:2007:261	03/05/2007	Advocaten voor de Wereld	Justice and home affairs	**2a c C**
62	C-265/05	Judgment (SUM, OP) ECLI:EU:C:2007:26	16/01/2007	Perez Naranjo	Social security	**4 g A**

Table 12.2 (*cont.*)

No.	Case no.	Ruling	Date	Parties	Area (courts category)	Category
63	C-192/05	Judgment (op, SUM) ECLI:EU:C:2006:676	26/10/2006	Tas-Hagen and Tas	Citizenship of the Union – Right of entry and residence	**6 a A**
64	C-77/05	Judgment (op) GS ECLI:EU:C:2007:803	18/12/2007	United Kingdom v Council	area of freedom, security and justice – Border checks	**2 c C**
65	C-53/05	Judgment ECLI:EU:C:2006:448	06/07/2006	Commission v Portugal	Freedom of establishment	**6 b C**
66	C-522/04	Opinion ECLI:EU:C:2006:632 Judgment ECLI:EU:C:2007:405	03/10/2006 05/07/2007	Commission v Belgium	Citizenship of the Union	**6 g B**
67	C-493/04	Judgment ECLI:EU:C:2006:167	09/03/2006	Piatkowski	Freedom of movement for workers	**4 b A**
68	C-414/04	Judgment (op) ECLI:EU:C:2006:742	28/11/2006	Parliament v Council	Energy	**3 e C**
69	C-413/04	Judgment (op) ECLI:EU:C:2006:741	28/11/2006	Parliament v Council	Energy	**3 e C**

70	Joined Cases C-266–207/04, C-276/04, C-321–325/04,	Judgment (op) ECLI:EU:C:2005:657	27/10/2005	Tout pour la maison, Komogo et al.	Competition – State aid	**5 b B**
71	C-209/03	Judgment (op) ECLI:EU:C:2005:169	15/03/2005	Bidar	Principles, objectives and tasks of the Treaties	**3 a A**
72	C-205/03 P	Judgment (op) ECLI:EU:C:2006:453	11/07/2006	FENIN v Commission	Competition – Agreements, decisions and concerted practices	**5 b A**
73	C-88/03	Judgment (op) ECLI:EU:C:2006:511	06/09/2006	Portugal v Commission	Competition – State aid	**3 b A**
74	C-46/03	Judgment (op) ECLI:EU:C:2005:725	01/12/2005	United Kingdom v Commission	Economic, social and territorial cohesion – European Regional Development Fund (ERDF)	**6 d C**
75	C-488/01 P	Order ECLI:EU:C:2003:608	11/11/2003	Martinez v Parliament	Provisions governing the institutions	**2 (other, other)**

Table 12.2 (*cont.*)

No.	Case no.	Ruling	Date	Parties	Area (courts category)	Category
76	C-486/01 P 488/01 P	Order ECLI:EU:C:2002:116	21/02/2002	Front national and Martinez v Parliament	Provisions governing the institutions	**2 (other, other)**
77	C-355, 354, 264, 306, /01	Judgment (Op, Sum) ECLI:EU:C:2004:150	16/03/2004	AOK-Bundesverband and Others	Competition – Agreements, decisions and concerted practices	**5 b B**
78	C-445/00	Judgment (op, order) ECLI:EU:C:2003:445	11/09/2003	Austria v Council	Transport	**4 j C**
79	C-389/00	Judgment (op, sum) ECLI:EU:C:2003:111	27/02/2003	Commission v Germany	Free movement of goods – Customs union –Charges having equivalent effect	**5 b B**
80	C-204/00 P - 205/00 P, C-211/00 P, C-213/00 P, C-217/00 P, C-219/00 P,	Judgment ECLI:EU:C:2002:337	07/01/2004	Cementir – Cementerie del Tirreno v Commission	Competition – Agreements, decisions and concerted practices – Concerted practices	**2 B b**

81	C-218/00	Judgment (op) ECLI:EU:C:2002:36	22/01/2002	Cisal	Competition – Agreements, decisions and concerted practices	**5 b B**
82	C-309/99	Judgment (op, SUM) ECLI:EU:C:2002:98	19/02/2002	Wouters and Others	Competition – Dominant position	**6 b B**
83	C-257/99	Judgment ECLI:EU:C:2001:491	27/09/2001	Barkoci and Malik	External relations – Association Agreement	**1 f D**
84	C-206/99	Judgment (SUM) ECLI:EU:C:2001:347	21/06/2001	SONAE	Taxation – Indirect taxation	**6 b B**
85	C-184/99	Judgment (SUM) ECLI:EU:C:2001:458	20/09/2001	Grzelczyk	Citizenship of the Union – Right of entry and residence	**2 a A**
86	C-120/99	Judgment ECLI:EU:C:2001:567	25/10/2001	Italy v Council	Agriculture and Fisheries – Fisheries policy	**3 h B**
87	C-107/99	Order (op) ECLI:EU:C:1999:338	29/06/1999	Italy v Commission	Economic, social and territorial cohesion – European Regional Development Fund (ERDF)	**1 d C**

Table 12.2 (*cont.*)

No.	Case no.	Ruling	Date	Parties	Area (courts category)	Category
88	C-56/99	Judgment (op) ECLI:EU:C:2000:236	11/05/2000	Gascogne Limousin viandes	Agriculture and Fisheries – Beef and veal	**4 h B**
89	C-50/99	Judgment (op) ECLI:EU:C:2000:288	25/05/2000	Podesta	Social policy	**6 B g**
90	C-302/98	Judgment (op) ECLI:EU:C:2000:322	15/06/2000	Sehrer	non-discrimination – Non-discrimination on grounds of nationality	**2 g B**
91	C-180/98	Judgment (op) ECLI:EU:C:2000:428	12/09/2000	Pavlov	Competition – Agreements, decisions and concerted practices	**6 b B**
92	C-34/98	Judgment ECLI:EU:C:2000:84	15/02/2000	Commission v France	Freedom of movement for workers	**2 g B**

Table 12.3 *Phase 3: Treaty of Maastricht to Treaty of Amsterdam (1994–2000) eleven cases – nearly two annually*

No.	Case no.	Ruling	Date	Parties	Area (courts category)	Category
93	C-219/97	Judgment (op) ECLI:EU:C:1999:437	21/09/1999	Drijvende Bokken	Competition – Agreements, decisions and concerted practices	**3 b B**
94	C-115–7/97	Judgment (op) ECLI:EU:C:1999:434	21/09/1999	Brentjens'	Competition – Agreements, decisions and concerted practices	**3 b B**
95	C-114/97	Judgment ECLI:EU:C:1998:519	29/10/1998	Commission v Spain	Freedom of movement for workers, freedom of establishment, freedom to provide services	**6 b B**
96	C-375/96	Judgment (op) ECLI:EU:C:1998:517	29/10/1998	Zaninotto	Agriculture and Fisheries – Wine	**3 h C**
97	C-84/96	Judgment ECLI:EU:C:1999:478	05/10/1999	Netherlands v Commission	Economic, social and territorial cohesion – European Regional Development Fund (ERDF)	**2a C d**

Table 12.3 (*cont.*)

No.	Case no.	Ruling	Date	Parties	Area (courts category)	Category
98	C-67/96	Judgment (op) ECLI:EU:C:1999:430	21/09/1999	Albany	Competition – Agreements, decisions and concerted practices	**5 b B**
99	C-55/96	Judgment (op) ECLI:EU:C:1997:603	11/12/1997	Job Centre	Freedom to provide services, competition law, abuse of dominant position	**5 b B**
100	C-248, 49/95	Judgment ECLI:EU:C:1997:377	17/07/1997	Stapf, SAM	Transport	**4 h B**
101	C-70/95	Judgment (SUM, op) ECLI:EU:C:1997:301	17/06/1997	Sodemare and Others	Freedom of establishment, freedom of services	**1 b A**
102	C-244/94	Judgment (op) ECLI:EU:C:1995:392	16/11/1995	FFSA	Competition – Agreements, decisions and concerted practices	**5 b B**
103	C-238/94	Judgment (SUM, ECLI:EU:C:1996:132	26/03/1996	García and Others	Freedom of establishment	**2 b B**

Table 12.4 *Phase 2: European Act to Maastricht Treaty (1987–93) seven cases (less than one annually)*

No.	Case no.	Ruling	Date	Parties	Area (courts category)	Category
104	C-159, 160/91	Judgment (op, SUM) ECLI:EU:C:1993:63	17/02/1993	Poucet, Pistre	Competition – Agreements, decisions and concerted practices – Concerted practices	**5 b B**
105	C-260/90	Judgment (op) ECLI:EU:C:1992:66	12/02/1992	Leplat	Free movement of goods – Customs union – Charges having equivalent effect	**1 f D**
106	C-240/90	Judgment ECLI:EU:C:1992:408	27/10/1992	Germany v Commission	Agriculture and Fisheries – Sheepmeat and goatmeat	**4 h B**
107	C-63/90	Judgment (op) ECLI:EU:C:1992:381	13/10/1992	Portugal v Council	Agriculture and Fisheries – Fisheries policy	**2a h C**
108	C-186/87	Judgment ECLI:EU:C:1989:47	02/02/1989	Cowan	Freedom to provide services	**6 g B**
109	C-203/86	Judgment ECLI:EU:C:1988:420	20/09/1988	Spain v Council	Agriculture and Fisheries – Milk products	**2a h C**
110	C-126/86	Judgment (op) ECLI:EU:C:1987:395	29/09/1987	Giménez Zaera	Social policy	**6 g B**

Table 12.5 *Phase 1: from the foundation of the EEC (1969–86)*

No.	Case no.	Ruling	Date	Parties	Area (courts category)	Category
111	C-295/84	Judgment (op) ECLI:EU:C:1985:473	27/11/1985	Rousseau Wilmot	Taxation – Value added tax	**5 tax C**
112	C-250/84	Judgment (op, SUM) ECLI:EU:C:1986:22	22/01/1986	Eridania	Agriculture and Fisheries – Sugar	**2a b B**
113	C-44/84	Judgment (op) ECLI:EU:C:1986:2	15/01/1986	Hurd	Accession	**6 f C**
114	C-72/83	Judgment (op) ECLI:EU:C:1984:256	10/07/1984	Campus Oil	Free movement of goods – Quantitative restrictions – Measures having equivalent effect	**2 b C**
115	C-75/82	Judgment ECLI:EU:C:1984:116	20/03/1984	Razzouk v Commission	Staff Regulations of officials and Conditions of Employment of other servants	**4 g B**
116	C-128/78	Judgment (SUM) ECLI:EU:C:1979:32	07/02/1979	Commission v United Kingdom	Transport	**2a, b C**

117	Avis 1/78	Opinions of the Court ECLI:EU:C:1979:224	04/10/1979	Commission	External relations – Commercial policy	**6 f D**
118	C-77/77	Judgment ECLI:EU:C:1978:141	29/06/1978	British Petroleum v Commission	Competition – Dominant position	**2a b C**
119	Avis 1/76	Opinions of the Court (SUM) ECLI:EU:C:1977:63	26/04/1977	Commission	External relations	**2a f C**
120	C-24/74	Judgment (op, Sum) ECLI:EU:C:1974:99	09/10/1974	Biason	Social security	**4 g B**
121	C-39/72	Judgment ECLI:EU:C:1973:13	07/02/1973	Commission v Italy	Agriculture and Fisheries – Milk products	**2a h C**
122	C-6/69	Judgment ECLI:EU:C:1969:68	10/12/1969	Commission v France	Conjunctural policy	**2a d C**

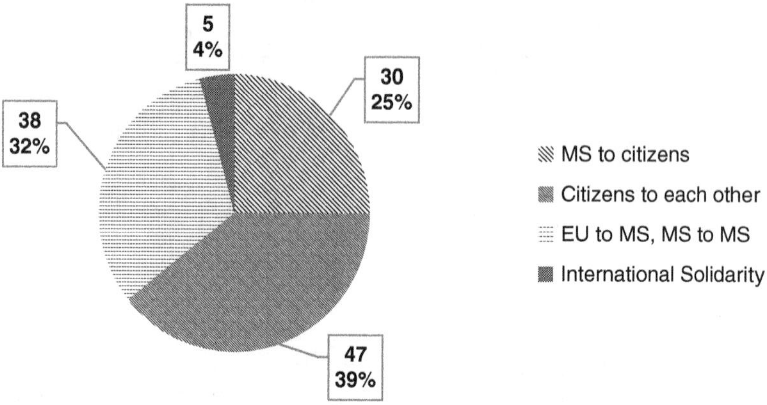

Figure 12.4 Dimensions of solidarity – frequency over time

Maastricht (in force in November 1993) introduced EU citizenship explicitly. The surge in cases after the Treaty of Amsterdam came into force by the end of 1999 seems attributable to two elements: first, EU citizenship had been recognised as obliging Member States to extend a certain degree of solidarity to citizens of other Member States, and second the heightened recognition of EU social policy through the re-integration of the 1993 protocol on social policy, and the creation of an employment chapter in 1997 may have promoted reasoning with social policy and solidarity considerations in order to curb individual rights as well as internal market rules. Overall, the EU internal dimensions of solidarity occur nearly equally, though international solidarity is very rarely used, as the pie chart above shows.

4.3 *Confirming the Types of Solidarity Actually Used by the Court*

In evaluating the case law, all five types of solidarity we expected to find were identifiable: the categorial types solidarity as charitable orientation without legal obligation (1), solidarity as mutually binding legal obligation (2) and solidarity as risk mitigation (3) alongside the functional types of solidarity embedding or restricting individual rights (4) or internal market concepts (5).

In addition to those five types, there was an unexpected instrumental use of solidarity by the Court, supporting the overall value of European integration. This is evidenced in two different ways. First, the Court used solidarity as an emanation of mutually binding legal obligation as a basis for supporting Member States' compliance with EU obligations, since compliance with obligations under EU law would enhance the mutuality of this organisation. In the very first case using the concept, decided in 1969, French attempts to mitigate the effect of the 1960s economic crisis by awarding rediscount rates for local business in contravention of EEC state aid law were branded as a violation of the solidarity base of Member States' obligations to the community.[50] Similarly, the legitimacy of quotas for production of agricultural goods is supported by the principle of solidarity between producers.[51] This use of solidarity is now occurring in the field of asylum and immigration, where the specific reference to Member States' solidarity to each other is used in recent judgments to underline the admissibility of legally enforceable quotas for admitting refugees.[52] Generally, this can be characterised as within the boundaries of the second categorial type of solidarity identified above, solidarity as mutual obligation, though with an integrationist twist. This was recognised by counting those cases as a (2a) category.

Second, the Court frequently has to react to Member States' and citizens' arguments relying on solidarity structures established at national level in order to justify an exception from or restriction of EU law concepts central to socio-economic integration. For example, Member States may argue that a certain benefit or institution is based on the specific bond of solidarity between citizens of the state, and refuse to extend that benefit to EU citizens from other Member States. Accepting such an argument would endanger the wider aim of creating solidarity bonds not only between Member States, but also between their peoples. In particular if derogations from obligations flowing from economic freedoms or competition law are at stake, the Court frequently stresses that the EU principles prevail over that local or national solidarity. Similarly, if claimants rely on national solidarity, the Court may refuse to recognise this kind of solidarity as a concept of community law.[53] We class this as an additional criterion (6), exposing more clearly where the Court rejects the central value of solidarity in favour of other EU values, although either the Court, or the Commission or the AG has recognised the relevance of the value.

Figures 12.6 and 12.7 illustrate how frequently each of these six types of solidarity appear. The pie chart on overall distribution exposes the

[50] Case 6/69 *Commission* v. *France* EU:C:1969:68.

[51] Case 250/84 Eridania EU :C :1986 :22.

[52] C-643/15 *Slovakia* v. *Council* CU:C:2-18:631.

[53] Case 44/84 Hurd EU:C:1986:2.

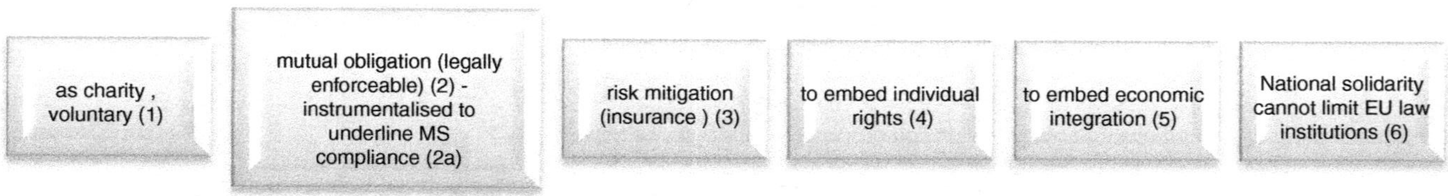

Figure 12.5 Types of solidarity – categorial (1–3) and functional (4–6)

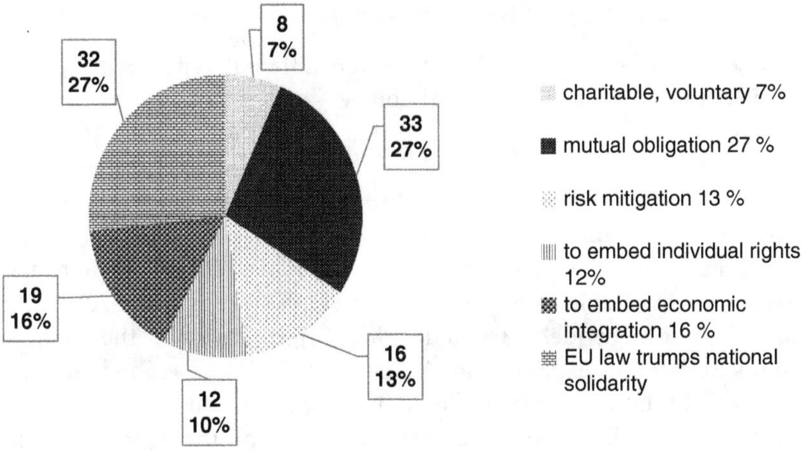

Figure 12.6 Types of Solidarity – overall

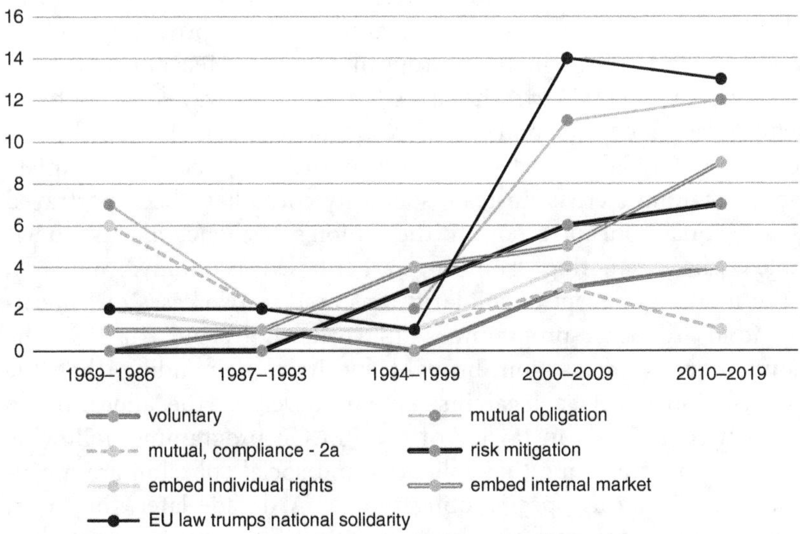

Figure 12.7 Types of solidarity over time, plus 2a category

dominance of the internal market category, while the next chart illustrates how the frequency of the different types of solidarity evolved over time. The overall frequency, depicted above in figure 12.7, was omitted in order to show the specific (2a) category as a dotted line.

4.4 *Exploring the Discourse within Six Types of Solidarity*

This section offers examples of how the different types of solidarity manifest in the Court's case law discourse.

4.4.1 Categorial Types: Solidarity as Charity, as Mutual Obligation and as Risk Mitigation

While there are only eight cases in which the Court embraced the traditional concept of solidarity as a voluntarily chosen benign act, based on charitable motives, this category trends upwardly and comprises some widely debated rulings. For example, the Pringle judgment[54] refers explicitly to Article 122 TFEU as embodying the spirit of solidarity between the Member States, only to reject that provision as a basis for financial assistance of the Union to the Member States, without any reference to the principle of solidarity. AG Kokott[55] relies on the fundamental position of solidarity among the EU's values for a narrow interpretation of Article 125 TFEU, which then does not exclude creating a fund providing aid to Member States through the European Stability Mechanism (ESM). However, as the Court, she does not in any way contribute to defining solidarity. In both instances, solidarity remains a nebulous concept potentially based on charity towards Member States suffering an economic crisis. Instead, solidarity could have been portrayed as a rational concept retaining the Union's resilience against inevitable risks emanating from a market-based economy. Similarly, a pre-modern concept of solidarity was used in two cases on allocating funds to peace-programmes in Northern Ireland. In 1999 the Court rejected an action brought by Italy, demanding that the Commission enacts a legal instrument to reduce the allocation to the structural funds in favour of the PEACE programme, following AG Mischo's reasoning that solidarity and social cohesion are incapable of engendering specific obligations.[56] A decade later, the Court uses the same rational for justifying the EC's contribution to the International Fund for Ireland.[57] At times the Court also retracts to this conservative and cautious reading of solidarity if activities at

[54] Case C-370/12 EU:C:2012:756, paragraph 115.
[55] View in case C-370/12 EU:C:2012:675, paragraphs 142-3.
[56] Case C-107/99 *Italy* v. Commission EU:C:1999:338.
[57] Case C-166/07, *Parliament* v. *Council*, ECLI:EU:C:2009:499.

national level of a social character are to be exempted from limitations, they would have to endure under EU Internal Market law. For example, in the Sodemare case, the Court exempted the statutory preference for non-profit organisation to provide locally funded care for the elderly from the control under EU state aid law because the system of social welfare was 'based on the principle of solidarity (in that it was) designed as a matter of priority to assist those who are in a state of need owing to insufficient family income';[58] and in the more recent Femarbel case[59] the 'activities essential in order to guarantee human dignity and integrity and are a manifestation of the principle of ... solidarity' were exempt from the restrictions imposed by Directive 2006/13.

While all these judgments justify initiatives that could be categorised as emanations of solidarity, they miss the opportunity to recognise that the exercise of solidarity is actually in the interest both of those in short term receipt of aid (whether Member States experiencing difficulty servicing their government debt, a region suffering from the aftermath of decades of neglect, or citizens lacking the income to lead a life in dignity) and those engaging in solidarity. This would have allowed the court to identify the mutual interest of maintaining the prosperity of the Union and its societies as a whole.

As mentioned, the category of solidarity as legally binding mutual obligation initiated the Court's solidarity case law, and was initially used as a basis for Member States obligations to comply with their treaty obligations, for example, by branding the UK's refusal to require lorry drivers to use tachographs in order to ensure compliance with working time rules as 'failure in the duty of solidarity' of Member States towards the EEC, which struck 'at the very root of the Community legal order'.[60]

The idea of solidarity as mutuality also underpins case law on EU citizenship. After first enunciating the slogan that Member States were required to extend a certain degree of (financial) solidarity to citizens of other Member States[61] without much reasoning, the Court

[58] Case C-70/95 *Sodemare et al.* ECLI:EU:C:1997:30, paragraph 27.

[59] Case C-57/12 *Femarbel* - ECLI:EU:C:2013:517, paragraph 43.

[60] Case 127/78 *Commission* v. *UK* EU:C:1979:32, paragraph 12, see also case 39/72 *Commission* v. *Italy* EU:C:1973:13 paragraph 25 and cases cited above in fn 50–2.

[61] Case C-184/99 *Grzelczyk* EU:C:2001:458, paragraph 44.

has increasingly relied on the 'genuine link' between the host Member State and the other EU citizen to support that obligation, thus injecting the criterion of mutuality. For example, in an infringement action concerning reduced fares for students against Austria, the Court conceded that 'it is legitimate for a host Member State to wish to ensure that there is a genuine link between a claimant to a benefit and the competent Member State',[62] though in the specific case being effectively enrolled in a publicly accredited higher education institution should be sufficient to establish this genuine link,[63] as was the fact that pensioners have moved to that Member State to enjoy their old age.[64] In the more recent case law on EU citizenship rights, the Court relies on liberal notions of citizenship instead of referring to solidarity and mutuality. One example is the Chavez-Vilchez litigation[65] on the right of non-EU mothers of Dutch children to remain in the Netherlands as carers. The last occasion when the requirement of Member States to extend a certain degree of solidarity towards citizens of other EU Member States in the area of residence rights was referred to was AG Wahl's opinion in the 2012 St Prix case.[66]

Recent rulings in the field of asylum and immigration policy demonstrate a more pronounced use by the Court and its advocates general of the principle of solidarity. The confidence of Member States in other states in the Schengen Area carrying out controls effectively and stringently becomes an emanation of solidarity between Member States under Article 67 TFEU in the ANAFE case.[67] AG Wathelet, in a case on international protection, is moved to base a suggestion for future legislation on the principle of solidarity, explaining 'that only the adoption of a genuine policy on international protection within the European Union with its own budget which would ensure uniform minimum living conditions for the beneficiaries of such protection

[62] Case C-75/11 *Commission* v. *Austria* EU:C:2012:605, paragraph 59.
[63] Ibid., paragraph 64.
[64] Case C-140/12 *Brey* EU:C:2013:565.
[65] Case C-133/15 (Grand Chamber), EU:C:2017:354, Opinion AG Spzunar EU:C:2016:659, referring to 'genuine enjoyment of the substance of rights conferred by virtue of their status' as EU citizens in the pivotal Ruiz Zambrano case (Case C-34/09 EU:C :2011 :124, paragraph 43).
[66] C-507/12 Opinion ECLI:EU:C:2013:841, St Prix.
[67] Case C-606/01 *ANAFE* EU:C:2012:348, paragraph 25.

would reduce, if not eliminate, the occurrence of cases such as that at issue in the main proceedings, by ensuring that the principle of solidarity and the fair sharing of responsibilities between Member States enshrined in Article 80 TFEU is a reality for the benefit not only of Member States, but above all of the human beings concerned'.[68] Nevertheless, relying on the law as it stands, he proposes for the Court to find that the Member State Germany must request a Gambian national to be retransferred to Italy, where he first made an application for international protection.[69]

The classical concept of solidarity as risk mitigating is obviously at the heart of social security provision in the EU's Member States. Accordingly, it is no surprise that the idea of solidarity as risk mitigation is referred to in the Court's case law on compulsory affiliation to social security bodies. The Kattner Stahlbau litigation is a prominent example, also because the term solidarity is found no less than twenty-two times in that ruling. The Court finds that the compulsory affiliation of employers to a liability fund providing for consequences of work accidents is necessary because 'different employers' liability insurance associations being grouped together in a risk community . . . enables them to effect an equalisation of costs and risks between them'.[70] The principle of risk sharing is also characteristic of social insurance institutions such as pension funds which accept members independently of the individual risks they present, and allocate pensions not in strict proportionality to contributions.[71]

The idea of risk sharing emerges in areas beyond social security as well. For example, in the 2017 judgment on the Slovakian challenge on the Council decision on redistributing those who fled war and destitution across the EU Member States, the Court stressed that the risk to be the first country of arrival for those migrant was unevenly distributed among Member States due to geographic realities, and that the resulting burdens 'must . . . be divided between all the other Member States, in accordance

[68] Opinion in case C-163/17, Jawo, EU:C:2018:613, paragraph 145.

[69] This is also reflected in the Court's ruling, though with the proviso that the first country may refuse to transfer the refugee if it obtains objective and credible evidence of a risk of degrading treatment in the country of first application (EU:C:2019:218).

[70] Case C-350/07 ECLI:EU:C:2009:127, paragraph.

[71] For example Case C-218/00 Cisal EU:C:2002:36, paragraph 39–40; C-219/97 *Drijvende Bokken* ECLI:EU:C:1999:437, paragraph 65.

with the principle of solidarity and fair sharing of responsibility'.[72] The Grand Chamber also rejected the Slovakian submission that solidarity only entails voluntary engagement to the extent the Member State decides without being bound by a legal obligation. Another example on the idea of risk sharing as an emanation of solidarity is found in the Medisanus case on the question whether a Member State may ban blood products using blood donated outside its borders.[73] Expanding on the concept of solidarity underlying Directive Dir 2004/18/EC, the Court explained that '(a)ll blood donors act in the interest of all individuals with whom they share the same interests by making it possible, together, inter alia to guard against the risks of insufficient quantities of medicinal products derived from blood or plasma.'[74]

4.4.2 Functional Types: Solidarity Embedding Internal Market Law Concepts or Individual Rights, while EU Law Concepts Cannot Be Curbed by National-based Solidarity

Both mutuality and risk sharing remain decisive in rulings where the Court uses functional types of solidarity.

Starting with the Poucet and Pistre case,[75] the Court has recognised national provisions protecting universal service providers from competition as justified through the principle of solidarity. For example, the Court argues that 'organisations involved in the public social security system fulfil an exclusively social function ... based on the principle of national solidarity and is entirely non-profit making. The benefits are statutory benefits bearing no relation to the amount of contributions'[76] in order to justify entrusting the postal services with the payment of retirement pensions.

Most frequently, solidarity serves to justify EU legislation limiting individual rights.[77] Yet, there are also cases where the limitation of EU rights is justified by the need to protect national-level solidarity bonds. This justification was used in two widely discussed cases on the question whether a Member State can withdraw its citizenship and thus EU

[72] Case C-643/15 *Slovakia* v. *Council* EU:C:2017:631 280-92.

[73] Case C-296/15 *Medisanus* ECLI:EU:C:2017:431.

[74] Ibid., paragraph 97.

[75] C-159, 160/91 *Poucet & Pistre* ECLI:EU:C:1993:63.

[76] C-185/14 *EasyPay and Finance Engineering* ECLI:EU:C:2015:716, paragraph 38.

[77] For example, the limits of transferring the payments for a national public pension fund into the EU pension fund are justified by the principle of solidarity informing the former (C-166/12 *Časta* ECLI:EU:C:2013:792).

citizenship. In both the Rottmann and the recent Tjebbes cases the Court relied on the legitimacy to protect the 'special relationship of solidarity and good faith between it and its nationals'[78]

Much more frequently, however, the national conceptions of solidarity are rejected as a justification for limiting EU rights. The reasoning of AG Cruz Villalon in the infringement action against Luxembourg on the question whether the office of a notary can be reserved for nationals of that Member State is particularly well developed in that it uses the solidarity bond between EU citizens in order to reject the priority of that same solidarity bond limited to the national level 'In so far as it has a transnational dimension, European citizenship is founded on the existence of a community of States and individuals who share a . . . commitment to solidarity. Given that, on being awarded the nationality of a Member State, an individual is introduced into that community of values, trust and solidarity, it would be paradoxical if membership of that very community were to constitute the ground for preventing a European Union citizen from exercising the rights and freedoms guaranteed by the Treaty.'[79] This reasoning supports European-level solidarity between all EU citizens and rejects a more limited national variety. However, there are also numerous examples of judgments where the Court rejects national emanations of solidarity without suggesting an EU level equivalent, thus effectively sacrificing solidarity on the altar of the EU internal market.[80]

5 Tentative Conclusions: Missed Opportunities Abound

It is startling to realise how frequently the Court misses the opportunity to explain specifically what is meant by solidarity, and in this way, clarify this key concept. By seizing that opportunity, the Court would be able to flesh out the EU's value base. Exploring the value of solidarity would be particularly suitable for countering the identity-based challenges of the EU integration project epitomised by Brexit as well as by the increasing

[78] Cases C-135/08 *Rottmann* EU:C:2010:104, paragraph 51; C-221/17 *Tjebbes et al.* ECLI: EU:C:2019:189, paragraph 33.

[79] C-51/08 *Commission* v. *Luxembourg* ECLI:EU:C:2011:336, paragraph 138.

[80] Widely criticised rulings such as Viking (Case C-438/05 International Transport Workers' Federation and Finnish Seamen's Union, EU:C:2007:772) Laval (Case C-351/05, EU:C:2007:809) and AGET Iraklis (Case C-201/15 EU:C:2016:972) are all among those where the parties as well as the AG stressed solidarity at national level as a potential justification to restrict economic freedoms, for example.

rejection of free movement of EU citizens and the refusal to exercise international solidarity in the field of migration.

The opportunity to highlight and explore the relevance of solidarity as one of the Union's core values is even missed in cases where it should be at the heart of the argument. For example, the circumstances leading to the ruling in Gusa[81] would have allowed the Court to explore the concept: the claimant entered Ireland initially being sustained by his children, before he worked as a self-employed builder for four years, contributing to social security and the tax base, only to be refused job seekers' allowance due to an alleged lack of being habitually resident in Ireland. While the Court holds that he can rely on his free movement rights to claim this very allowance, the reference to mutuality of contributions remains unexplored.

Another example can be found in the DEB case on the question whether national legislation requiring a special public interest test to be satisfied before a legal entity can claim legal assistance for representation in court.[82] Germany had claimed, in defence of the rule, that legal assistance is organised on the basis of solidarity, which cannot be extended to legal entities instead of natural persons. This argument, which bordered at limiting solidarity to a charitable emotion, was countered by AG Kokott and the Court with reference to the fact that Article 47 Charter of Fundamental Rights of the European Union (CFREU), from which the right to legal assistance derives, was not placed in the Charter's solidarity chapter. This formal argument is inherently unconvincing, in particular as the CFREU's Chapter IV (Solidarity) also contains Articles 27 and 28 endowing works councils and trade unions with rights. Thus, the question is rather which legal entities would profit from legal assistance: those created to represent natural persons, or rather legal entities such as businesses which are removed from their natural owners through institutions such as shares. Accordingly, the Court has missed an opportunity to fill the term 'solidarity' with life.

More concerning, in the Wightman ruling on the UK's option to unilaterally revoke the notification of its intention to withdraw from the Union,[83] the Court relied on citizenship as a fundamental status to support its argument. However, free movement – a liberal right – is presented as the most important aspect of citizenship, and not the partial

[81] Case C-442/16 EU:C:2017:1004.
[82] Case C-279/09 *DEB* EU:C:2010:811.
[83] Case C-621/18 *Wightman and Others* EU:C:2018:999.

extension of solidarity from the host Member States towards those EU citizens who dare using their free movement rights.[84] The Full Court's grandiose reference to Article 2 TEU including the sentence on solidarity thus rings hollow in this regard, as the Court missed an opportunity to elaborate on the practical relevance of this principle.

Observing and evaluating the case law using the term of solidarity, we have exposed a high degree of inconsistency. Evaluating from a normative perspective the Court's approach to this 'cardinal value of the European Union', one would hope that the Court follows the example of some of its advocates general and specifies the application of this principle in those cases where citizens expect to be included in the Union's solidarity. The frequent reference to the solidarity between the Member States to each other and to the Union should not lead to obscuring the fact that solidarity is based on mutual support of persons, which can only lead to effective risk mitigation if there is a sufficient number of persons and the willingness of the better off to shoulder burdens communally. Thus, the Court could make more of the principles of solidarity in the field of EU citizenship, social policy, anti-discrimination law and allow solidarity structures at national, transnational and European level to conquer adverse effects of internal market law. There is a long way towards developing a consistent approach to the principle, which can be used in more cases than presently. Such uses could contribute to supporting a more inclusive constitutional discourse on European integration than the mere reliance on liberal constitutional principles.

Solidarity in ECJ Case Law – Documentation of Coding

Up to March 2019 – only closed cases, those where solidarity was not relevant are eliminated.

The column 'category' uses the type of solidarity as a number, the dimension of solidarity as a capital letter, and the policy field as a normal letter.

Types of solidarity: (1) Solidarity as charity, voluntary engagement based on ethics, (2) Solidarity as mutual obligation, legally enforceable [(2a) supporting MS compliance with EU law], (3) Solidarity as risk mitigation, insurance, (4) Solidarity to embed individual rights, (5) Solidarity to embed economic integration, (6) national solidarity recognised, though it does not trump EU law obligations

[84] Ibid., paragraph 64.

Dimensions of solidarity: A Member States towards citizens (of other MS, or their own, especially if they have moved), B Citizens' direct solidarity towards each other, C EU and its Member States towards each other D International Solidarity (EU and/or its Member States to other states)

Policy fields: (a) EU citizenship, (b) law of economic integration, (c) immigration, asylum, area of security, freedom and justice, (d) economic policy, including cohesion funds, (e) energy policy, (f) external relations, (g) anti-discrimination law and social law and policy, (h) agricultural policy, (i) other

13

Civic Solidarity in Transnational Spaces

Organisation and Institutionalisation of Solidarity Within the European Union

CHRISTIAN LAHUSEN

1 Introduction

Solidarity is a firm reference point of modern societies. It is not only part and parcel of caring relations within informal groups and communities (families, kinship, peers, neighbourhoods and so forth), but also a well-established principle of European nation states. Also, the European Union (EU) has committed itself to this principle by introducing it into its legal framework. Following the Treaty of the European Union (TEU) (Article 130a-e) and the Treaty on the Functioning of the European Union (TFEU) (2007), the community is devoted to enhancing social cohesion, cooperation and solidarity among its Member States in some policy fields, even as an explicit reference point of coordinated action (for example, asylum and immigration, economic cooperation, energy and security). The political aim of this principle is obvious: to guarantee the co-operation of Member States in regard to policy issues that transcend the problem-solving capacity of single nation states, thus requiring joint efforts. While European law primarily addresses institutional actors, namely governments and the European institutions, the treaty also expresses the desire to deepen solidarity between European peoples, thus acknowledging that the principle and spirit of solidarity among institutional actors depends also on the willingness of the European citizens to support public policies and/or actively engage in additional or complementary activities.

Against this backdrop, it is necessary to address the level of citizens' actions and to engage in an analysis of social or civic solidarity within the EU. This topic is a highly relevant area of research within the social sciences in general, and within sociology in particular, because solidarity

This chapter is also available as Open Access.

is intimately linked to the social integration of modern societies. Following the seminal work of Durkheim[1] and later Parsons,[2] it is known that solidarity plays a key role in societal integration. In addition, research in the tradition of de Tocqueville[3] has stressed that citizens' initiatives, groups and organisations have helped to establish a public sphere of civil society that is devoted to solidarity and integration at the national and grass-roots level.[4] However, while research has provided several insights into the ways complex societies organise, institutionalise and stabilise solidarity, it is unclear whether this wisdom applies to the EU as a multinational community with a marked multilevel structure.

In the aim of this chapter is to develop a sociological framework for the analysis of civic solidarity within multi- and transnational spaces. I will argue that solidarity in modern societies is organised and stabilised on various levels of aggregation and institutionalisation (informal networks, civil society, welfare states), and I will highlight that these various levels are interrelated in a more or less complementary manner. This situation changes, however, once transnational solidarity comes to the fore, given that solidarity relations transcend national borders and need to bridge spatial and social distances. Against this backdrop, I will focus on transnational solidarity within Europe, arguing that the EU furnishes an instructive case that enables us to better understand the challenges, structures and dynamics of transnational civic solidarity. In fact, European citizens have been actively engaged in cross-national activities of support, particularly in reaction to the various EU crises (for example, the Great Recession or the so-called refugee crisis). Moreover, the EU seems to provide a partially beneficial context, given the existence of Europeanised informal networks, organised civil societies and citizenship rights. The analysis will show, however, that the situation of transnational solidarity within Europe shows some deviation from the national situation. It will be argued that the interrelations between the various levels of aggregation and institutionalisation are much more fragmentary, unstable and contradictory, thus leading to a more segmented and fragile form of European civic solidarity.

[1] E. Durkheim, *The Division of Labor in Society*, trans. W. D. Halls. (New York: Free Press, 1997).

[2] T. Parsons, *The Social System* (Glencoe, IL: Free Press, 1951).

[3] A. de Tocqueville, *Alexis de Tocqueville on Democracy, Revolution, and Society* (Chicago, IL: University of Chicago Press, 1982).

[4] E.g., R. Putnam, L.M. Feldstein and D. Cohen, *Better Together: Restoring the American Community* (New York: Simon & Schuster, 2003).

2 Conceptual and Theoretical Issues

Solidarity is a specific type of social relation. Recurrently, scholars define solidarity as mutual help or support between members of a group.[5] This support can be based on charitable donations (for example, the sharing of time, goods, money or knowledge). However, these examples are a rather restrained aspect of a more general commitment to act and speak out on behalf of others (for instance, raising awareness for their needs, supporting their political claims or legal rights). Solidarity thus implies that individuals recognise each other's needs and claims as a shared concern and task. In this sense, solidarity is a social relation that is marked by three elements: reciprocity, mutual responsibilities and obligations, and group commitments.

Scholarly works have underscored the importance of these components. In the first instance, they stress that solidarity is a social relation based on mutuality and reciprocity.[6] Everyday life observations might indicate that this is not necessarily the case, because specific acts of solidarity are very often marked by an asymmetric relation of giving and receiving help. These observations are close to the notion of altruism, philanthropy or empathy. All of them assume that somebody is in need of support, while others are able to provide help. However, these suppositions do not reflect the specific traits of solidarity. On the one hand, the provision of support is a responsibility and/or obligation of individuals by which they recognise the situation of others as marked by legitimate needs and interests. On the other hand, the relation of support is reciprocal because one's own and the other's situations are interchangeable. The support of others implies the expectation that others will help oneself when in need of support later on. Solidarity is thus based on the notion of mutual responsibilities and obligations as members of (imagined) communities or groups. Or in other words, solidarity is tied to membership in specific communities and groups, whose members are called on to

[5] S. Stjerno, *Solidarity in Europe. The History of an Idea* (Cambridge: Cambridge University Press, 2012); S. A. Hunt and R. D. Benford, 'Collective identity, solidarity, and commitment', in D. A. Snow, S. A. Soule and H. Kriesi (eds.), *The Blackwell Companion to Social Movements* (Oxford: Blackwell, 2004), pp. 433–57; A. E. Komter, *Social Solidarity and the Gift* (Cambridge: Cambridge University Press, 2005).

[6] L. D. Molm, J. L. Collett and D. R. Schaefer, 'Building solidarity through generalized exchange: a theory of reciprocity', *American Journal of Sociology*, 113 (1) (2007), 205–42; H. Lengfeld, S. Schmidt and J. Häuberer, 'Is there a European solidarity? Attitudes towards fiscal assistance for debt-ridden European Union Member States', Report No. 67, University of Leipzig (2015).

safeguard and maintain the groups' integrity by replicating and defending shared ideas, norms and rights.

This conceptualisation helps us to understand why the discussion about egoism versus altruism, and voluntarity versus involuntarity is of secondary importance when addressing solidarity. On the one hand, solidarity is a social relation enabling egoistic and altruistic intentions and motives at the same time. This is due to the reciprocal structure of solidarity mentioned before. Supporting others can be an ego-centred investment in a relation from which one expects to benefit in the future.[7] However, solidarity is a risky investment not necessarily guaranteeing future 'returns'. Even if we assume some sort of immediate 'gratification', solidarity always involves costs and thus some sort of sacrifice to a common good or goal.[8] In this sense, it is highly probable that civic solidarity is driven by various norms at the same time. Helping others might be driven by the rationale calculation of *quid pro quo*, arguing that solidarity is a mutual exchange of help that in the long run is beneficial for everybody.[9] At the same time, however, support might also be propagated as a civic duty that limits cost–benefit calculations in the name of norm-conformity and sacrifices to common welfare.[10]

On the other hand, solidarity also involves different degrees of voluntarity. At first sight, solidarity presupposes the voluntary commitment of individuals to help others. However, this voluntarity is not that easy to ascertain, given that solidarity is based on the notion of mutual responsibilities and obligations. In line with Parsons, we might expect that these obligations are fulfilled 'voluntarily' by group members only as long as they have internalised group norms and values. According to Parsons, it is not force but 'voluntary action' that allows for the mobilisation of individual commitments in a sustained manner, thus guaranteeing the reproduction of groups and communities in the long run.[11] However, even Parsonian 'voluntarism' argues that sanctions are a correlate of normative expectations and roles. Indeed, it is difficult to conceive of a situation that is free of social pressures; at least some sort of soft, informal sanctions granting or withdrawing esteem, reputation or status

[7] M. Hechter, *Principles of Group Solidarity* (Berkeley, CA: University of California Press, 1988).

[8] M. Hoelzl, 'Recognizing the sacrificial victim: the problem of solidarity for critical social theory', *Journal for Cultural and Religious Theory*, 6(1) (2004), 45–64.

[9] Hechter, *Principles of Group Solidarity.*

[10] Hoelzl, 'Recognizing the Sacrificial Victim'; Lengfeld et al., *Is There a European Solidarity?*

[11] T. Parsons, *The Structure of Social Action* (New York: McGraw-Hill, 1937).

will be in place even in cases where participants stress the voluntarity of their support. Consequently, rather than focusing on the question of voluntarity or involuntarity, which are difficult to measure empirically, it is necessary to focus on the different degrees of bindingness of mutual responsibilities and obligations. Mutual support can be stipulated in a group as: an optional ('can'), a desired ('should') or an obligatory ('must') commitment. The third is clearly the most binding the inherent assumption is that the degree of formalisation and institutionalisation will grow from optional to obligatory commitments, and with it the degree to which related commitments will be organised and regulated. In some communities and groups, solidarity might be imposed on members, for instance, by compulsory contributions that are not necessarily made willingly. In these cases, however, membership contributions are only a valid measure of civic solidarity, as long as the related norms and expectations are internalised by group members. In these cases, it is thus important to assess the degree to which group members perceive solidarity obligations as acceptable and/or legitimate.

The assumption that solidarity is tied back to groups does not exclude the possibility that individuals engage in supporting 'outsiders' living within their immediate surroundings (social distance) and in far-off places (spatial-social distance). Local, national and transnational solidarities are not necessarily opposing dispositions and practices. The contrary seems to be the case. In fact, studies have shown that European citizens engaged in solidarity activities within their own country are also more likely to be active on behalf of individuals living in other European countries or outside Europe, while citizens refraining from transnational solidarity are less likely to be active in regard to their fellow citizens.[12]

Moreover, in conceptual terms, there is little reason to separate transnational solidarity strictly from other expressions of solidarity. In fact, this type of support can also be defined as group-bound social relations. Transnational solidarity only diverges in scope and size, when compared with more spatially restricted forms, given that it is tied to bigger entities, possibly even to the most encompassing (imagined) group: humankind. Individuals commit to 'borderless' transnational solidarity because they believe that distant others are part of humanity; and as members of this community, individuals are called to act in solidarity in order to conform

[12] C. Lahusen and M. Theiss, 'European transnational solidarity: citizenship in action?', *American Behavioral Scientist*, 63(4) (2019), 444–58; J. Kiess and H. J. Trenz, 'Ties of solidarity and the political spectrum: partisan cleavages in reported solidarity activity across Europe', *American Behavioral Scientist*, 63(4) (2019), 459–74.

to global rights, obligations and responsibilities. In this regard, notions of cosmopolitanism, global civil society and democracy are widely discussed as a normative reference point of transnational and/or universal solidarity.[13]

What makes transnational solidarity unique, is it universalist orientation (Gould, Chapter 2 in this volume). Any other, more specific solidarity involves a more particularistic approach, because it ties and limits solidarity to specific social entities (for example, groups, communities, societies). Particular solidarities thus limit the membership, and this implies that 'others' will be excluded from solidarity relations. Particular solidarities thus have integrative and disintegrative implications. Solidarity is an integrative force because it establishes reciprocal relations, responsibilities and obligations among its members, while erecting group borders between insiders and outsiders. Solidarity unleashes disintegrative forces, because different groups and (imagined) community (for example, nation states, regions, localities, transnational diasporas, subcultures, professions or corporations) start to compete with each other by mobilising and organising solidarity among their members. This means that a proper understanding of civic solidarity needs to take the integrative aspects into consideration as much as the disintegrative, contentious and conflict-related dimensions. As we will see, this is particularly important for an analysis of solidarity within larger and complex social formations, such as the EU.

3 Solidarity Within the 'Container' of the Nation State

On this conceptual basis, I propose to define solidarity as dispositions and activities of mutual support within (imagined) groups that are tied to group-specific norms and expectations, rights and obligations. Moreover, solidarity is enacted and organised on various levels of aggregation: Social solidarity is enacted at the micro-level on the basis of face-to-face interactions and immediate social relations (informal solidarity); it is an organised practice that is facilitated, co-ordinated and regulated at the meso-level in terms of voluntary groups, civic associations and networks (civil society solidarity); and it is institutionalised at the macro-level by means of (redistributive) policies, programmes and measures (welfare state solidarity). These levels share the basic traits of solidarity,

[13] H. Brunkhorst, *Solidarity. From Civic Friendship to Global Legal Community* (Cambridge: Cambridge University Press, 2005).

but exhibit a different degree of organisation and institutionalisation. What distinguishes the macro- and meso- from the micro-level is the degree of formalisation and codification. Solidarity develops an increasingly impersonal trait because it leaves the face-to-face interactions space for the sphere of organisational and/or fiduciary solidarity. Individuals either participate in organised forms of solidarity tied back to specific associations, membership rolls and action repertoires, and/or they delegate solidarity to public authorities, whose activities they support through financial or symbolic means. Solidarity is thus exposed to a gradual abstraction and generalisation of mutual responsibilities and obligations. At the same time, it becomes patterned and more strongly mediated by law and legally defined rights and obligations, as well as formally defined relations of support.

This analytical argument is well founded in empirical research within the social sciences. There are numerous studies published in this context, but a closer inspection shows that most strands of research conform to the various levels of analysis presented before. First, solidarity has been extensively studied at the micro-level. Many of these studies have dealt with forms of interpersonal help and support.[14] Sociological analyses argue that solidarity relations are an important ingredient in group-formation and reproduction, and that much of everyday life is patterned by these relations of reciprocal action.[15] In particular, the analysis of social capital has evidenced that interpersonal support and norms of reciprocity provide the 'glue' for social cohesion, essential for maintaining social relations, informal networks and/or larger communities.[16]

Research has shown, however, that informal solidarity at the micro-level is tightly patterned by the organisational fields of civil society and the institutional structure of welfare states. In fact, informal solidarity seems to interact with associational involvement, for instance, in terms of associational membership and participation in civil society organisations.[17] Additionally, the macro-level matters as well, in

[14] D. Schroeder, A. Penner, A. Louis, J. F. Dovidio and J. A. Piliavin, *The Psychology of Helping and Altruism: Problems and Puzzles* (New York: McGraw-Hill, 1995); P. Scheepers and M. T.Grotenhuis, 'Who cares for the poor in Europe? Micro and macro determinants for alleviating poverty in 15 European countries', *European Sociological Review*, 21(5) (2005), 453–65.

[15] Hecter, *Principles of Group Solidarity*; Komter, *Social Solidarity and the Gift.*

[16] Putnam et al., *Better Together: Restoring the American Community.*

[17] W. van Oorschot, W. Arts and J. Gelissen, 'Social capital in Europe. Measurement and social and regional distribution of a multifaceted phenomenon', *Acta Sociologica*, XLIX (2006), 149–67.

particular when speaking about the impact of the welfare state. Research findings are inconclusive, but tend to suggest that the crowding-in and crowding-out effects of the welfare state on informal solidarity are to be expected. On a general level, evidence shows that higher levels of welfare provision stimulate associational involvement and social capital by increasing the availability of resources, encouraging generalised trust and spurring feelings of social responsibility.[18] At the same time, however, social-democratic welfare states tend to substitute private forms of philanthropy with public programmes more often when compared to liberal welfare states,[19] and conservative and residual welfare regimes tend to promote solidarity within 'natural entities' like the family and the neighbourhood. Informal solidarity is not necessarily crowded out, but patterned and shaped by the organisational and institutional context in which citizens reside.

A second strand of research has centred on the meso-level of civil societies and social movements.[20] Solidarity is not only a mission of civil society organisations and social movement networks, but also a prerequisite for the development of their collective actions.[21] These organisations and networks need to arouse identity and solidarity among their members.[22] These forms of organised solidarity are an established pattern of mobilising and sustaining solidarity in modern societies. They also have palpable effects on individual solidarity, because the latter is often motivated and sustained by the affiliation, membership and/or adherence to specific organisations, networks or movements. The latter provide incentives to participate, role models for acting, and norms and

[18] J. Gelissen, J. H. Wim, W. van Oorschot and E. Finsveen, 'Does the welfare state influence individuals' social capital? Eurobarometer evidence on individuals' access to informal help', *European Societies*, 2012 (2012), 1–25; S. Kumlin and B. Rothstein, 'Making and breaking social capital: the impact of welfare-state institutions', *Comparative Political Studies*, 38(4) (2005), 339–65.

[19] Scheepers and Grotenhuis, 'Who cares for the poor in Europe?', p. 11.

[20] H. K. Anheier and L. M. Salamon, 'Volunteering in cross-national perspective: initial comparisons', *Law and Contemporary Problems*, 62(4) (1999), 43–65; M. Giugni and F. Passy, *Political Altruism? Solidarity Movements in International Perspective* (Lanham, MD: Rowman & Littlefield (2001); J. Smith, 'Bridging global divides? Strategic framing and solidarity in transnational social movement organizations', *International Sociology* 17 (4) (2002), 505–28.

[21] Hunt and Benford, 'Collective identity, solidarity, and commitment'.

[22] E.g. J. Bandy and J. Smith (eds.), *Coalitions Across Borders. Transnational Protest and the Neoliberal Order* (Lanham, MD: Rowman & Littlefield, 2005); D. della Porta and M. Caiani, *Social Movements and Europeanization* (Oxford: Oxford University Press, 2009).

identities to motivate and/or justify solidarity.[23] This allows for the decoupling of organised solidarity from the (potentially erratic) support of individuals, for instance, by widening constituencies, formalising membership rolls and contributions, and relying on the strategic planning of full-time staff.

Scholarly writing has shown that these organisational dynamics open the door to cooperation and alliances across organisations, networks and fields,[24] while remaining responsible for arousing tensions between competing and/or antagonistic organisations or movements that struggle to mobilise and sustain solidarity for different issues and missions.[25] Hence, organisations might be the basis for expanding and sustaining solidarity across borders, that is, organising solidarity transnationally.[26] However, they expose transnational solidarity to the fragmentations, cleavages and contentions prevailing within and between countries. Moreover, scholarly writing has shown that national differences between civil society and social movement organisations are quite marked, because their missions and functions are patterned by political and institutional factors. Volunteering for associations diverges considerably between welfare state regimes, depending on whether service provision is a matter for the state, or delegated to welfare associations and/or individual philanthropy.[27] Moreover, social movement organisations tend to reflect the political and institutional opportunities provided by their national environment.[28] Hence, we need to take into consideration that organised solidarity, even when reaching out beyond national borders,

[23] E. L. Hirsch, 'The creation of political solidarity in social movement organizations', *The Sociological Quarterly*, 27(3) (1986), 373–87; D. C. Minkoff, 'Producing social capital. national social movements and civil society', *American Behavioral Scientist*, 40(5) (1997), 606–19.

[24] C. Chase-Dunn, C. Petit, R. Niemeyer, R. A. Hanneman and E. Reese, 'The contours of solidarity and division among global movements', *International Journal of Peace Studies*, 12(2) (2007), 1–15; C. Lahusen, M. Kousis, U. Zschache and A. Loukakis, 'European solidarity in times of crisis: comparing transnational activism of civic organisations in Germany and Greece', *Österreichische Zeitschrift für Soziologie, Supplement 1/43: Power and Counter-Power in Europe* (2018), 173–97.

[25] C. K. Ansell, *Schism and Solidarity in Social Movements. The Politics of Labor in the French Third Republic* (Cambridge: Cambridge University Press, 2004).

[26] Della Porta and Caiani, *Social Movements and Europeanization*.

[27] Anheier and Salamon, 'Volunteering in cross-national perspective: initial comparisons'.

[28] H. Kriesi, R. Koopmans, J. W. Duyvendak and M. G. Giugni, 'New social movements and political opportunities in Western Europe', *European Journal of Political Research*, 22(2) (1992), 219–44; S. Tarrow, 'States and opportunities: the political structuring of social movements', in D. McAdam, J. D. McCarthy and M. N. Zald (eds.), *Comparative Perspectives on Social Movements* (Cambridge: Cambridge University Press, 1996).

will reflect national compartmentalisations, for instance, in terms of breadth and intensity, topics and claims, as well as normative orientations and missions.

Finally, social science research has insisted on the assumption that solidarity in complex societies is organised and institutionalised by means of redistributive policies and measures, and is thus basically institutionalised in the form of the modern welfare state.[29] Conversely to traditional charity and care, as provided by the family, church, neighbourhood or nobility, solidarity is a legally codified right, thus implying enforceable obligations and entitlements on the side of recipients and contributors. What we learn from empirical research on the public support of the welfare state, however, is that institutionalised and legally codified solidarity is an empty shell if not enforced, re-enacted and legitimised by societal actors. Hence, not the legal provisions themselves, but rather the active and/or passive support of these rights, policies and measures by citizens is what matters most.[30] The prospects of institutionalising solidarity within the EU are thus dependent on the arousal of sufficient public support from citizens.[31] In this respect, research has insisted on the contentiousness of institutionalised solidarity, because citizens tend to diverge in the amount of support they express. Additionally, research has devoted itself to the analysis of public discourse in the mass media to show that the principle of solidarity is highly contested, particularly when speaking about the economic and fiscal crisis, and the European measures to assist countries most severely hit by them, such as Greece.[32]

[29] E.g., K. Banting and W. Kymlicka (eds.), *The Strains of Commitment: The Political Sources of Solidarity in Diverse Societies* (Oxford: Oxford University Press, 2017).

[30] S. Svallfors, 'Worlds of welfare and attitudes to redistribution: a comparison of eight western nations', *European Journal of Sociology*, 13(3) (1997), 283–304; P. Rehm, J. S. Hacker and M. Schlesinger, 'Insecure alliances: risk, inequality and support for the welfare state', *American Political Science Review*, 106(2) (2012), 386–406.

[31] S. Mau, 'Democratic demand for a social Europe? Preferences of the European citizenry', *International Journal of Social Welfare*, 14(2) (2005), 76–85; J. Gerhards, H. Lengfeld, Z. S. Ignácz, F. K. Kley and M. Priem, 'How strong is European solidarity?', *Berlin Studies on the Sociology of Europe* (BSSE), 37 (2018), 1–37.

[32] Y. Mylonas, 'Media and the economic crisis of the EU: the 'culturalization' of a systemic crisis and *Bild-Zeitung*'s framing of Greece', *tripleC*, 10(2) (2012), 646–71; P. Wilde, A. de Michailidou and H. J. Trenz, *Contesting Europe. Exploring Euro-scepticism in Online Media Coverage* (Colchester: ECPR Press, 2013); S. Papathanassopoulos, 'European media views of the Greek crisis', in S. Schifferes and R. Roberts (eds.), *The Media and the Financial Crises. Comparative and Historical Perspectives* (New York: Routledge, 2015), pp. 103–18.

Overall, previous research findings have testified that solidarity is aggregated, organised and stabilised at various levels of analysis. Additionally, it shows that intensities and forms of solidarity at the micro-, meso- and macro-levels are interrelated. To a varying degree, national welfare states codify binding rights and obligations, delegate service provision to civil society, and promote normative expectations about active social citizenry, while civil societies provide an organisational field of voluntary groups and associations that arouses, organises and sustains citizen involvement in solidarity activities. At the same time, however, civil societies and welfare states also depend on the readiness and ability of citizens to engage in organised activities and to morally and financially support public policies and programmes of redistribution.

4 Solidarity within the European Union

The assumption that solidarity is aroused, organised and institutionalised at different levels also applies to the EU, given that a significant share of the European citizenry subscribes to the idea of European solidarity,[33] that an organised field of European associations and networks has been established,[34] and that the EU has included the principle of solidarity in its legal framework.[35] However, the current state of solidarity and its prospects are very different when compared to the situation within the European Member States, given that the EU is a much more complex social formation. This also means that the mobilisation, organisation and institutionalisation of solidarity at the micro-, meso- and macro-levels will most probably be exposed to a different set of constraints and limitations. These limitations are related to the sheer size of the

[33] Mau, 'Democratic demand for a social Europe?'; Gerhards et al., *How Strong Is European Solidarity?*; S. Baute, B. Meuleman and K. Abts, 'Welfare state attitudes and support for social Europe: spillover or obstacle?', *Journal of Social Policy* (2018), 1–19; C. Lahusen and M. T. Grasso (eds.), *Solidarity in Europe. Citizens' Responses in Times of Crisis* Cham: Palgrave Macmillan, 2018).

[34] S. Smismans, *Civil Society and Legitimate European Governance* (Cheltenham: Edward Elgar, 2006); R. Balme and D. Chabanet, *European Governance and Democracy. Power and Protest in the EU* (Lanham, MD: Rowman & Littlefield, 2008); B. Kohler-Koch and C. Quittkat, *De-mystification of Participatory Democracy. EU-governance and Civil Society* (Oxford: Oxford University Press, 2013).

[35] M. Ross and Y. Borgmann-Prebil (eds.), *Promoting Solidarity in the European Union* (Oxford: Oxford University Press, 2010); E. di Napoli and D. Russo, 'Solidarity in the European Union in times of crisis: towards "European Solidarity"?', in V. Federico and C. Lahusen (eds.), *Solidarity as a Public Virtue. Law and Public Policies in the European Union* (Baden-Baden: Nomos, 2018), pp. 195–248.

European community, but also to the fact that the EU is composed of various nation states that provide targets and arenas of civic solidarity, and thus might monopolise solidarity dispositions and activities. Consequently, European solidarity has to overcome problems associated with the size and structure of the EU. A closer inspection along the heuristic model introduced before promises to identify the main challenges and core implications.

First, informal solidarity at the citizens' level is particularly demanding, because the EU provides few possibilities for rooting civic solidarity in individual, face-to-face relations of cross-border help and exchange. Previous research even suggests that social solidarity is strongly attached to grown communities, where proximity seems to play a certain role. The readiness to support others seems to be stronger in regard to those who feel closer and share a sense of identity and belongingness, thus distinguishing between countrymen and foreigners.[36] This is associated with the underlying notion of reciprocity, which privileges relations of solidarity among people that maintain direct or close social relations.[37] This evidence, however, does not rule out the possibility that citizens engage in European solidarity all together. Two arguments can be extracted from previous research. On the one hand, studies on transnationalism provide ample evidence that proximity, identity and reciprocity are not necessarily tied back to a physical territory, because contact networks and everyday life practices can transcend national borders.[38] These studies insist that European integration and globalisation promote transnationalism, because they establish new opportunities that increase cross-national mobility, communication and networking.[39] On this basis, transnationalisation might create horizontally opened spaces of mutual support and

[36] W. van Oorschot, 'Who should get what, and why? On deservingness criteria and the conditionality of solidarity among the public', *Policy & Politics*, 28(1) (2000), 33–48; M. Coenders, M. Lubbers and P. Scheepers, 'Support for labour-market discrimination of migrants in Europe', in W. Arts and L. Halman (eds.), *Value Contrasts and Consensus in Present-day Europe. Painting Europe's Moral Landscapes* (Boston, MA: Brill, 2013), pp. 73–94; E. B. Peral and A. Ramos, 'Neighbours: determinants of whom Europeans want to keep at a distance', in W. Arts and L. Halman (eds.), *Value Contrasts and Consensus in Present-day Europe. Painting Europe's Moral Landscapes* (Boston, MA: Brill, 2013), pp. 117–41.

[37] Molm, Collett and Schafer, 'Building solidarity through generalized exchange'.

[38] J. Delhey, E. Deutschmann, T. Graf and K. Richter, 'Measuring the Europeanization of everyday life: three new indices and an empirical application', *European Societies*, 6(3) (2016), 355–77.

[39] E. Recchi and A. Favell, *Pioneers of European Integration. Citizenship and Mobility in the EU* (Cheltenham: Edward Elgar, 2009); S. Mau and J. Mewes, 'Horizontal Europeanisation

help. On the other hand, we might expect national forms of solidarity to spill over at the European level.[40] Citizens supportive of redistributive policies within the nation state seem to be more sympathetic to extending solidarity measures at the EU level.[41] It is thus to be expected that the levels of public support for European solidarity thus mirror local and national contexts.[42] Welfare countries with higher rates of approval of institutionalised solidarity would be more supportive of European solidarity policies, but also countries with a greater need for solidarity, such as the crisis countries.[43] Consequently, we must expect that informal European solidarity will be highly fragmented both between countries along the opportunities and constraints that national contexts provide, as well as within each country along the divisions between proponents and opponents.

Second, organised civil society plays a particularly important role in arousing and stabilising European solidarity under these circumstances. Research has corroborated that this field of organisation has grown substantially at the EU level as a consequence of the construction of the EU.[44] It thus provides organisational agency and entrepreneurship in order to mobilise, organise and maintain civic solidarity across borders. Several studies have testified to the ability of these European associations, multinational networks and issue coalitions to co-ordinate support and protest activities transnationally in different issue fields.[45] However, this form of organised solidarity also has limitations. In the first instance, the organisational field is mainly devoted to political advocacy and interest representation, and is thus strongly accommodated in the institutional structures and working procedures of the EU.[46] The organisations

in contextual perspective. What drives cross-border activities within the European Union?', *European Societies*, 14(1) (2011): 7–34.

40 Baute et al., 'Welfare state attitudes and support for social Europe: spillover or obstacle?'.

41 Baute et al., 'Welfare state attitudes and support for social Europe: spillover or obstacle?'; Gerhards et al., *How Strong Is European Solidarity?*.

42 Mau and Mews, 'Horizontal Europeanisation in contextual perspective'.

43 Gerhards et al., *How Strong Is European Solidarity?*; Lahusen and Grasso, 'Solidarity in Europe. Citizens' responses in times of crisis'.

44 Smismans, *Civil Society and Legitimate European Governance*; Kohler-Koch and Quittkat, *De-mystification of Participatory Democracy.*

45 Balme and Chabanet, *European Governance and Democracy*; Della Porta and Caiani, *Social Movements and Europeanization.*

46 D. Rucht, 'Lobbying or protest? Strategies to influence EU environmental policies', in D. Imig and S. Tarrow (eds.), *Contentious Europeans: Protest and Politics in an Emerging Polity* (Lanham, MD: Rowman & Littlefield, 2001), pp. 125–61; Kohler-Koch and Quittkat, *De-mystification of Participatory Democracy.*

represent multinational fields of associations and groups, and they co-ordinate locally rooted solidarity activities, but their ability to mobilise transnational solidarity activities ultimately depends on the readiness of local activists to engage in these transnational campaigns. In fact, the locus of activities remains national and local, and this means that the organised field of civil societies stays segmented in regard to issue fields and countries.[47]

Third, the degree of institutionalisation of solidarity in terms of European treaties and public policies at the EU level is rather low.[48] References to the principle of solidarity are included in the TEU in regard to the general objectives of the Union (Article 3), and in regard to different policy areas, such as border checks, asylum and immigration (Article 80), economic policy and energy (Articles 122 and 194), and security and disaster relief (Article 222). But this institutionalisation has various specificities. On the one hand, the principle of solidarity is addressed as governments and calls the Member States explicitly to co-operate more closely in order to co-ordinate policy measures and secure a fair burden share of issues that require joint problem solving. The ability to pressure Member States into burden sharing is low, as evidenced by the incapacity of the EU to agree on a quota system for refugees and asylum seekers since 2015. On the other hand, the EU has only minor competencies in the field of social policies, and is thus unable to regulate the relations between states and citizens in terms of social rights and benefits. Social policies remain a matter for the Member States, and European programmes are rather geared to increase cooperation and harmonisation, for example, through the Open Method of Coordination or the European Semester.[49] The EU has not set up any social security schemes or programmes targeting European citizens, because nation states are exclusively in charge of this field. Additionally, the EU is unable to make use of civil society organisations as a subsidiary agent of redistribution, because the delegation of service provision to civil societies as an instrument of welfare generation remains in the hands of the nation

[47] H.Johansson and S. Kalm, *EU Civil Society. Patterns of Cooperation, Competition and Conflict* (Houndmills: Palgrave Macmillan, 2015); Lahusen et al., 'European solidarity in times of crisis'.

[48] di Napoli Russo, 'Solidarity in the European Union'.

[49] M. Jessoula, 'Europe 2020 and the fight against poverty – beyond competence clash, towards "hybrid" governance solutions?', *Social Policy & Administration*, 49(4) (2015), 490–511; P. Copeland and M. Daly, 'The European Semester and EU social policy', *Journal of Common Market Studies*, 56(5) (2018), 1001–18.

state. As a consequence, European solidarity is institutionalised only in terms of policy co-ordination, thus restating the importance of Member States and the subsequent disparities in legal frameworks and public policies.[50] Additionally, the EU promotes civil society organisations both financially and symbolically, but at the same time, it is unable to establish a European statute of associations, and thus to detach transnationally active initiatives and organisations from specific national legal and institutional contexts.

These observations conclude that European solidarity is subjected to a low degree of transnational organisation and institutionalisation. Against this backdrop, we expect that the public sphere, and in particular the mass media, will play a more noticeable role. They might be treated as 'functional equivalents': If the level of organisation and institutionalisation of solidarity is low at the EU level, then it might be plausible to assume that the mass media will have a much higher impact on mobilising, stabilising, questioning and discouraging European solidarity. The mass media is an important 'gatekeeper' and agenda-setter, meaning that it is important in raising awareness for issues and in shaping public opinion. Research has confirmed that the mass media plays a crucial role in public discourse about European solidarity, and that it thus influences the ideas and expectations citizens have about its meaning and meaninglessness, such as fiscal solidarity measures in support of countries affected by the financial and economic crisis.[51] In analytic terms, it is to be expected that the mass media will increase the volatility and fragmentation of European solidarity considerably. On the one hand, mass mediated debates about European solidarity should be exposed to cycles of attention: The more intense the focus of debates on specific grievances, target groups and solidarity activities, the more marked the decline of attention will be once other issues emerge. On the other hand, public discourse about European solidarity should follow the structure of the European public sphere: Given the existence of different language areas, mass media markets and national regulations, there might be common events, issues and claims; nevertheless, distinct national debates about them will emerge.[52]

[50] V. Federico and C. Lahusen (eds.), *Solidarity as a Public Virtue. Law and Public Policies in the European Union* (Baden-Baden: Nomos, 2018).

[51] Mylonas, 'Media and the economic crisis of the EU'; Wilde, Michailidou and Trenz, *Contesting Europe. Exploring Euro-scepticism in Online Media Coverage*; Papathanassopoulos, 'European media views of the Greek Crisis'.

[52] C. Bee and E. Bozzini, *Mapping the Public Sphere. Institutions, Media and Civil Society* (London: Routledge 2010).

In summary, available evidence suggests that care must be taken when drawing conclusive statements about European (civic) solidarity. What the previous observations show is that European solidarity is a widely diffused latent normative principle, activated only under specific circumstances. In this sense, European solidarity in action is expected to be fragile, contested, volatile and fragmented. It is contested because the degree of institutionalisation is low, and the number of institutional proponents defending its cause have limited powers. It is fragile because it cannot build on a well-developed organisational field that has a transnational structure and outreach, volatile because it is not a fixed point on public agendas, but rather an issue surfacing in emergency situations where immediate action is required. Lastly, it is fragmented because European solidarity is not a cross-cutting principle of action within the EU, and thus left to the discretion of citizens with their specific preferences, and to civic organisations with their issue-specific foci of attention and memberships.

5 Empirical Evidence: the Momentum of European Solidarity

These conceptual and analytical observations require empirical evidence in order to testify to their plausibility. For this purpose, data from TransSOL, an EU-funded research project, will be used.[53] Among others, this project conducted a systematic mapping of civic initiatives and associations engaged in solidarity activities in three different issue fields, namely: disabilities, unemployment and asylum/refugees. The selection of these issues fields was led by the assumption that structures and dynamics of civic engagement and organised civil societies might diverge not only between countries, but also between policy domains and social problems, given that solidarity dispositions are – according to previous research[54] – influenced by concepts of social proximity and deservingness (privileging people with disabilities against refugees), and neediness (favouring refugees and/or the unemployed depending on circumstances).

[53] The data employed in this paper were collected as part of the European Horizon 2020 Project 'European paths to transnational solidarity at times of crisis: Conditions, forms, role models and policy responses' (TransSOL) led by the University of Siegen. This project has received funding from the European Union's Horizon 2020 research and innovation programme under grant agreement No. 649435.

[54] Van Oorschot 'Who should get what, and why?'; W. van Oorschot, 'Making the difference in social Europe: deservingness perceptions among citizens of European welfare states', *Journal of European Social Policy*, 16(1) (2006), 23–42.

Data was collected in eight countries (Denmark, France, Germany, Greece, Italy, Poland, Switzerland and the UK) and extracted from 300 randomly chosen organisational websites (100 for each of the three fields), following a standardised content analysis based on a cross-nationally co-ordinated and tested codebook.[55] It is noteworthy that this sample does not mirror the organisational field of civil society in its fullness, because it focuses on solidarity groups and organisations that have a transnational element in at least one of eight criteria. We only selected transnational solidarity organisations (TSOs) and groups with (1) branches, (2) activities, (3) beneficiaries, (4) volunteers, (5) participants and supporters, (6) partners, (7) sponsors from another country, and (8) a transnational mission and spatial outreach. Excluded were commercial entities or public institutions.[56] Finally, online sources allowed for the inclusion of more recently established organisations, as well as more informal groups that are usually not part of public directories or formal lists, and are thus capable of painting a more comprehensive and diverse picture of organised solidarity.[57] Data retrieval was completed in mid-2016, thus allowing us to depict developments up until that point.

The data from this organisational survey are a good basis to assess the structure of European solidarity, because civic initiatives and organisations are a more demanding manifestation of solidarity, when compared to the individual dispositions and opinions respondents report during opinion polls and surveys. They give us an impression of solidarity in action. In this regard, the data unveil that solidarity initiatives are mainly active at the local level, with 72 per cent of all TSOs indicating this scope of activity. Differences are marked because French groups are less often active at this level (that is, 22 per cent), while in other countries, this is the rule (for example, 84 per cent in Greece, 95 per cent in Germany, 96 per cent in Italy and 97 per cent in the UK). The prevalence of local initiatives is not surprising, given that this survey was not only interested in large, formal organisations, but also in informal groups which are most often active in their immediate locale. In this sense, our comprehensive

[55] M. Kousis, M. Giugni and C. Lahusen, 'Action organization analysis: extending protest event analysis using websites', *American Behavioral Scientist*, 62(6) (2018), 739–57; Lahusen et al., 'European solidarity in times of crisis'.

[56] TransSOL, *Integrated Report on Reflective Forms of Transnational Solidarity*. Siegen (2016) Project deliverable 2.1, available at: https://transsol.eu/outputs/reports/ (accessed: 29 October 2018.

[57] See also Kousis, Giugni and Lahusen, 'Action organization analysis'.

mapping of organised civil society allows us to paint a picture of an organisational field with a strongly decentralised grass-roots structure. This did not exclude other forms of activities, given that TSOs indicated across country activities at the national (42 per cent), European (16 per cent) and global (11 per cent) levels. Additionally, most TSOs indicated partnerships in other countries (63 per cent with one to ten, and 8 per cent with 11+) as well. Differences between countries and issue fields were small, even though in the field of disabilities, transnational co-operation was more diffused when compared to the field of migration and unemployment. Overall, we thus see that solidarity work is mainly a local and decentralised activity, embedded in transnational webs of cooperation. This picture is not unexpected, given that it conforms to findings on citizens' initiatives and social movements.[58]

Against this backdrop, it is advisable to look more carefully at how these fields of civic solidarity engagement developed across time. This question is pivotal to fully grasp the dynamics that European civic solidarity is exposed to, and it will allow us to check whether the analytical framework, introduced before, is empirically plausible. In this regard, the organisational data provides important insights because information on the TSOs' year of establishment was extracted from websites. This information allows for reconstructing the development of the organisational fields across countries, even though this picture excludes all those organisations that have ceased to exist and thus ignores the volatility of these fields. It needs to be highlighted that these data only provide information on the organisational entities, that is, on organised civic solidarity. The number of organisations says something about the dynamics of the organisational field itself, but it does not mirror what the individual organisations or groups do, and how many individuals they mobilise or address. We are thus unable to mirror solidarity activism in itself, but we are able to unveil the organisational manifestation of this activism.

Figure 13.1 gives some interesting insights into the history of the current fields of civic organisations. Some organisations are considerably old, as they were established before 1900. However, most other TSOs are younger, and waves of establishments diverge considerably between issue fields. TSOs in the field of disabilities started their work mostly in the

[58] Bandy and Smith, *Coalitions Across Borders*; Della Porta and Caiani, *Social Movements and Europeanization*, p. 15; Tarrow, 'States and opportunities: the political structuring of social movements', p. 168.

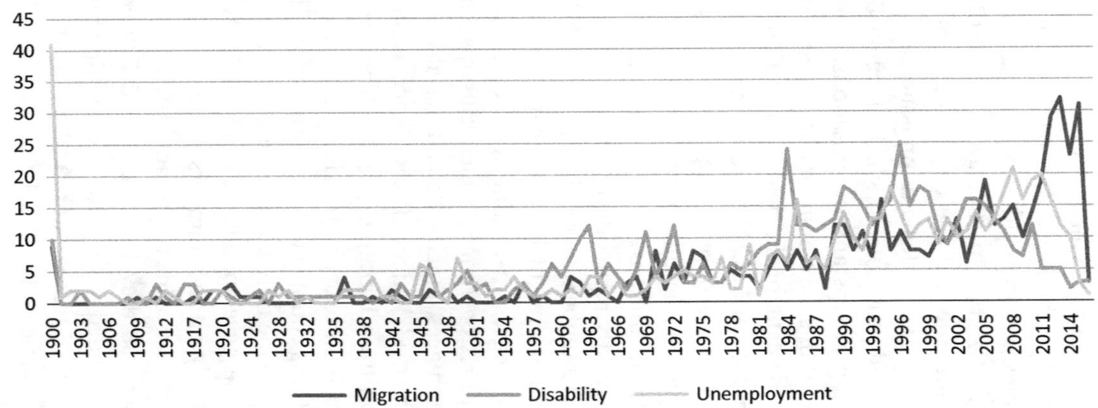

Figure 13.1 Year of establishment across all countries (three issue fields; n = 1,764)

1980s and 1990s, with fewer organisations joining since then. In the field of unemployment issues, organisations and groups started to emerge during the 1980s, and further waves are perceivable for the 1990s, and since 2008, reflected in the development of mass unemployment across Europe, with average unemployment rates running at almost 10 per cent during that period. And in regard to migration and refugees, the data unmistakably testifies that the field of organised civil society reacted to the waves of forced migration, particularly since 2012.

These findings indicate that the development of the organisational field of civic solidarity greatly depends on issues, and thus also on issue-specific grievances and problems, to which citizens obviously try to find solutions by forming groups and organisations. Additionally, a closer inspection shows that this development also depends on location. Figure 13.2 disaggregates the data for the field of migration; for clarity's sake, it restricts itself to five countries. The most obvious finding is the emergence of German citizens' groups devoted to solidarity work for refugees, which reflects the 'welcoming culture' of the years 2015 and 2016. Also in Greece, the number of initiatives increased dramatically, even though this growth is not strictly related to the estimated number of incoming refugees, given that numbers were higher before 2010 and after 2014. However, these findings might indicate that citizens committed themselves to helping refugees in a context of economic crisis, austerity policies and welfare retrenchment, which caused substantial grievances for the incoming refugees. Finally, Poland has also experienced a more recent growth in the field, which reflects the accession to the EU and the strong immigration from Ukraine. The development of the Italian and Danish fields is much more even, surprising in the case of Italy given the strong exposure of this country to forced migration since the 2000s.

These findings provide only a very rough and tentatively constructed representation of the development of civic solidarity in Europe, given that they focus merely on the numbers of newly formed organisations and groups. These data provide important insights into the dynamic side of civil society, because they indicate at which times (and in which countries) citizens decided to respond to upcoming problems and crises in a collective and concerted manner. And in this regard, the data show that the organisational field of civic solidarity seems to respond to urgent needs and upcoming grievances in specific contexts and locations. While many groups persist, it is obvious that civil societies tend to stop growing once other social problems and needs emerge. This has to do with the specific orientation of civic engagement, as portrayed by our data. Most

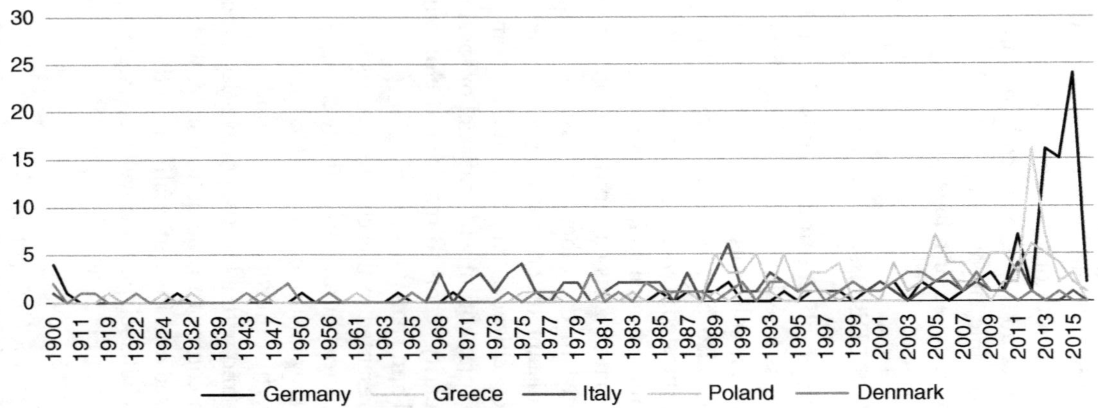

Figure 13.2 Year of establishment (TSOs in the field of migration, n = 534)

citizens' groups and organisations are engaged in political advocacy, but they also provide services and goods to the needy. Additionally, they operate primarily at the local level, albeit maintaining working relations with other groups in other countries. Hence, civic solidarity is transnationally organised, but its main locus of activity is the grass-roots level. This orientation seems to motivate the uneven growth of the organisational field: Citizens seem to engage in collective and organised forms of solidarity when palpable needs emerge, be they among people with disabilities, the unemployed or refugees.

6 Discussion and Conclusion

A closer inspection of citizens and organised civil society reveals that European solidarity is a reality. Recent studies have evidenced that the principle of European solidarity is supported by a wide strata of the population, in part also by majorities,[59] even though this support is conditional and contested.[60] Additionally, research findings show that global, European and national solidarities are not necessarily opposed to each other, given that citizens committed to one of them are also more likely to be engaged in the other expressions, while inactive citizens disengaged from distant others are also more likely to be inactive in regard to their fellow citizens.[61] Global and European solidarities are thus not necessarily in competition with national or local ones, even though transnational solidarity seems to require more organisational efforts in overcoming social and spatial distances.

The evidence presented in this chapter proves that citizens' initiatives and organisations across Europe are actively engaged in service provision and political advocacy in support of troubled groups. A closer inspection showed, however, that European civic solidarity is confronted with various challenges and with a less supportive (legal, political and institutional) context. In contrast to the nation state, where civic solidarity is supported, organised and institutionalised on the level of informal networks, organised civil societies and welfare systems, these elements are little developed at the EU level. This unbalanced context makes it very

[59] Gerhards et al., *How Strong Is European Solidarity?*.

[60] Baute et al., 'Welfare state attitudes and support for social Europe'; Lahusen and Grasso, *Solidarity in Europe*; Christian Lahusen, *Citizens' Solidarity in Europe. Civic Engagement and Public Discourse in Times of Crisis* (Cheltenham: Edward Elgar, 2020).

[61] Kiess and Trenz, 'Ties of solidarity and the political spectrum'; Lahusen and Theiss, 'European transnational solidarity'.

likely that civic solidarity will remain a very lively and dynamic, yet, local, fragmented and fragile phenomenon.

The empirical evidence presented in this chapter corroborates this picture. On the one hand, empirical data evidence that citizens are committed to solidarity work, and that an organisational field is being established that aims to respond to upcoming problems and grievances. In fact, there has been a spread of solidarity groups responding to incipient mass unemployment across Europe, particularly since 2008, and the same applies to the inflow of forced migrants since 2011, who needed urgent assistance and help. On the other hand, civic solidarity is primarily a decentralised grass-roots phenomenon, even though these groups and organisations are embedded in national and transnational structures of co-operation. This decentralised structure reproduces fragmentations while guaranteeing flexibility and fluidity, and thus assures the diffusion of issues and ideas, solidarity norms, repertoires of actions and organisational skills and tools across borders.[62] Ultimately, it allows civic solidarity to be highly responsive to upcoming problems, grievances and needs.

European citizens and organised civil society have thus proven to be Europe's emergency services, given that they react in times of urgent need, often providing assistance and voice where public authorities have trouble reacting with alacrity. Additionally, they have proven to advocate for those groups that have difficulties being heard, particularly in regard to the economic and financial crisis since 2008, and the crisis of the European immigration and asylum system. These findings illustrate that citizens and solidarity groups jump in when governments become entrenched in an inability to agree on policy solutions.

However, this political, legal and institutional context is not without risks for European civic solidarity. On the one hand, it is highly probable that civic solidarity will remain a local, fragmented and fragile phenomenon. Solidarity is highly organised and institutionalised within the nation state, when referring to constitutional principles, public policies, funding schemes, welfare and voluntary associations. This means that civic solidarity within the nation state is encouraged legally, financially, organisationally and symbolically, while obstacles predominate over incentives where transnational solidarity is concerned. On the other

[62] A. Mattoni and D. della Porta, 'Adapting theories on diffusion and transnational contention through social movements of the crisis: some concluding remarks', in Kivanç Atak et al. (eds.), *Spreading Protests. Social Movements in Times of Crisis* (Colchester: ECPR Press, 2014), pp. 277–92.

hand, it is very likely that the current level of organisation and institutionalisation might increase the volatility of European civic solidarity. The lack of political and institutional responses to upcoming crises forces citizens to act on whatever problems require urgent solutions. Citizens' engagement might be overstrained under these circumstances, leading to cycles of mobilisation and demobilisation. The mass media contribute to these developments, as evidenced by the German 'welcoming culture', which ended abruptly as a publicly visible phenomenon once criticism and populist mobilisations gained momentum. The arousal and stabilisation of European civic solidarity are thus not only dependent on the individual motivations and intentions of citizens. What is required is a concerted effort to strengthen the organisational and institutional fabric within which European solidarity can thrive and evolve.

PART IV

Creating New Forms of Transnational Solidarity in Europe

14

Free Movement and Social Citizenship

Towards a Politically Constructed Understanding of Solidarity Across Borders

CHENCHEN ZHANG

1 Introduction: Free Movement and Social Citizenship in the EU

The relationship between freedom of movement and the evolvement of variegated citizenship regimes in the European Union (EU) has long been a subject of vigorous debate in both political and academic discourses. Brexit, the rise of radical right parties across Europe advancing anti-immigration and Eurosceptic agendas, and the restrictive interpretation of the social rights of economically inactive citizens in recent citizenship jurisprudence of the Court of Justice of the European Union (CJEU) have all contributed to the perception that freedom of movement is increasingly 'under attack'[1] from both the left and the right. While right-wing populist parties in Europe typically combine their support for the national welfare regime with nativist resentment against immigrants from both within and outside the EU,[2] some observers from the left have also been concerned with the possible detrimental impact of the European regime of free movement and immigration in general on the norms and mechanisms of national solidarity.[3]

[1] F. de Witte, R. Bauböck and J. Shaw (eds.), 'Freedom of movement under attack: is it worth defending as the core of EU citizenship?', EUI Working Papers, 2016.

[2] C. Mudde, *Populist Radical Right Parties in Europe* (Cambridge: Cambridge University Press, 2007).

[3] A. J. Menéndez, 'European citizenship after Martínez Sala and Baumbast: Has European law become more human but less social?', ARENA working paper, 11 June 2009, available at: www.sv.uio.no/arena/english/research/publications/arena-working-papers/2001–2010/2009/WP11_09_Online.pdf; M. Höpner and A. Schäfer, 'Embeddedness and regional integration: waiting for Polanyi in a Hayekian setting', *International Organization*, 66 (2012), 429–55, at 429; W. Streeck, 'Exploding Europe: Germany, the refugees and the British vote', 31 SPERI paper, 2016, available at: http://speri.dept.shef.ac.uk/wp-content/uploads/2016/09/SPERI-Paper-31-Wolfgang-Streeck-Exploding-Europe.pdf.

One central aspect of the debate is the perceived tension between open borders and social solidarity that underpins redistributive institutions previously established at the national level, known as a 'progressive dilemma'[4] in migration and welfare research. In a sense, EU legislation and jurisprudence on free movement and equal treatment offer a 'multilevel and transnational answer' to the progressive dilemma by conferring transnational social rights on individual mobile citizens and thereby 'rescaling solidarity'[5] beyond the nation state. From a liberal cosmopolitan perspective, the emergence of a 'rights-based approach to freedom of movement' paves the way towards constructing a European political community of equal citizens as rights bearers[6] or enables individual emancipation from the domination of national boundaries.[7] However, from a republican or communitarian perspective on citizenship that emphasises democratic solidarity, the rights-based and individualist approach to forging transnational citizenship has been considered inadequate or even problematic.[8] Höpner and Schäfer, for instance, argue that 'while court rulings can strengthen individual rights, they cannot create the norms of reciprocity and solidarity that underpin redistribution'.[9] The ambiguous attitudes towards the welfare rights of economically inactive EU citizens in EU (case) law, which are characterised by an oscillation between favouring the individual citizen's right to equal treatment and the Member State's interests in protecting national systems of social cohesion,[10] have further

[4] O. Parker, 'Critical political economy, free movement and Brexit: beyond the progressive's dilemma', *The British Journal of Politics and International Relations*, 19(3) (2017), 479–96, at 479.

[5] R. Bauböck, 'Why liberal nationalism does not resolve the progressive's trilemma: comment on Will Kymlicka's article: "Solidarity in diverse societies"' *Comparative Migration Studies*, 4(10) (2016), 1–6, at 5.

[6] W. Maas, *Creating European citizens* (Lanham, MD: Rowman & Littlefield, 2007), p. 27.

[7] F. de Witte, 'Emancipation through law?', in L. Azoulai, S. B. des Places and E. Pataut (eds.), *Constructing the Person in EU Law: Rights, Roles, Identities* (Oxford: Hart Publishing, 2016), pp. 15–33.

[8] M. Everson, 'A very cosmopolitan citizenship: but who pays the price?', in M. Dougan, N. Nic Shuibhne and E. Spaventa (eds.), *Empowerment and Disempowerment of the European Citizen* (Oxford: Hart Publishing, 2012), pp. 145–67; A. Somek, *The Cosmopolitan Constitution* (Oxford: Oxford University Press, 2014); R. Bellamy, 'A duty-free Europe? What's wrong with Kochenov's account of EU citizenship rights', *European Law Journal*, 21(4) (2015), 558–65.

[9] M. Höpner and A. Schäfer, 'Embeddedness and regional integration', p. 430.

[10] D. Thym, 'The elusive limits of solidarity: residence rights of and social benefits for economically inactive Union citizens', *Common Market Law Review*, 52(1) (2015), 17–50.

complicated the picture.[11] Scholars hold that the restrictive interpretation of the conditionality for economically inactive citizens to access benefits exemplifies the logic of 'earned citizenship' that underscores the 'individual citizen-outsider's responsibility to' contribute to the host society and may reinforce social exclusion.[12]

This chapter seeks to bring in the insights of critical citizenship theory to reflect on the relationship between free movement, social citizenship and solidarity. Critical citizenship studies focus on acts, performances and claim-makings outside formal institutions of participations as processes of political subjectivisation through which the citizen subject is brought into being. Rather than a fixed collection of social rights, social citizenship can be understood as a 'fluctuating reality' shaped by relations of social forces[13] and open-ended collective struggles for 'translating' needs into rights.[14] This approach also helps us rethink the concept of solidarity, a term frequently referred to in public and political discourses on citizenship and migration, the meaning of which is nonetheless not always specified. Gould distinguishes between a 'classic' form of intragroup solidarity that characterises a relationship 'binding all the members of a single cohesive group' and a new notion of transnational solidarity based on 'overlapping networks'.[15] In the national context, solidarity implicates a notion of shared responsibility that has become institutionalised to varied degrees through social policies and

[11] For the application of the EU law on free movement and welfare rights in Member States administrations, see, e.g., A. Heindlmaier and M. Blauberger, 'Enter at your own risk: free movement of EU citizens in practice', *West European Politics*, 50(6) (2017), 1198-1217 and D. S. Martinsen, G. Pons Rotger and J. S. Thierry, 'Free movement of people and cross-border welfare in the European Union: dynamic rules, limited outcomes', *Journal of European Social Policy*, 29 (1) (2019), 84–99.

[12] D. Kramer, 'Earning social citizenship in the European Union: free movement and access to social assistance benefits reconstructed', *Cambridge Yearbook of European Legal Studies*, 18 (2016), 270–301, at 270; D. Schiek, 'Perspectives on social citizenship in the EU: from *status positivus* to *status socialis activus* via two forms of transnational solidarity', in D. Kochenov (ed.), *EU Citizenship and Federalism: The Role of Rights* (Cambridge: Cambridge University Press, 2017), pp. 341–70; E. Spaventa, 'Earned citizenship – understanding Union Citizenship through its scope', in D. Kochenov (ed.), *EU Citizenship and Federalism: The Role of Rights* (Cambridge: Cambridge University Press, 2017), pp. 204–25.

[13] É. Balibar, 'Antinomies of citizenship', *Journal of Romance Studies*, 10(2) (2010), 1–20, at 10.

[14] H. Dean, 'The translation of needs into rights: reconceptualising social citizenship as a global phenomenon', *International Journal of Social Welfare*, 22 (2013), S32–S49.

[15] C. C. Gould, 'Transnational solidarities', *Journal of Social Philosophy*, 38(1) (2007), 148–64, at 148, see also Chapter 2.

redistributive mechanisms of the welfare state. Beyond the national community, the idea of (transnational) solidarity is often associated with looser networks of actions and discourses in support of distant others.

While distinguishing between relatively 'thick' and 'thin' forms of solidarity is analytically useful for discussing issues such as global justice and transnational social movement, it is also important to note that solidarity emerges as a way to 'imagine commonality' and 'negotiate difference in heterogeneous struggles'[16] also within the national context. The sources of national solidarity should not be reduced to a common membership based on categories such as cultural and ethnic similarity and 'somehow anterior to political action or its legitimation'.[17] A politically constructed conception of solidarity can be understood in two dimensions. First, it implies that solidarity emerges in the process of 'emancipatory political action rather than its indispensable condition of possibility'.[18] Second, it also emphasises that, rather than simply gestures of sympathy, solidarity movements produce a space for resistance within increasingly transnationalised structures of power relations. For Brunkhorst, 'joining together in common action against the proliferation' of 'hegemonic global laws' is a potent source of global solidarity.[19] With regard to migration, solidarity practices are transnational in nature not only because the networks of support are geared towards those without formal membership of the respective national community (namely citizenship), but also because they are enacted against racialised border regimes that routinely produce violence, illegality and precarity.

There has been an increasing interest in examining and conceptualising the politics of solidarity among scholars of migration and citizenship studies.[20] This literature, however, has been focused mainly on

[16] M. Tazzioli and W. Walters 'Migration, solidarity and the limits of Europe', *Global Discourse: An Interdisciplinary Journal of Current Affairs*, 9(1) (2019), 175–90, at 179.

[17] C. J. Calhoun, 'Imagining solidarity: cosmopolitanism, constitutional patriotism, and the public sphere', *Public Culture*, 14(1) (2002), 147–71, at 156.

[18] L. Ypi, 'Politically constructed solidarity: the idea of a cosmopolitan avant-garde', *Contemporary Political Theory*, 9(1) (2010), 120–30, at 121.

[19] H. Brunkhorst, *Solidarity: from Civic Friendship to a Global Legal Community* (Cambridge, MA: MIT Press, 2005), p. xi.

[20] E.g. I. Ataç, K. Rygiel and M. Stierl, 'Introduction: the contentious politics of refugee and migrant protest and solidarity movements: remaking citizenship from the margins', *Citizenship Studies*, 20(5) (2016), 527–44; M. Stierl, 'Contestations in death – the role of grief in migration struggles', *Citizenship Studies*, 20(2) (2016), 173–91; Tazzioli and Walters, 'Migration, solidarity and the limits of Europe'.

movements of solidarity with undocumented migrants, refugees and asylum seekers rather than legal migrants. Whereas, the debate on free movement and social citizenship tends to treat solidarity more as an established common identity that underpins redistributive social policies than relationalities emerged from political practices. To bridge this gap, this chapter considers how a politically constructed understanding of solidarity could shed light on questions of legal migration and social rights, specifically within the framework of EU free moment. I argue that comprehending rights and solidarity as co-occurrent in political actions allows us to move beyond the individualist approach to transnational rights in liberal cosmopolitanism and the static approach to solidarity in the defence of national closure. Other conceptual tools have been proposed to think constructively about the tension between economic integration, social solidarity and democratic citizenship in the EU such as Schiek's socially embedded constitutionalism[21] and Blokker's proposal on a 'bottom-up constitutional order'.[22] This chapter contributes to this line of inquiry by drawing attention to largely non-institutionalised avenues for reconstructing and enacting social citizenship through struggles over mobility. Mobilisations centred on the social rights of EU migrants (and beyond) both challenge the neoliberal political economy of free movement and construct new forms of solidarity across a plurality of boundaries.

The article is structured as follows. It starts by reviewing criticisms of EU free movement that are centred on democratic boundedness and analyses of market citizenship. They hence point to the limits of the individualistic approach to supranational rights, the negative implications of economic integration for labour standards, and regulatory changes that deepen the precarity of vulnerable migrants and atypical workers. I then illuminate how critical citizenship theory could contribute to the debate by offering a perspective on social citizenship as a contingent crystallisation of relations of social forces within ongoing processes of political struggles rather than a finalised national project. In the last section, the article

[21] D. Schiek, 'Re-embedding economic and social constitutionalism: normative perspectives for the EU', in D. Schiek, U. Liebert and H. Schneider (eds.), *European Economic and Social Constitutionalism after the Treaty of Lisbon* (Cambridge: Cambridge University Press, 2011), pp. 17–46.

[22] P. Blokker, 'Constitutional alternatives to the crisis: a political-sociological approach to European "anti-politics"', in H.-J. Trenz, C. Ruzza and V. Guiraudon (eds.), *Europe's Prolonged Crisis: the Making and Unmaking of a Political Union* (London: Palgrave, 2015), pp. 63–82, at 76.

considers two interrelated fields of contestation that challenge the institutional configurations of free movement – one focused on social inclusion and the other industrial citizenship – and how they bear upon the notion of solidarity across borders. I argue that the contestations politicise the social question in the transnational space and establish relations of solidarity and reciprocity across various boundaries.

2 Free Movement and its Critics: Democratic Boundaries and (Stratified) Market Citizenship

Having emerged as an initiative to facilitate the circulation of goods, capital and workers in building the common market, free movement has now evolved into a defining character of and an essential right associated with EU citizenship – listed as the first right enjoyed by Union citizens in Article 20(2) of the Treaty on the Functioning of the European Union (TFEU). Although free movement of persons in earlier periods were restricted to workers or economically active citizens, its gradual decoupling from the mobile citizen's economic status through Directive 2004/38/EC and the CJEU's jurisprudence has been considered instrumental for advancing the normative and political dimensions of EU citizenship.[23] Moreover, the project of constructing Union citizenship through free movement entails that the latter should not merely amount to the right to travel freely to another country, but also involve 'the enjoyment of a legal status' that confers on the mobile citizen the right to be treated equally without discrimination.[24] In the scenario of international migration, precarious migrant workers are often forced to accept a 'trade-off' between their mobility (entry to the labour market of the host country) and the rights available to them, known as a 'numbers versus rights' dilemma in temporary migration programmes. As Dauvergne and Marsden have pointed out, the ideology of temporary labour migration takes advantage of the subordinate position of migrant workers and frames their subordination as somehow 'natural and inevitable'.[25] Mobility *without* equal treatment

[23] D. Kostakopoulou, 'Ideas, norms and European Citizenship: explaining institutional change', *The Modern Law Review*, 68(2) (2005), 233–67.

[24] S. I. Sanchez, 'Free movement as a precondition for integration of third-country nationals in the EU', in E. Guild, K. Groenendijk and S. Carrera (eds.), *Illiberal Liberal States. Immigration, Citizenship and Integration in the EU* (Farnham: Ashgate, 2009), pp. 205–19, at 206.

[25] C. Dauvergne and S. Marsden, 'The ideology of temporary labour migration in the post-global era', *Citizenship Studies*, 18(2) (2014), 224–42, at 234.

hence reinforces unequal employment relations in the labour market and facilitates the exploitation of migrant labour whose profitability is derived from vulnerable legal status.

It is against this background that the implementation of free movement begs critical questions regarding the portability of social rights and the boundaries of national solidarity. On the one hand, the principle of equal treatment under conditions of cross-border mobility offers an opportunity to construct transnational social citizenship through 'the universalist aspirations of European law'.[26] One of the best known formulations of such an aspirational universalism is from the *Grzelczyk* case: 'Union citizenship is destined to be the fundamental status of nationals of the Member States, enabling those who find themselves in the same situation to enjoy the same treatment in law irrespective of their nationality, subject to such exceptions as are expressly provided for.'[27] On the other hand, however, the institutional framework of free movement is also marked by ambiguities and contradictions that pose challenges to democratic citizenship in both normative and practical terms. There has been a vast literature on the limitations of the ways in which free movement, both as citizenship rights and as market freedoms, is governed in EU law and political economy.[28] This section briefly reviews two interrelated theses emerged in the criticisms: the question of democratic boundedness and the stratification of market citizenship.

The normative assumption that democratic citizenship demands certain forms of territorial and membership closure can be defended from liberal, republican and social democratic (redistributive) perspectives. Within the debate on free movement and transnational citizenship in the European context, the latter two perspectives have offered most pertinent criticisms of the liberal cosmopolitan approach that emphasises individual rights and autonomy beyond national boundaries. In an earlier intervention, Bellamy articulates a republican conception of citizenship based on belonging, rights, and participation, and argues that the attempt to develop belonging at the European level 'from an attachment

[26] Everson, 'A very cosmopolitan citizenship', p. 148.

[27] Case C-184/99.

[28] J. E. Dolvik and J. Visser, 'Free movement, equal treatment and workers' rights: can the European Union solve its trilemma of fundamental principles?', *Industrial Relations Journal*, 40(6) (2009), 491–509; I. Wagner and N. Lillie, 'European integration and the disembedding of labour market regulation: transnational labour relations at the European Central Bank construction site', *JCMS: Journal of Common Market Studies*, 52(2) (2014), 403–19; Kramer, 'Earning social citizenship in the European Union'; Schiek, 'Perspectives on social citizenship in the EU'.

to' supranational rights would be neither plausible nor desirable.[29] In contrast to the transcendental view of rights as moral claims, Bellamy's political constitutionalism indicates that rights do not lie outside politics but requires 'democratic justification' via a political, democratic process.[30] The republican perspective thus stresses on the reciprocity between rights and duties as well as the role of 'political obligations' to democratic structures of the Member States in realising the 'status of citizens as equal rights bearers'.[31] In legal scholarship, the implications of the CJEU's judicial decision making for the democratic legitimacy of the EU and redefining the relationship between citizens and states have also been questioned.[32] According to Everson, the 'universalist impulses' of the Court's jurisprudence that aim to facilitate market freedoms and expand the scope of transnational rights for citizen free movers fail to acknowledge the particularism of citizenship traditions developed in bounded communities and hinder the redistributive dimension of national citizenship.[33] For critics, the problem thus concerns not only the difficulty in envisioning a political understanding of citizenship as democratic self-governance rather than the enjoyment of individual rights beyond the national community, but also the challenges of open borders to redistributive social rights, which from the conventional point of view are particularly dependent on bounded solidarity that seems to be the exclusive territory of the national community.[34]

This leads us to another, related theme in the critical literature. In both legal and political economic research, it has been argued that the governance of free movement in the EU produces a neoliberal market citizenship with the construction of the citizen as *homo economicus* at its very centre.[35] Somek contends that the Court's jurisprudence renders

[29] R. Bellamy, 'Evaluating Union citizenship: belonging, rights and participation within the EU', *Citizenship Studies*, 12(6) (2008), 597–611, at 597.

[30] R. Bellamy, 'Rights as democracy', *Critical Review of International Social and Political Philosophy*, 15(4) (2012), 449–71, at 449.

[31] Bellamy, 'A duty-free Europe?', p. 558.

[32] Menéndez, 'European citizenship after Martínez Sala and Baumbast'; A. Somek, 'Solidarity decomposed: being and time in European citizenship', The University of Iowa Legal Studies Research Paper, 13 June 2007; Everson, 'A very cosmopolitan citizenship'.

[33] Everson, 'A very cosmopolitan citizenship'.

[34] A. Somek, 'From workers to migrants, from distributive justice to inclusion: exploring the changing social democratic imagination', *European Law Journal*, 18(5) (2012), 711–26.

[35] D. Kramer, 'From worker to self-entrepreneur: the transformation of *homo economicus* and the freedom of movement in the European Union', *European Law Journal*, 23(3–4) (2017), 172–88; M. Dani, 'The subjectification of the citizen in European public law', in

citizenship a 'resource' and freedom a 'freedom of choice in the private sphere', such as 'a place to receive an education, to spend one's retirement years',[36] and above all to seek employment opportunities. In Dani's view, when citizens are perceived of primarily as *homo economicus*, workers' rights are no longer 'meant to protect the individual from the risks of markets' but to offer them opportunities to participate in transnational markets.[37] It needs to be pointed out that not all forms of worker mobility are considered a matter of citizenship rights and adjudicated on the basis of Article 20 of the Treaty and Directive 2004/38/EC. Labour mobility may also be governed as an element of market freedoms (free movement of service and freedom of establishment), and it is this aspect of the Court's judicial decision making that has been especially condemned for compromising existing structures of national social solidarity. In the much-discussed *Laval* case,[38] for example, the Latvian workers posted to Sweden were not excising their citizenship rights of free movement in the eye of the law; their mobility was rather attached to the employer's freedom of providing services across borders. The Court held that any restrictions on the implementation of free movement must be proportionate in the light of legitimate objectives such as the protection of fundamental rights. Given that the Swedish law does not lay down a minimum wage, forming 'a national context characterised by a lack of provisions … which are sufficiently precise and accessible',[39] it found that the negotiations on wage the trade unions sought to advance did not constitute a legitimate restriction on market freedoms. This decision and other cases involving collective bargaining and the employment of foreign workers have received wide-ranging criticism, which often point to the neoliberal rationality of EU economic governance and the prioritising of supranational rules at the cost of downplaying national welfare models. In other words, observers from the left worry that the opening of

L. Azoulai, S. B. des Places and E. Pataut (eds.), *Constructing the Person in EU Law: Rights, Roles, Identities* (Oxford: Hart Publishing, 2016), pp. 55–88. For a summary of criticisms of open immigration regimes in the political economy literature, see Parker, 'Critical political economy, free movement and Brexit'.

36 Somek, *The Cosmopolitan Constitution*, p. 205.

37 Dani, 'The subjectification of the citizen', p. 63.

38 C. Woolfson, J. Fudge and C. Thörnqvist, 'Migrant precarity and future challenges to labour standards in Sweden', *Economic and Industrial Democracy*, 35(4) (2014), 695–715; A. Bücker and W. Warneck (eds.), *Reconciling Fundamental Social Rights and Economic Freedoms after Viking, Laval and Rüffert* (Baden-Baden: Nomos, 2011).

39 C-341/05, para. 110.

labour market and welfare borders leads inevitably to social dumping in host countries.

Whereas, if we look at the implications of cross-border mobility from the perspective of the migrants, especially those in precarious employment and the 'economically inactive', the market citizenship engendered by the European regime of free movement is more stratified than universalist or cosmopolitan. The degree of protection enjoyed by EU migrants is conditioned by legal categories, employment forms and socio-cultural mechanisms of bordering (for example, the social exclusion of the Roma people). It is worth noting that neither the legislative instruments nor the case law has unequivocally allowed unconditional access to social benefits for mobile EU citizens.[40] The free movement directive provides that Member States may deprive the right to free movement from Union citizens on grounds of 'public policy, public security or public health'. This conditionality rule mainly affects the rights of the groups of people who have already been marginalised and criminalised in their host societies.[41] Recent regulatory changes in the eligibility of worker status and case law on the rights of economically inactive citizens to social benefits[42] have brought in focus the increasing stratification of social citizenship, which must be 'earned' by EU migrants through assuming their 'individual responsibility to fulfil the economic, social and cultural conditions of membership'.[43] In the controversial *Dano* case, the supranational Court states that a Union citizen can claim equal treatment 'only if his or her residence . . . complies with the conditions for lawful residence' laid down in the free movement directive. The retrenchment has been criticised not only for contributing potentially to the social exclusion of vulnerable migrant citizens in their host society, but also for undermining the coherence of EU law.[44] Indeed, scholars warn that the increasing conditionality of equal treatment means that the status of EU citizenship resembles more that of a migrant than that of a citizen.[45]

40 Thym, 'The elusive limits of solidarity'.

41 J. S. Gehring, 'Free movement for some: the treatment of the Roma after the European Union's eastern expansion', *European Journal of Migration & Law*, 15(1) (2013), 7–28; O. Parker, 'Roma and the politics of EU citizenship in France: everyday security and resistance', *Journal of Common Market Studies*, 50(3) (2012), 475–91.

42 G. Alberti, 'A new status for migrant workers: restrictions of the free movement of labour in the EU', *Mondi Migranti*, 3 (2017), 33–49.

43 Kramer, 'Earning social citizenship'.

44 N. Nic Shuibhne, 'Limits rising, duties ascending: the changing legal shape of Union citizenship', *Common Market Law Review*, 52(4) (2015), 889–937.

45 Spaventa, 'Earned citizenship'.

To summarise, the complex impact of free movement on both national solidarity and the prospect for transnational social citizenship has been subject to various criticisms. Even though commentators might share similar critiques of neoliberal market citizenship and agree on the importance of the redistributive dimension of citizenship, some stress on democratic boundedness while others defend the norm of equality in transnational settings. On the one hand, it has been argued that the expansive approach to transnational citizenship through individual rights might undermine the structure of national solidarity or fails to address the question of democratic legitimacy. On the other hand, the nationalist approach that prioritises the Member State's interest in maintaining welfare boundaries is criticised for enhancing civic stratifications and betraying the normative principles of EU citizenship. At the theoretical level, the debate highlights the tension between the republican concept of citizenship as democratic practice, the cosmopolitan aspiration for transnational rights and open borders, and the social democratic ideal of redistributive justice. In the following sections, I reflect on how critical citizenship theory could help us rethink the relationship between rights, solidarity and social citizenship, whereby recognising the transformative potential of mobility/migrancy to open up a space for constructing transnational solidarity.

3 Social Citizenship Revisited: Rights, Solidarity and Democratic Contestations

Theories of citizenship generally approach the concept in terms of several interrelated components or dimensions: status, rights, practice and belonging/identity. As noted earlier, different normative traditions differ in their emphases on each of the components: the liberal tradition analyses citizenship primarily as legal status and rights, whereas the republican tradition conceptualises citizenship as practice and civic identity, and the communitarian tradition emphasises forms of belonging not limited to political identity. Over the last few decades, however, critical scholarship on citizenship has been pushing the boundary of the field beyond studying formal rights, institutional participations and national belongings, redefining this key concept of modern politics through a range of new theoretical lenses such as insurgency, governmentality, ambivalence or performative claim-making.[46]

[46] E.g. J. Holston, *Insurgent Citizenship: Disjunctions of Democracy and Modernity in Brazil* (Princeton, NJ: Princeton University Press, 2008); G. Procacci, 'Governmentality and

Critical citizenship studies shift focuses away from the existing distribution of status and rights to the processes – 'those constitutive moments, performances, enactments and events'[47] – through which the 'outsiders' constitute themselves as political beings and hence citizens. One productive conceptual and methodological tool that has been developed in this direction is 'acts of citizenship'.[48] Isin argues that the category of acts differs from that of 'practices', as the latter is a privilege or obligation of someone who is *already* recognised as a citizen, whereas the former is staged in the very making of citizenship.[49] In other words, 'acts produce actors that do not exist before acts'.[50] The idea of 'acts of citizenship' thus has been employed to register the political subjectivity of those formally excluded from the citizenship regime – such as irregular migrants, refugees and stateless people – and to capture the significance of 'creative ruptures and breaks' in the given order.[51] Conversely, another strand of the critical literature also illuminates how citizenship as a technology of government functions to produce differentiations, stratifications, and structures of inclusion and exclusion. It is important to note that citizenship as 'acts' and as managerial regimes are inherently intertwined with one another, which can be depicted as 'a mobile surface of engagement between the practices of government and the universe of the governed which constantly tends to escape their grasp'.[52] Historically, as Sassen has noted, it is the insurgent claim-makings of the excluded groups that have continuously forced changes in the juridical and institutional scope of citizenship.[53] However, the incorporation of the achievements of popular

citizenship', in K. Nash and A. Scott (eds.), *The Blackwell Companion to Political Sociology* (Oxford: Blackwell Publishing, 2004), pp. 342–51; A. McNevin, 'Ambivalence and citizenship: theorising the political claims of irregular migrants', *Millennium – Journal of International Studies*, 41(2) (2013), 182–200; I. Bloemraad, 'Theorising the power of citizenship as claims-making', *Journal of Ethnic and Migration Studies*, 44(1) (2018), 4–26.

47 W. Walters, 'Acts of demonstration: mapping the territory of non-citizenship', in E. F. Isin and G. M. Nielsen (eds.), *Acts of Citizenship* (London: Zed Books, 2008), pp. 182–206, at 192.

48 E.F. Isin and G. Nielsen (eds.) *Acts of Citizenship* (London: Zed Books, 2008).

49 E.F. Isin, 'Theorizing acts of citizenship', in E. F. Isin and G. M. Nielsen (eds.), *Acts of Citizenship* (London: Zed Books, 2008), pp. 15–43.

50 Ibid., p. 37.

51 Ibid., p. 36, for examples of applying this approach to the discussion of European citizenship, see E.F. Isin and M. Saward (eds.) *Enacting European Citizenship* (Cambridge: Cambridge University Press, 2013).

52 J. Donzelot and C. Gordon, 'Governing liberal societies – the Foucault effect in the English-speaking world', *Foucault Studies*, 5 (2008), 48–62, at 51.

53 S. Sassen, *Territory, Authority, Rights: from Medieval to Global Assemblages* (Princeton, NJ: Princeton University Press, 2006).

contestation into the juridico-institutional regime of citizenship and rights does not mean a teleological movement towards 'citizenship for all', as democratic struggles are constantly 'reappropriated by the play of the governmental machine itself'[54] and becoming included in the citizenship regime may lead to reproducing hegemonic modalities of exclusion based on nationality, ethnicity, productivity and so on.

Along these lines, it is particularly instructive to consider Balibar's theorisation of social citizenship as a 'fluctuating reality' shaped by the power relations among social classes and subject to alternating 'advances and retreats'.[55] According to Balibar, social citizenship is best understood as a 'contingent co-occurrence of rights and social movements that are themselves more or less institutionalised' and that has resulted in the relative neutralisation of class antagonism,[56] rather than being reduced to 'a collection of social rights granted from above to "weak" individuals who should be seen as passive beneficiaries'.[57] In this respect, Marshall's classic account of social citizenship centred on the evolvement of civil, political and social rights also posits that the social dimension of national citizenship has not been developed primarily by 'creating' social rights, but through 'the exercise of political power' by the working class.[58] The historical struggles for political, labour and social rights not only expanded the meaning of citizenship, but also challenged the liberal tradition of rights underpinned by the distinction and distribution of the public and the private. Rancière interprets the claim of the 'right to work' made by workers of the nineteenth century as first of all a demand to de-privatise the relations of work and reconstitute work as a 'structure of collective life'.[59] In other words, these collective forces redefined the aspects of social life pertaining to human needs that were previously considered private, such as work, housing and education, as legitimately *political*. In Marshall, the reconfiguration of the social as political means that citizenship now implies the right to 'share to the full in the social heritage and to live the life of a civilised being according to the standards prevailing in the society'.[60]

[54] J. Rancière, 'Democracy, republic, representation', *Constellations*, 13(3) (2006), 297–307, at 299.
[55] É. Balibar, *Citizenship* (Cambridge: Polity, 2015), p.51.
[56] Ibid., p. 52.
[57] Balibar, 'Antinomies of citizenship', p. 9.
[58] T. Marshall, *Citizenship and Social Class* (London: Pluto Press, 1992), p. 43.
[59] Rancière, 'Democracy, republic, representation', p. 300.
[60] Marshall, *Citizenship and Social Class*, p. 11.

However, the bounding of access to social rights with national belonging through the development of what Balibar calls the 'national-social state' is both inclusive and exclusive. The nationalisation of previously fragmented systems of social assistance – what Marshall describes as a process of geographical fusion and functional fusion – implies the conflation of 'the national' with 'the social', which renders national boundaries the most important mechanism of exclusion.[61] However, the institution of social citizenship also operates through other kinds of differentiations. As Bhambra and Holmwood have recently explicated, the development of solidarity in European welfare states – especially major colonial powers such as Belgium, France, the Netherlands, and the UK – has its roots in hierarchical relations between the metropole and the colonies as well as racialised inequalities within the 'national' society[62]. Moreover, as Balibar notes, the constitution of labour or work as an 'essentially human capacity' central to the notion of social citizenship also involves contradictory logics. Although the politically constructed solidarity of the community of worker-citizens is potentially emancipatory and universalist, its institutional forms are also potentially stratifying by 'distinguishing between useful and useless, active and inactive, or productive and unproductive workers'.[63] The incorporation of social rights into the regime of national citizenship is accompanied by socioeconomic and discursive differentiations along various lines such as class, gender, ethnicity and race. On this account, critical theorists also go beyond the category of labour and reconceptualise social citizenship as constituted by competing discourses of needs[64] and claims about the right to social inclusion[65].

If we take social citizenship as a contingent crystallisation of power relations of social classes and shaped by the ongoing dynamics of the recognition of rights and the struggles over needs and social inclusion, then social rights are 'never won irreversibly'.[66] The neoliberal

[61] C. Zhang, 'Governing neoliberal authoritarian citizenship: theorizing hukou and the changing mobility regime in China', *Citizenship Studies*, 22(8) (2018), 855–81.

[62] G. K. Bhambra and J. Holmwood, 'Colonialism, postcolonialism and the liberal welfare state', *New Political Economy*, 23(5) (2018), 574–87, at 583.

[63] É. Balibar, *Equaliberty: Political Essays* (Durham, NC: Duke University Press, 2014), p. 115.

[64] N. Fraser, *Unruly Practices: Power, Discourse and Gender in Contemporary Social Theory* (Minneapolis, MN: University of Minnesota Press, 1989).

[65] M. Somers, *Genealogies of Citizenship: Markets, Statelessness, and the Right to Have Rights* (Cambridge: Cambridge University Press, 2008).

[66] Balibar, *Equaliberty: Political Essays*, p. 113.

retrenchment of welfare in recent decades indicates that the Marshallian ideal of social rights as 'an absolute right to a certain standard of civilisation' regardless of an individual's economic value[67] has not gone uncontested. Furthermore, the increasing flow of international migration, a phenomenon that has its roots in economic globalisation and the international hierarchies of power, has brought about an 'increasingly complex system of civic stratifications with differential access to civil, economic and social rights'[68] within national welfare states. Meanwhile, from the vantage point of migrant agency, researchers have also explored how new forms of solidarity are being forged through concepts such as 'mobile commons'[69] or 'mobile solidarities'[70] against exclusion, exploitation and the proliferation of borders.

What are the implications of critical citizenship studies for the debate about EU free movement reviewed in the first section? First, the relational and processual approach to citizenship highlights its incomplete nature and questions its association with national closure as a natural and finalised project. This problematises the framing of the 'progressive dilemma', which has been appropriated by the populist right to present immigrants and ethnic minorities as scapegoats for the declining economic security of the white, working class. Rich empirical evidence indicates that assuming a simplistic relation between welfare policies and openness for immigration or ethnic diversity is misleading.[71] In the European context, it has been shown that EU migrants are fiscally 'net contributors' rather than a 'welfare burden' to the host country in some of most universalistic welfare states, such as Denmark and Sweden.[72] However, framing the relationship between national solidarity and immigration as an inherent dilemma is problematic not only because

67 Marshall, *Citizenship and Social Class*, p. 43.

68 E. Kofman, 'Citizenship, migration and the reassertion of national identity', *Citizenship Studies*, 9(5) (2005), 453-467, at 453.

69 N. Trimikliniotis, D. Parsanoglou and V. S. Tsianos, 'Mobile commons and/in precarious spaces: mapping migrant struggles and social resistance', *Critical Sociology*, 42(7–8) (2016), 1035–49.

70 V. Squire, 'From community cohesion to mobile solidarities: the city of sanctuary network and the strangers into citizens campaign', *Political Studies*, 59(2) (2011), 290–307.

71 R. Bauböck and P. Scholten, 'Introduction to the special issue: solidarity in diverse societies: beyond neoliberal multiculturalism and welfare chauvinism', *Comparative Migration Studies*, 4(4) (2016), 1–7.

72 D. S. Martinsen and G. Pons Rotger, 'The fiscal impact of EU immigration on the tax-financed welfare state: testing the 'welfare burden' thesis', *European Union Politics*, 18(4) (2017), 620–39; J. Ruist, 'Free immigration and welfare access: the Swedish experience', *Fiscal Studies*, 35(1) (2014), 19–39.

of the lack of systemic evidence. Understanding national social citizenship as a fixed and finalised institution, such a framing tends to ignore that solidarity within the nation state has been politically constructed and involved racialised and gendered forms of exclusion. Labour mobility has been integral to the collective movements that have driven the institutionalisation of social rights. Presuming a dichotomous opposition between international migration and national solidarity also disregards the fact that mobility as a 'particular form of sociality' has the potential to promote intersubjective understandings and mobility-based struggles could create solidaristic relationships among members of different collective constructs such as nation, ethnicity and class.

Second, while critics of liberal cosmopolitanism correctly note that the codification of transnational rights alone does not necessarily bring about norms of solidarity across borders, solidarity can emerge in the process of taking part in collective actions rather than 'its indispensable condition of possibility'.[73] Furthermore, although I agree with the republican argument that rights do not originate outside political processes, the democratic verification of rights is not confined to official and established venues of participation.[74] Critical citizenship studies draw attention to how status non-citizens enact citizenship and the rightless claim rights through democratic struggles that contest the governmental regimes of citizenship and rights. As to be shown in the next section, migrants and 'sedentary' citizens enact transnational rights both within and against the institutional frameworks of free movement in a number of ways and spaces. Lastly and relatedly, critics of free movement correctly argue that the prioritising of economic integration over social protection and the increased barriers for economically inactive Union citizens to access welfare benefits produce a neoliberal and stratified notion of citizenship. However, just as the 'progressive's dilemma *need not* be real',[75] the reduction of human mobility into a factor of market relations and a resource for the privileged private citizen need not be the only way of understanding mobility. When conditions of globalisation effectively displace social antagonism on the international level,[76] confusing the critique of neoliberal globalisation with

[73] Ypi, 'Politically constructed solidarity', p. 121.

[74] C. Zhang, 'Between postnationality and postcoloniality: human rights and the rights of non-citizens in a "cosmopolitan Europe"', in N. Dhawan (ed.), *Decolonizing Enlightenment: Transnational Justice, Human Rights and Democracy in a Postcolonial World* (Opladen: Barbara Budrich Publishers, 2014), pp. 243–60.

[75] Parker, 'Critical political economy', p. 488, emphasis in original.

[76] Balibar, *Citizenship*, p. 54.

the defence of national closure risks forming a 'misplaced alliances between capital/business and labour' against the projected 'enemy' of foreign workers[77], which would only reinforce processes of racialisation and marginalisation in societies that have always already been characterised by heterogeneity. Collective struggles against misplaced alliances, social exclusion and precarious employment bring into being politically constructed solidarity across a plurality of borders.

4 Re-envisioning Solidarity Through Acts of (Social) Citizenship

The remainder of the chapter considers the strategies of reconfiguring the relationship between cross-border mobility and social rights against the individualistic and differentiated approach to free movement in the supranational and national governance of intra-EU mobility. I focus on the 'acts of citizenship' outside formal political and legal institutions without dismissing the crucial role parliamentary democracy, social policy and law should play in reconciling the trilemma between economic integration, social protection and democratic legitimacy. However, the purpose here is to bring to the fore how alternative views on free movement, rights and solidarity are articulated 'from below' in other increasingly transnational spaces: such as migrant activism and trade unionism[78]. Two aspects of the institutional limits of free movement are being contested in these mobility struggles: (1) the first concerns the juridico-institutional restrictions on free movement and access to social rights imposed on vulnerable EU migrants; and (2) the second pertains to the impact of market integration on precarious employment – or the 'trade-off' between mobility and rights mobile workers are often forced to accept. The former dimension thus addresses social exclusion by engaging in a politics of needs and equality; and the latter is oriented towards building transnational industrial citizenship 'based on inclusive forms of worker solidarity'.[79]

[77] Ó. G. Agustín and M. B. Jørgensen (eds.), *Solidarity without Borders: Gramscian Perspectives on Migration and Civil Society Alliances* (London: Pluto Press, 2016).

[78] This chapter focuses on the relationship between free movement and social citizenship, and therefore looks specifically at mobility-related struggles. See, for example, Blokker for a theoretical analysis of other civil society movements that seek to address the questions of social solidarity and democratic legitimacy. He considers them as part of an emerging 'bottom-up constitutional order', Blokker, 'Constitutional alternatives to the crisis', p. 76.

[79] V. Doellgast, N. Lillie and V. Pulignano, 'From dualization to solidarity: halting the cycle of precarity', in V. Doellgast, N. Lillie and V. Pulignano (eds.), *Reconstructing Solidarity: Labour Unions, Precarious Work, and the Politics of Institutional Change in Europe* (Oxford: Oxford University Press, 2018), pp. 1–41, at 34.

As noted earlier, the rights to mobility and equal treatment of Roma EU citizens have been particularly disadvantageously affected by instituted restrictions on free movement in EU law and national administration. Their right to residence in other Member States are either completely denied, as in the case of forced removals and forced 'voluntary returns', or severely circumscribed to the degree that they are 'effectively without access to social rights and pathways to permanent residence'.[80] However, in contrast, mobilisation networks against the othering of Roma populations as 'semi-citizens'[81] offer an opportunity to verify the inscription of transnational rights through democratic practices and thereby to enact European citizenship within and against its institutional arrangements. Some forms of mobilisations contest the variegated regime of rights by appealing to the universalistic principles of EU citizenship, while others bring the (transnational) social question into the picture and deploy the language of solidarity as a critique of neoliberal citizenship. Protesting the expulsions of Roma in France in 2010, for example, a group of Roma non-governmental organisations formed their campaign around 'a simple motto, ROMA = CITIZENS', emphasising that such measures clearly violated EU law such as the free movement directive and that 'Roma persons are citizens enjoying full rights in the European Union'.[82] Nonetheless, the instrumental use of the established discourse of rights and citizenship often both ruptures and re-inscribes the structures of inclusion and exclusion they seek to challenge.[83] Thus as

Schiek usefully distinguishes receptive solidarity from participatory solidarity in her discussion of transnational social citizenship: the former refers to the relationship between the benefactor (such as the state) and the citizens as passive recipients of certain benefits that relieve them from 'constant worry about their mere existence', whereas the latter enables citizens to directly engage with each other and 'gain the right to improve their position in the markets' through collective actions, Schiek, 'Perspectives on social citizenship in the EU', pp. 349–50. This distinction roughly corresponds to the two loci of mobility struggles discussed here. However, even though some practices concentrate on questions of receptive solidarity and others on participatory solidarity, I emphasis the participatory dimension in *both* fields.

80 M. Tervonen and A. Enache, 'Coping with everyday bordering: Roma migrants and gatekeepers in Helsinki', *Ethnic and Racial Studies*, 1(18) (2017), 1114–31, at 1114.

81 J. Sardelić, 'The position and agency of the 'irregularized': Romani migrants as European semi-citizens', *Politics*, 37(3) (2017), 332-346.

82 Fundación Secretariado Gitano (FSG) and the European Roma Policy Coalition (ERPC), 'Letter to the Non-Profit Social Sector'. Available at www.gitanos.org/citizens/bu/roma_citizens.pdf. See also Parker, 'Roma and the politics of EU Citizenship in France'.

83 McNevin, 'Ambivalence and citizenship'; B. Anderson, 'Mobilizing migrants, making citizens: migrant domestic workers as political agents', *Ethnic and Racial Studies*, 33(1) (2010), 60–74.

Aradau et al. have shown, activists also make claims in ways that go beyond the 'institutional scripts' of European citizenship and minority rights.[84] Scholars illustrate this simultaneous enactment and disruption of the official framing of citizenship and free movement through the example of a demonstration that took place in Italy in 2008. As a Roma activist put it, '[W]hen I talk about rights I am referring to education, work but also the possibility of having an active role in society.'[85] These reformulations of mobility rights resist the privatised notion of free movement as a resource for the autonomous, free moving individual and activate an understanding of mobility as a 'form of sociality' enabling exchanges between strangers[86] and claims to social rights.

Another example could be drawn from a Swedish online network named 'Solidaritet med EU migranter!' (SOM), recently documented and analysed by Morell.[87] The online community was founded by local activists to support vulnerable EU migrants by providing shelter, advocating against criminalisation and discrimination, improving their living conditions materially, and fighting 'for their cause politically'. The network criticises the unjust border regime that essentially views some people as having 'less right to life opportunities than others' and maintains that their activism is not driven by humanitarian sentiment, but rooted in a 'a practical solidarity between all of us who were hit by the crises of capitalism independent of where we are from'. Furthermore, members of the SOM deny the misplaced alliance by positing themselves, the 'Swedes', as victims of the same system of exploitation that has shaped the experiences of vulnerable migrants prior to and after their migration.[88] The language of solidarity is thus employed in such a way that explicitly distinguishes itself from that of humanitarianism and inscribes itself within a political economic analysis of the power structures that deepen migrant precarity. Crucially, it is precisely the

[84] C. Aradau, J. Huysmans, P. G. Macioti and V. Squire, 'Mobility interrogating free movement: Roma acts of European citizenship', in E. Isin and M. Saward (eds.), *Enacting European Citizenship* (Cambridge: Cambridge University Press, 2013), pp. 132–54, at 141.

[85] Ibid., p. 147.

[86] C. Aradau and J. Huysmans, 'Mobilising (global) democracy: A political reading of mobility between universal rights and the mob', *Millennium: Journal of International Studies*, 37(3) (2009), 583–604.

[87] I. A. Morell, '"Solidarity not alms": civil rights movements contesting the evictions and denial of social rights from vulnerable European Union citizens in Sweden', *Local Economy*, 33(2) (2018), 147–71.

[88] Ibid., pp. 153–4.

recognition that both sedentary citizens and migrants are subject to the hegemonic power of the transnational market and the supranational law that has become a starting point for reformulating solidarity across borders.

The second locus of mobility struggles revolves around the empowering of migrant workers through the exercise of industrial citizenship, which has been institutionalised within the national context as processes of organisation and participation through which to negotiate class interests and to assert 'social control over market forces'.[89] As noted earlier, the dynamics between collective actions and the recognition of rights have driven the development of national social citizenship within territorially exclusive communities. Against the background of market integration and the informalisation of labour, the inclusion of migrant workers into institutions of collective bargaining and workplace representation provides an important platform for forging transnational solidarity and fighting against precarious employment within increasingly transnationalised relations of capital and labour. Clearly, efforts to unionise migrant workers face various obstacles ranging from the temporary contracts of migrants and the nationalist attitudes of unions to certain aspects of EU regulation.[90] However, recent research in industrial relations and labour studies has documented a growing number of successful instances where EU *and* non-EU migrant workers are represented and integrated into systems of social dialogue.[91] Despite difficulties, the unionisation and other forms of organisation of migrant workers not only seek to enhance labour rights and improve working conditions, but also enable migrants to exercise industrial citizenship and gain a 'right to have rights' in the socioeconomic field, which is above all the right to have a political voice and take part in collective actions. Moreover, the prospect for a transnational industrial citizenship highlights emergent forms of solidarity and identities based on 'social interdependency' and 'the dynamics of the claiming process'.[92] Such emergent

[89] C. Zhang and N. Lillie 'Industrial citizenship, cosmopolitanism and European integration', *European Journal of Social Theory*, 18(1) (2015), 93–111, at 98.

[90] V. Doellgast, N. Lillie and V. Pulignano (eds.), *Reconstructing Solidarity: Labour Unions, Precarious Work, and the Politics of Institutional Change in Europe* (Oxford: Oxford University Press, 2018).

[91] For one of the latest collections of case studies, see Doellgast, Lillie and Pulignano (eds.), *Reconstructing Solidarity.*

[92] Dean, 'The translation of needs into rights', p. 32.

solidarity constitutes both a source and a democratic justification of transnational social rights.

These different fields of contestation aimed at renegotiating the relationship between mobility and social rights redefine the concepts of social citizenship and solidarity in the transnational setting. First of all, they are acts of citizenship that either demand recognition and inclusion in the existing regime of EU citizenship or a radical 'staging of a non-existent right'[93], such as the right of non-nationals to social inclusion. It is essentially through acts or, in Arendtian terms, the 'performance itself',[94] that the process of subjectivisation brings into being the citizen subject as equal and political beings. Furthermore, the examples of mobilisations of both sedentary and migrant citizens discussed above insist on the *social* dimension of transnational citizenship and challenge the individualistic logic of neoliberal cosmopolitan citizenship. If questions of social inclusion and labour rights have been de-privatised and politicised through collective struggles within the national context, the 'transnational social question'[95] remains largely determined by the power of market interests or regulated by juridical and administrative procedures. Mobilisations focused on the social rights of mobile workers constitute democratic forces that politicise the social question within transnational regimes of labour migration that organise and condition precariousness.

Acts of social citizenship in the context of cross-border mobility spell out the politically constructed nature of solidarity in the two senses of being 'political' mentioned in the introduction. First, practices of migrant solidarity with regard to social rights, whether being providing basic services of livelihood or integrating migrant workers into national frameworks of industrial citizenship, are more than expressions of hospitality and compassion external to politics.[96] They are rather situated within connected and different strategies of resistance against the neoliberal logics of labour migration regimes that produce shared experiences of precarity and naturalise 'trade-offs' between mobility and rights. Second, the struggles over transnational social rights outside formal channels of

93 J. Rancière, *Dis-agreement: Politics and Philosophy* (Minneapolis, MN: University of Minnesota Press, 1999), p. 25.

94 H. Arendt, *The Human Condition* (Chicago, IL: University of Chicago Press, 1998), p. 206.

95 T. Faist, 'On the transnational social question: how social inequalities are reproduced in Europe', *Journal of European Social Policy*, 24(3) (2014), 207–22.

96 Tazzioli and Walters 'Migration, solidarity and the limits of Europe'; R. Kelz, 'Political theory and migration: Concepts of non-sovereignty and solidarity', *Movements: Journal für kritische Migrations-und Grenzregimeforschung*, 1(2) (2015), 1–18.

democratic participation open up terrains for new forms and relations of solidarity to emerge, precisely through political actions.[97] This also engenders an alternative understanding of human mobility rooted in social interactions and sensitive to the spatialised power relations that circumscribe it. In contrast with the individualist approach to free movement as the right of the autonomous individual to enter freely into the transnational labour market, cross-border mobility is reformulated as a medium for constructing solidaristic intersubjective relations beyond the statist space. Solidarity practices create connections not only among the people on the move and between 'immobile' and 'mobile' EU citizens, but also more broadly between EU citizens and third-country nationals – whether the latter are 'legal', 'illegal' or with ambiguous legal status. This has been displayed in both Roma solidarity movements and trade union organisations.[98] It is of crucial importance that the democratic contestations that redefine free movement as the right to inclusion and participation also questions the dichotomy of internal and external mobility in the citizenship and border regimes of 'EUrope', especially in a time marked by growing anti-refugee and anti-immigration anxieties.

5 Conclusion: Towards Politically Constructed Solidarity Across Borders

This chapter started by reviewing some of the criticisms of EU free movement, especially in relation to social citizenship and the national welfare state, from normative, legal and political economic perspectives. Those emphasising democratic boundedness argue that the expansion of individual rights beyond national borders through law is insufficient to create relations of reciprocity and solidarity underpinning political and republican understandings of citizenship. Another strand of critique points out that the neoliberal governance of free movement produces

[97] Ypi, 'Politically constructed solidarity'.

[98] For example, Çağlar writes that after a group of Roma families and supporters squatted in a Berlin church because of possible police eviction in 2009, they received voices of support from a wide range of civil society organisations such as the Refugee Council of Berlin and the Sans Papiers from Paris, A. Çağlar, 'Displacement of European citizen Roma in Berlin: acts of citizenship and sites of contentious politics', *Citizenship Studies*, 20(5) (2016), 647–63. Tapia and Holgate have shown how traditional unions have over time developed strategies to support undocumented migrant workers in the UK, France, and Germany, M. Tapia and J. Holgate 'Fighting precariousness: Union strategies towards migrant workers in the UK, France and Germany', in Doellgast, Lillie and Pulignano (eds.), *Reconstructing Solidarity*.

a market citizenship that, on the one hand, prioritises economic freedoms over social protection and, on the other hand, increases civic stratification through a variegated regime of rights. The chapter then reflected on how critical citizenship theory could help us move beyond the individualist approach to mobility rights in liberal cosmopolitanism and the static conceptualisation of solidarity in the defence of national closure. Drawing on the work of Balibar, social citizenship could be understood as a contingent crystallisation of relations of force within ongoing processes of struggles over social inclusion and human needs. In this account, solidarity and rights are co-occurrent in the open-ended political processes through which individuals constitute themselves as citizens and establish reciprocal relations – in their coming together to form a 'common world'.[99]

In this light, the last section of the chapter considered the theoretical significance of two interrelated fields of contestation over the social rights of intra-EU migrants: those against exclusion and rightlessness; and those enacting industrial citizenship. Their theoretical implications for the concepts of both social citizenship and solidarity in the transnational setting were reflected on. As acts of social citizenship, they politicise the question of social rights in the context of cross-border mobility and resist the market logic naturalising 'trade-offs' between mobility and rights. As solidarity movements, these practices spell out the political nature of solidarity not only because they are positioned within transnationalised socioeconomic structures and heterogeneous constellations of resistance, but also in that they open up terrains for new forms and relations of solidarity, which traverse the boundaries of the national, the European and the legal, to emerge through political actions.

[99] É. Balibar, '(De)constructing the human as human institution: a reflection on the coherence of Hannah Arendt's practical philosophy', *Social Research: An International Quarterly*, 74(3) (2007), 727–38, at 732.

15

New Opportunities for Transnational Solidarity Mobilisation

The Role of the Media

HANS-JÖRG TRENZ

1 Introduction: Media and Transnational Solidarity

Mass media are commonly held responsible for strengthening bonds of national solidarity and supporting relationships of mutual support among citizens as members of a political community. Solidarity relationships as established within a membership community of equals are described as thick or reciprocal, whereas the support that is granted to distant strangers is often reduced to forms of charity in a non-reciprocal relationship of inequality. At the same time, mass media increasingly raise questions of global justice and through their coverage of distant suffering confront audiences with their moral responsibility to provide assistance to strangers. The notion of solidarity as grounded in global justice is therefore not only an abstract normative and legalistic principle but, sociologically speaking, is also linked to an expansive logic of building solidarity relationships of modern society as a community of strangers. The transition from solidarity as enshrined in the private relationships of kinship to solidarity as a public relationship among strangers is underlying the social struggles for an expansion of rights, citizenship and equality. This leaves us with the problem of how the needs and concerns of the others can be communicated in a way to formulate reciprocal commitments of a community of strangers.

To investigate this relationship between the media and (trans)national solidarity, this chapter discusses the communicative infrastructure that allows for the formulation of such mutual obligations and responsibilities, and for the validation of claims for solidarity in the light of the requirements of global justice. Such a communicative infrastructure for the validation and expansion of globalised solidarity is provided by the modern public sphere. In the following, I will investigate how a particular normativity has been inscribed into the public sphere, which works at the same time as a social mechanism of commitment towards strangers. The public sphere is in this sense seen as the horizon for the dynamic unfolding of global solidarity among strangers. In the second part, the chapter discusses the role played by the media in establishing solidarity relationships among individuals across established borders of political community. I will give examples of mediated solidarity discourses in which mutual obligations between states and equal rights of citizens across borders are discussed controversially. I shall argue that the Janus-faced nature of the media as a transmission mechanism for universal notions of justice (representing the world) and as the filter for the consolidation of thickened and contextualised relationships of solidarity within a community of equals (representing the nation) offers an opportunity for transnational solidarity mobilisation.

2 The Modern Public Sphere: Solidarity Among Strangers

To account for the distinctiveness of solidarity in the modern age it is useful to investigate how mutual obligations and responsibilities are communicated and hold valid among individuals who are not familiar with each other. The classical answer given by early sociology is that modern society emerged by detaching solidarity from the bonds to community.[1] Modernisation is not simply the history of an expansion of solidarity from community to society, it is also a shift of meaning of solidarity from the community of intimate friends to the society of strangers.[2] With the advancement of industrialisation, capitalism and individualisation, solidarity bonds had to be established among people who do not work in the same profession, do not live in the same household and do not share the same faith or tradition. Individuals who are strangers to each other will not be able to rely on shared sentiments and affection but will need to strive more actively at rational agreement to co-ordinate their activities based on competing goals and interests. Solidarity is then no longer the essence of the community (*Wesenswille*, in terms of Tönnies), but a collective will based on the reciprocity of transactions that needs to be communicated and mobilised to be held

[1] É. Durkheim, *The Division of Labor in Society* (New York: The Free Press, 1964 [1893]).

[2] H. Brunkhorst, *Solidarity: From Civic Friendship to a Global Legal Community* (Cambridge, MA: MIT Press, 2005).

valid (*Kürwille*, in terms of Tönnies).[3] Solidarity as based in the reciprocity of transactions relies on the possibility to convince others about the possibility of shared benefit and to raise promises of paybacks. Solidarity occurs in public communication. It is not private but public; not intimate, but anonymous; not an emotion, but an agreement, not a verdict, but a conviction. It is also never fully materialised, but always invigorated as a future promise. Solidarity unfolds, in the words of Habermas, as a discourse that is validated by the communicative rationality of the public sphere.[4]

The specific mode of building solidarity relationships in modern society is thus grounded in the activation of a new type of public communication that binds strangers together through generalised claims of validity. Solidarity is to be considered as a general case of engagement with difference beyond a horizon of global justice.[5] This is the classical constellation of the public sphere as it emerged at the end of the eighteenth century. In the enlightenment period, a public–private distinction was introduced, which established solidarity relationships in the form of communicative bonds among the anonymous members of society. These communicative bonds to the 'significant others' within society were seen as distinct from the direct and intimate relationships of mutual help and assistance within the family. The intimacy of kinship or family relationships in the pre-modern era could then be reinterpreted not simply as private, but also as non-civic, as detached from public duties and dissolving from other obligations towards strangers.[6] It was only by grounding solidarity relationship in the public realm, that the modern notion of solidarity could be used progressively to build social bonds and to expand the boundaries of the social. While solidarity in the pre-modern era was, in the words of Durkheim, mechanically applied, the modern notion of solidarity allowed society to self-organise through internal differentiation and external expansion. The public sphere became the carrier of shared meaning and common expectations that committed the society of strangers to solidarity, while at the same time the intimate spaces of privacy could be confined, controlled and protected.

[3] F. Tönnies, *Community and Society* (New Brunswick, NJ: Transaction Publisher, 1988 [1888]).

[4] J. Habermas, *The Theory of Communicative Action: Volume One. Reason and the Rationalization of Society* (Boston, MA: Beacon Press, 1981).

[5] Brunkhorst, *Solidarity: From Civic Friendship to a Global Legal Community.*

[6] Ibid., p. 11.

Solidarity is in this sense approached in this chapter as a form of engagement with the needs of others. In the public sphere the moral mechanism of this form of engagement applies to social relationships established by anonymity and distance.[7] Public discourse is used to exchange information about the needs of others and the moral obligations and commitments that follow from it from a perspective of social justice. This opens the possibility of communication about experiences of injustice of people who are not present, or who even live at a distance but who are nevertheless included in a discourse of moral commitment and thus recognised as carriers of rights and legal subjects. The problem of how such bonds of solidarity to non-present others can be maintained over space and time has been settled within the nation state in the form of a legal and political commitment of citizenship, which, at the same time, remains tied to the justificatory requirements of global justice.[8] In the democratic nation state citizenship and human rights are closely entwined. There is in other words an inbuilt transnationalising mechanism in the way politically confined solidarity relationships are constantly challenged and exposed to criticism by reference to the justificatory requirement of global justice.[9] In the light of this criticism, the political space within which solidarity relationships are established can always be considered as transitory and opened up to external linkages. Driven by the expansive logic of the public sphere, solidarity engagement becomes transnational. To the extent, that such external linkages become institutionalised and translate into solidarity practices beyond the national, we can speak of transnational solidarity as a network of relationships among people who support each other over distance and over national borders (see Gould, Chapter 2, in this volume). In this chapter, I wish to explore how such networks of transnational solidarity can also expand through discursive links that define commitments among distant groups of people. Such a widening of our horizon of moral commitment relies on the availability of a mediating infrastructure to bring distant events to our attention and make them relevant for us. The solidarity of the public sphere builds on the mass media, which are not just a neutral transmitter of information about what is happening at a distance but also a forum of

[7] J. Habermas, 'The public sphere. An encyclopedia article (1974)', *New German Critique*, 3 (1974), 49–55.

[8] D. Miller, *National Responsibility and Global Justice* (Oxford: Oxford University Press, 2007).

[9] J. Habermas, *Between Facts and Norms. Contributions to a Discourse Theory of Law and Democracy* (Cambridge: Polity Press, 1996).

critique and of normative debate about the interpretation of these events and their relevance for our moral self-understanding.

Historically speaking, the condition for the diffusion of transnational solidarity networks through a discourse of global justice were met with the appearance of critical journalism and the technical means to bring distant events to the immediate attention of local audience. Systematic evidence for distant pain and suffering was first widely distributed in the famous case of war photography in the second half of the nineteenth century.[10] Translating such evidence into mediated experiences of injustice through media outlets such as newspapers and photographs was also a core condition for the mass worker movement to unfold and to call for international solidarity.[11] The public sphere of mass media facilitated not only almost instant global dissemination, but also turns information about distant events into news that are discussed by underlying common criteria of relevance.[12] The shared world of news is in this sense also a world of shared concern and commitment. Responses to images of the pain of others and their translation in a political language of commitment follows established and institutionalised narratives that structure our social relationships to strangers and justify our moral stance towards them.[13] The 'repertoire of justifications' on which we can base our moral commitment is limited and, in itself, can only claim generalised validity through mediated discourse. Solidarity as a discourse follows narrating structures that are hold valid over time and across social context.

Solidarity as discourse in the public sphere is further linked to particular social positions that become relevant in communication among strangers. There are, first of all, the moral entrepreneurs who call for solidarity providing the basic information about distant events and the needs of people in distant places. Solidarity entrepreneurs are, however, not just those who inform about the needs of others but also seek to promote a particular normative stance or a behaviour of benevolence towards these others. There are, second, the targets of solidarity, usually particular categories of social actors in need of assistance. The question arises, whether these targets are mainly treated as objects, whose needs

[10] S. Sontag, *Regarding the Pain of Others* (London: Penguin Books, 2013).

[11] M. Davis, *Comrade or Brother? A History of the British Labour Movement* (London: Pluto Press, 2009).

[12] F. Neidhardt, *Öffentlichkeit, öffentliche Meinung, soziale Bewegungen* (Opladen: Westdeutscher Verlag, 1994).

[13] L. Boltanski, *Distant Suffering: Morality, Media and Politics* (Cambridge: Cambridge University Press, 1999).

are defined by others and represented in public discourse or whether they appear in a more active role as subjects with the power to self-define their needs and negotiate the conditions under which they receive assistance. There are, third, media organisations and mediating institutions, such as journalism, that facilitate flows of information, create the conditions for the selective visibility of the suffering and the needs of others and selectively amplify the calls of solidarity. Finally, there are the passive audiences of those who listen to or are addressed by solidarity discourse. It is important to stress that the relationship between these social positions is asymmetrical: there is an infinite number of potential targets of solidarity, who are only brought selectively to the attention of the public. Calls for solidarity are further dependent on successful strategies of agenda setting that relate to power positions of moral entrepreneurs, who compete for attention in the public arena. Selective attention of the media institutions further narrows down our horizon of pity and compassion and what passes through the media as a solidarity filter encounters an audience that shows only vague interest and generally low willingness to engage. The challenge of solidarity mobilisation towards strangers correlates with the challenge to address an audience of strangers and to commit individuals within that anonymous audience to engage in solidarity action.

3 *The Janus-faced Nature of Mass Media: Turning Strangers into Fellow Citizens*

The understanding of mass media as a facilitator of transnational solidarity relationships is not simply based on a technical reading of the means of mass communication and their capacities to transmit messages around the globe. Mass media are also to be considered as the infrastructure of the public sphere, which puts moral demands on the building of stranger relationships and the recognition of 'strangers' as 'significant others', whose needs and demands deserve our attention. 'Recognition' of equality as the basic condition for building solidarity relationships[14] works here at the basic level of 'recognising' the existence of others. Through the notion of the public, we can recognise people around us belonging to the world, not as kin or comrades, but as strangers. Belonging to the public nevertheless turns these strangers 'significant'

[14] A. Honneth, *The Struggle for Recognition: The Moral Grammar of Social Conflicts* (Cambridge: Polity Press, 1995)

to the minimum degree that we recognise them as belonging to a 'shared world'.[15] Such a 'media solidarity rhetoric' is like a background noise that works as a constant reminder of our obligations towards others to be treated fairly and to avoid their degradation and humiliation.

Media create nevertheless a sensitivity for injustices occurring anywhere in the world, for the 'instances of suffering' that challenge our shared moral horizon as humans. Our obligations towards these 'others' may often not be further defined. These are obligations towards others as 'humans' and not yet as 'fellow citizens'. Yet, there is an expansive logic inherent in this media solidarity rhetoric'. Mass media open up the *world of solidarity* with the possibility of an expansion of the social bonds towards all 'humans' that are brought to our attention and that are included in media discourse. Media facilitate solidarity through the extension of content and consequently of our views of the worlds. More precisely, solidarity become possible through *shared* experiences of witnessing injustice, cruelty and distant suffering. The media rhetoric of solidarity unfolds in the form of *shared* public attention to such instances of human suffering and engages us in a *shared* interpretation of these mediated experiences under the premise that suffering should not feature prominently, that it affects us as 'humans', that responsibilities can be ascribed and that measures should be taken to avoid it. Solidarity of the media is here in the sense of Rorty a 'minimal universalism', but also a 'putative universal force'.[16] It is expansive, because our obligations to human beings should, in principle, not be limited by borders, but also because the very demand of solidarity raised in the public requires us to create a more extensive view of the suffering of others and of its possible remedies.[17]

Turning now to the role of political journalism more specifically, we can detect this 'media solidarity rhetoric' in the daily routines of news making, but also in the shared professional understanding of journalists and the ethical standards that guide their working practices. Journalists are, first of all, the gatekeepers of the public attention market that, in principle embraces the world, but in practice can only pay selectively attention to events that are to be considered of public relevance. Among

[15] M. Warner, *Publics and Counterpublics* (New York: Zone Books, 2002).

[16] S. E. Cole, 'Evading the subject: the poverty of contingency theory', in H. W. W. Simons and P. M. Billig (eds.), *After Postmodernism: Reconstructing Ideology Critique* (London: Sage Publications, 1994), p 46.

[17] R. Rorty, *Contingency, Irony, and Solidarity* (Cambridge: Cambridge University Press, 1989).

the news criteria that guide the practice of news selection, attention to human suffering and disaster ranks high.[18] Media expose victims of crime, violence or disaster to evoke our compassion or indignation with the injustice or with the wrongdoing of the perpetrators. At the same time, the media solidarity rhetoric proceeds highly selectively in the way the needs of others are brought to our attention. Mass media are not more than a straying spotlight that rests on some few events on the scene but leaves many others obscure and also quickly moves on in search of new events that deserve our attention.

The media attention market has been found to be highly unreliable but still indispensable to the forming of solidarity in a political community. At this point, another, cultural logic of news making, comes into play restricting the horizon for the work of journalism to the realm of local culture and audiences to be addressed within established state structures. Publicity as the principle of global attention management needs to be locally embedded. The institutionalisation of journalism took place within the structures provided by democratic nation states, which allowed journalists to reach an audience that shared a language, culture and identity. Newspapers and journalism serve the nation, as this has been called emphatically.[19] Within the national public sphere, journalistic practice of news making is guided by another news criteria based on proximity and distance that is used to filter the political news stream, for example, in the distinction between domestic and foreign news.[20] The solidarity horizon of the world is in this sense narrowed down by daily journalistic routines and practices. The national segmentation of the news media enabled the institutionalisation of a national public sphere and the constitution of national publics who pay selective attention to news of shared relevance. In this sense, the news media are commonly hold responsible for representing and contributing to the national solidarity community of fellow citizens.

As a motor of nation building, the news media have indeed played the key historical role of turning strangers into fellow citizens and building new grounds of commonness, not least related to the standardised

[18] B. Höijer, 'The discourse of global compassion: the audience and media reporting of human suffering', Media, Culture & Society, 26(4) (2004), 513–31

[19] D. A. Copeland, *The Media's Role in Defining the Nation: The Active Voice* (Bern: Peter Lang, 2010).

[20] P. J. Shoemaker, J. H. Lee, G. Han and A. A. Cohen, 'Proximity and scope as news values', in E. Devereux (ed.), *Media Studies: Key Issues and Debates* (London: Sage, 2007), pp. 231–48.

language of mass communication, to become the shared language of the nation.[21] The national segmentation of journalism is further backed by the commercial logic of the news media and their dependency on national markets. Global media companies sustain rather than transcend national niche markets. Journalistic practice often embraces nationalism also in a more explicit and emphatic sense, for instance, in storytelling that focuses on the defence of national interests, the promotion of the well-being of the nation and the sympathy towards fellow citizens. Ettema and Glasser identify solidarity as one of the values that informs journalism practice in the spirit of supporting patriotism, attachment to the nation and national interest.[22] Journalists sustain the nation not only ideally but also in a more practical way by facilitating social cohesion of everyday life, for instance, by reaching out to the whole nation, by setting the agenda for political talk or by creating inclusive social and cultural events (such as television shows or televised sports events).[23] Collective identification is further promoted through the targeting of potential threats to our solidarity community, for instance, in crime coverage.[24] In a wider sense, the symbolic inclusion and exclusion of mass media are closely related to the inclusive and exclusive mechanisms that are at work within the solidarity community in their daily decisions about 'deservingness' – of who gets what and who its entitled to rights and privileges. At the end, mass media made us believe that our lives were firmly enshrined within national solidarity communities, made us believe to share the same destiny and to be obliged to each other within the borders of the nation state.

Based on this distinction between journalism as a promoter of social bonds, cohesion and democracy within a nationally confined public sphere and journalism as a selective window to the world that is reinterpreted by underlying criteria of national relevance, the media solidarity linkage is de-facto nationalised. This does not exclude the possibility of media engagement in transnational solidarity mobilisation. Such forms of campaigning through old and new media can be very efficient, for instance, in the mobilisation of humanitarian aid in cases of disaster of famine.

[21] B. Anderson, *Imagined Communities. Reflections on the Origins and Spread of Nationalism* (London: Verso, 1991); M. Billig, *Banal Nationalism* (London: Sage, 1995).

[22] J. S. Ettema and T. L. Glasser, *Custodians of Conscience: Investigative Journalism and Public Virtue* (New York: Columbia University Press, 1998).

[23] P. Schlesinger, 'Wishful thinking: cultural politics, media, and collective identities in Europe', *Journal of Communication*, 43(2) (1993), 6–17.

[24] D. McQuail, *Journalism and Society* (London: Sage, 2013), p. 68.

Transnational solidarity mobilisation through mass media remains, however, sharply distinguished from the reciprocal solidarity among equals and finds expression mainly as a form of charity that is conditional of the selective attention paid to distant events and instances of distant suffering.[25] Through media campaigns, ad hoc assistance in emergency situations can be mobilised quickly, without that further commitment need to follow from this. This form of selective aid remains confined to the realm of international humanitarian aid and, as such, it is meant to be distinguished from the solidarity of mutual obligations and commitments.

The questions then are: how such a distinction between the world of solidarity among equals and the world of humanitarian aid towards outsiders can be sustained in public discourse? And, what role mass media play in drawing the lines between the 'domestic' and the 'international'? The exceptional character of news coverage about instances of distant suffering follows from the rules of the media attention market. The translation of such instances into cases of 'charity' and not of 'solidarity' comes, however, at the price of disabling the reflexivity of the public sphere and the critical force of discourse of which the media are part and parcel. Translating evidence of global injustice into charity, is in itself a media construction, which is based on a self-imposed restriction of solidarity discourse. It results from the application of different filters and different schemes of interpretation that determine what media see when they look at the word and what they highlight as public-political and private-non-political. If the necessity of acts of charity towards the world is highlighted in media discourse, such mobilisation is usually meant to be only temporary and limited to single, exceptional instances. Calls for charity work well, because they offer a short, yet incomplete translation of evidence of human suffering into a language of pity that (temporarily) evades the political. At the same time, the very fact that charity is seen as exceptional, indicates that mass media and journalism remain committed to global justice as the normative horizon of the public sphere. A 'politics of pity'[26] can only be made meaningful as part of the media morality that relates us to the world of solidarity.[27] Once the media agenda for human suffering is set, the critical

[25] D. Pallotta, *Charity Case: How the Nonprofit Community Can Stand Up For Itself and Really Change the World* (San Francisco, CA: Wiley, 2012); R. Andersen and P. L. de Silva, *Routledge Companion to Media and Humanitarian Action* (London: Routledge, 2017).

[26] Boltanski, *Distant Suffering: Morality, Media and Politics.*

[27] R. Silverstone, *Media and Morality: On the Rise of the Mediapolis* (Malden, MA: Polity, 2006).

standards of public discourse apply translating charity into political talk and recoupling it to the ethics of mutual obligations and responsibilities.

The very ethics of journalism provide an inbuilt safety belt for the constant regeneration of global justice discourse in the form of a critical scrutiny of evidences of distant suffering. This opens an ever-present potential for transnational solidarity mobilisation that can be taken up at any moment by the journalists themselves or by other actors who communicate by applying the standards of critical discourse. While journalism work and practice remain grounded in the realm of the national, the ethical standards of journalism cannot be detached from the principle of global responsibility. There is thus a tension in the work of journalism to serve the well-being of the nation and the world. Journalists need to be Janus-faced to look inside and to look outside, while, despite the constraints of the media attention market, applying the same critical standards and mechanism of truth finding to both their inwards and outwards facing perspectives. Newspapers and journalism can then, indeed, be hold responsible for the nationalisation of our solidarity relationships. Yet, they also remain our window on the world, relating us to strangers and making their needs visible and known to us. The basic function of mass media, of turning strangers into 'significant others', therefore remains intact, independently so of whether the news media highlight stories of national interest or whether they relate us to the world. Those out there in the world who deserve our temporary attention are included, at least to the minimum degree that their status as humans with the rights to be treated as equals cannot be denied to them.

The ethics of journalism constitute in this sense not just an external yardstick for the critical assessment of the work and performance of journalism, but also an internal critical standard that guides journalistic practice. Journalism ethics are based on international agreements and codifications.[28] They are institutionalised in a way that journalism work becomes standardised across the globe.[29] Journalism ethics are further formulated in the establishment of various control mechanisms of journalism practice: they are used as common criteria for media self-control and for external control by regulatory bodies and courts or supervision by international organisations, such as the Council of Europe. The work of journalists and foreign correspondents is conditioned by these

[28] See, for instance, The Declaration of Principles on the Conduct of Journalism by the International Federation of Journalism, available at: www.ifj.org/about-ifj/ifj-code-of-principles/ (accessed 12 September 2018).

[29] R. Smith, *Ethics in Journalism* (Malden, MA: Wiley, 2011).

universal norms, when they cover, for instance, victims of crime, war and disaster who deserve our attention as targets of solidarity. This includes, in particular, the reversal of humiliation and the reconstitution of human dignity of victims to be recognised as legal subjects with equal rights. Journalists also often side with the victims or engage in a discourse of global responsibility to point out our duties towards them. Especially foreign correspondents, who are themselves a class of transnational migrants and as such likely to socialise in a cosmopolitan expat environment where global solidarity with strangers becomes routinised.[30] Their contributions are therefore often written in a 'cosmopolitan spirit', with a sensitivity to global problems and justice beyond the particular interpretation of national interest.

It is further noteworthy how the rule of objectivity as the cornerstone of good journalistic practice meets with a particular moral code of human dignity. Objectivity in news coverage means that the journalist is not driven by an affective attitude of love and hate towards the chosen protagonists of news but maintains an objective distance to be able to assess their protagonists' performance and to evaluate their particular needs and demands. Such an operation of objective distance is, however, at the same time the condition to treat others as equals and to restore the dignity of those whose basic rights as equals have been violated. In turning their attention to 'significant others', media deliver the empirical and practical knowledge that allows us to identify social needs and our own possibilities of action, but media also provide us with moral knowledge that is used to assess these situations and define our obligations. Media are thus a sensor for injustices that are turned into news stories. They portray the others as persons whose rights to be treated as equals need to be recognised, while appealing at the same time to the moral responsibility of their audiences. Media coverage creates a forum for publicly raising demands and making the needs of others salient (being 'cognisant' of someone or *Zurkenntnisnahme*), but it is only through the reception of these media messages that the condition for recognition or *Anerkennung* are met, which requires that there are also felt concerns towards the other, not just passive tolerance of their presence.[31] The media solidarity link requires in this sense a well-functioning public sphere through which journalists can selectively draw our attention and

[30] U. Hannerz, *Foreign News. Exploring the World of Foreign Correspondents* (Chicago: University of Chicago Press, 2004).
[31] Honneth, *The Struggle for Recognition*, p. 112.

allow us to be 'cognisant' of the needs of the others and, at the same time, engage us in a moral discourse about their 'recognition' as equals. This public sphere as the realm of mutual respect on which to base solidarity relationship in a society of equals remains however incomplete. Mass media coverage and audience attention remain selective in the way they relate us to strangers and engage us in moral discourse. Nevertheless, mass media and journalism set the critical standards through which we can address the existing asymmetries in our mediated solidarity relationships and contest the moral demands that are directed towards the 'other'.

Media are in this sense seen as constitutive of any solidarity relationship among strangers in the way they inform audiences about the needs of the others, define collective responsibilities and direct moral demands towards them. Media can however only provide the infrastructure for solidarity discourse that needs to be inscribed into social relationships. Precisely because solidarity is understood to be more than charity, it also needs to be conceived as a reciprocal relationship to the 'other' who receives particular services but also 'talks back' or 'pays back' in future relationships. In a mediated relationship of solidarity, the conditions for 'talking back' are not only met by giving 'voice' to the victims of injustice, but also by addressing a third part as a moral spectator of solidarity relationships. At this stage, we need to turn from the media as a promoter of solidarity discourse to the various ways of addressing, activating and engaging the audience.

4 Mediated Solidarity Relationships: the Audience as Moral Spectator

The audience of solidarity discourse is admittedly under-researched. In principle, they comprise all those who can be addressed by solidarity discourse or who can reply to it. In our modern media landscapes, this is the world; for solidarity discourse in its appeals to social justice can only address the world. Still, the audiences of solidarity discourse are severely restricted, as their constitution depends on spaces of appearance, that is, the media[32] and the selective attention mobilised within these spaces of appearance. The audiences of solidarity discourse are in this sense brought together by an expectation of global reach that is nevertheless restricted by the availability of existing media infrastructures. In practice,

[32] Silverstone, *Media and Morality*, p. 25.

the audience of solidarity discourse is constituted by all those who are not present and initially unaffected by the incidence of distant suffering but can be asked to pay attention and can agree to express affection and concern.[33] Their morality as spectators is based on such an agreement to build a solidarity bond with the victim of distant suffering without being self-interested and without being forced into it.[34]

In abstract terms, the audience can be approached as the third part in a mediated solidarity relationship among strangers. As such, the audience is constitutive to mediated solidarity. Claims for building a solidarity relationship towards strangers are raised in a way to come to the attention of an audience. There are two ways of including an audience in the solidarity relationship: first, by 'calls for attention', and, second, by 'paying attention' and demanding to be included. In the first case, the audience is addressed and targeted, by particular solidarity entrepreneurs who mobilise support for specific target groups. In the second case, they are bystanders who pay attention to particular instances of human suffering and demand to be included in a mediated solidarity relationship, not necessarily as donators or as recipients of services but as anonymous members of an audience who simply demand to be informed. Ideally the addressed audience and the audience that pays attention are identical: you listen because you are addressed, but also because you are potentially affected by an occurrence that 'deserves' your attention. As such, the reception context is confined by a particular sender–receiver relationship that is often institutionalised over time, for instance, in the form of a newspaper's readership who receives daily news. In a transnational public sphere, there are, however, frequent instances of 'dispersed attention': audiences, who are addressed by solidarity campaigns are often indifferent and might only show little interest to be included in a mediated solidarity relationship, while others who are unknown to campaigners for or against solidarity, can show a sudden interest in remote events and claim for inclusion in the mediated solidarity relationship (for example, by asking for more information or by communicating their emotions, such as affection and pity for the case). Transnational solidarity is therefore not only distinguished by the broader reach of solidarity towards strangers (the targets of solidarity in distant places) but also by the broadened reception context of solidarity discourse and the floating attention of anonymous audiences (the

33 Warner, *Publics and Counterpublics*

34 K. Tester, *Media Culture & Morality* (London: Routledge, 2013), p. 83.

globally dispersed audiences that are not reached through the structures of national public spheres and escape the institutionalised solidarity relationships within the nation state). The strangers in the mediated solidarity relationship are duplicated: they can be the targets of solidarity (for example, refugees in need of protection), but also those bystanders in remote places who become witness through media coverage and, as such, involved as a 'third part' in the solidarity discourse. The audience of solidarity is distinguished by a minimum degree of moral engagement (for example, emotional affection by the suffering of others), but it remains at the same time an audience of strangers, whose selective attention can hardly be turned into political engagement. In a public sphere of transnational solidarity discourse, the spaces of dispersed audience attention are never congruent with the spaces to which solidarity is politically confined. The solidarity of the national community of citizens is either too small or to big when confronted with the audiences of public attention of solidarity discourse. Moral spectators do not belong to space and community; they are bound together by sharing the same emotional affection as voluntary or involuntary witnesses of distant suffering, and not by pre-established bonds of community and citizenship.

In the tradition of audience research, solidarity is often considered as an emotional state or a shared feeling among the recipients of uniformly raised media messages. As such, it is discussed as a form of audience identification, which is facilitated by media framing and shared experiences of media consumption.[35] The audiences of solidarity discourse appear in this sense as the passive recipients of pre-fabricated media content. Their solidarity is considered as a manifestation of collective identity, and as such it is also analysed through methods of media reception studies that measure emotional attachment or aggregated individual attitudes towards particular groups of people as targets of solidarity. Luc Boltanski's path-breaking contribution on the construction of media morality significantly went beyond this narrower focus on the emotional state of audiences as aggregates of individual media consumers.[36] Boltanski is interested instead in the possibility that the observation of distant suffering through the media is translated into political talk and collective action. On the one hand, the spectators of

[35] A. E. Williams and C. M. Toula, 'Solidarity framing at the union of national and transnational public spheres', *Journalism Studies*, 18(12) (2017), 1576–92.

[36] Boltanski, *Distant Suffering*.

distant suffering are detached, uninvolved and impartial. They are sheltered, for instance, from the war action that takes place in the distance and have no prior communal commitment to the victim, who is neither friend nor foe. As media spectators, they remain invisible and uncontrolled by others, which means that they could safely ignore the victim, switch off the screen and stop witnessing. On the other hand, media spectatorship facilitates a relationship of moral commitment to the suffering stranger. Media spectators cannot escape the media morality in the form of involvement into a 'politics of pity', which requires them to take a stance, for instance, to translate pity into humanitarian commitment. Media involve spectators only as anonymous members of an audience, but even this anonymity creates expectations of 'taking sides' that follow particular moral codes. It is precisely this latent possibility of a swing to commitment, that distinguishes 'moral spectatorship' from impartial observation or passive media consumption. The audiences of solidarity discourse are committed to a shared discourse of responsibility and justice. Boltanski defines this swing to commitment from an impartial to a morally engaged observer as the 'political moment par excellence':

> So in the ideal of the public sphere a local suffering can be conveyed without deformation in such a way that it is there for anyone to examine it, that is to say, for all those who, from the fact of their reciprocity arising from their lack of prior commitment, are free to examine this suffering and find themselves sufficiently affected by it to become committed and take it up as their cause.[37]

Media play a key role as the main provider of images of distant suffering and inhumanity but also as the main translator of such images into representations of shared responsibility, civility and humanity.[38] Yet, the mediated image (or information) about distant suffering is only part of the message that is conveyed by moral spectatorship and does not constitute in itself the bonds of solidarity between the potential benefactor and the victim. The public sphere also carries the broader repertoire of meaning that allows the interpretation of these images and identification of ethically acceptable or normatively justifiable responses to it (for Kant, such responses are categorical; Boltanski speaks of 'orders of justification'). Precisely because the distant spectator and the victim cannot rely on a notion of primordial solidarity of belonging to the same

[37] Boltanski, *Distant Suffering*, p. 31.
[38] Silverstone, *Media and Morality*, p. 25.

emotional community (like a family or a nation), the moral commitment that is underlying their relationship requires some form of involvement in *public speech*. For members of the audience who take the role of a 'moral spectator' of distant suffering, involvement in public speech opens the possibility to bridge the distance and the asymmetry that is underlying their social relationship.[39] In a public speech situation, the morality of the media witness refers back to generalisable principles and to the validity of arguments that reach beyond the particular case. As we have argued previously, such a generalisable principle that allows moral spectators to translate their media experiences of witnessing human suffering into humanitarian action is found in references to *justice*. There must be a notion of *injustice* attached to the incidence of distant suffering to be turned into an object of moral spectatorship that affects distant spectators politically and not just personally.

Boltanski insists further that these 'politics of solidarity' are fundamentally different from 'politics of identity' within pre-established community, precisely, because they break with our local everyday social relationships, expand the horizon of justice and require justification beyond what is considered as taken for granted. In such a mediated relationship between potential benefactors and recipients of solidarity action, the 'victim' or the 'person in need' is no longer someone we know or feel close to. 'Conveying suffering in a public sphere takes a different form because the public sphere constitutes itself against a communitarian sphere.'[40] In the Habermasian sense, the public sphere allows the crossing from inhumanity to humanity. The selective and incomplete audiences of media attention are linked back to a notion of the 'public', which implies awareness of problems, shared concern and some minimal degree of moral engagement (for example, through the attribution of responsibility).[41]

The question to be answered then remains how volatile audiences of dispersed attention are turned into a 'public' of moral engagement. This translation process from dispersed audience attention into a solidarity relationship can be described in three steps[42]: First, media recipients are

[39] Ibid., p. 37.

[40] Ibid., p. 34.

[41] S. Splichal, *Transnationalization of the Public Sphere and the Fate of the Public* (New York: Hampton Press, 2012).

[42] E. O. Eriksen, 'Structural injustice: the Eurozone crisis and the duty of solidarity', in A. Grimmel and S. M. Giang (eds.), *Solidarity in the European Union* (Berlin: Springer, 2017) pp. 97–118.

not isolated individuals but included in the discursive context for the detection of social problems, which is the public sphere of shared attention: we witness the suffering of 'others' and receive information about who did what to whom. Second, the shared attention of the public sphere allows for the identification of injustice: we apply particular interpretative filters that turn the 'other' 'significant' and describe our own responsibilities towards them. Third, the 'public' comes into being as an agent that translates the shared experiences of injustice into a moral duty of solidarity. Such a 'public' is therefore always more than an aggregation of audience attention. It is rather unified through the practice of moral criticism, which consists in identifying injustices, ascribing political responsibilities and calling for the moral duty of solidarity. The media solidarity link is in this sense not simply a normative postulate, but inscribed in the logics of news reception. Whenever indignation and guilt are triggered in the public sphere, a moral duty of solidarity follows.[43]

In the following, I wish to briefly illustrate the changing context of media reception in a world of global interdependencies where spectatorship is no longer defined in a one-to-many relationship of hierarchical mass media that reach out to a unified (and mainly nationally confined) mass audience but a relationship opened up to new connective and interactive forms of relating to media content.

5 Social Media: New Opportunities for Transnational Solidarity Mobilisation

When Roger Silverstone published his book on the rise of the mediapolis in 2007, social media were still in its infancy. Silverstone nevertheless left no doubt that the mediapolis could only be conceived as global space of communication, in which the basis for our relations towards strangers were established and our moral obligations towards them contested. The mediapolis is built on global connectivity in a double sense: technically, in the sense of connecting the world through media channels and content; and culturally, in the sense of facilitating the imagination of world culture through arts, visuals and the translation of text.[44] The mediapolis

43 Ibid.

44 A. Hepp, *Mediatized Worlds, Culture and Society in a Media Age* (Basingstoke: Palgrave, 2014); N. Stevenson, *The Transformation of the Media: Globalisation, Morality and Ethics* (London: Routledge, 2014).

is of global reach and of cosmopolitan intent. It dynamically unfolds through global networks and global culture.

The Internet and social media are believed to accelerate media globalisation.[45] Yet, their effects on solidarity bonds are ambivalent. In the literature, the destabilisation effects of the Internet, and particularly of social media on existing communication systems are emphasised, undermining the economic viability of legacy media (for example, through the sharing of content) and the civicness of political communication and debate (for example, through hate speech).[46] The 'uncivic online sphere' would thus be a major threat to established solidarity relationships. Others emphasise new opportunities of the Internet as a stimulus for agenda setting, more inclusive deliberation and identity building. Political debates are more global, inclusive and accessible, empower disadvantaged groups and pluralise the public sphere in various ways.[47] New opportunities for transnational solidarity mobilisation, are for instance described, in the forms of 'moral spectatorship' through visuals that are shared through social media and translated into political speech that claims solidarity with victims and ascribes responsibility.[48] Social media moral spectatorship can built more immediate relationships to victims while at the same time activating critical capacities of online users-citizens.[49] Chouliaraki, for instance, describes how social media

45 N. Couldry, *Media, Society, World. Social Theory and Digital Media Practice* (Cambridge: Polity, 2012).

46 J. Gerhards and M. S. Schafer, 'Is the internet a better public sphere? Comparing old and new media in the US and Germany', *New Media & Society*, 12(1) (2010), 143–60; A. Michailidou, H. J. Trenz and P. De Wilde, *The Internet and European Integration. Pro- and Anti-EU Debates in Online News Media* (Opladen: Barbara Budrich, 2014); T. Rasmussen, 'Internet and the political public sphere', *Sociology Compass*, 8(12) (2014), 1315–29.

47 P. Dahlgren, *The Political Web: Media, Participation and Alternative Democracy* (Basingstoke: Palgrave, 2013); A. Rauchfleisch and M. Kovic, 'The internet and generalized functions of the public sphere: transformative potentials from a comparative perspective', *Social Media + Society*, 2(2) (2016), https://doi.org/10.1177/2056305116646393

48 L. Chouliaraki, *The Ironic Spectator. Solidarity in the Age of Post-Humanitarianism* (Cambridge: Polity, 2013); L. Chouliaraki and T. Stolic, 'Rethinking media responsibility in the refugee "crisis": a visual typology of European news', *Media, Culture & Society*, 39 (8) (2017), 1162–77; M. Mortensen and H. J. Trenz, 'Media morality and visual icons in the age of social media: Alan Kurdi and the emergence of an impromptu public of moral spectatorship', *Javnost. The Public*, 23(4) (2016), 343–62.

49 H. J. Trenz, V. K. Brändle, M. Cinalli and O. Eisele, 'PART 2: comparative report on social media commenting over the "refugee crisis"', in TransSOL 5.1, available at: https://transsol.eu/files/2018/05/deliverable-5-1.pdf.

users engage in a collective interpretation of texts and visual contents. She describes the 'performance' of media texts by social media user in itself as a form of collective action that constitutes audiences as publics. The audience finds itself in a new performative role with texts, which constitutes them as publics of possible action.[50] In our own analysis of user commenting in response to the so-called refugee crisis, we found, for instance, frequent critic of speech for its ineffectiveness ('only words') as part of users' exchanges of political content. The social media users thus turn critical against themselves and express their shame or bad conscience of being only a voyeur of distant suffering.[51] It is only through an engagement in altruistic speech that the integrity of the spectator can be restored and the suspicion to be passive or 'heartless' be reverted. Such altruistic speech is paired with demands for collective action: 'we shall', 'let's do'. In a community of Facebook users who self-identify as 'friends', and who share feelings of pity and indignation in witnessing distant suffering, speech becomes easily more committing. Users do frequently motivate and encourage each other to swing to commitment and to group each other around a cause. This does not mean that users necessarily become militant protesters, yet they engage in public speech in a way to spread alarm and to call for solidarity, not least because they believe that their strong feelings of pity and indignation might have an impact on shaping political responses, that is, that their voice is heard by political decision makers. The 'civic online sphere' would thus allow for a further expansion of solidarity bonds beyond the exclusively defined community of the nation state.

Given this inbuilt ambivalence of the online public sphere, any a priori assumption about the disruptive or constructive dynamics of online political communication on the expansion of transnational solidarity bonds seems impossible. The online media and legacy media are also not two distinct spheres but increasingly interwoven in the way solidarity relationships are build and given meaning in particular contexts. On the one hand, the social media solidarity linkage is increasingly context bound and depends on the affordances provided by particular social media platforms, the collective action repertoire available at a particular moment and the opportunities offered for political mobilisation. On the other hand, social media indicate a structural transformation

[50] L. Chouliaraki, 'Global representations of distant suffering', in N. Coupland (ed.), *The Handbook of Language and Globalization* (Malden, MA: Wiley, 2010), pp. 608–24.

[51] Mortensen and Trenz, 'Media morality and visual icons', p. 343.

of the public sphere in terms of ownership, control and reception of political content. Especially the disruptive effects of social media are not only seen as context bound but also structural in terms of a colonisation of the social media lifeworlds by commercial powers with new possibilities of commodification of content and surveillance.[52] Instead of a global public sphere of common interest mediation, we would assist the resurgence of an 'imperialist private sphere'.[53]

We encounter here the old Janus-faced nature of the media to confine solidarity relationships to particular places while at the same time unbounding them from place and embracing the global. Social media are at the same time very modern and pre-modern. Through their connectivity, they establish basic solidarity bond towards strangers and thus revive the original expansive logic of solidarity in the public sphere that was blocked by the nationalising logic of legacy media. A new form of 'civic cosmopolitanism'[54] unfolds through media engaging citizens across the borders. In a similar vein, also Gould (Chapter 2, in this volume) identifies a 'cosmopolitan requirement' for social movements who fight historical or temporary injustices. Even though such groups often fight locally and their solidarity claims remain contested, it is precisely through such conflicts over the generalised validity of their claims that these solidarity movement become tied into a transnational network. At the same time, we can observe how social media build on a new intimacy of solidarity relationships, foster segmented online communities that close themselves off the world and, all too often, are held responsible for the spread of an exclusive rhetoric towards strangers or even hate towards fellow citizens. The question of how 'unsocial' social media are and thus the extent to which un-solidarising forces of online political communication prevail is ultimately not simply an empirical question, but a question that confirms the validity of the critical yardsticks of the public sphere as they became institutionalised 200 years ago. The social media thus become the object of moral criticism that involves a global community of online users. Raising such critical questions, translating them into shared concerns and asking for political solutions, will keep the transnational public sphere of solidarity alive, even though its institutional structures and performances are currently found to be highly deficient.

[52] C. Fuchs, 'Social media and the public sphere', *Journal for Global Sustainable Information Society*, 12(1) (2014), 57–101.

[53] Ibid., p. 65.

[54] P. Dahlgren, *The Political Web: Media, Participation and Alternative Democracy* (Basingstoke: Palgrave, 2013)

6 Conclusion: Opportunities or Threats for Transnational Solidarity Mobilisation?

Solidarity is a key notion in understanding the bounding and unbounding forces of mass media communication in modern society. It allows the binding of people together as strangers at the global scale, while at the same time separating them into imagined communities of belonging. Solidarity and justice are the grammar of public speech, but the particular translations in the application of this grammar to the ongoing events in the political process remain contested. Solidarity contestations in the public sphere are the indicator for the application and constant actualisation of this grammar. The very fact that solidarity remains contested serves as a constant reminder of the 'unfinished' character of the political community in the light of a global society of equals. Such solidarity contestations in the media are driven by two countervailing forces of a re-nationalising and highly selective news culture (making events relevant for particular audiences) and the global outlook of news journalism as the window to the world with its dedication to truth, impartiality and equality. A journalism that detaches itself from global responsibilities becomes contradictory and non-viable. The needs of distant people also continue to make 'good news stories' in the mediapolis, which adds a commercial dynamic of media globalisation to the normative horizon of global responsibility that drives the work of journalists.

Online and social media replicate this inbuilt ambivalence of mass media as a facilitator for the imagination of community and as a window of the world. On the one hand, the online public sphere is occupied by global civil society and critical journalism promoting a discourse of global responsibility, on the other hand, it is increasingly fragmented, becoming the playground for all kind of anti-modern forces and their promotion of exclusive, nativist or racist discourse. Audience fragmentation in the offline and online media world is an additional challenge for those who have ambitious solidarity projects, because it erodes processes of political will formation within established national democracies and beyond. An online world that is constituted by fragmented 'sphericules'[55] would however remain unstable not only because the boundaries of such sphericules are necessarily porous, but, above all, because they contradict the very logic of public and media

[55] T. Gitlin, 'Public sphere or public sphericules', in T. L. A. J. Curran (ed.), *Media, Ritual and Identity* (London: Routledge, 1998), p. 168–74.

discourse which consists in communication to strangers and thus turning them 'significant' and deserving our attention.

More threatening than public sphere fragmentation is therefore a possible scenario of public sphere disruption. Disruptive public sphere dynamics can themselves become a globalising force, not least through professional news management and spin that entail misinformation, rumour and conspiracy.[56] Digital networks that bypasses truth oriented public discourse often feed back into mainstream public debates and the news in a way that does not only fragment public sphere(icules) but also fundamentally challenges the character of post-truth democratic politics.[57] The omnipresence of such 'exclusivist, nativist, or racist discourse' challenges transnational solidarity discourse not so much by invalidating the principle of global justice but rather by distorting the rules of the democratic game through which such discourses can claim generalised validity.

Against this threat of public sphere distortion, a genuine public sphere of globalised media communication remains the normative horizon for the unfolding of critical discourse through transnational solidarity networks. Such critical discourses are distinguished by their efforts of making the moral standard explicit, on the basis of which we relate to strangers, pay them attention or ignore them, provide them assistance or deny it. It is this justificatory logic of the public sphere and the never-ending contestations following from it that provide the universal moral grounds for solidarity.[58] Solidarity therefore continues to exist in the public sphere and not as a private relationship between the benefactor and a person in need of assistance. As such, it becomes reflected and generalised, no longer a private matter of interpersonal sympathy and empathy, but a shared responsibility. Solidarity as grounded in the communicative rationality of the public sphere is in this sense always political. It requires 'an active, engaged, collective response to injustice or oppression'.[59] Yet, it is also more than just political, it is

[56] W. L. Bennett and B. Pfetsch, 'Rethinking political communication in a time of disrupted public spheres', *Journal of Communication*, 68(2) (2018), 243–53.

[57] B. McNair, *Fake News: Falsehood, Fabrication and Fantasy in Journalism* (London: Routledge, 2017).

[58] J. Kapeller and F. Wolkenstein, 'The grounds of solidarity: from liberty to loyalty', *European Journal of Social Theory*, 16(4) (2013), 476–91.

[59] S. J. Scholz, *Political Solidarity* (University Park, PA: Penn State University Press, 2008), p. 70, see also pp. 65 and 252–60.

revolutionary in the sense that it can be turned against any form of domination.[60] The contested solidarity of the public sphere is progressive and expansive, it exists when it is articulated and found public expression, and it ceases to exist when it is taken for granted or disabled from expanding beyond the particularity of community.

60 Eriksen, 'Structural injustice'.

16

Changing Normativity and Solidarity

European Legal and Trans-Religious Perspectives

HANNE PETERSEN

1 United We Stand – A Memorial Service

On Wednesday, April 6th [2016] at 17.00 hrs, a memorial Service commemorating the victims of all recent terror attacks will be held at the Vor Frue Kirke, Nørregade 8, 1165 Copenhagen.

Since the tragic events in Brussels, Belgium, terror has already stricken elsewhere. Iraq and Pakistan were the most recent victims. In March, blood was shed in Turkey, Iraq, Nigeria and Côte d'Ivoire.

Together with the Embassies of Belgium, Côte d'Ivoire, Pakistan and Turkey, the Cathedral of Copenhagen welcomes all who want to share a moment to meditate or to express solidarity.

In the presence of dignitaries, both civil and religious, Vr. Rev. Anders Gadegaard, Dean of the Cathedral, will lead the service, *transcending religions, races and cultures.* A number of personalities, including Minister of Justice Mr. Søren Pind, Ambassador of Belgium Mr. Pol De Witte and the author Mr Jens Christian Grøndahl will address the audience. Hodja Hüseyin Gültekin will recite the sura 'Al Fatiha'.

Hymns will be sung by all including the Copenhagen Royal Chapel Choir. Parvaiz Akhtar will perform Sufi Music poetry in Punjabi. Bach's Ave Maria will be played on violin and cello by Anna and Igor Egholm. All participants are invited to write a word of prayer or sympathy when entering the Cathedral. They can also light a candle and leave it on the stairs to the choir in the church.

United we stand both in mourning the victims, in solidarity with all afflicted and in condemning terrorism.[1]

[1] Kirken I København, 'United we stand', was available at: http://kirkenikbh.dk/kalender/mindegudstjeneste-united-we-stand (accessed 29 October 2018). Emphasis added here.

The above announcement of an international and inter-religious memorial service in the Cathedral of Copenhagen in April 2016 was still on the homepage of the Church at the time of writing, more than two and a half years after the service took place. The announcement used the term solidarity twice underlining the links between countries' different religious affiliations, embassies and their international representations. In addition, present at the service were ministers and politicians as well as authors and artists in a joint reaction against terror, and to share in the mourning of victims and express solidarity with the afflicted.

This was not an everyday event and it was particularly exceptional in the way it employed the concept of solidarity.

Solidarity is a concept strongly linked to the twentieth century and its burning issues of conflicts between capital and labour[2] in a secularised world. The remembrance service demonstrated that in the twenty-first century, solidarity has moved beyond secularity and the field of production of paid work. The pressing issues of the beginning of the twenty-first century transcend secularity and pose challenges for a post-secular, globalised world of migration and movements of refugees.

Since the end of the Cold War, and especially since 9/11 in 2001, the re-emergence of (often conservative) religions and the role of religious affiliations have given rise to many reflections and motivated many research projects, not least in the European Union (EU), on issues related to conflicts, minorities and religious perspectives. I have myself participated in some of these research projects, mainly in a Danish and EU context. This chapter reflects on the challenges, difficulties and potentials for trans-religious expressions and forms of solidarity based among others on this earlier research.[3]

[2] É. Durkheim, *Om den sociale arbejdsdeling* (København: Hans Reitzels Forlag, 2000). The original *De la division du travail social* was first published in 1893, and later republished in 1902 with a second, long introduction by Durkheim on the role of associations.

[3] I have participated in the interdisciplinary research area of the University of Copenhagen on *Religion in the 21st Century* (2003–7), see the book L. Christoffersen, H. Raun Iversen, H. Petersen and M. Warburg (eds.), *Religion in the 21st Century. Challenges and Transformations* (Farnham: Routledge, 2010).

I was also a participant in the Danish team in an EU-financed research project called 'RELIGARE. Religious Diversity and Secular Models in Europe. Innovative Approaches to Law and Policy' (2010–13). See CORDIS, 'Final Report Summary – RELIGARE (Religious Diversity and Secular Models in Europe – Innovative Approaches to Law and Policy)', available at: https://cordis.europa.eu/result/rcn/143814_en.html (accessed 29 October 2018).

2 Kassel, Germany 2012, dOCUMENTA 13

> Visitors for dOCUMENTA (13) may not necessarily experience Ana Prvacki's contribution as a tangible work of art, but they will benefit from an enhanced atmosphere of politeness, friendliness, and hospitality. Prvacki, whose work is an ongoing investigation into our increasingly dematerialized economy of services and ideas, has hired a team of professional coaches and etiquette instructors to train as many people as possible working for and with documenta in the public services – guides, guards, ticket sellers, cloakroom people etc. – in etiquette and civility prior to the opening of the exhibition. One might think that such social skills are a given, but in fact they have to be learned and practiced, the more so since they differ from culture to culture.[4]

Documenta is an exhibition of contemporary art which takes place every five years. It was started in one of the many German cities bombed by the Allied Forces during the Second World War. In 1955, as a reaction to war, moral collapse and the Nazi regime's rejection of modernity, among other phenomena represented in contemporary modern art of the time, the city of Kassel held the first *Documenta* exhibition. The aim was to signify a new beginning after the breakdown of a totalitarian regime, and to familiarise the public with the cultural expressions of the *entartete Kunst* (the 'degenerate Art') that had been banned by the Nazi regime. The exhibition was a success from the beginning with 130,000 people visiting in 1955. The first exhibition in Kassel took place in coincidence with the establishment of new institutions signifying a will to change Europe's and the world's institutional architecture towards a more democratic, transnational and inclusive landscape. These instruments and institutions are now well known.[5]

The situation in the early part of the twenty-first century may arguably not represent quite as dramatic a collapse of a world order, of states and regimes, and of values as the shift in the mid-twentieth century. However, in the last three decades Europe has experienced the fall of the Soviet Union and with it the political idea of state socialism, the collapse of the bipolar world, as well as the spill over from a serious economic crisis felt worldwide (with particularly deep ramifications in Greece in the EU). Several states

[4] dOCUMENTA (13) 2012, Das Begleitbuch/The Guidebook. Katalog/Catalogue 3/3, Verlag Hantje Cantz, Introduction to all artists. This quotation is from the information about artist Ana Prvacki (born 1976 in Pančevo, Serbia).

[5] The establishment of the United Nations in 1945, the UN Declaration on Human Rights from 1948, the Council of Europe from 1949, the European Convention of Human Rights from 1950, the Rome Treaty from 1957 creating the European Economic Community (also called the Common Market), and the European Court of Human Rights established in 1958.

have disappeared or disintegrated, some have reappeared or re-emerged and reunified. The world has experienced the highest number of refugees since the Second World War, and the Mediterranean Sea has been called a Sea of Death. In 2015, the EU was almost paralysed by the sheer number of groups of refugees leaving unstable Mediterranean Middle Eastern countries, especially Syria. Refugees, who were predominantly Muslim, were heading towards wealthy and comparatively welcoming European states, particularly Germany and Sweden. The stability of inter-state order was once again questioned. In 2016, the EU experienced the first decision of a (small) majority of practising voters in the UK to leave the EU, further terrorist attacks in French and German cities, coup and counter-coup in Turkey, and the unforeseen election of Donald Trump as the forty-fifth president of the United States of America. These processes have been accompanied by, and interconnected with, a re-emergence of religious, spiritual, national(ist) and often neo-conservative movements, ideas and practices. Perhaps all of these developments have been attempting to fill voids of values, ideas, ideals and ideologies. European and other normative traditions and cultures have, for a decade, been 'challenged' by globalisation(s), a term which was hardly used before the turn of the millennium. There is a clear need for developing new ways of addressing these challenges. Providing the people of Europe with civility and social skills could perhaps be one small way, among others, to initiate this change. Updating the concepts, practices and places of solidarity in a post-secular world might produce intangible but felt results.

Ana Prvacki was born in 1976, and grew up in both Yugoslavia and Romania, which were among the countries where atheism was performed as a unifying ideology. She has lived in Singapore, and now lives in Los Angeles. She has been presented as:

> an artist whose work draws on daily practices and social research. Her interventions are meant to transform the viewer's perception and experience of daily life and routine, providing solutions to our everyday problems, worries, and fears. She explores social anxiety and the comedic potential of faux pas as well as the sociopolitical significance of welcoming the 'other'.[6]

She belongs to the post-Cold War cosmopolitan generation, for whom cultural interconnection – and not least conflict – has become lived reality, and for whom solutions to conflicts are not necessarily expected to emerge from a national context through legal instruments. Solutions

[6] Was available at www.art.northwestern.edu/calendar/visiting/prvacki.html> (no longer accessible).

are also sought in markets, media, migration (transnational) religions, interpretations, art, business practices and ethics as well as in other arenas.

3 European Normative Landscapes in Transition

In 2011, Jacques Delors, former head of the EU commission, gave an interview to a German magazine entitled 'In search of Europe'. The first question was whether there was such a thing as European society, and what he thought the circumstances were in which European social relations could be seen and identified as such. His answer was:

> From a purely intellectual point of view, yes, there is still such a thing. European society has its own values that are deeply rooted in Greek democracy, the Judaeo-Christian tradition, the Reformation and, in France of course the Revolution. But these values also owe something to the contribution that Islam made through its great influence on southern Europe – something that we tend to forget. You can find its traces in Spain and elsewhere. But you will also find these values in Ukraine, and, to some extent – although some people might not agree – in Turkey as well. We have inherited these historical traditions. There is a European way of thinking about things, a way that is linked to this heritage.[7]

Europe has a complex heritage of secular and religious political and cultural ideas, ideals, traditions and models, which are increasingly interconnected and have interacted, overlapped, conflicted and co-existed in different and changing balances over centuries. Solidarity and its interrelation with religious beliefs is one of these heritages, as discussed by the Norwegian Professor Steinar Stjernø in his 2004 book, which included important reflections on religious solidarity in Catholicism and Protestantism as well as on the idea of solidarity among Christian Democratic parties in Europe.[8]

When the great expansion of the EU took place in 2004, following the collapse of the Soviet Union and of the former communist regimes in Eastern Europe, eight of the former Eastern European states became EU members (the Czech Republic, Estonia, Hungary, Latvia, Lithuania,

[7] J. Delors, N. Tietze and U. Bielfeld 'In search of Europe. An interview with Jacques Delors', available at: www.eurozine.com/in-search-of-europe/ (accessed 15 January 2020). Original in French, translation by Mike Routledge. Contribution by Mittelweg 36 (German version February 2011). English version published by Eurozine 1 July 2011.

[8] S. Stjernø, *Solidarity in Europe. The History of an Idea* (Cambridge: Cambridge University Press, 2004), see especially chs 3, 6, 7 and 9.

Poland, Slovakia and Slovenia) together with two small Mediterranean countries (Malta and Cyprus). This expansion introduced a number of Member States who had recent economic and political histories and heritages that were different from the original EEC/EU Member States, including in their relations between secular and religious normative cultures. Religion and religious institutions in post-socialist former Eastern European countries and communities have (re)gained legitimacy and received support (in economic and other terms) from Western regimes and institutions.

The German professor of philosophy, Kurt Bayertz, published an early and influential anthology on *Solidarität, Begriff und Problem* in 1998,[9] which was quickly translated into English and has, among other things, inspired many authors from different fields to address this topic. One of them was Johannes J. Frühbauer, who in 2007 published an article on solidarity in Islam, Buddhism and Confucianism, searching for building blocks for an inter-religious social ethic.[10]

4 Ambivalence, Fear, Confusion and Adaptation to Change

Another German professor of sociology, Hans Joas, has addressed issues of solidarity and morality in a chapter in a book on one of the most important early writers on solidarity, Émile Durkheim.[11] He finishes his chapter with a quote from the last piece Durkheim (1858–1917) was to write dealing with morality:

> Only ages characterised by a split on moral questions are creative in the domain of morality. If traditional morality is not thrown into question, if no need is felt to innovate it, moral reflection withers away.[12]

Our time seems increasingly to be one that is split on moral questions – and perhaps thus creative in the domains of both morality and solidarity. The collapse of the bipolar world caused considerable anxiety, insecurity and fear in large parts of Europe. The replacement of collectivist ideas and ideologies with (neo-)liberal and individualist ideologies has led to

[9] Kurt Bayertz (ed.), *Solidarität–Begriff und Problem* (Berlin: Suhrkamp Verlag 1998).

[10] J. J. Frühbauer, 'Solidaritët in Islam, Buddhismus und Konfuzianismus. Bausteine für eine interreligiöse Sozialethik', *Jahrbuch für Christliche Sozialwissenschaften*, 48 (2007), 105–20, available at: www.jcsw.de.

[11] H. Joas, 'Durkheim's intellectual development: the problem of the emergence of a new morality and new institutions as a leitmotif in Durkheim's oeuvre', in S. Turner (ed.), *Emile Durkheim: Sociologist & Moralist* (London: Routledge, 1993), pp. 223–38.

[12] Ibid., p. 236.

moralistic and sometimes doctrinal reactions to the challenges which members of communities and societies have been facing during the last decades. Demand for symbolic representation[13] and visibility in the public sphere may be a reaction to insecurity and fear[14], as well as being part of an effort to secure authority[15], protection and good/better conditions for children and adults alike. It may also lead in different conservative directions, including gender conservative politics often linked to religion, as highlighted in a recent report published by German Friedrich Ebert Stiftung, *Gender as Symbolic Glue. The Position and Role of Conservative and Far Right Parties in the Anti-Gender Mobilizations in Europe.*[16] In the present era, secular arguments are no longer as persuasive and influential as they were in the twentieth century, even in Northern Europe. Modernity has not been able to deliver the protection and betterment of people's lives which it seemed to promise and under the present (economic) conditions there is no strong conviction that it may do so in a future globalised world. This may lead to increasing conflicts between generations and groups influenced by respectively 'secular' and 'religious' values. We may also witness new conflicts emerging as earlier ones fade away. But Durkheim and Joas may also give us hope that new forms of morality, cohesion and solidarity could emerge.

Other explanations for the present situation may perhaps be found in comparisons to 'fictitious' representations of major societal changes. In her novel, *The Fourgated City* (published in 1969), which takes place in post-Second World War London, Nobel Laureate Doris Lessing, describes the reconstruction of material surroundings and mental lives after the ideological and material collapse during the war.[17] The book is the last in the series, Children of Violence, which contains autobiographical elements, especially in the earlier novels, describing the development of the central character from the interwar period onwards. The novel has been described as both a *Bildungsroman*, as

[13] This representation may be pious, nationalist, conservative and/or traditional as well as fundamentally secular or an expression of corporate loyalty or militarism.

[14] See M. C. Nussbaum, *The New Religious Intolerance. Overcoming the Politics of Fear in an Anxious Age* (Harvard, MA: The Belknap Press of Harvard University Press, 2012).

[15] S. Mahmood, *The Islamic Revival and the Feminist Subject* (Princeton, NJ: Princeton University Press, 2005).

[16] E. Kováts and M. Põim (eds.), *Gender as Symbolic Glue. The Position and Role of Conservative and Far Right Parties in the Anti-Gender Mobilizations in Europe* (France, Germany, Hungary, Poland, Slovakia) (Bonn: Friedrich Ebert Stiftung, 2015).

[17] D. Lessing, *The Four-Gated City* (London: first published by MacGibbon & Kee, 1969).

well as the beginning of Lessing's science fiction writing, and is thus a mixing of genres. The novel describes the arrival and disoriented stage of the protagonist, Martha, coming from colonial South Africa to a bombed city, and the phases both Martha and her surroundings experience in the transition from the 1950s through the 1960s. It vividly portrays how difficult it is to tell when one phase begins or when it ends, but at some point a 'bad time' and a certain public concern or moral panic (related to communism, the atomic bomb, youth criminality, drug abuse among other things) seems to be fading to be replaced by new concerns, panics, worries or hopes. The author's description of how one moral concern is followed by the next is of clear contemporary relevance. It is also clearly influenced by her studies of Sufism which began in the mid-1960s. The book contains several quotes and brief stories from her Sufi teacher, Idries Shah, whom she was following for a longer period. One of them describes a Sufi understanding of the world as characterised by 'hope, fear and repetition'.[18] This novel could be seen as an example of new insights emerging from periods of collapse, split and change, and of hope following periods dominated by fear, as has been the case in Europe for the last decades.[19] It may also be understood as an example of an individual incorporating different religious and moral insights into their work.

Martha Nussbaum relates directly to the role of fear in the title of her 2012 book *The New Religious Intolerance. Overcoming the Politics of Fear in an Anxious Age.* She is very critical of the European approaches to a 'fear of religion', and (at the time of writing) saw a difference between the USA and Europe in the observation that 'European nations tend to conceive of nationhood and national belonging in ethno-religious and cultural linguistic terms', and she further considered that 'Europe urgently needs to engage in a deep and searching debate about equality and what equal respect for citizens entails in the area of religion'.[20]

[18] Lessing, *The Four-Gated City*. M. Galin *Between East and West. Sufism in the Novels of Doris Lessing* (New York: State University of New York Press, 1997) draws attention to the role of Sufism in her work.

[19] One major example of this relation between hope, collapse and fear is the three volumes by German (and later East German) philosopher Ernst Bloch, *Das Prinzip Hoffnung [The Principle of Hope]*, written while Bloch was in exile in the US from 1938 to 1947 and published during the 1950s, is described as being fundamental to a dialogue among Christians and Marxists, see Wikipedia, 'The Principle of Hope', available at: https://en.wikipedia.org/wiki/The_Principle_of_Hope (accessed 29 October 2018).

[20] Nussbaum, *The New Religious Intolerance*, p. 223.

At the end of 2018, this is perhaps also valid in the context of the increasingly divided and fearful USA.[21]

The second decade of the twenty-first century may be a period where the 'panic' about religion, which dominated the first decade of the twenty-first century, has become perhaps even more explicit and exploited. The inter-religious memorial service at the Copenhagen Cathedral could be a small sign of a new practical solidarity emerging in spite of growing divisions and tensions.

5 Subversive Traditionalism or Symbols of Transition?

Where are the signs of hope in the sense of emerging models and practices reflecting societies adapting to a new era and its concerns? Etienne Balibar claims that:

> If we are to articulate a 'politics of hope' in contemporary Europe, then we must revisit such problematic concepts as 'populism', 'democracy', and 'Europe', formulating a new language that can register the fact that the coexistence of an anti-democratic Europe and an anti-European exploitation of fears and frustrations, are two sides of the same coin.[22]

Art is a field which deals with both emerging tensions and models. A young curator, Nav Haq, who has worked in Antwerp, was invited to work on the Göteborg International Biennial for Contemporary Art (GIBCA) for 2017. In an interview on his appointment, he commented that:

> ... GIBCA has been extremely positive in responding to my thoughts about the next edition in 2017, for which I will look to engage with some fundamental questions about Europe, the formalisation of its values, and the fine line between protection and violence. I will place emphasis on a subject of core socio-political relevance – that of secularism. What happens to secularism during moments of crisis? What role should secularist thought have in society today? And what might culture do when failed by political regimes? Perhaps it might form some unexpected alliances in working towards new modes of secularism.[23]

New modes of secularism and of post-secular sites for both religious and spiritual encounters and solidarity may emerge in the years to come. For

[21] See D. Moïsi, *The Geopolitics of Emotion: How Cultures of Fear, Humiliation, and Hope are Reshaping the World* (New York: Random House, 2009).

[22] E. Balibar 'Our European incapacity', available at: www.opendemocracy.net/etienne-balibar/our-european-incapacity.

[23] GIBCA, 'Nav Haq', available at: www.gibca.se/index.php/en/2017/curator (accessed 29 October 2018).

many years, media focus has been on conflicts between different religions, between fundamentalist expressions of religiosity and/or between fundamentalist secularism and religious beliefs. The interview material gathered by the RELIGARE research[24] dealt, in particular, with issues concerning family law, labour law, public space and public funding (tax issues). The interviews in five national reports revealed that *intra-religious* tensions and conflicts between conservative and reform oriented parts of the same religion(s) with their wider religious communities were found across all the monotheistic religions, which dominate the religious landscape in Europe.[25] The pattern of conservation versus reform thus seemed to form a kind of 'unity in religious diversity'. The research material also indicated a need for a more nuanced understanding of (religious) conservatism. Conservatism could be directed towards a static reproduction of traditional authority and power, but it was also under considerable pressure to adapt to external conditions including diverse and changing value sets.

What emerges out of the transformation of social structures, state structures and belief structures that take place alongside major technological changes might be understood as a situation of *paradoxical conservatism or subversive traditionalism*. This is a conservatism and traditionalism that continues to demand access to the benefits of modernity and 'modern life', while at the same time seeking to preserve a traditional or conservative (gender) order. The demand for access to modernity often equates to families' demands for access to education, especially for girls and young women.

This is clearly reflected in a quote from the Turkish RELIGARE report:

> The core issue is that religious conservative women now request being present in the public space, at university, want higher education. Before 1980 this was not the case. When women started to be more visible through modernization, the reaction was 'what is going on?' But they were always there, they just became more visible. And not with the traditional

[24] See note 3 on RELIGARE.

[25] The national *reports* from five countries (Bulgaria, Denmark, France, Turkey and the UK) were earlier accessible for download on the original RELIGARE website (but are no longer accessible). They were described as: 'The research to be carried out in this team will focus in the first place on significant actors well acquainted with conflicts between religious and secular values in their countries, and who by shaping the ideological and political approaches to these conflicts influence policy-making on these issues. Interviews will cover issues/controversies related to conflicts between religious and secular values . . . .' The *case* database is now accessible from http://religaredatabase.cnrs.fr/ (accessed 29 October 2018).

> headscarves, but in a fashion that emerged with modernity. This change became a very ideological discussion topic in politics. I think that it has been corrupted by politics. Today, the headscarf is still used for politics.[26]

But subversive traditionalism may also demand the right for 'modern women' to live non-stereotypical modern lives. In her article, 'The right to bare arms: reading Michelle Obama's public image', M. Michaela Hampf wrote about the mixed emotions and stereotypical, anxious perceptions of the American public towards the now former first lady.

> White feminists tended to view the First Lady's new public image as 'the nation's stylish first mom' with criticism: An Ivy League-educated former executive has been 'pushed into this stereotypically feminine box' until it is only her style and her being a mother that is discussed.[27]

Hampf reminded us that black and white working women have not been playing on the same team.

> The gender norms that have relegated women to the domestic sphere were generally white middle-class ones. While they have limited white women's opportunities for education, employment and career, women of color and working class women have faced other challenges.[28]

Hampf also claimed that there was 'something powerful, subversive, and new in Michelle Obama's traditionalism'.[29]

> She has repeatedly been cast in the stereotypical roles white America had invented for African American women during and after slavery. She has managed to successfully escape and subvert them. Yet at the same time she has to a certain extent conformed to 'safer' stereotypes in order to make her husbands and her public image appear less threatening in post-9/11 American culture.[30]

The highly educated women who continue to wear headscarves may also (gradually) appear less threatening in their own communities, cultures and families.

[26] RELIGARE: Turkish Socio-Legal Research Report: Challenges of Religious Accommodation in Family-Law, Labor-Law and Legal Regulation of Public Space and Public Funding on file with author (see note 23). TDV-KFM – a Turkish Religious Foundation / Centre for Women's Activities, interview with the female director.

[27] M. M. Hampf, 'The right to bare arms: reading Michelle Obama's public image', in B. Christ and G. Olson (eds.), *Obama and the Paradigm Shift. Measuring Change* (Heidelberg: Universitätsverlag Winter, 2012), p. 65.

[28] Ibid., pp. 65–6.

[29] Ibid., p. 72

[30] Ibid., pp. 72–3.

The movements back and forth between spheres, worlds and experiences do present glimpses of new complex orders and meetings in intimate and international as well as spiritual relations, which will require an innovation in moral reflection and forms of solidarity across religions, races, genders and social classes.

An increased presence of children (often girls) from 'conservative' parental backgrounds in the public sphere can be seen as a sign or symbol of a postmodern and post-secular condition where conservatives opt in to a 'modern sphere' but at the same time require this sphere to adapt to a more conservative, 'safe' and 'traditional' expression which is amenable to community life. The 'conservative position' is especially challenged through the female exit from the private family life and (religious) girls' and women's access to the 'public sphere' and the labour market. The 'modern' spheres are in turn challenged through demands for visible symbols of (religious) conservatism. These paradoxes create the postmodern conditions that knowledge should deal with which Jean-Francois Lyotard suggested a generation ago in his famous book *The Postmodern Condition: A Report on Knowledge* from 1979.[31] According to Lyotard, the task for postmodern science was to research instabilities and to show an interest in the 'undecidable' in the limits of control, in conflicts with insufficient information, in 'fracta' and catastrophes, and in 'pragmatic paradoxes'.[32] Perhaps 'progressive conservatism' and/or 'subversive traditionalism' are pragmatic paradoxes significant for contemporary Europe in the field of religion but also beyond it. Perhaps they can also produce sites for the development of trans-religious solidarity.

The paradox here consists of a demand that aims at securing a conservative and hierarchical gender order in the family, while at the same time leading to an increased level of education for girls and women. The consequences of the latter may be increased cultural independence from the ('traditional') family through increased economic and personal independence achieved via (female) paid labour in the public sphere. These consequences may be contested but may also be sought after in changing societies and family structures. The statistician Philippe Fargues, wrote already in 1997 about the situation in the Middle East, more specifically about Egypt, '(J)ust as gender hierarchy is losing little by little, the hierarchy of generations, the foundation which gave a triple advantage to the

[31] J. F. Lyotard, *The Postmodern Condition: A Report on Knowledge* (Minneapolis, MN: Minnesota University Press, 1984). The French original is from 1979

[32] J. F. Lyotard, *Viden i det postmoderne samfund* (Aarhus: Sjakalen, 1982), p. 114.

man – age, education and economic activity – is likewise offset by the diffusion of education.'[33] This development may lead to a feeling of solidarity between women with different religious backgrounds as well as between feminists from different cultural and religious contexts. It is my experience from having worked with women in the Middle East and North Africa (MENA) region, and especially in Morocco in North Africa between 2008–14, that this was indeed the case.[34]

Professor of semiotics Per Aage Brandt, wrote in 2010 – apropos the Danish Cartoon Crisis from 2005/6 – that symbols may become mitigated and subdued and that we have attempted to create a 'low-symbolized public space'.[35] According to Brandt, the bearer of symbols signals to others (also bearers of symbols) that they are dealing with a person who wants to be treated as part of the story in question and that they consider it exemplary. 'Symbolization starts with bodily expressions: gestures, hair, painting and dress. Symbols challenge the viewer – and describe how the bearer of symbols wants to look, what s/he wants to belong to and wants to do.'[36] Symbols refer to the authority in the story from which they emerge. They are ordering and they may be provoking, but this provocation may decrease as users of the public space get used to diverse representations and performances in such spaces. Trans-religious solidarity will have to deal with issues of symbolic representation and will have to 'bridge' differences between symbolic expressions.

6 Innovative Approaches to Solidarity, Religion, Law and Policy?

6.1 *Changing Mentalities in Europe? Reflexive Majorities and Considerate Minorities?*

The RELIGARE project (from 2010 to 2013) did not explicitly investigate generational or inter-generational views of religious traditions and secular models. Since the generation born during the 1980s might be carrying

33 P. Fargues, 'From Demographic Explosion to Social Rupture', in N. S. Hopkins and S. E. Ibrahim (eds.), *Arab Society. Class, Gender, Power and Development* (Cairo: The American University in Cairo Press, original 1997, here quoted from 3rd edition, 2003), p. 82.

34 See more on this project initiated by an NGO in Denmark KVINFO, available at: http://kvinfo.dk.linux150.unoeuro-server.com/mena/morocco/?lang=en (accessed 29 October 2018). I also participated in KVINFO co-organised seminars and made own interviews in Lebanon, Egypt and Jordan during the same period.

35 P. A. Brandt, 'I symbolernes vold – apropos *Danish Cartoons*', 4 April 2010 (Politiken, Danish newspaper).

36 Ibid.

less antagonistic views about the relationship between religious and secular expressions than the situation which formed the basis for the legal models and religions that dominated the twentieth century, such investigations would be very valuable. Practices and experiments which surface from some of the research material indicate such changes.

A young female, who was then Copenhagen's mayor of integration and herself a lawyer, established a council of co-operation between the Christian Lutheran bishop of Copenhagen, the Jewish rabbi and an imam in order to contribute to the prevention of violent clashes between radicalised members of these communities. The involved and interviewed members considered this move very favourably. The mayor also underlined the need for less biased education on religious issues.[37]

In the Netherlands, Yasmine el Ksaihi, a young female former president of the Polder Mosque in Amsterdam, said about visits of non-Muslims to the mosque that:

> Generally speaking, we also had a lot of discussions about whether you have to wear a headscarf in the prayer room. Well, religiously our view was that a Muslim woman should wear a headscarf and that a non-Muslim woman shouldn't have to wear one [when just visiting the mosque]. My personal view is that if you don't want to wear a headscarf, you do not have to. That often led to conflict, but we had welcomed a lot of groups in between prayers and then the prayer room was empty. It was actually really adorable to see that a lot of non-Muslim women were prepared, and had brought some kind of scarf. I always appreciate it when someone's intentions are respectful. At a certain moment in time, we tried to handle it very strategically and we made sure it was planned in between prayer times, and that these people had left before the next prayer started. Then you do not insult the elderly and you do not have to keep discussing whether it was right or not. At a certain point in time, we decided that during the Friday prayer people needed to bring a scarf or at least wear concealing clothes, because it was much busier and because there were men and women attending the Friday prayer, but I have to say that it all worked out smoothly.[38]

If similarly flexible arguments were used in relation to teenage girls or women wanting not to wear or later deciding to wear a veil (or a cross, or other symbols) for instance, such changes – including changes in belief and personality – would perhaps not present the difficulty they seem to

[37] Danish RELIGARE report on file with author, p. 101. The then mayor of Copenhagen, Anna Mee Allerslev, was born in South Korea in 1984, and is an adopted child (see note 23 above).

[38] Dutch RELIGARE report on file with author, p. 41.

currently. Religious identities have often been understood as fixed and stable identities which do not move over time and/or according to differing conditions. However, identities – including identities providing a legal status – are increasingly fluid and changeable. The approaches to identities may be more or less fundamental or foundational, but they may also be complex, shifting and context or purpose specific. This could enable and promote temporary and contextual forms of solidarity.

Rabbi Miriam Berger, a female rabbi from the reform movement, described some of the differences *within* Judaism, where, for example, issues of a woman's right to divorce and the *get* document create difficulties in Orthodox communities, but not in the reform movement:

> These are not issues within the reform movement. The reform movement for many years have ensured that there is equal partnership – that either men or women can apply for a *get* (Jewish divorce). The reform Jewish law court are responsible for accepting a divorce even if the other side have refused one. Within the reform movement, you can't get stuck in a marriage where there is no mutual consent to it.[39]

In the French context, the heritage of *laicité* is apparent. A legal department manager from Force ouvrière, Véronique Lopez Rivoire, was one of only two women interviewed for the French report. Her comments showed recognition of the growing pluralism which requires practical and pragmatic compromises.

> Indeed, with the effect of growing religious and cultural pluralism, certain companies must face requests of a religious nature (days off for religious festivals, places for prayer . . .); either compromises are regulated by company agreement or the compromises are reviewed on a case-by-case basis. From a legal point of view, these compromises must be treated in good faith by the employer, i.e. with sincerity and seriously (good faith has to govern the execution of the contract of employment, according to Article L. 1222–1 of the Labour Code); but with religious practices having an impact on the organisation of work and the working environment, employers' decisions can be based on the interest of third parties.[40]

A female Danish labour union leader of a public sector union, which organises an important number of women, expressed similar views on issues of 'proper' work place dress. She underlined the necessity to respect both institutions and the citizens the female worker serves.

[39] UK RELIGARE report on file with author, p. 39. Emphasis in original.
[40] French RELIGARE report on file with author, p. 62.

> Yes, I generally feel that if you work in a public office then you need to have respect for the institution you are at and respect for the people that come there. I don't condone low cuts or jewellery all over the place or tight highs or even making much of a ruckus about your own faith to the people that come there. They need to have the feeling that in this place, things are handled by unbiased people who know the rules and not much else . . . but you have to be able to see the hands and carry a sensible and present conversation that doesn't involve you sitting there and thinking, I wonder what's going on underneath all that. Then you shouldn't have such a job. Also, it's a choice that you make if you feel like showing off your religion because you're also choosing to not work with certain jobs.[41]

The historical Roman law concept of *decorum* comes to mind in this relation regarding proper dress and behaviour. A very similar approach was taken by Achmed Baâdoud, a member of Partij van de Arbeid (the labour party) and the district mayor of New West, one of the largest city districts in Amsterdam:

> In our city district New West, our vision is to promote the separation of church and state . . . In New West, you are free to believe what you want, but you are also free to not believe at all. If you are one of the civil servants in New West who refuses to marry homosexuals, then you have probably chosen the wrong profession. That freedom also means that if you make a choice to work somewhere, and if you know that there are also homosexual customers, and that it is a neutral services provider, without any selectivity, that still means that you have the freedom to be who you want to be and to live in the way you want to live. Nonetheless, it is not the community that has to take you into consideration. If you want a job, and you know in advance that you will have to deal with all kinds of people with different kinds of religions, or if you want to wear a burka, then you just shouldn't apply for certain positions.[42]

A female expert from the Bulgarian Confederation of Trade Unions mentioned an example of more direct inter-religious solidarity in a case where a Muslim granted a Christian church to a town.[43]

A female member of the Turkish Democratic Party criticised the uniformity of models and wondered why discussions and ideas, which were once accepted, had become taboos.

> When we look to the 14th century we see that there were many different ideas, why do you impose only one form and one practice today? We do not even have the discussions they had in the 9th or

41 Danish RELIGARE report on file with author, pp. 42–3.

42 Dutch RELIGARE report on file with author, p. 33.

43 Bulgarian RELIGARE report on file with author, p. 22.

> 10th century, they became a taboo. Why? Because we are afraid, because when you express different interpretations you face exclusion. It is really hard for me to understand how ideas of the 10th, 11th, 12th century were turned into taboos ... Islam has plurality at its centre; it combines various ways of thinking. We need to create a meta-language. But via the Diyanet, our pluralistic society moves towards a policy of uniform thought.[44]

All the research reports, as well as other material, reflect images of societies undergoing considerable technological and economic changes. Marriages are performed by telephone, and are no longer only organised according to a male breadwinner model, female participation has become important in all social and religious groups in both politics and in the labour force, technology influences all spheres of life including (not least) the public sphere, and the traditionally privileged relations between states and dominant religious communities all over Europe are increasingly contested. Emerging forms of solidarity may be linked to adaptation to changing conditions and negotiations about how to act, compromise and react.

7 Concluding Remarks on The Paradox of Confusion, Disorientation and Liberation

> We think of history as ordered around the year zero of the birth of Christ, and more specifically as a serial train of events in the life of peoples from the 'centre', the West, the place of civilization, outside of which are the 'primitives' and the 'developing' countries.[45]

As early as 1992, the Italian philosopher, Gianni Vattimo, claimed that the European ideal of humanity has been revealed as one ideal among others 'not necessarily worse, but unable, without violence, to obtain as the true essence of man, of all men'.[46] According to Vattimo, mass media plays a decisive role in the birth of a postmodern society where the emerging ideal of emancipation is 'based on oscillation, plurality and, ultimately, on the erosion of the very "principle of reality"'.[47] Media has clearly had a keen focus upon conflicts where religious issues and clashes with secular models have appeared. The emancipation based upon the

[44] Turkish RELIGARE report on file with author, p. 79.

[45] G. Vattimo, '*The transparent society*', in *The Postmodern: A Transparent Society?* (Cambridge: Polity Press, 1992), ch. 1, at p. 2

[46] Ibid., p. 4.

[47] Ibid., p. 7, see also his Chapter 4 in this book on 'Art and Oscillation'.

erosion of the principle of reality consists in *disorientation* 'which is at the same time also the liberation of differences, of local elements, of what could generally be called dialect'.[48] 'To live in this pluralistic world means to experience freedom as a continual oscillation between belonging and disorientation.'[49] This *disorientation* has been described above as the confusion often related to existential anxiety.[50]

This experience is not specific to late or postmodernity and therefore also holds for earlier ages. We are witnessing changes occurring and we do not know what changes may take place during the historical eras to come, but we do know some of the likely future challenges and we can be sure that there will be further changes. Adaptation to change is important for all communities, societies and relationships.

The European normative landscape is in flux. This gives rise to considerable anxiety, but there are also glimpses of hope for a peaceful co-existence and solidarity between secular and religious values as well as across religions. New 'panics' may replace older ones be they panics concerning large-scale tax evasions and tax fraud undermining welfare or even more existential climate changes undermining the living conditions of populations all over the world. Co-existence is not only required for groups, but also increasingly among individuals. In practice, pluralism prevails and it often gives rise to pragmatic compromises and solutions. There are many overlapping experiences, arguments and concerns in the countries studied in the research project. There are also many differences due to political and historical heritages, but for this author the overlapping concerns and the interconnections between countries and communities and the problems emerging from the research material seem striking.

Besides the fact that the EU does not have competence to regulate in the area of religion, general legal regulations as such may be inadequate. Growing complexity and considerable changes may demand that moral and 'cultural guidelines' develop the social skills necessary for solidarity and peaceful co-existence in pluralist societies. Economic support, together with cooperation in practical projects and dialogues with broader groups and representatives, may open new avenues.

[48] Ibid., p. 8.
[49] Ibid., p. 10.
[50] Vattimo discusses the role of art in producing anxiety and disorientation in Chapter 4 on 'Art and Oscillation' in this book, see pp. 50ff.

Over the last decades, the United Nations has developed a practice of integrating non-governmental voices in conferences and consultations. Some of the quotes in the last part of this presentation indicate that new practices of consultation, communication and education – highly facilitated by social media – might be among the avenues to be studied as part of reforms and developments of social skills and new forms of trans-religious and social solidarity.

17

Transnational Solidarity Among European Cities

HELLE KRUNKE AND KATARINA HOVDEN

> Cities today are the laboratories where many innovative solutions are emerging to address the biggest economic, social and environmental challenges facing our societies today.
>
> David O'Sullivan, European Union Ambassador to the United States, 2014–19

1 Introduction: Building Transnational Solidarity Between Cities

In this chapter, we study the growing phenomenon of transnational co-operation between and among cities in Europe. This co-operation is driven by other actors than state-level actors, is (or at least claims to be) closer to the citizens, and is based on specific challenges facing cities in different countries. Central to the development is an increased legal and political role for the city transnationally. At a time with multiple challenges to solidarity, our aim is to assess whether co-operation initiatives between and among cities in Europe could be a means through which to create or contribute towards a European transnational solidarity. Our focus is on cities within the territorial space of the European Union (EU). That being said, the phenomenon of intercity co-operation is by no means confined to Europe (or to the EU) and we therefore include prominent global initiatives in which European cities participate at the end of the chapter.

In 2016, more than one-half of the global population lived in cities. By 2030, the United Nations (UN) has projected that six out of ten people will be urban dwellers.[1] Europe is certainly no exception to this global trend; already in 1950, over one-half of the European population lived in

[1] United Nations, Economic and Social Council, 'Report of the Secretary-General. Progress towards the Sustainable Development Goals' (2016) E/2016/75, available at: https://unstats.un.org/sdgs/files/report/2016/secretary-general-sdg-report-2016–en.pdf (accessed 15 March 2019).

urban areas.[2] Since then, there has been a steady increase in the concentration of populations in the urban relative to the rural areas, totalling 73 per cent population in 2014. By 2050, the EU projects that 80 per cent population will live in urban areas.[3]

The dense accumulation of populations in cities gives rise to numerous challenges – ecological, social and economic. Cities, because they house such vast proportions of the population, are inevitably responsible for a large proportion of the human strain on natural systems: water, land, habitats, species populations and more. Cities are also vulnerable. While pressures on infrastructure, resources and limited space are by no means new challenges for cities, the contested and unpredictable era of climate change and natural disasters amplifies existing challenges. In the 2018 Global Risks Report produced by the World Economic Forum, transnational environmental threats dominated. 'Extreme weather events', 'natural disasters', and the 'failure of climate-change mitigation and adaptation' appeared in both the list over the top five most likely and the top five most impactful global risks.[4] These are all risks that pose particular challenges for cities.

Many of these are non-national by their very nature, highlighting the need for transnational co-operation and mutual support – possible building blocks, one might think, for transnational solidarity. Yet, if we look at Europe, the geographical focus of our chapter, we have the impression that the reality of interconnection and interdependence is not always translating to an actual feeling of solidarity between people. Instead, solidarity in Europe appears to be challenged, as evidenced by the growth in populist movements and isolationist agendas, and the falling support for the EU in some Member States. The reasons therefore are no doubt many, and it is not the aim of this chapter to suggest what they might be. What we can suggest is that the presumed (or imposed) bonds of solidarity between the Member States of the EU, as laid down in the Treaties[5] (the preamble to the Treaty on the Functioning of the European Union [TFEU], for example, announces an intention 'to confirm the solidarity which binds Europe

[2] Urban Europe, Statistics on Cities, Towns and Suburbs (Brussels: Eurostat, 2016), p. 8; United Nations, Department of Economic and Social Affairs, Population Division, 'World urbanization prospects: the 2014 revision' (2015) ST/ESA/SER.A/366, available at: https://esa.un.org/unpd/wup/publications/files/wup2014-report.pdf (accessed 15 March 2019).

[3] Urban Europe, *Statistics on Cities, Towns and Suburbs*', p. 8.

[4] World Economic Forum, *The Global Risks Report 2018*, 13th edition, available at: www3.weforum.org/docs/WEF_GRR18_Report.pdf (accessed 15 March 2019).

[5] The Treaty on European Union (TEU) mentions solidarity fourteen times and the Treaty on the Functioning of the European Union (TFEU) ten times, in the preamble and operative parts of the treaties.

and the overseas countries'[6]), no longer appear to be enough (if they ever were) to build coherence in Europe.

Against this background, cities are emerging (or, perhaps more accurately, re-emerging[7]) as global actors and participants in global governance. Re-emerging because, as Pluijm and Melissen remind us, 'city diplomacy' – which they define as 'the institutions and processes by which cities, or local governments in general, engage in relations with actors on an international political stage with the aim of representing themselves and their interests to one another'[8] – is not new; such '[d]iplomacy . . . existed before the existence of states'.[9] As we will discover later in the chapter, cities have been self-advocating for their greater involvement in international politics, most prominently in matters related to sustainable development. Successful, it turns out, since cities are explicitly encompassed by the UN Sustainable Development Goals (SDGs) and Agenda 2030. Goal 11 is to '[m]ake cities and human settlements inclusive, safe, resilient and sustainable.'[10] More than that, the SDGs and accompanying Agenda 2030 mainstream the idea of multi-level stakeholder *participation* in achieving the global goals, including by the local levels of government.[11] To that end, 'Local2030' is one of the partnerships set up under the SDGs, aiming to bring the wide gamut of stakeholders together 'to collaboratively develop and implement solutions that advance the SDGs *at the local level*'.[12]

[6] Consolidated version of the TFEU [2008] OJ C115/47, 7th preambular statement.

[7] J. E. Nijman, 'Renaissance of the city as global actor: The role of foreign policy and international law practices in the construction of cities as global actors', in G. Hellman, A. Fahrmeir and M. Vec (eds.), *The Transformation of Foreign Policy: Drawing and Managing Boundaries from Antiquity to the Present* (Oxford: Oxford University Press. 2016), pp. 209–39.

[8] R. V. D. Pluijm and J. Melissen, City Diplomacy: *the* Expanding Role of Cities in International Politics (The Hague: Netherlands Institute of International Relations, Clingendael, 2007), p. 6.

[9] Ibid., p 5.

[10] United Nations Economic Commission for Europe, 'Day of cities', available at: www.unece.org/housing/dayofcities.html (accessed 15 March 2019); United Nations Economic Commission for Europe, 'Day of cities provisional agenda', available at: www.unece.org/fileadmin/DAM/hlm/Meetings/2019/04_8_Day_of_Cities/Day_of_Cities_Provisional_Agenda_Updated_20.02__1_.pdf (accessed 15 March 2019).

[11] United Nations, General Assembly, 'Transforming our world: the 2030 agenda for sustainable development' (2017) A/RES/70/1, available at: www.un.org/en/development/desa/population/migration/generalassembly/docs/globalcompact/A_RES_70_1_E.pdf (accessed 15 March 2019), para 45.

[12] United Nations, 'Local2030' (Partnerships for the SDGs: Global Registry of Voluntary Commitments & Multi-Stakeholder Partnerships), available at: https://sustainabledeve

2 Cosmopolitan Big Cities versus Small Towns in the Provinces

Let us return for a moment to the population statistics that were projected at the outset, for they do not tell the full story. While the biggest capital cities, such as London and Paris, are expected to bear a disproportionate portion of the projected increase, the smallest cities in Europe, those that barely qualify for city status, may be more prone to population drains.[13] People tend to migrate to the city, as they have historically done, 'in search of a job and an improved quality of life'.[14] Thus, the discrepancies in population trends between cities of different sizes may be explained by the fact that economic activities tend to be highly concentrated in large cities.[15] Moreover, it is often the case that countries have just one, or a few, such mega-hub(s) of economic activity – most obviously, the capital city. It is unlikely that this will change in the years to come. In fact, de-industrialisation or post-industrialisation, that is to say, 'the transition that has occurred in advanced industrial nations from a manufacturing-based to services-driven economy',[16] may encourage an even greater concentration of economic activities in large or capital cities. In the era of the so-called knowledge economy, in which there is a 'greater reliance on intellectual capabilities than on physical inputs or natural resources', proximity to the land or resources beyond the city is simply not a necessity for a vast proportion of jobs.[17] With these statistics and projections, we uncover one of the reasons why cities may be encouraged to co-operate with other cities across borders: simply, they may find that they have more in common with their transnational counterparts than those within their own country.

A city may find it has more in common with cities in other countries, which for example are of a similar size and climate, or which have similar geographical features, than it does cities in its own country. Linking cities together in transnational dialogue might thus be a tool with which to strengthen the solidarity of EU citizens and thereby a contribution to EU

lopment.un.org/partnerships/local2030 (accessed 15 March 2019), para. 52, emphasis added.

[13] European Commission, *Eurostat Regional Yearbook: 2018 Edition* (Brussels: Eurostat, 2018), p. 178, available at: https://ec.europa.eu/eurostat/documents/3217494/9210140/KS-HA-18-001-EN-N.pdf/655a00cc-6789-4b0c-9d6d-eda24d412188 (accessed 15 March 2019).

[14] Ibid.

[15] Ibid.

[16] W. W. Powell and K. Snellman, 'The knowledge economy', *Annual Review of Sociology*, 30 (2004), 199–220, at 201.

[17] Ibid.

solidarity as such. However, it is important to be aware that there currently seems to be a tension between, on the one hand, capitals and big cities and, on the other hand, smaller cities and rural areas in the countryside. Nations are split between cosmopolitan citizens who think solidarity across borders and citizens who turn towards the nation state as the main ground for solidarity. We see a general trend of globalised cities and more inward-looking provinces in the countryside. It is a trend across Europe, but we also see it in many countries outside Europe, for instance in the USA. It finds its expression through among others national referenda and elections, and in elections for the European Parliament. At the same time, large groups, including the younger generations, refuse to express themselves through the established political system as we have recently seen in the UK Brexit referendum.

What does all of this mean for our study of co-operation between and among cities as a means to build European solidarity? It means that the solidarity crisis in Europe is not only a transnational crisis; it is also a solidarity crisis within different groups in the individual Member States, geographically expressed as a conflict between large cities and provinces. As an example to illustrate the extent of the contrasts: in the Danish elections in 2015, approximately 80 per cent of the voters in Nørrebro, which is a large district in Copenhagen, voted for the three left-wing parties, which among others have a strong green focus, while 40 per cent of the voters in a small town in Jutland at the border to Germany voted in favour of Dansk Folkeparti, which is the most right-wing party in the Danish Parliament that among other things has a strong focus on migration. Though this might be a particularly polarised example, it still provides a good picture of how deep the distance can be between capitals and small towns, which focus on different challenges. Conversely, if cross-border co-operation between cities can be extended not just to cover co-operation between and among big cosmopolitan cities, but also to cover transnational co-operation between small cities, which face the same challenges, then it might actually be possible to establish more transnational solidarity between the citizens of Europe, and perhaps even a richer European discourse on the different challenges, which Europe is facing.

3 State of the Art and the Focus of Our Study

While the literature has focused on showing the emergence of cities and transnational associations of cities in the international arena,[18] studying it from a multi-level governance perspective,[19] as part of a globalisation trend,[20] in the light of international politics,[21] and through an international law prism where cities increasingly take part in transnational legal processes,[22] we focus on the possible role of cities in contributing to transnational solidarity in Europe.[23] In a moment of solidarity crisis, and dwindling support for the traditional political apparatus, we are interested to know whether the city could have a role to play in building transnational solidarity. Since co-operation initiatives between and among cities in Europe connect people across borders in an alternative way to treaties, it seems they could be one way to strengthen European transnational solidarity.

The literature has especially emphasised that cities are closer to the citizens than the state when discussing their emerging role on the international stage.[24] This is also the reason provided by the cities themselves and international organisations as a justification for the new influence of cities in a global context. City proximity to the challenges felt at the local level, so the argument goes, necessitates their participation in global conversations about the solutions that would adequately and appropriately address those challenges. The principle of subsidiarity is sometimes referred to. It should be noted that the described development is not without critics. For example, it has been put forward that cities

[18] Y. Blank, 'The city and the world', *Columbia Journal of Transnational Law*, 44 (2006), 868–931; Y. Blank, 'Localism in the new global legal order', *Harvard International Law Journal*, 47 (2006), 263–81; G. E. Frug and D J. Barron, 'International local government law', *The Urban Lawyer*, 38 (2006), 1–62.

[19] K. Kern and H. Bulkeley, 'Cities, Europeanization and multi-level governance: governing climate change through transnational municipal networks', *JCMS: Journal of Common Market Studies*, 47 (2009), 309–32.

[20] P. J. Taylor, B. Derudder, P. Saey and F. Witlox, *Cities in Globalization: Practices, Policies and Theories* (New York: Routledge, 2006); P. J. Taylor and B. Derudder, *World City Network: A Global Urban Analysis* (New York: Routledge, 2015).

[21] Pluijm and Melissen, *City Diplomacy*; N. J. Toly, 'Transnational municipal networks in climate politics: from global governance to global politics', Globalizations, 5 (2008), 341–56.

[22] J. Lin, *Governing Climate Change: Global Cities and Transnational Lawmaking* (Cambridge: Cambridge University Press, 2018).

[23] Theory exists on the special case of 'town twinning', where the collaboration between twin towns is studied empirically through among others interviews. See, for instance, J. Jańczak, 'Town twinning in Europe. Understanding manifestations and strategies', *Journal of Borderlands Studies*, 32 (2017), 477–95.

[24] I. M. Porras, 'The city and international law: in pursuit of sustainable development', *Fordham Urban Law Journal*, 36 (2009), 537–601.

alone cannot solve challenges of climate change.[25] Moreover, Porras cautions that cities, 'despite their democratic credentials ... are increasingly losing their strong public government function as traditional public services are privatized and cities begin to resemble private corporations'.[26]

4 On Concepts: The City, Co-operation and (Transnational) Solidarity

This chapter engages with three central concepts: the city, co-operation, and (transnational) solidarity. As the reflections in the preceding section may have suggested, we want to focus on *cities* in different sizes. This way we might transgress a common understanding of the city as referring to a quite large town and in some cases even to the centre of a large city. As a minimum, there must be a certain structure and organisation, which allows the city to enter into agreements with other cities abroad. This will normally also mean that we are talking about either a good number of inhabitants and/or an area of a certain size.

In the United Nations 2016 Data Booklet on the World's Cities, the following definitions are offered:[27]

> Most people can agree that cities are places where large numbers of people live and work; they are hubs of government, commerce and transportation. But how best to define the geographical limits of a city is a matter of some debate. So far, no standardized international criteria exist for determining the boundaries of a city and often multiple different boundary definitions are available for any given city.
>
> One type of definition, sometimes referred to as the 'city proper', describes a city according to an administrative boundary. A second approach, termed the 'urban agglomeration', considers the extent of the contiguous urban area, or built-up area, to delineate the city's boundaries. A third concept of the city, the 'metropolitan area', defines its boundaries according to the degree of economic and social interconnectedness of nearby areas, identified by interlinked commerce or commuting patterns, for example.[28]

[25] Ibid.

[26] Ibid., p. 539.

[27] United Nations, Department of Economic and Social Affairs, Population Division, 'The world's cities in 2016 – data booklet' (2016) (ST/ESA/SER.A/392), available at: www.dx.doi.org/10.18356/8519891f-en (accessed 15 March 2019).

[28] Ibid., p 1.

Since we are interested in cities as legal entities, those that can enter into agreements with other cities abroad, the 'city proper' definition, with its emphasis on administrative boundaries, is most appropriate for our study. On this view, the city is by no means a single actor; rather, it encapsulates numerous actors that are competent to represent the city in different matters. These actors include local governments, municipalities, city councils and mayors, to name a few.

Moving on, to co-operation and (transnational) solidarity. Since we are studying the extent to which various co-operation initiatives may aim at, contribute to or reflect, solidarity, it is apparent that we are operating under the premise that co-operation and solidarity are distinct concepts and that one does not necessarily entail the other. The *Oxford English Dictionary*'s definition of *co-operation* as 'the action of co-operating, i.e. of working together towards the same end, purpose, or effect; joint operation' is descriptive of the manner in which we conceive co-operation. Moreover, it is our view that co-operation is an element of, and one means by which to express, solidarity, but that it is neither necessary nor sufficient for solidarity. That being said, since we are assessing solidarity in relation to co-operation initiatives, we are necessarily exploring the links between the two concepts for the purposes of this chapter.

What about the concept of *solidarity*, then? Many definitions of solidarity exist; all with a different focus.[29] Barbara Prainsack's and Buyx's definition of solidarity, which emphasises that solidarity builds on practices, is interesting because it opens up for many different practices with a multitude of actors and different kinds of 'costs' (financial, social, emotional or otherwise).[30] However, for our purpose we need to add a transnational dimension. Having done so, we reach the following understanding of transnational solidarity: Transnational solidarity signifies practices reflecting a commitment to carry 'costs' (financial, social, emotional or otherwise) to assist others **across borders** with whom we recognise similarities in a relevant aspect.

[29] We refer to the discussion of different definitions of solidarity and transnational solidarity in the Introduction and the Concluding Thoughts sections of the book.

[30] See B. Prainsack and A. Buyx, *Solidarity in Biomedicine and Beyond* (Cambridge: Cambridge University Press, 2017).

5 On Method

The purpose of this chapter is to illuminate transnational co-operation between and among cities in Europe, considering in particular whether such co-operation initiatives could be a means through which to create or contribute towards a European transnational solidarity.

We approach this by first shedding light on the different possible types of city co-operation and their characteristics. Intercity co-operation – in contradiction to interstate co-operation – is carried out at the local level, closer to the citizens, in a more informal way, and often addresses a concrete current challenge for the cities involved in the co-operation (in other words a challenge that is visible and relevant for the local politicians, citizens and companies).

We are mostly interested in whether the studied intercity co-operation initiatives include an element of transnational solidarity. We do not engage in measuring precisely the extent to which the co-operation initiatives create or contribute to transnational solidarity. The latter could be the object of further study in another research project. Following Prainsack's definition of solidarity, we are looking for a commitment component and a willingness to carry 'costs' of different kinds.

It has not been possible to find and research all initiatives between European cities in this chapter. Instead, we have chosen a selection of case studies. In case study selection, we applied a 'most different' approach: searching for multiple expressions of city co-operation. The idea behind applying a 'most different' criterion is to try to show that transnational solidarity exists in many different forms of cross-border city co-operation.[31] Besides a 'most different' criterion, we based our selection on the existence of co-operation between cities, the involvement of cities in at least two nation states in the co-operation, and a degree of formalisation of the co-operation. After having selected the case studies, we assessed whether they included an element or elements of transnational solidarity. We have structured the case studies into three groupings: initiatives with a European reach, thematic initiatives and geographically delimited initiatives.

[31] Ran Hirschl uses the term 'most different' cases criterion. According to his theory, the purpose is to prove a hypothesis by showing that even if the 'most different' cases are compared, similarities exist as regards the component reflected in the hypothesis. See R. Hirschl, 'The question of case selection in comparative constitutional law', *The American Journal of Comparative Law*, 53 (2005), 125–56, at 139.

6 Sampling Transnational Co-operation Initiatives Between European Cities

6.1 Initiatives with a European Reach

In what follows, we discuss three co-operation initiatives that have a European reach, including not only EU Member States but also countries within the wider geographical space of Europe, and, in the case of the first initiative, also (some of) Europe's neighbours.

EUROCITIES

EUROCITIES was founded in 1986 by the mayors of six large cities: Barcelona, Birmingham, Frankfurt, Lyon, Milan and Rotterdam. Today, EUROCITIES is a network of more than 140 of Europe's largest cities and over forty-five partner cities, collectively governing 130 million citizens across thirty-nine countries. Cities of different sizes participate, but full membership requires cities to be located in the Member States of the EU or the European Economic Area (EEA), to be 'an important regional centre with an international dimension', and usually to have a population of at least 250,000 inhabitants.[32] For instance, Copenhagen and Aarhus are the only Danish cities to participate (and also the two largest cities in Denmark). Associate membership is open to cities of the same size and character as full members, but which are located outside the EU or EEA, while partner status is available to 'local authorities or organisations that are not eligible for full or associate membership'.[33] Finally, EUROCITIES has a membership category for business partners.

Ultimately, EUROCITIES emphasises its character as 'the main a political platform' for the mayors and leaders of major European cities towards the EU institutions, highlighting that it has been 'making cities' voices heard in Europe since 1986'.[34] EUROCITIES has a strong focus on how to solve challenges at the local city level, and the organisation attempts both to co-operate with the EU and to influence EU law and policy in matters relevant to city governance:

> Well-performing cities and metropolitan areas are crucial not just for the local, regional and national level, but for Europe as a whole. Their

[32] EUROCITIES, 'Membership categories', available at: www.eurocities.eu/eurocities/members/membership_categories (accessed 15 March 2019).
[33] Ibid.
[34] EUROCITIES, 'Why join', available at: www.eurocities.eu/eurocities/members/why_join (accessed 15 March 2019).

> performance is critical both to Europe's global competitiveness and to its democratic legitimacy.[35]

Its strategic framework for 2014–20 identifies the following themes: jobs and sustainable growth, diverse and creative cities, green and healthy cities, smarter cities and urban innovation. The focus areas are all topics, which try to solve major challenges for cities and the citizens living in them.[36] They deal with challenges, to which the citizens can relate. EUROCITIES moreover emphasises the need for cohesion policy as being vital for economic growth and social cohesion across Europe and links it to a need for more EU structural funds to cities.

How close to the citizens does the EUROCITIES co-operation take place? The main purpose seems to be to 'work with all levels of government to ensure cities' interests are taken into account when EU policies affecting local and regional governments are developed'.[37] It also claims that its work with the EU institutions is an effort to 'respond to common issues that affect the day-to-day lives of Europeans'.[38] Despite working on matters that are close to European citizens, EUROCITIES looks more like an interest group for cities and city actors than it does a network, which is attempting to involve citizens directly across borders. Its objectives confirm this view. EUROCITIES seeks to 'reinforce the important role that local governments should play in a multilevel governance structure', 'shape the opinions of Brussels stakeholders', and ultimately 'shift the focus of EU legislation in a way which allows city governments to tackle strategic challenges at local level'.[39] Thus, it seems that EUROCITIES is more focused on re-balancing the relative power of the city vis-à-vis the nation state than it is connecting citizens of the EU across cities and borders.

However, EUROCITIES' character as an interest group does not make it irrelevant to solidarity. Quite to the contrary, interest groups are normally characterised by a sense of solidarity. They share common interests and challenges, which they together attempt to promote and

[35] EUROCITIES, 'EUROCITIES strategic framework 2014–2020: towards an EU urban agenda for cities' (2015), available at: www.eurocities.eu/eurocities/publications/EUROCITIES-strategic-framework-2014–2020-towards-an-EU-urban-agenda-for-cities-WSPO-9T2CS9 (accessed 15 March 2019).

[36] Ibid.

[37] EUROCITIES, 'Cooperation', available at: www.eurocities.eu/eurocities/forums/cooperation&tpl=home (accessed 15 March 2019).

[38] EUROCITIES, 'About EUROCITIES', available at: www.eurocities.eu/eurocities/about_us (accessed 15 March 2019).

[39] Ibid.

solve. To that extent, elements of transnational solidarity are present in the EUROCITIES endeavour, but appear to be retained largely in the relations between the cities and not to trickle down to the citizens, which the cities represent.

As a good example, EUROCITIES is involved in the Solidarity Cities initiative on the management of the refugee crisis and on the integration of refugees. Solidarity Cities was launched by the city of Athens under the framework of the EUROCITIES network, and is structured around four pillars: (1) information and knowledge exchange on the refugee situation in cities; (2) advocating for better involvement and direct funding for cities on reception and integration of refugees; (3) city-to-city technical and financial assistance and capacity building; and (4) pledges by European cities to receive relocated asylum seekers.[40]

There seems to be a clear element of solidarity in the description of this concrete initiative in the field of refugees, not only as regards knowledge-sharing and common policies, but also as regards 'financial assistance' and the 'relocation of asylum seekers'. Here we can identify a clear commitment and willingness to bear costs in the form of sharing knowledge as well as technical, financial and capacity building expertise. Interestingly, the described solidarity initiative concerns a field, which it has proven difficult to handle at the formal EU political level (namely, burden-sharing among Member States in the field of asylum seekers).

URBACT

Another interesting cross-border co-operation between cities is URBACT. Unlike EUROCITIES, URBACT is a EU creation, one of the Interreg initiatives under the European Grouping of Territorial Cooperation (EGTC) programme, and part of the Union's regional and cohesion policy. URBACT has been conceived in the context of the EU's economic strategy 'Europe 2020', which seeks smart, sustainable and inclusive growth.[41] Despite its temporal limitations and nature as a programme, URBACT is structured with a degree of permanence and

[40] Solidarity Cities, 'About', available at: https://solidaritycities.eu/about (accessed 15 March 2019).

[41] URBACT, 'URBACT at a glance', available at: https://urbact.eu/urbact-glance (accessed 15 March 2019); European Commission, 'Europe 2020: a strategy for smart, sustainable and inclusive growth' (2010) COM(2010) 2020, available at: http://ec.europa.eu/eu2020/pdf/COMPLET%20EN%20BARROSO%20%20%20007%20-%20Europe%202020%20-%20EN%20version.pdf (accessed 15 March 2019).

looks much more like an organisation, with its secretariat in Paris and National URBACT Points in most Member States.

URBACT's main beneficiaries are cities from the EU Member States, Norway and Switzerland. URBACT employs a broader notion of city than EUROCITIES, which covers 'cities, municipalities, towns (without limit of size), infra-municipal tiers of government, metropolitan authorities as well as organized agglomerations'.[42] Its other beneficiaries include 'local agencies, provincial, regional and national authorities; universities and research centers'.[43] As of January 2019, URBACT III had 415 beneficiaries.[44] URBACT carries out three types of activities: transnational exchanges, capacity building, and capitalisation and dissemination.[45]

> Since 2002, URBACT has provided alternative solutions to addressing key urban challenges by promoting sustainable integrated urban development through exchange and learning. URBACT supplies cities with tools and methods to develop strategies and solutions to high-priority urban issues. As these challenges are shared across the European Union (EU), URBACT is financed by the European Commission and contributes to the delivery of its strategy to prepare the EU economy for the next decade. URBACT does not finance physical investments, nor does it carry out pilot projects. Rather, URBACT uses resources and know-how to strengthen the capacity of cities to build solid strategies and action plans that respond to all the different kind of economic, environmental and societal challenges they are facing today. The main target participants of the programme include urban practitioners, city managers, elected representatives, stakeholders from other public agencies, the private sector and the civil society.[46]

Compared to EUROCITIES, URBACT is especially interesting in two aspects. First, URBACT has quite a strong focus on the inclusion of citizens as participants in the programme (see the quote above) – this is among others achieved through summer schools – and on engaging citizens in cross-border solidarity. URBACT for instance carried out a project on cross-border conurbations, which dealt with

[42] European Union, European Regional Development Fund, 'URBACT III operational programme' (2015) 11, available at: https://urbact.eu/sites/default/files/u_iii_op_oct_2015.pdf (accessed 15 March 2019), p. 36.

[43] Ibid.

[44] URBACT, 'List of URBACT III beneficiaries', available at: https://urbact.eu/files/list-urbact-iii-beneficiaries (accessed 15 March 2019).

[45] URBACT, 'URBACT at a glance'.

[46] URBACT, 'URBACT III – 2016 citizens' summary', available at: https://urbact.eu/sites/default/files/air_2016_-_citizens_summary.pdf (accessed 15 March 2019).

the challenges of developing inhabitants' feeling of belonging to a cross-border area and involving civil society within the cross-border public life. The project analysed how the EGTC, which is today the only European legal tool able to establish a multi-level governance, can be a reference tool to support the governance of cross-border conurbations.[47] As an example of such a cross-border co-operation, the Öresund region is mentioned:[48]

> The example of the co-operation that is led within the Öresund, between Malmö (Sweden) and Copenhagen (Denmark), two cities linked by a bridge since 2000, has demonstrated, following the setting-up of an online forum dedicated to the citizens of the cross-border region, that 99% of them are interested in cross-border co-operation for very practical questions related to their daily lives (job ads, movie time schedule, cultural agenda . . .).

While URBACT undoubtedly seeks to foster and facilitate co-operation between actual citizens (and not merely cities) across borders, one might question whether the underlying motivation is to build solidarity between and among European citizens (unless solidarity-building is reduced to the pursuit of the 'common' European economic objectives of smart, sustainable and inclusive growth). Nevertheless, given that the activities and programmes connect people across borders in sharing among others knowledge, it is certainly possible that the activities and programmes it facilitates create the space for solidarity-building through a commitment and a willingness to carry 'costs' across borders.

As indeed URBACT promotes on its homepage: 'We enable cities to work together to develop solutions to major urban challenges, reaffirming the key role they play in facing increasingly complex societal changes.'[49] Targeted challenges are in the areas of integrated urban development, the economy, the environment, governance and inclusion.

[47] A. Decoville, F. Durand and V. Feltgen, *Opportunities of Cross-Border Co-operation between Small and Medium Cities in Europe* (Luxembourg: Luxembourg Institute of Socio-Economic Research (LISER)/Department of Spatial Planning and Development – Ministry of Sustainable Development and Infrastructure, 2015).

[48] URBACT, 'EGTC seminar: involvement of civil society within cross-border conurbations' (2017), available at: https://urbact.eu/egtc-seminar-involvement-civil-society-within-cross-border-conurbations (accessed 15 March 2019).

[49] URBACT, 'URBACT at a glance', available at: https://urbact.eu/urbact-glance (accessed 15 March 2019).

URBACT is especially interesting in one more regard. In the URBACT III programme, cross-border implementation networks are established with regard to the size of the city:

> *Cities of similar size* which have already developed a strategy or an action plan to tackle a challenge gather in a network to jointly tackle the issue at stake. As partners in such networks, cities share experiences, problems and possible solutions, generating new ideas and learning from one another to manage the switch from theory to practice, from building an action plan to implementing it.[50]

In the European context, this is significant, since 'Europe is characterised by a more polycentric and less concentrated urban structure compared to the USA or China'.[51] Taking this into account, URBACT sets out to 'respect the diversity of the [*sic*] European settlement system and will target all kinds of European cities and towns including small- and medium-sized [*sic*] ones which tend to have less capacity and fewer specialised staff'.[52] This fits nicely with our comments on how the size of cities matter and that we need transnational co-operation among cities based on size. Furthermore, the transnational solidarity elements in this co-operation among cities can be seen in the sharing of knowledge, experience and solutions to common challenges. Together, the cities can generate new ideas.

Twinning

The town twinning movement started shortly after the end of the Second World War. The Council of European Municipalities and Regions (today, also a member of the prominent global network 'UCLG', which we will return to later in the chapter) has been at the forefront of advocating for the twinning movement. Initially, twinning partnerships were established between towns that had been divided because of to war.[53] Twinning partnerships blossomed again as Greece, Portugal and Spain were preparing to join the EU, as well as after the fall of the former communist regimes in Eastern Europe, which led to a new wave of accession to EU membership.[54] Non-EU countries, such as Norway

[50] URBACT, 'URBACT III – 2016 citizens' summary', p. 3, emphasis added.

[51] European Union, European Regional Development Fund, 'URBACT III operational programme', p. 11.

[52] Ibid.

[53] Twinning, 'History', available at: www.twinning.org/en/page/history#.XIxB7ChKhPZ (accessed 15 March 2019).

[54] Ibid.

and Switzerland, also participate. By 2010, the total number of twinning partnerships was estimated at over 20,000.[55] Twinning takes place between conurbations of varying size, from small villages, to towns, counties and cities proper.

Intended to emulate the friendship between two cities, twinning is a commitment based on mutual awareness. A commitment to co-operate on for example the arts, culture, sustainable development, social inclusion and more. Active participation by the citizens is highlighted as key to a successful twinning partnership. Twinning partnerships are intended for the long term, meaning they should survive political changes, and the partners should support one another in times of need (for example, natural disasters).[56] Given these underlying objectives, it is clear that the purpose is to establish transnational solidarity through a commitment and willingness to bear 'costs'. Notable examples include the city twinning projects that were set up between Western cities and South African townships in the 1980s, to show 'solidarity with the black population in South Africa in the fight against apartheid'.[57]

6.2 *Thematic Co-operation Initiatives*

Another group of initiatives were thematic in nature. Although the constraints of space did not permit a detailed analysis of all of them, a number are worth mentioning, for the sake of highlighting the breadth of initiatives. The European Association of Historic Towns and Regions, with its membership of over 1,200 historic and heritage towns, cities and regions in thirty-two European countries, was formed by the Council of Europe and seeks to 'promote the interests of historic towns and cities across Europe' through international cooperation, the sharing of experiences and good practices, and promoting 'vitality, viability and sustainable management'.[58] To the extent that there are elements of knowledge

[55] Council of European Municipalities and Regions, 'Table showing the number of twinnings in wider Europe in 2010', available at: www.twinning.org/uploads/assets/news/Number%20of%20twinnings%20in%20Europe%20in%202010.pdf (accessed 15 March 2019). Note that the table inputs all twinning points, which is why the total figure is close to 40,000. Since we are looking at the number of partnerships entered into by two cities, the relevant figure is half of the total, that is, just under 20,000.

[56] Twinning, 'A quick overview', available at: www.twinning.org/en/page/a-quick-overview#.XIxDLChKhPa (accessed 15 March 2019).

[57] Pluijm and Melissen, *City Diplomacy*, p. 15.

[58] European Association of Historic Towns and Regions, 'Who are we?', available at: www.historic-towns.org/about-us/ (accessed 15 March 2019).

sharing in the initiative, its solidarity potential is of a similar kind as that in EUROCITIES and URBACT. The same could be said for the European Alliance of Cities and Regions for the Inclusion of Roma and Travellers, which was launched in 2013. Set up by the Council of Europe's Congress of Local and Regional Authorities, the alliance includes 130 cities and regions from twenty-nine countries. It aims to promote projects and policies for the inclusion of Roma and Travellers, and to fight anti-gypsyism, which it does through condemning hate speech against Roma and Travellers; recognising anti-gypsyism as a form of racism; enabling co-operation and the sharing of good practices for political engagement, lobbying and advocacy; and working to improve the dialogue between local authorities, non-governmental organisations, as well as between Roma and Traveller residents and the rest of the population.[59] Here, the commitment to sharing expertise and good practices suggests burden-sharing in an effort to address a matter of common societal concern.

The Covenant of Mayors

The Covenant of Mayors is an example of a transnational co-operation initiative among cities on one specific topic. It is the world's largest movement for local climate and energy actions, bringing together 'thousands of local governments voluntarily committed to implementing EU climate and energy objectives ... and achieving and exceeding the EU climate and energy targets'.[60] Gathering more than 7,000 local and regional authorities across 57 countries, and 'drawing on the strengths of a worldwide multi-stakeholder movement and the technical and methodological support offered by dedicated offices', its success 'quickly went beyond expectations'.[61]

This initiative is built on a transnational vision and on the desire for solidarity among cities as a means of implementing the EU's climate and energy objectives. The cities voluntarily enhance environmental, climate and energy actions with a shared environmental goal.

[59] European Alliance of Cities and Regions for the Inclusion of Roma and Travellers, 'About us', available at: www.roma-alliance.org/en/page/33-about-us.html (accessed 15 March 2019).

[60] Covenant of Mayors for Climate & Energy, available at: www.covenantofmayors.eu/en (accessed 15 March 2019).

[61] Ibid.

The European Charter for the Safeguarding of Human Rights in the City

The European Charter for the Safeguarding of Human Rights in the City is an initiative through which European cities co-operate on the respect, protection and fulfilment of human rights at the local level. It 'strives to make municipal administration more accessible and effective to city dwellers. It aims to improve the collective use of public space and to guarantee human rights for all.'

The co-operation started in Barcelona in 1998 in the framework of the Conference 'Cities for Human Rights', which was organised to commemorate the 50 Anniversary of the Universal Declaration of Human Rights:

> Hundreds of Mayors participated in the event and united their voice to call for a as key actor in safeguarding human rights. Participating cities adopted the 'Barcelona Commitment, which defined a roadmap aimed at drafting a political document that fostered the respect, protection and fulfilment of human rights at local level in Europe. During the next two years, the European Charter for the Safeguarding of Human Rights in the City was drafted as the result of a dialogue between European cities, civil society and human rights experts. The draft was discussed and finally adopted in Saint-Denis in 2000. [62]

At the time of writing, the Charter had been signed by approximately 400 cities. This is an interesting initiative in several ways. Human rights conventions such as the European Convention of Human Rights are binding on the states. Municipalities are of course part of the state and when they execute administrative power they must comply with the conventions to which their nation states are contracting parties. Since human rights conventions are normally ratified by states, it might seem that compliance with human rights in municipalities is to a large extent a relationship between the state and its municipalities. However, in this initiative, municipalities across borders co-operate in order to promote compliance with human rights in cities across Europe. By so doing, the cities take upon themselves a shared responsibility for safeguarding human rights at the local level. Another observation in relation to this initiative is that the involved cities step into the arena as key actors in lifting and solving important, comprehensive and complex societal

[62] UCLG Committee on Social, Inclusion, Participatory Democracy and Human Rights, 'European Charter for the Safeguarding of Human Rights in the City' (United Cities and Local Governments), available at: www.uclg-cisdp.org/en/right-to-the-city/european-charter (accessed 15 March 2019).

challenges, which have traditionally been viewed as the responsibility of states. In a field such as human rights, where not all European countries have implemented all the UN conventions, there is even room for the cities to provide a better human rights protection than the state has provided, if they wish to do so. This could for instance be relevant in the field of disability rights, and the rights of woman and children. The described co-operation seems to satisfy the definition of transnational solidarity.

6.3 Geographically Delimited Co-operation Initiatives

Several co-operation initiatives were delimited by geographic area. The Union of the Baltic Cities, for example, is a network of around 100 cities in the Baltic Sea region, drawn from the countries of Denmark, Estonia, Finland, Germany, Latvia, Lithuania, Norway, Poland, Russia and Sweden. Self-described as a 'voluntary, proactive network mobilizing the shared potential of its member cities, the Union works across seven Commissions, focusing on culture, inclusivity and health, planning, safety, prosperity, sustainability and youth'.[63] A second example is the Council of Danube Cities and Regions, established in 1998, with a membership of around forty cities and regions in the Danube region at the time of writing. In addition to highlighting its respect for democracy and human rights, the Council, in its mission statement, states that it is founded on the belief that powers between the state and regions should be apportioned 'in accordance with the principles of political decentralization and subsidiarity', and that 'functions should be exercised at the level as close to the citizen as possible'.[64]

Nordic Safe Cities

In the spirit of 'most different', Nordic Safe Cities stands out as an initiative with a strong agenda towards solidarity building. Geographically limited to the Nordic countries (Denmark, Finland, Iceland, Norway and Sweden), twenty-five cities and municipalities (as well as several organisations) across the Nordic participated in its activities in 2016–17. The co-operation network is funded by the Nordic Council of Ministers, which also took initiative for its creation. It appeals to Nordic values, in particular

[63] Union of the Baltic Cities, available at: www.ubc.net/ (accessed 15 March 2019).

[64] Council of Danube Cities and Regions, 'Mission & vision', available at: www.codcr.com /about-up/mission-vision/ (accessed 15 March 2019).

to democracy, human rights, openness, trust and tolerance. The focus is particularly on the prevention of radicalisation and violent extremism, which are considered both threatening to cities' safety and ability to be tolerant, as well as to challenge Nordic values as such.[65]

> Violent extremism is a fundamental challenge. Not only because of the immediate physical danger that it poses, but because it challenges our democracies and way of life. It challenges the very essence of the societies we have built – the trust in our citizens. A society closing its doors around itself is an excluding society where people become suspicious of each other's motives. It is a society where we ultimately become less tolerant to other people's ideas and convictions. Nordic Safe Cities is doing the opposite [Dagfinn Høybråten, Secretary General of the Nordic Council of Ministers].[66]

Nordic Safe Cities has formulated 'six ambitions', focus areas, for its work on making cities safe and preventing 'radical and violence-promoting behaviour': safe urban spaces, a safe online sphere, strong families, safe public institutions, a strong youth engagement and safe communities.[67] It is also interesting to note that the network collaborates with the Radicalisation Awareness Network, set up by the European Commission (also known as RAN),[68] in an effort to scale up the Nordic approach, and to share its knowledge and experiences with the wider Europe.[69] Nordic Safe Cities is a collaboration based on a commitment and willingness to bear costs among the Nordic countries, and also involves knowledge-sharing.

7 Linking Europe to the Rest of the World

Though our focus in this chapter has primarily been on solidarity initiatives among cities in the EU and the wider geographical space of Europe, we will now provide a few examples of how solidarity among cities goes beyond the EU and Europe. One might say that this is not surprising, since many of the major challenges of our time are global rather than

[65] The Nordic Council of Ministers, 'The Nordic safe cities guide' (2017), available at: https://nordicsafecities.org/wp-content/uploads/2017/03/nsc_guide_download.pdf (accessed 15 March 2019).

[66] Ibid., p. 6.

[67] Ibid., p. 9.

[68] European Commission, 'Radicalisation Awareness Network (RAN)' (Migration and Home Affairs), available at: https://ec.europa.eu/home-affairs/what-we-do/networks/radicalisation_awareness_network_en (accessed 15 March 2019).

[69] Nordic Safe Cities, 'Nordic safe cities in Europe', available at: https://nordicsafecities.org/local-concepts-2/nordic-safe-cities-europe/ (accessed 15 March 2019).

regional or local. Thus, for example, C40 is a 'network of the world's megacities committed to addressing climate change'. Connecting (the mayors of) '94 of the world's megacities to take bold climate action', C40 is present in cities which together house over 700 million citizens. C40 convenes networks, conducts programmes on barriers to climate action (for example, inclusivity, finance and planning), carries out research and develops tools and frameworks for action based on its research.[70] Another notable initiative is the International Cities of Refuge Network (ICORN), which offers 'shelter to writers and artists at risk, advancing freedom of expression, defending democratic values and promoting international solidarity'. ICORN member cities offer long-term shelter to those 'at risk as a direct consequence of their creative activities'. Currently more than seventy cities have joined the network.[71] While ICORN is not an initiative involving cities coming together to work on a shared problem they face in their respective locality, it is an initiative that brings cities together because of their shared belief in the very notion of transnational solidarity, in particular as it pertains to respect for human dignity, life and the protection of individuals' freedom of expression.

7.1 *United Cities and Local Governments*

By far the most prominent on the global scene is United Cities and Local Governments (UCLG). UCLG seeks to represent and defend the interests of local governments on the world stage, including in the UN and other global fora. To that extent, it is similar in kind to EUROCITIES. Created in 2004, after local and regional authorities decided to 'unite their voices before the international community',[72] the UCLG network comprised 240,000 towns, cities, regions and metropolises in 140 nation states, representing 5 billion people or 70 per cent global population by 2015.[73]

By supporting international co-operation between cities, and facilitating networks, partnerships and learning to build the capacities of local governments, UCLG works towards its mission statement: 'To be the united voice and world advocate of democratic local self-government . . .'.

[70] C40, available at: www.c40.org/ (accessed 15 March 2019).

[71] International Cities of Refuge Network (ICORN), 'ICORN cities of refuge', available at: www.icorn.org/icorn-cities-refuge (accessed 15 March 2019).

[72] United Cities and Local Governments (UCLG), 'Who are we?', available at: https://issuu.com/uclgcglu/docs/uclg_who_we_are (accessed 15 March 2019).

[73] Ibid.

UCLG has a decentralised structure, with nine sections. Seven of these are regional, including the prominent European section, namely the Council of European Municipalities and Regions (CEMR),[74] whose work we have already mentioned in relation to two of the above-discussed initiatives. The first is the twinning movement, of which the CEMR was the brainchild. The second is the European Charter for the Safeguarding of Human Rights in the City, which the Committee on Social Inclusion, Participatory Democracy and Human Rights of the UCLG was involved in and promoted. Eleven years later, in 2011, UCLG's World Council adopted a global equivalent, the Global Charter-Agenda for Human Rights in the City.[75] To relate to an introductory discussion, the UCLG was actively involved in advocating for SDG 11 on sustainable cities,[76] and continues to be active in this field, working along with UNDP and UN-Habitat on a toolkit for 'localizing the SDGs'.[77]

7.2 The Strong Cities Network

This network among cities from all over the world is a very good example of a common global initiative aiming at preventing and solving one of the most pressing challenges of our times, namely terrorist attacks.[78] This is of course a serious matter, which is normally dealt with by national state institutions such as the police, intelligence service and foreign ministry – in co-operation with other states. In the Strong Cities Network (SCN), however, cities from all continents are attempting to solve a global challenge:

> Launched at the United Nations in September 2015, the Strong Cities Network is the first ever global network of mayors, municipal-level

[74] The Council of European Municipalities and Regions (CEMR) was established in 1951 and thus predates the United Cities and Local Governments (UCLG).

[75] UCLG Committee on Social, Inclusion, Participatory Democracy and Human Rights, 'Global charter-agenda for human rights in the city', available at: www.uclg-cisdp.org/sites/default/files/CISDP%20Carta-Agenda_ENG_0.pdf (accessed 15 March 2019).

[76] Global Taskforce of Local and Regional Governments, 'Local and regional voices on the global stage: our post-2015 journey' (United Cities and Local Governments (UCLG)), available at: www.uclg.org/sites/default/files/our_post-2015_journey.pdf (accessed 15 March 2019).

[77] Localizing the SDGs, available at: http://localizingthesdgs.org/ (accessed 15 March 2019).

[78] Strong Cities Network (SCN), 'About the SCN', available at: https://strongcitiesnetwork.org/en/about-the-scn/ (accessed 15 March 2019).

policymakers and practitioners *united in building social cohesion and community resilience to counter violent extremism in all its forms* [79]

Led by ISD[80] and comprised of more than 120 cities, the SCN builds collaboration between mayors, political actors and frontline teams to tackle polarisation, hate and violence in local communities in every major global region. The network catalyses, inspires and multiplies community-centric approaches and action to counter violent extremism through peers learning and expert training. It operates with a set of fundamental principles, agreed by all members, which protect and promote human rights and civil liberties in all aspects of its work to prevent violent extremism.

This is a good example of a network that aims at building transnational solidarity globally.

8 Citizen-Driven Initiatives

Finally, it should be mentioned that not only cities take transnational solidarity initiatives. Citizens also start such initiatives, which are typically less formal and last less long. An interesting example is *Venligboerne*, which is the Danish group created in 2013 in response to the migration and refugee flows that reached Europe during this period.[81] While some citizens and politicians were worried and/or critical towards migrants and refugees coming to Denmark, *Venligboerne* decided to create a positive, open and inclusive alternative. Their key idea was to meet other people with kindness, curiosity and respect. Interestingly, transnational solidarity is reflected in two ways in this initiative. First, a form of transnational solidarity with the migrants and refugees is clearly expressed in the initiative. Second, *Venligboerne* also exists in other European countries such as in France, Germany, Greece, Italy, Norway, Sweden and the UK. Hence, there is a degree of transnational solidarity among the different national groups working under this initiative. A further and important reflection is that *Venligboerne* is an example of an initiative, which has sub-groups all over Denmark, and both big and small cities in its steering committee. This shows that with the right cause and aim, it is possible to create a solidarity that breaks down the big city vs. small city divide and which at the same time is based on transnational solidarity.

79 Ibid., emphasis added.
80 Institute for Strategic Dialogue, available at: www.isdglobal.org/ (accessed 15 March 2019).
81 *Venligboerne*, available at: www.venligboerne.org/ (accessed 15 March 2019).

9 Conclusion

Despite their differences, the analysed case studies on intercity co-operation all turned out to be geared towards transnational solidarity in some form. The involved actors, commitments and costs differed from case to case but they all fell within our definition of transnational solidarity. This shows how widespread such intercity co-operation is and the broad spectrum of topics it involves. We have not attempted to measure the actual impact of such initiatives; however, it is clear that we are facing an increasing trend of 'bonding' between European cities and beyond. While this trend might to some extent reflect that cities and their inhabitants are not satisfied with how the EU (and nation states) are handling contemporary challenges, the created transnational bonds, might still strengthen Europe's emotional coherence and in this way provide the EU with a stronger basis. It is noteworthy that cities in Europe and beyond are joining forces in a common quest to take responsibility for and attempt to solve global challenges such as environmental problems and terrorism threats. Serious problems, which are normally solved by states alone and in co-operation for instance in the EU or the UN.

Many big cities are bigger than small states. This makes them not only powerful political players, but it also strengthens the feasibility of their ambitions as actors with the potential to contribute to the solution of some of the most pressing challenges facing humanity in the twenty-first century. Many of the case studies also seem to reflect that solidarity is definitely no longer a national issue. Big cities seek other big cities with the same identity and challenges. Cities – including smaller cities – around the Arctic zone or the Baltic Sea, which, for instance, share geographical, geopolitical and environmental characteristics, also seek each other out. There seems to be a greater awareness of other people across borders, who live under similar conditions, and a shared belief that together such transnational groups can actually solve problems and benefit from each other. Obviously, this seems to reflect a new kind of transnational bond and solidarity, which in many of the studied cases appear outside the EU treaties and other state-created legal instruments. In some cases, we see an interplay between the city-led initiatives and the EU, either through EU funding or when cities try to influence EU policy in relevant fields. Finally, there are also initiatives, which were originally initiated by the EU to promote co-operation among cities in the EU. Examples of these include the European Capitals of Culture initiative, which among others aims at 'increasing the European citizen's sense of belonging to a common cultural area',[82] and the European Green Capital Award, 'which recognises and rewards local efforts to improve the environment, the economy and the quality of life in cities'.[83] The EU seems aware that co-operation among cities might strengthen a feeling of transnational European solidarity.

Ironically, such a new transnational city solidarity also seems to hold the potential to split Europe into big and small cities. This split at the national level is already a reality in many Member States. Transnational solidarity between alike cities might build cross-border solidarity and identity – however, it might also strengthen the cultural and political gap between cosmopolitan cities and more remote and rural areas. While it is conceivable that this form of transnational solidarity, which transgresses geographical, legal and political borders, might emerge, it is also conceivable that new, physically invisible borders, which do not follow any geographical, legal or political formalities, might appear within Member States. This development must be seen in the light of the citizen-led initiative *Venligboerne*, which illustrated the potential for uniting citizens from big cities and small cities across countries and across borders in solidarity – in this case, in solidarity with migrants and refugees from countries far from Europe. Another example could be the recent protest marches demanding a political reaction to the environmental challenges by school children from all over Europe, originally sparked by a Swedish student, Greta Thunberg. Such examples seem to show a positive potential for a transnational solidarity, which transgresses all borders: legal, political, geographical and cultural – within and across states.

[82] European Commission, 'European capitals of culture', available at: https://ec.europa.eu/programmes/creative-europe/actions/capitals-culture_en (accessed 15 May 2019).

[83] European Commission, 'European green capital', available at: http://ec.europa.eu/environment/europeangreencapital/about-the-award/policy-guidance/ (accessed 15 May 2019).

Concluding Thoughts

Concept, Challenges and Opportunities

HELLE KRUNKE AND HANNE PETERSEN

1 Conceptual Reflections

Part I contributes to a richer understanding of the conceptual aspects and conditions of transnational solidarity. The first five chapters raise crucial questions. What is the history of the concept of solidarity? How can transnational solidarity be defined and understood? What are the symbols and myths of transnational solidarity? How can different solidarities co-exist and how do we choose between conflicting solidarities? Through philosophical, sociological, historical, political, anthropological, psychological and ancient Greek thought, we are drawn into an interdisciplinary universe with transnational solidarity at the heart.

Liedman, in Chapter 1, explains the historical background and development of the concept of solidarity from the Roman law of obligations to its use in the sixteenth century over the Labour movement, Marx, the Catholic Church, Giddens and Tony Blair's New Labour to present movements led by young activists, such as Greta Thunberg, and solidarity with young and future generations. His analysis shows how the concept of solidarity – though understood in different ways over time – has engaged us for 500 years. The reason for this longstanding engagement is probably that we are social beings living together in societies, and in contemporary times also in a globalised world. While the world population is increasing, the global living space is decreasing because of climate change (the desert is expanding and many areas have become very difficult to live in because of extreme weather causing flooding and other disasters). Furthermore, we are becoming increasingly dependent on the behaviour and actions of other countries and continents. Pollution affects the entire globe. Wars, poverty and starvation in one country or region leads to flows of refugees and migrants to other countries and continents. In other words, we all impact each other and we all depend on each other and therefore solidarity is no longer a concept relevant only to a small-scale group, society or a country, it is now a concept that is much more far-reaching and at the same time much more complex.

Carol C. Gould, in Chapter 2, defines transnational solidarities as overlapping networks of relations between individuals or groups and distantly situated others, individuals or groups, in which the former aim to support these latter through actions to eliminate oppression or reduce suffering. Such solidarity networks may be based on empathy or fellow feeling or else shared interest. According to Gould, network solidarity is not necessarily transnational but it often is. Furthermore, conflicting solidarities may appear for instance between national solidarity and transnational solidarity. This difficult situation is treated in Gould's chapter. In order to better underpin the situation of conflicting solidarities, Gould introduces the notion of 'web', which may better reflect the interrelatedness of people and groups within social movement contexts or even social structure (compared to the notion of 'network'). However, the web metaphor (like the network metaphor) does not do justice to the power discrepancies, which mark human social relations (especially between groups and society). When discussing conflicting solidarities, Gould draws a picture with overlapping and sometimes conflicting solidarities at the local, national, regional and global levels. While local and national solidarity can be characterised as assigned responsibility and builds on a presupposed shared historic and cultural universality, regional and global solidarity are choice-based forms of solidarity, which are often more project-oriented; aiming at the realisation of shared goals. When it comes to how one might choose between conflicting solidarities, she draws on, among others, historical injustice and its contemporary effect, systems of structural and institutional injustices, and cosmopolitan principles and requirements.

Adding to the conceptualisation of solidarity Hauke Brunkhorst in Chapter 3 defines solidarity as comprehensive democratic inclusion with cosmopolitan democracy as an ideal. According to Brunkhorst self-legislation, solidarity and justice are equally universal concepts and all (and not just national citizens) who are affected by a legal norm should be able to understand themselves as authors of that norm. In this way Brunkhorst does not distinguish between national and transnational solidarity: solidarity is cosmopolitan/global in its nature. Brunkhorst's rich chapter contributes to the concept, challenges and opportunities of solidarity and therefore we shall draw upon him again later in these concluding thoughts.

Interestingly, Nathalie Karagiannis's Chapter 4 uses as a point of departure the old meaning of solidarity in Roman law: responsibility *in solidum* applied to debtors and creditors. According to Karagiannis, solidarity cannot be considered without the violence that produces it and without the violence it produces. She shows how solidarity originates from violence or revolt and how this at the same time creates a longstanding debt, for instance, as regards Europe's roots in colonialism. She distinguishes between an Ur-violence, which builds on patricides, and an Ur-violence, which builds on fraternal killing, drawing on the foundational myths of ancient civilisations such as Greece and Rome, in which the killing of brothers is the original violence leading to solidarity between non-brothers. Debt towards 'fathers' (and gods) pertain a hierarchical type of solidarity, and a solidarity that builds on cohesion, integration and homogeneity among its members (Durkheim's mechanical solidarity), while debt towards fellow human beings pertains to a fraternal type of solidarity in which social integration is due to complementarity and differentiation (Durkheim's organic solidarity). Since the brother can be a stranger, the organic solidarity is open to a wider 'community'. Using the metaphors of cement and glue, she states that solidarity and debt are intricately related, because they both hold the relations between people. Viewing debt from an anthropological, non-utilitarian point of view, Karagiannis shows the double belonging of the debt to the historical and non-historical universe, which she states is fundamental to understand the co-existence between different types of solidarity. Karagiannis talks of the chains of solidarity highlighting that solidarity can 'limit freedom' and 'keep things imprisoned'. According to her, we must see solidarity as something other than trade unionism and the welfare state. We must acknowledge that solidarity is founded in violence and bears the scars of violence and revolt in order to capture the constant overlap between different types of solidarity – which is the key to understanding the different co-existing solidarities in European integration. Solidarity has nothing to do with equality (contrary to Brunkhorst). She underlines that chains of solidarity can be established, interrupted and cut away. Finally, Karagiannis present us with two possibilities of solidarities, which establish a new language and reflect a new way of thinking and practising transnational solidarity (and interrupt other chains of solidarity). First, a solidarity built on our *in solidum* debt to the violence we have shown towards the environment, and which we must pay back. Second, a solidarity built on sorority and the unfailing concern for the more vulnerable.

Drawing on Gould's definition of transnational solidarity, Ian Manners in Chapter 5 writes of the symbols and myths of European transnational solidarity. Symbols include 'official and non-official images and representations of the EU'. By myths he means 'cultural and political narratives that provide meaning to the EU in society'. He analyses symbols and myths within the EU, across the EU's borders and beyond, making a distinction between communitarian, cosmopolitan and cosmopolitical solidarity. This way, he reveals how solidarity has different meanings, expressions, initiators and so forth, within the EU, across the EU's borders and beyond. Manners shows how cosmopolitical transational EU solidarity exists through grass-roots activist groups and networks in the EU aiming, among other things, to support refugees and initiate climate action. Through a number of images accompanying the text, Manners brings a visual expression of solidarity – and thereby another dimension – into the conceptual analysis of solidarity in the first part of the book.

Coming from different academic backgrounds and representing different academic positions, the authors in Part I offer different definitions and understandings of solidarity and transnational solidarity and emphasise different aspects. These definitions span the traditional understanding of solidarity in Roman law with a shared debt (Karagiannis), over comprehensive democratic inclusion (Brunkhorst) to overlapping networks of relations between individuals or groups and distantly others (individuals and groups) in which the former aim to support these latter through actions to eliminate oppression or reduce suffering (Gould). They also offer different metaphors to describe solidarities, such as network or web (Gould), glue, cement, chains (Karagiannis) and even images (Manners). They attach importance to different aspects when understanding transnational solidarity, such as violence, debt and language (Karagiannis), global democratic inclusion politically and socially (Brunkhorst), networks of relations among individuals and groups and distantly situated others (Gould), curiosity (Liedman), symbols and myths (Manners). However, the five authors share a cosmopolitical hope, that (young) people around the globe through their protests and actions against climate change will build a new transnational solidarity. We seem to be living in – and are part of – an important moment and window of opportunity for cosmopolitical transnational solidarity.

Central elements appear across the five chapters in the Part I. As regards *the past*, Gould, Brunkhorst and Karagiannis all offer colonialism a central role in their theories, however in different ways. Gould highlights historical injustice, such as that of colonialism, as a reason for prioritising cosmopolitan solidarity over national solidarity (when they are in conflict). Although she applies a different conceptualisation than Karagiannis, it seems to link up with Karagiannis's solidarity and debt theory. Karagiannis mentions colonialism as one among other elements of violence on which Europe and European solidarity is built. Europeans share a common debt towards the old colonies. Finally, Hauke Brunkhorst emphasises the heritage of colonialism as one of the two main problems for the constitutional state, which was democratised between 1940 and 1990 and thereby solving the twofold problem of growth and social exclusion through social inclusion. This way, the authors tell us, that we must understand transnational solidarity in the light of our historical past.

The present meaning and impacts of the crises, which have faced Europe and beyond have a different meaning for the authors of the conceptual contributions. For Liedman 9/11, the invasion of Iraq, the financial crisis, the refugee crisis and the environmental crisis have all led to a break with Gidden's optimistic solidarity theory, which was built on a different political context. Gould is concerned with the new global trend of heads of state who primarily focus on the well-being of their own country and on how that effects cosmopolitan solidarity, which is the background for her analysis of conflicting solidarities and how one chooses between them. Moving on to Brunkhorst, the crises we witness are among other things based on inequality in society (social, economic and political). Which is also why 'massive redistribution of wealth to the lower and middle classes is the only hopeful perspective'. In Liedman's chapter, fighting economic inequality is also mentioned as the solution to many contemporary problems. Karagiannis, in contrast, has a stronger focus on 'moral economy'. Her theory seems to embrace both cohesion practices and practices that revolt against cohesion and cause disunity – though she emphasises that chains of solidarity can be interrupted and even cut in relation to the trends of nationalism and populism. Her theory builds on the observation that many types of solidarity co-exist. Crisis becomes an acknowledged and integrated phenomenon in her theory. Manners highlights how the financial and economic crises 'exposed serious differences and absence of European community solidarity on questions of financial regulation and intra-Eurozone transfer mechanisms' in his analysis of communitarian solidarities within the EU. Other challenges are Brexit and the regionalisation crisis. As regards cosmopolitan solidarity across the EU's borders, the failure of the EU's attempt to introduce burden sharing of refugees, showed 'an iconic moment in the collapse of cosmopolitan solidarity across the borders of the EU'. Finally, cosmopolitical solidarities beyond the EU have arisen from the climate crisis through, for instance, School strikes initiated by Greta Thunberg and actions by theExtinction Rebellion.

As regards *the future* opportunities, the environment is central to Liedman, Gould, Brunkhorst, Karagiannis and Manners. Liedman emphasises Greta Thunberg – the young Swedish environmentalist – as building/kick-starting a new global solidarity movement focused on solidarity with the young and future generations, thereby adhering to a more long-term perspective in politics. Liedman also offers other examples of how global opposition can create a new global solidarity. There seems to be a link between these examples exhibiting protest at the existing political environment and Karagiannis' emphasis the link between solidarity and revolt/violence. Interestingly, Brunkhorst also mentions the younger and future generations as a hope for the future and a more cosmopolitan solidarity and democracy. Furthermore, he mentions green growth as the only realistic solution to the environmental problems. Gould mentions natural disasters as a situation where 'call for solidarity by outsiders may well overwhelm state-based solidarities and rightly take priority over them'. Karagiannis believes that the environmental crisis offers an opportunity to develop a new language, which might create a new way of thinking and practising transnational solidarity. Manners shows how cosmopolitical solidarities beyond the EU have been born out of grass-roots reactions to the climate change crisis. Such networks are co-ordinated via social media. As mentioned, there seems to be a mutual agreement among the authors of the importance of the grass-roots protests against climate change for the future of cosmopolitical transnational solidarity. Maybe we are witnessing a 'constituting moment' of a new strong transnational solidarity, which has the strength to make heads of states and European and global institutions and organisations listen to a sixteen-year-old. Greta Thunberg has certainly had an impact and Liedman, Gould and Manners all refer directly to her in their chapters. Hanne Petersen has elsewhere called Greta Thunberg a 'Jeanne d'Arc' of our times. One might even call her a 'cosmopolitical Jeanne d'Arc', because she fights not just for her own country but for the globe, supported by networks of young people and bringing hope to people around the world. This way her 'crusade' becomes important not just in relation to the cause itself (saving the environment) but also in relation to our understanding of solidarity, democracy and politics.

2 The Case of Europe: Reflections on the Challenges

Part II focuses specifically on the challenges that Europe has faced in the past ten years. The authors analyse a number of these crises and their impacts on transnational solidarity in Europe: the financial and economic crisis, the refugee crisis, the Brexit crisis and the regionalisation crisis.

Starting with the economic crisis, in Chapter 5 Neergaard analyses the role of the term 'solidarity' in general in EU primary law and in the specific context of the Economic Monetary Union (EMU). She then analyses how solidarity has materialised itself in the context of the EMU after the crisis broke, dividing the analysis into two periods: that under the first and second Barroso Commissions and that under the Juncker Commission. Her analysis shows that during the first period, initiatives to combat the crisis were introduced gradually and solidarity between the member states was given substantive weight and seemingly increasingly over time. In the second period, references to solidarity increase even more. However, its use was primarily characterised by political statements rather than concrete legal action. This way, viewed through a legal lens, solidarity among member states has been legally emphasised in the EMU. Butler and Snaith (Chapter 7) make a distinction between positive solidarity (involving acting genuinely in the interests of the whole out of a sense of duty) and negative solidarity (involving acting in a way that may be superficially aligned with the interest of the whole, while being primarily and self-evidently driven by a self-interest). Starting with these definitions, they analyse the course of the financial crisis in the EU and conclude that the Eurozone member states are willing to engage in redistributive efforts in extremis but if, and only if, their own self-interest would be threatened if invention did not occur. As might be recalled, in her definition of transnational solidarity, Gould states that support can build on 'empathy or fellow feeling with these affected others, or else on shared interest'. Since Gould includes 'shared interest' it seems that the behaviour of the Eurozone member states still falls within Gould's definition of transnational solidarity. Chapter 8 by Thielemann falls nicely in line with this. After describing the course of the refugee crisis, he analyses how a more effective responsibility-sharing initiative could be designed. One of the cornerstones in this analysis is the use of 'public good' theory to gain insight into large-scale refugee crises. The key to better responsibility-sharing of refugees in large-scale refugee crises is member states being convinced that responsibility-sharing of refugees will provide more stability and security benefits for all Europe including their own country. Just as it was the case in the economic crisis example, 'shared interests' (not only empathy) is at stake. The refugee crisis no doubt played an important role in the British referendum on its continued membership of the EU in 2016. Young analyses the Brexit crisis and the possible future challenges for cross-border solidarity, which cover a broad range of areas. Besides the obvious challenges which might occur if the four freedoms are fully removed through a hard Brexit, Young (Chapter 9) also mentions more indirect potential effects, such as other member states beginning to question the role of the EU. Her analysis also includes the legal cultural heritage of EU membership encompassing judicialization of the UK constitution, constitutionalisation and multi-layered constitutionalism. The point is that even after leaving the EU, the UK will carry elements from the EU and trans-border solidarity in its legal culture in important areas. She ends her chapter with a hope, that this will enable the UK to address tensions that have arisen between the component nations of the UK through the Brexit process as well regarding the future relationship between the UK and its European neighbours. The situation of Scotland and Wales is mirrored in the last chapter of Part II on session and transnational solidarity. Beginning with an article by Joseph Weiler on Catalonian independence and the EU from 2012, Ninet in Chapter 10 discusses the relationship between transnational solidarity and secession. Whereas Weiler sees secession as a challenge to transnational solidarity, Ninet argues that this is not necessarily the case, emphasising EU principles on fairness, non-discrimination and sincere co-operation and challenging an understanding of placing sovereignty in the member states and not in the Union as such.

One key point arising from the chapters is that some kinds of crisis and challenges seem to affect transnational solidarity more than others. In the EU context, the refugee and migrant crisis has, particularly, challenged transnational solidarity and the ability to politically agree on responsibility-sharing. The refugee and migrant crisis is also one of the main drivers behind the result of the referendum in the UK in 2016, which led to Brexit. Another area that has turned out to be especially challenging was economic redistribution among member states during the economic crisis. Economy in the form of how much the UK pays to the Union and how much it receives from the Union was also one of the main discussion and campaign points in the UK during the run up to the referendum and throughout the Brexit process.

Another key point arising from the chapters on the challenges that Europe has faced during the past ten years seems to be that, even though the EU has been under severe pressure economically and financially, a large number of refugees and migrants have arrived at its borders from Africa and the Middle East. In spite of this and the challenges from nationalism, populism and those member states that oppose the fundamental EU principles (such as rule of law, judicial independence and human rights), secession claims in some EU member states and the UK's Brexit, the EU is still probably the best example in the world of effective transnational solidarity based on legal treaties and close political co-operation. No doubt, progress can be made and the EU can show even more solidarity, for instance, as regards responsibility-sharing of refugees and economic redistribution. Undoubtedly, there are wounds left after the recent crises and the North–South and West–East divides are stronger than ever. While, the EU crisis narrative is often presented by some as a story of member states that did not show solidarity when it was really necessary, and an EU that barely survived the many crises it has faced during the past ten years and which could fall apart any minute, an alternative narrative could be that of an EU that actually survived this extreme period of crises and despite its flaws remains a good example of well-functioning transnational solidarity in the world.

Finally, some of the mentioned crises, especially the refugee crisis, mobilised civic society across borders in Europe in protest against the political actors' unwillingness to aid the refugees and their incapability to agree on trans-border solutions to the problem. These reactions from civic society may also be seen as manifestations of transnational solidarity. This way the crisis indirectly sparked new transnational solidarity initiatives.

3 The Case of Europe: Reflections on (Re)establishing Transnational Solidarity Within Existing European Institutions and Political Settings

Part III discusses, how transnational solidarity can be strengthened within the existing European institutions and political setting, while

Part IV discusses how new forms of solidarity can be created outside the existing European institutions and political setting.

Alexander Somek's Chapter 11 adds to conceptual chapters by using 'friendship' as the starting point for understanding solidarity. The chapter is inspired by Aristotle and reflects on the conditions for transnational solidarity, namely the construction of a shared cultural heritage. The chapter could have been placed in the first part of the book. However, Somek's chapter also offers us a key to understand the possible limits of EU integration and the costs that must be paid if we are to exceed these limits. Following the friendship metaphor, we must think of other people – even the ones we do not know – as good people and likeminded on matters such as reciprocity and fairness in order for democratic politics to invest in a shared social policy in the EU. According to Somek too much heterogeneity is present in Europe for this to happen. Therefore, a postnational Europe might be lively, but not socially significant, and he sees no reason to believe we still have to engage in an effort to build a postnational democracy. The cost would be an exclusion of the 'others', among them Russia and Turkey. Though, Somek's analysis is intended to show the difficulties, limits and costs of further EU integration especially in some fields, such as social politics, it at the same time offers a key to understanding what is needed for transnational solidarity in the EU to be taken further. Somek emphasises the significance of a constructed cultural heritage for citizens in a given nation to feel they belong together. In other words, it is a narrative that needs some kind of cultural artefacts with which to refer. Within the nation differences existing among its citizens, however, once the narrative on common inheritance is in place 'everyone is free to seek shelter for his or her own cultural way in order to have it shielded by the nation'. Through this process 'relatively free-floating ways of life become aggregated, even if only loosely, into one bounded "national" culture'. It should be noted that large nations exist and that they sometimes embrace many different peoples, religions and cultures. Therefore, one might ask, why it should not be possible for Europe to construct a common narrative, which can provide citizens of Europe with a common cultural heritage? Such a narrative could be built on, for instance, a shared history, a shared intellectual heritage or maybe even how we together stood through the many crises? After all, when travelling outside Europe, it is easy to realise that Europeans in fact do share some cultural and historical features and experiences. Somek reflects that 'overcoming common mistakes' would perhaps 'be the most plausible focus for a narrative anchoring European identity'. As

Manner's chapter shows, myths and symbols have played a big part in the way EU integration is communicated and constructed, and maybe the EU has actually managed to build at least some common feeling of shared culture and identity through this? One might also argue that the longer the EU exists – and the longer the member states share this EU history – a shared history and culture is actually present and continues to build. It must be remembered that some member states have only been part of the EU for a short time. Importantly, the myths and symbols – sometimes expressed through images – which Manners shows us go far beyond the abstract values mentioned in Article 2 of the Treaty of the European Union (which Somek refers to) and appear much more concrete and assessable to ordinary people. However, if the myths and symbols appear too fragmented they might not be effective enough – as Somek points out a more grand narrative might be needed. Setting up such a grand narrative – which actually appeals to ordinary people across member state borders – should be undertaken by the political institutions of the EU and this way it is an opportunity, which builds on the current institutional design.

Schiek (Chapter 12) has analysed the case law of the European Court of Justice in order to establish how the Court applies the EU principle of solidarity. While the result of this analysis is that the Court 'frequently misses opportunities to fill the concept of solidarity with life', 'flesh out the EU's value base' and counter 'the identity-based challenges of EU integration', Schiek at the same time shows us the opportunities, which lie with the Court. Bearing in mind the ability shown by the European Court of Justice in the past to introduce new principles into the EU legal order and develop them over time with great impact for the efficiency of EU law and EU integration as such, it seems very likely that the Court could make a real difference in the field of solidarity in the EU. Schiek points out its potential in the fields of EU citizenship, social policy, anti-discrimination law and in conquering the adverse effects of internal market law at the national, transnational and European levels. This way Schiek's chapter contributes with an important opportunity for the EU to strengthen solidarity drawing on the already existing institutional setup. Interestingly, Brunkhorst mentions that courts of international public law such as the European Court of Justice, though often 'insufficient, decoupled from democratic legislation and often mentally complying to the interests of the global ruling and propertied classes', can be converted into institutions of increasing democratic solidarity (together with other bodies of public law [not civil law] such as the European Parliament and the UN Assembly). In this way, Brunkhorst also sees possibilities of strengthening transnational solidarity through existing institutions.

Having discussed how the EU might be able to strengthen transnational solidarity through the creation of a grand narrative on cultural heritage or using an existing institution, the European Court of Justice, to do so, we now move on to how civic society in the EU can contribute to strengthening transnational solidarity in Chapter 13. Lahusen emphasises the integrative aspects of civic solidarity (not just the disintegrative, contentious and conflict-related dimension). Solidarity establishes reciprocal relations, responsibilities and obligations among its members. Local, national and transnational solidarities are not necessarily opposing dispositions and practices. Lahusen refers to studies that have shown that European citizens who engaged in solidarity activities within their own country are also more likely to be active on behalf of individuals living in other European countries or outside Europe, while citizens refraining from transnational solidarity are also more likely to be inactive in regard to their fellow citizens in their own country. This brings Lahusen to argue that in conceptual terms there is little reason to separate transnational strictly from other expressions of solidarity. What makes transnational solidarity unique is its universalistic orientation (with reference to Gould). Lahusen distinguishes between three forms of interrelated solidarity: informal solidarity at the micro-level, civil society solidarity at the meso-level and welfare solidarity at the macro-level – on this scale the degree of organisation, institutionalisation, formalisation and codification distinguishes the macro- and meso-levels of solidarity from the micro-level. Lahusen analyses solidarity in the EU based on the empiric data from the EU funded TransSOL project. His conclusions are that civic society is transnational as organised in the EU but its main focus is the grassroots level – this means that citizens engage in collective and organised forms of solidarity when palpable needs emerge. While civil society is often organised and institutionalised at the nation state level, the level of organisation and institutionalisation is low at the EU level. Therefore, civic society transnational solidarity in the EU is often fragmented, and fragile. On the positive side it is flexible, fluid and highly responsive to problems and needs. In conclusion, the EU would probably gain more transnational solidarity by supporting such transnational civic society co-operation organisationally and institutionally like the nation states do at the national level, where civic society is a more integrated part of political decisions.

Besides adding to the conceptual framework, Part III has provided three concrete opportunities[1] for a strengthened transnational solidarity in Europe which may be applied within the existing institutions and political settings: (1) creation of a grand narrative of shared cultural heritage among the EU member states; (2) using the European Court of Justice to flesh out solidarity in the EU; and (3) strengthening the institutionalisation and organisation of transnational civic society in the EU.

4 The Case of Europe: Reflections on Creation of New Forms of solidarity in Europe

Leaving the safe and well-known institutional and political structure of the EU, Part IV turns towards the opportunities for creating new forms of solidarity in Europe.

Zhang in Chapter 14 argues in favour of a politically construed understanding of solidarity across borders. She highlights two strands of critique – from a liberal cosmopolitan perspective and from a republican and communitarian perspective – that have been raised against EU free movement in relation to social citizenship and the national welfare state. As a solution, Zhang introduces critical citizenship theory to reflect on the relationship between free movement, social citizenship and solidarity. Critical citizenship theory focuses on *acts, performances and claim makings outside formal institutions of participation*. Social citizenship is not thought of as fixed individual social rights but 'as a "fluctuating reality" shaped by relations of social forces and open-ended collective struggles for translating needs into rights'. Zhang's goal is to consider reconfiguration strategies for the relationship between cross-border mobility and social rights against the individualistic and differentiated approach to free movement in the supranational and national governance of intra-EU mobility. In doing so, she draws on the case of free movement of Roma EU-citizens and the mobilisation of networks against the 'othering' of Roma populations as 'semi-citizens', which appeared as a reaction to instituted restrictions to the free movement in EU law and national administration. Reformulations of mobility rights 'activate an understanding of mobility as a "form of sociality"

[1] It should be born in mind that Somek's aim is actually to explain why solidarity is easier at the national level than in the EU a.o. because of the heterogeneity of member states. Nevertheless, his chapter at the same time inspires the reader to a better understanding of what it would take to strengthen transnational solidarity in the EU.

enabling exchanges between strangers and claims to social rights'. The other case, is local activists who support vulnerable EU migrants by fighting for their cause politically and joining forces with them in a fight for better conditions for workers. The recognition that both citizens and migrants are subject to 'the hegemonic power of the transnational market and the supranational law' becomes the starting point for reformulating solidarity across borders. According to Zhang, as social movements, these practices draw out the political nature of solidarity because they are positioned within transnational socioeconomic structures and heterogeneous constellations of resistance, and they open up terrains for *new forms and relations of solidarity*, which traverse the boundaries of the national, the European and the legal, to emerge through political actions. The transnational solidarity, which grows out of actions of civic society, appears in many chapters of the book, among them Gould, Brunkhorst, Manners and Lahusen. However, whereas Lahusen argues in favour of further institutionalisation and organisation of civil society at the EU level, Zhang proposes that the new forms and relations of solidarity must be sparked as political actions outside the institutional structures of the EU.

Trenz in Chapter 15 brings media including social media into the arena of our discussion of transnational solidarity. Do media especially social media bring new opportunities for transnational solidarity mobilisation? Interestingly, Trenz argues that the social media may at the same time both facilitate transnational solidarity and disrupt it. He refers to the 'Janus-faced' nature, a metaphor for traditional media's national/local focus when covering news, on the one hand, but also its role in bringing the world to the audience, one the other. The new social media have the ability to connect distant people (strangers) to transnational relationships 'a new form of civic cosmopolitanism', social movements which fight injustice. However, at the same time social media also serve other purposes, namely, to spread a discourse of hate speech, racism, radicalism and nationalistic messages sometimes in closed internet groups and sometimes in the open public sphere on the Internet. To this list can be added fake news. This 'exclusivist, nativist or racist discourse' challenges transnational solidarity discourse by distorting the rules of the democratic game through which such discourses can claim generalised validity'. Such disruptive public sphere dynamics can themselves become a globalising force.

While religion has historically and contemporarily caused wars, divided countries and led to terrorism, Petersen's Chapter 16 presents religious solidarity across different religions and between secular and religious values as a new kind of transnational solidarity. According to Petersen, solidarity is a concept strongly linked to the twentieth century and its burning issues of conflicts between capital and labour in a secularised world, but in the twenty-first century, 'solidarity has moved beyond secularity and the field of protection of paid work'. Updating the concepts, practices and places of solidarity in a post-secular world might produce 'intangible but felt results'. Drawing upon a memorial service held in the Cathedral of Copenhagen in solidarity with all afflicted by and in condemnation of terrorism, an interview with Jacques Delors, former head of the Commission, in which he explains the significance of religion in the European cultural heritage (the Judaeo-Christian tradition but also the contribution from Islam), art and literature on inter-religious social ethic (across Islam, Buddhism and Confucianism), symbols, solidarity theory, fear of religion and the EU-funded RELIGARE-project, Petersen shows how religion and solidarity are linked in the postmodern world and how we see 'glimpses of hope for a peaceful co-existence and solidarity between secular and religious values as well as across religions'. Interestingly, religion like media (as explained by Trenz) has two faces. On the one hand, Petersen explains how we currently see a re-emergence of religious, spiritual, *national(ist)* and often neo-conservative movements, ideas and practices. On the other hand, Petersen offers religion as a new kind of transnational solidarity.

Through case studies in Chapter 17 Krunke and Hovden analyse whether transnational solidarity is present in intercity co-operation. While the main focus is co-operation between European cities, they also analyse some initiatives between European cities and cities outside of Europe in other words more global initiatives. The outcome of the analysis is that all the case studies – selected through a 'most different' criteria, the involvement of cities in at least two nation states and a degree of formalisation of the co-operation – despite their differences are geared towards transnational solidarity in some form. The involved actors, commitments, topics and costs might differ. The co-operations often attempt to solve important societal and global challenges, such as climate change or upholding human rights, which would normally have been handled by nation states alone or in co-operation with other nation states or international organisations. It seems that this kind of intercity co-operation holds the potential to strengthen Europe's emotional bonds since the initiatives are taken close to the citizens and regards challenges, which their city currently faces.

Through the co-operation with other cities citizens understand and feel that citizens in other cities struggle with the same challenges and have much in common with themselves. Such emotional transnational bonds established through city co-operation might strengthen the EU – even if the city initiatives in some cases represent a critique of the EU and/or the nation states. An important perspective is that while transnational solidarity is established among cities, many countries are split internally in cosmopolitan cities with citizens with a global outlook and small towns/rural areas with citizens who focus on the nation state. This way internal solidarity might be lacking in many countries not just in Europe but worldwide. Therefore, it is important that transnational solidarity among cities does not only involve cosmopolitan cities – intercity co-operation should also be established between small cities that face the same challenges. The chapter ends with the positive potential we have seen in the citizen-led protests against refugees and climate change, including the school strikes initiated by Greta Thunberg, which transgresses all borders: legal, political, geographical, cultural and generational within and across states. This way the chapter links up to the cosmopolitical hope expressed in many other chapters including the conceptual chapters in Part I.

In Part IV we search for new opportunities for transnational solidarity. Opportunities in the form of a politically construed understanding of solidarity across borders, new opportunities for transnational solidarity mobilisation brought by social media, the opportunities brought by religious solidarity across different religions and between secular and religious values as a new kind of transnational solidarity, and opportunities of transnational solidarity among cities are all explored. To this list can be added the new opportunities for transnational solidarity created through transnational citizen-led protest against climate change. The opportunities analysed in this part of the book either stretch beyond Europe or seem to be directly applicable beyond Europe.

An interesting aspect is the two-faced Janus metaphor introduced in Trenz's chapter, which seems to apply to several of the opportunities. Social media sparks a new form of civic cosmopolitanism, but it is also used to spread a nationalistic discourse. While religious nationalist movements re-emerge, trans-religion might also be seen as a new kind of transnational solidarity. While intercity co-operation creates transnational solidarity, differences between big and small cities in nation states might lead to lack of internal solidarity. This reflects how complex the new forms of transnational solidarity are and that while they hold great opportunities for future cosmopolitical transnational solidarity, they also hold possibilities for nationalism.

5 Concluding Reflections

Looking around us we see two major trends. The first is a strengthened transnational grass-roots community – a cosmopolitan movement – that protests primarily (but not only) against climate change. We also see people fighting for democracy and human rights in Hong Kong,Russia, and other places. The protestors' actions repower, revitalise and bring new life to traditional political freedoms, such as the right of expression and the rights of assembly. In the case of the school strikes, a classic labour protest tool has been given new vitality. The second trend is nationalistic and populistic movements. In countries such as Brazil, Hungary, Italy, Poland, Romania, Turkey, the UK and the USA, this trend is reflected in the current governments. Interestingly, we also find nationalists in protest groups such as the Yellow Vests in France. The Yellow Vest movement started as a protest against increased prices on gasoline. Weekend after weekend protest marches filled the streets of Paris, co-ordinated on social media. The protests lead to confrontations with police in several cases (thus leading to violence). Other examples are protest marches in Germany organised by AfD.

We see two very strong opposing trends, which both have their roots in revolt and in some cases even violence, building on traditional tools, such as protest marches and strikes. The strength of these democratic tools is reflected in the fact that the politicians listen and even in some cases change their actions. For example, Greta Thunberg was invited to speak at, among other significant venues, the European Parliament and the United Nations. The bill that the citizens of Hong Kong protested against, was stalled, and Macron gave up the idea of higher prices on gasoline.

The positive implication of the revitalised protest spirit is that emotions and passion are involved at both the individual and group level and in some cases across borders in the EU and globally. Something important is at stake in the eyes of both groups. Manners in his chapter provides us with many examples of grass-roots groups such as Pulse of Europe, which demonstrates in favour of a united Europe in opposition to the decline of European democracy (and the nationalistic trend) and which can be seen as an expression of cosmopolitical solidarity. Together with other examples, such as the climate protests, we see evidence that Gould's understanding of transnational solidarity is actually playing out. The protest element also connects well with Karagiannis's revolt theory: solidarity is built on revolt or violence. While the Second World War is slowly becoming a distant memory to many, the present collision between nationalists and cosmopolitans is much more real for people. The interesting thing is that since these trends are global (not just European) transnational solidarity reaches outside Europe for both groups. People follow protests abroad and take an interest in how elections and referendums – nationally and regionally in the European Parliament – turn out in other countries/regions. In general, we see globally an overrepresentation of support for cosmopoliticalism in big cities and an overrepresentation of support for a more nationalistic mindset outside those cities in the more rural areas. Obviously, the clash between the cosmopolitical trend and the nationalistic trend at the same time relates to the discussion of how different solidarities co-exist and how we chose between conflicting solidarities when necessary.

Finally, returning to the question that we asked in the introduction to the book: whether and how transnational solidarity is possible? Based on the analyses in this book, we may answer the question in a positive manner. Both the theoretical and the empirical chapters show that transnational solidarity exists. It exists in many forms, including new forms, at many levels (formal and informal) and involves many different actors. The solidarity networks and practices overlap, co-exist and sometimes conflict with each other. When institutionalised they have a more permanent form, when no institutional or organisational support exists they have a more fragmented and short-term character. When attempting to answer the main question whether and how transnational solidarity is possible, we must underline that it is not a zero-sum game. At a certain time, the level of transnational solidarity will depend on the sum of the commitments by all the involved actors and networks. Solidarity is playing and will be played out at different levels and in different forms and as mentioned, there will also be practices, which are counter-productive to building transnational solidarity. Furthermore, specific challenges such as the ones the EU has faced the past ten years, which several chapters of the book analyse, affect the strength and extent of transnational solidarity at a certain point in time. This does not mean that transnational solidarity in Europe does not exist. Following our model of explanation, it means that some practices are in crisis but at the same time, other practices exist and new practices appear (for instance, grass-roots networks) within and outside the EU system.

Europe is still a very good example of a quite strong transnational solidarity. Even when the UK leaves the EU, it will still be part of this transnational solidarity not only through its potential new agreements with the EU but also through other international organisations and through transnational solidarity initiatives by civic society, individuals and cities. European transnational solidarity is deeper than the EU and involves more practices. The advantage of institutionalised solidarity is that it delivers a stable setting for all the practices – institutionalised solidarity might enjoy more support in some periods and less in other periods but it creates continuity and stability in transnational coherence. The more informal transnational solidarity movements bring new life and ethos to transnational solidarity often as a protest against the establishment. It seems that right now we are experiencing an important moment: the creation of new strong transnational solidarity networks in protest against climate change. A first step that could in the future spread to other topics of global relevance – a development that brings a new cosmopolitical hope.

INDEX

www.ingramcontent.com/pod-product-compliance
Lightning Source LLC
LaVergne TN
LVHW010340220926
848484LV00004BB/985
* 9 7 8 1 1 0 8 4 8 7 3 6 8 *